THE
YEAR
OF YES!

....

WHAT IF YOU SAID YES! TO EVERYTHING YOUR SOUL TOLD YOU TO DO FOR ONE YEAR?

BY TRACEE SIOUX

Copy editor Stephanie Gunning
Cover design by Audrey Christie McLaughlin,
Intuitive Marketing Genius
Cover image & author images by Looking Glass Studio
Book layout © 2013 by BookDesignTemplates.com

Lyrics of "Bittersweet" from *The Unknown* album are reprinted with permission of Sea Stars. Copyright © 2013 by Sea Stars.

Ordering Information:
Special discounts are available on quantity purchases by corporations, associations, and others. For details, contact yes@traceesioux.com.

The Year of Yes/ Tracee Sioux. — 1st ed.
978-0-9907762-0-8 (paperback)
978 0-9907762-1-5 (ebook)

For my Soul,
and yours

Dear Klint,

Please do not read this book.

~Tracee

THE DEMONS FEED ON SHAME.

THEY FEED ON THE SECRETS HIDDEN IN THE DARKNESS.

TURN ON THE LIGHT.

~Tracee Sioux

I WANT A DIVORCE

In the fall of 2012 I found myself staring at the peace lily in front of the kitchen sink as I washed dishes by hand. I noticed something. The incessant voice inside my head had gone silent. I was filled with a deliciously simple sense of profound peace and calm within myself. The twelve-year struggle was over.

I want a divorce.

I want a divorce.

I want a divorce.

I want a divorce.

I want a divorce.

I want a divorce.

I want a divorce.

I want a fucking divorce.

This was the incessant plea from my Soul to be set free from a marriage that was confining her, keeping her from her purpose. My husband wasn't a bad man; in fact, he's a good man. A good provider, a good father. He wasn't even particularly difficult to be married to. But he was in constant conflict with my Soul and her purpose. She wanted to serve the world with her writing. He knew I would fail and demanded I give up my dream and "get a job." She wanted to help others as an entrepreneur with a coaching business. He didn't think I was a worthy investment.

Spouse. Soul.

Spouse. Soul.

I was in constant conflict, unable to appease both at the same time, and it made me miserable and unhappily married.

But I didn't want to want a divorce, so I pushed her down, told her to hush, made bargains with myself, sucked it up, pushed through, and tried my damnedest to "make the marriage work."

There was an enormous pull from my ego to maintain my financial security within the marriage. To leave—having been a stay-at-home mom (SAHM) and work-at-home-mom (WAHM) for twelve years, completely dependent on my husband's breadwinning—seemed a terrifying financial risk. I had been doing writing piecework, a few bucks here and there, and it was *nothing* I could live on. Having been out of the workforce for so long I found that no one wanted to hire me.

My Soul revolted at the mere thought of going out and "getting a job." Which was the one thing that my husband said would make him happy. *Quit your "delusional dream" and go get a customer service job or a teaching certificate or something,* he'd plea/demand.

It had been the constant battle of our marriage: Would I do what he wanted me to do or would I listen to the pleas of my Soul to serve her purpose for this lifetime? Sadly, he won out more often than not. I often gave in so I could avoid his repetitive harassment and demands that I quit, but primarily did so because he adamantly refused to invest in me and my "ridiculous dream" of being a writer and life coach. Thus, I "failed," over and over, by not being able to manifest a successful business with what felt like zero resources. I got the message: "So quit already and accept your fate like a normal person. You're never going to make it."

Soul or Spouse?

Suddenly, there doing dishes, I realized that I no longer faced an inner struggle. I was *free.*

I was at a crossroads. Turning forty soon, I had put my Soul's purpose on hold, unable to bring it to fruition without investing in it. Suddenly, that wasn't an issue. I could invest in whatever I wanted. Even *myself.* I had almost no money, I was bringing in about $600 a month doing shitastic writing piecework and my *was*band was essentially paying the mortgage with maintenance and child support. I had only four point two five years to "get it together" and manifest my dream. However, I finally was in control of the money I *did* have. Which felt very powerful.

My Soul is eventually going to get anything she wants, was my dishwashing epiphany. *If I resist her, I'll suffer terrible internal conflict. But if I surrender and say YES! to what she asks, I'll get profound peace.*

What if I said YES! To everything my Soul told me to do? What would my life look like? I speculated. *Who would I be?*

The funny thing about being free at rock bottom is that you really can take any turn you want. I could have gotten a craptastic job. I could have continued my work as a struggling writer, banging my head against a wall that only seemed to get harder as the years rolled on and my "market value" plummeted. I could have set out on a hunt for a husband to save me. I could have run home and lived in my parents' basement, playing the desperate single mom role.

Or I could listen to my Soul and trust three things that ultimately would keep me going during my *Year of YES!* experiment:

1.   My Soul knows where she is going.

2. She knows the fastest, easiest way to get there.

3. She will never, ever steer me wrong.

I committed. In 2013, I would say YES, enthusiastically, to everything my Soul told me to do. Even if it was terrifying. Even if it looked and felt impossible. I would not argue, rationalize her to death, or try to reason her out of what she wanted. I would not listen to outside voices: family, religion, neighbors, society, culture, feminism, political parties, money demons, friends, or even my kids. I would not demand to know the outcome before following her promptings. The only voice that would matter during my Year of YES! was my Soul's.

❧

THIS MEMOIR—my personal journal—chronicles my Year of YES! experiment. It is intentionally raw and unedited. Aside from changing names and identifying characteristics, I have left the Crazy in. The spiritual path, the Soul's quest for God, purpose, and meaning is messy. I chose not to sanitize it for the reader. *This is my real dark and painful shit.*

Writers face a dilemma with autobiographical works. We have to write about other people—because other people are meaningful in our lives, in our journeys, and in our spiritual growth. My intention is not to hurt anyone, and my prayer is that those who are written about here, including my family, friends, and lovers, will find healing in these pages. All of those mentioned in this book are loved on some level by me. I hope that they will at least understand that this book is a critical part of my own healing process, my own salvation, and critical to my Soul's purpose.

Demons like addiction, abuse, and limiting beliefs can only survive in the dark; they feed on shame, secrets, and silence. They survive generation after generation, passed down like genetic code swaddled in secrecy and shame, protected and nurtured. If we never tell the truth about ourselves to ourselves or others, we believe the Inner Liar's constant chant, *You're not good enough.* Yet, when we face our demons square in the eye, shining light on them with compassion for self and others, shame dissipates and love begins anew. I tell this truth for myself, to free me. And I tell this truth to free my children and their children of the demons my family has been passing down for generations. I'm turning on the light.

A memory is nothing more than a memorized and flawed interpretation of how shit went down. This book is a memoir. It is based on my own memory. Memories change over time for the simple reason that perspectives and perceptions shift over time. The intention of my Year of YES! was to shift my perspective and perceptions. This means that how I saw events in the beginning was different than how I see them now. The experiment was a success.

Everything in this book is drawn from my own limited perspective. I did not write it in an attempt to be fair or objective. This book isn't fair. And it isn't "true." It is an exploration of *me, my Soul, and my experience of the human incarnation of Tracee Sioux.* I don't attempt to represent anyone else's experience.

This is what happened, what it felt like, what I struggled with to heal myself of forty years of *etheric garbage,* as my friend and client Bina Mehta terms the energetic junk we pick up along the way. This is what it was like to rebuild my life after a divorce, to discover my Soul anew, to push past my money shit, and to reconcile my relationship history. It is an unflinching look at how *I* created *my* life. It's also a book about reinventing Self and setting one's Self free. It's a head-on look at how I've created my life, but more importantly, it's the conscious creation of my future. *Where do I want to go? How am I going to get there?*

Some of it is ugly and paints me in a terrible light. I expose my shadow to the Light, in the hope of freedom from my shame. Some of it is sweet and tender, exposing the wounded raw places of my heart to be seen. It is raw and vulnerable by intention.

Within these pages, you'll see that I struggled with my past, painfully. I struggled with my marriage(s) and my family of origin. I struggled with my place in the world. I struggled as a mom. I struggled with my money (poverty) consciousness. I struggled with my sexuality and my desire. I struggled with my spirituality, conventional wisdom, cultural beliefs, and my own Selfness. Most of all, I struggled to heal my heart and learn to trust my Soul.

This was a spiritual journey—and I don't want to gloss over what a spiritual journey is. It's fraught with all kinds of shit and some of it isn't pretty. Doubt, disbelief, anger, resentment, frustration, grief, sadness, despair, lust, and longing are married to a quest for light, healing, joy, friendship, love, happiness, forgiveness, money, success, intimacy, faith, and the manifestation of a million sweet little gifts from the Universe.

I don't feel the same now about almost everything in this book. Why? I experienced healing in every area of my life, I let go of this stuff. The experiment—and the process of writing this book—healed me, which is why I now offer a Year of YES! coaching program: I know this work is transformative. I lived it and my clients live it. It works. It can change the way you live forever.

My Soul took me to healers all over the world; showed me how to build a profitable, sustainable coaching business; helped me let go of my past shame and guilt and torment; took me to past lives, illuminating and healing some of my most traumatic experiences, and transforming them into some of the most beautiful; and introduced me to playing in the Spirit Realm. I built a tribe, a profitable business, a healthier body, and a simple joy.

Had I tried to transform my life alone, I couldn't have done it. I had God and my Soul's guidance. I had no power *to* do it.

The Year of YES! wasn't my easiest year, but it was one of the most transformative of my life. For during it, I transformed, transmuted, and was resurrected.

ONE

JANUARY 16, 2013

I'm sitting in Starry Night, a coffee shop in Old Town Fort Collins, Colorado. I have detoured from my usual routine of dropping the kids off at school, hitting the gym, and returning home where I guilt myself about not doing the "right thing," look around in a daze, and realize I don't know, really, what it is I believe I should be doing.

I have spent twelve years of my marriage creating a lifestyle in which I run as quickly as possible on a treadmill going nowhere to please a husband, Alex, who stalwartly refused to be pleased, unless I abandoned my Soul's plan in favor sitting in a cube somewhere making $13 an hour doing things that don't matter to me, which makes me hate them, which makes me suicidal. This is what Alex considered possible for my life.

Which really, really hurt my feelings, and made me exert a phenomenal amount of effort in order to prove to him that I could do and be so much more, and make so much more money, if only I were allowed to follow my Soul's purpose. A path he was sure I would fail at because it involved writing and people caring what I had to say enough to read said writing—and that's before I even brought up the idea of being a life coach, which brought out in him a villainous reaction and the utter certainty of my failure.

This is pretty much why I had wanted a divorce.

I have strayed from my routine because my Soul told me to come to Starry Night. *Write a memoir: The Year of YES!* she said. The Year of YES! will be the year that I listen closely to my Soul and say YES! to everything she tells me to do. I will simply obey her and go where she wants to go. Without questioning, without reasoning, without rationalizing or demanding an explanation.

Lately, my life and the feedback from either listening to or ignoring this voice is quick. For example, I'll be at the bank and hear, *Deposit more money.* I'll think, *But I only have this many bills to pay and I had planned other things for this money.* Then I go home, I order something on Living Social, and before I can enter the payment information for my checking account it automatically overdraws the wrong account. This happened three times during the holiday season. With the message, *For God's sake keep a one hundred-dollar cushion in your checking account! Aren't you tired of living from hand to mouth? Money is a reflection of your true values. If you value security and prosperity, change your money habits!*

Don't answer the phone, she said.

But it's my friend Susan, I answered. I dropped the phone onto the icy driveway. Shatter. I had been repeatedly told to buy an Otter Box case. *I don't have the money, they are so expensive. I'll do it later* (my standby excuse for everything involving money).

When I listen to the voice, I also get rapid positive feedback. My divorce, which happened six months ago, is an example. For many years my Soul was demanding a divorce. I'd hear, *I want a divorce,* repeatedly, sometimes many times a day. But I didn't want to fail at marriage, I was economically dependent, I was terrified and worried about the effect divorce would have on my eleven-year old daughter, Madigan, and my six-year old son, Charlie.

I want a divorce, get a divorce. I want a divorce. I shouldn't be married to this person. I hate being married to this person. I want a divorce. Why am I still married to a person who isn't in love with me? Why am I married to a person who doesn't believe in me?

If I'm being honest, my Soul had told me there would be an enormous price if I married Alex, but that I would get beautiful, wonderful children. Since I wanted those babies in a desperate way, I made the bargain. By the time we divorced, both of us just wanted to end our long struggle and live peaceful lives.

The *aaahhh* I felt when the divorce was final was so peaceful and calm that I couldn't believe how terrified I'd been. The constant pain I carried in my heart for over a decade almost immediately vanished. I had tried to heal that pain through various forms of therapy and bodywork, kinesiology, and prayer—believing something was wrong with me. That if I just tried hard enough, I could fix it and be contentedly married. But it was the divorce that finally dissipated the pain.

The Soul always gets what the Soul wants. If I listen to my Soul, things will go smoothly, miracles will drop from the blue right into my lap, things I want to manifest will manifest swiftly and easily, the pain in my heart will vanish, I'll feel good, I'll be healthy, and I'll be living the life I was meant to live and following the path my Soul has laid out for me. Conversely, if I ignore what my Soul wants, I will be miserable in a million ways. I'll be living a life that's not really meant for me, I'll be driven to addiction and depression and anxiety, I'll be manifesting things that I don't want, and I'll be unhappy—and I probably won't even know why.

The frightening part is that you really have no control over your Soul's purpose. Your Soul came here with it. You think you're in control and that you get to choose anything you want. To some degree, this is true: You can decide to resist your Soul's purpose, you can tune out the voice and instead listen to the noise of society, the media, and familial and cultural expectations. But it won't make you very happy and you'll always experience discontent, even if your life looks good on paper.

My marriage and my divorce were both instrumentally instructive in this way. And I am at peace—finally. My life is a clean slate. I'm practically swimming in the joy of being single again.

࿏

ONE OF THE WORST THINGS about being in my marriage was that my Soul's vision was in constant conflict with my wasband's vision for my life. I would get a prompting from my Soul and then I'd have to convince *him* to get on board with my Soul's plan.

I am a writer. I don't mean that I want to be a writer or that I could take or leave it. I mean that I *am* a writer. It is what I was meant to do, it has always been my intention to follow this path, I never in a million years would leave the profession. Although some parts of it suck—like the rejection and the fact that everybody in the world thinks they can do it, so they do it for free, and it lacks the stability and the steadiness of other professions—I am 100 percent committed to it. It is my Soul's purpose. The one period in my life where I quit writing drove me to rehab, extreme depression, and suicidal thoughts. My life lacked purpose and purpose is vital to living. My Soul must express herself through the creation of story and the written word. It simply must.

My husband made it his mission to make me stop being a writer and take a job as an administrative assistant or substitute teacher or *any* other mundane, but steady job I could find. He absolutely, 100 percent opposed my Soul's purpose. It became his obsession. He was discouraging at every turn. It is no wonder my Soul wanted out of the marriage. She wanted to pursue her path and he was making it a million times harder than it had to be.

❧

I AM A DEDICATED STUDENT of the Law of Attraction. As such, becoming a Martha Beck life coach has been on my dream boards and vision statements since 2009. Alex was vehemently opposed to my becoming a life coach, certain of my failure. His reaction to my suggestion that we invest in certification and building a business could be described as disgust. Now that I'm no longer married my yearning for this experience has resuscitated itself and taken on new energy. The only thing I lack is a pile of cash.

I've been toying with the idea of taking coaching clients to pay for the $8,000 Martha Beck life coaching training, which is relatively expensive if you look at certifications that really carry no legal meaning whatsoever, and relatively inexpensive if you look at what a master's program in psychology might cost. I really like the synchronicity of my coaching paying for my coaching training, in the same way that I loved buying Apple stock and then paying for my iPhone and MacBook with the profits. I have even gone so far as to create a coaching page on my website, although I made it invisible. Still, it is a step toward the dream and a way of acting "as if," a declaration of my intention.

Declaring yourself a coach without certification takes *audacity*.

I'm afraid.

❧

IN DECEMBER, I WAS ON the elliptical machine and my Soul told me to move forward: *Redesign the website. Pay the designer four hundred dollars NOW.* This was the only $400 I had and it was the last rent check from my tenant, who is moving out. It's a week before Christmas, I don't have all my kids' shopping done, and I'm wondering how I'm going to pay my bills.

In my former life as a wife, I would have had to go home and justify the expense of this $400 redesign to market my services as a life coach, a career my wasband adamantly didn't want me to pursue. I would have had to convince and cajole. It would have resulted in a fight and an adamant refusal, and I would have suffered the angry silent treatment through the whole holiday. I wouldn't have spent the money and I would have resented it and my Soul would have screamed once again, *I WANT A DIVORCE!!!*

But I already had my divorce.

I sent my designer $400 that day.

It is impossible to describe how good it felt not to have to justify listening to my Soul to a man who doesn't believe in inner wise women. The exuberant high I got from sending that money, taking that risk, and stepping toward my dream by declaring my intention with a physical manifestation of cash was liberating.

And you know what? My kids had a great Christmas, the money rolled in to pay my bills, and $200 arrived in my mailbox from anonymous angels. *Phew.*

I'm so excited and curious to find out what else will manifest for me during this Year of YES!

TWO

JANUARY 28, 2013

Among my New Year's Intensions, along with listening to and saying yes to my Soul, is to do a lot of healing body work: massages, energy work, yoga; generally a lot of lying on a table and letting healers touch and rub me. Twelve years of chronic stress is very hard on the body. My thyroid has suffered and I have adrenal exhaustion from chronic stress. I broke my shoulder in the middle of 2012, putting an end to virtually all physical adventure and enforcing my need to rest and stop frantically rushing through my life. *SLOW DOWN*, a message repeatedly harped on by my Soul, came in the form of three traffic tickets and falling down the stairs while doing three things on my iPhone and breaking my clavicle. My eyesight is struggling, my weight has fluctuated up and down and up and down, sometimes so rapidly that I am in shock. And my hormones are wackadoo.

I recently had a reading by a divine feminine high priestess of some sort. I think the first deck she used was a tarot deck and the second was an oracle deck featuring spirit animals. She said that my ego was bruised, which may be from my divorce, but could just as well be from my recent visit to my parents' house when my dad told me he doesn't like being "milked," and that he felt I had been taking advantage of his generosity.

I was so embarrassed, humiliated even, to hear this. I was acting from a place of lack and fear. I had been feeding my children from the food bank for several months in 2012, so when my parents took me to Sam's Club for groceries I simply told myself that my dad was feeling his "masculine protect and provide" instinct for us, while I got on my feet. I had been wrong about his intentions and that hurt my feelings. So yes, my ego was bruised. I'm now changing my thinking to, *I'm an adult, I can take care of my family.* A beautiful phrase borrowed from my brother, Jason.

This priestess prophesied that I would be a healer, but that this year I should focus on healing myself. She said I am highly psychic and a high priestess. She told me to go to the library and check out some books on developing psychic abilities. So I did. While there, I found a book titled *The 7 Secrets of Synchronicity.* In the "how this book was born" section at the beginning there as a mention of a "fam trip," essentially free trips for journalists in an effort to get press coverage.

I used to go on those, I said to myself.

Why don't I do that anymore? asked me.

Because I had a baby and 9/11 happened and the travel industry basically shut down, I explained. *The doors closed.*

Why don't I do that now? Where would I want to go if I went on a fam trip? I queried.

I want to go to spiritual places: John of God; Landolozi with Martha Beck; the Raj Spa in Vedic City in Fairfield, Iowa; a tut.com cruise; the Omega Institute; an ashram in India, I fantasized.

Who would let me write a spiritual travel column? I wondered. *Linda from BellaSpark magazine would probably let me write one. All I need is a magazine that guarantees publication and I can start soliciting fam trips,* I thought. So I emailed Linda and she said yes and asked me to write something within three days. Thankfully, I had been to a program in 2009 called *Discovery* in Dallas, Texas, which fit the criteria for my new column "Soul Trek." I don't love the name, but I love that I listened to my Soul's voice to follow up on the spiritual travel column idea and it happened immediately.

A few days after being told by the psychic woman that I would be a healer, I went to a bodywork/spiritual energy session. *Go see C.J. McDaniel*, my Soul repeated while I was on other massage tables. Over and over I heard the message, *Go see C.J.* As soon as she started working on me she said that my spiritual guides were telling her that I was being *initiated as a healer*.

Several other healers have mentioned that angels and winged ones are highly prominent in my life. The palm reader who came to my divorce/thirty-ninth birthday party, Myrna Lou, said I have six angels helping me and that I should make a come-hither gesture when I need something and they would help me get it. C.J. McDaniel also said that the angels Ariel (the angel of manifesting dreams and of the natural world) and Ezekiel were prominent for me. Evidently, I have many spiritual beings on my side.

∾

MYRNA LOU WAS SURPRISED that I am not currently experiencing hieros gamos with my twin soul. *Hieros gamos*—the Sacred Marriage—is an ancient Greek sexual practice that acts out the marriage of a god and goddess. Many, including myself, believe that Jesus Christ and Mary Magdalene were married and shared hieros gamos. To me it's the ultimate in sacred sexuality and marriage. It is my longing and my ideal. *Yum.*

Myrna predicted that I will have a very short wildee time (a period in which I get to be a wild woman, and sow some wild oats), but then a "hunk" with something to bring to the table will come into my life. It will be easy and we'll enjoy each other for fifty years.

A relationship is missing from my dream board. I have not spent energy describing or attracting the man I want. I've gone on a couple of dates, but it's obvious that I'm not serious about it. I am *loving* being alone. I love my free time. I love making decisions by myself. My Soul was in constant conflict with my wasband's lack of soul. To simply listen to my inner voice is so liberating that I am not rushing out to find another man with whom I will need to negotiate my life. No, this man will have to be impeccably special for me to give up the independence that is mine now.

Still, I am horny and have been love starved for many years. Soon my thirst for a relationship will likely rekindle itself. For now, I'm happy not to have found him yet. My wildee time looks like it will take place at spiritual retreats rather than in bars and bedrooms, which suits me perfectly.

❧

I MET JAKE WHEN I was in college. It was as if I knew him or we knew each other immediately. We kept trying to place each other. We, of course, fell in love and it was wonderful and terrible. He was married and then could not divorce because he was part coward and part honorable. I couldn't stop being tormented by dreams of him.

Eventually we moved on, getting jobs elsewhere, but always finding ourselves in touch somehow. I married. I had kids. When I had my son, Jake called to tell me he had finally divorced. I was in no mood. Also I was angry at him for having phone sex with my best friend, Viveka Moon. Because I'd deluded myself that he only acted shamefully with his pseudo-cheating with *me*. Evidently not. In fact, I strongly suspect he made a profession out of it.

Now that I've finally divorced, Jake is quite happily married again. Still, he still seeks me out to flirt with me on Facebook and via phone calls and text messages. He is not someone I want to find myself married to, but my attraction to him is pervasive. It's silly, too, because I don't even find him that physically attractive, it was his pheromones. When relationship issues come up—especially when a psychic mentions that the man for my future is already in my life—it is Jake I wonder about. God save me from this fate, I fear it will be less fun for me than I have imagined for fifteen years.

Jake tends to love his ego being stroked, though he doesn't stroke mine as much. He is surely a selfish lover. I prefer to be the worshipped one in a relationship. It is a woman's prerogative. Besides, I haven't been in his physical presence for a decade. I probably am not even attracted to him anymore.

Lord, bless me with hieros gamos and spare me anymore love disasters. And help me stop thinking about Jake and romanticizing him into something he is not.

THREE

JANUARY 30, 2013

My children are spoiled. The positive reinforcement parenting thing is kind of bullshit. When I tell people over fifty how my children talk to me, they can't believe it. "I was scared to death of my parents, I never would have talked to them like that," they say. I am considered "mean" by my kids for all acts of *parenting,* such as asking them to pick up their own shit, telling them they have to be full participants with the housework, and telling them to *try harder* when they do anything mediocre. I am evidently not allowed to think them mediocre at anything and am certainly forbidden to point out that their efforts are lazy.

I would like to take my children to an impoverished third-world country to show them just how blessed their lives really are and to point out what a good fucking mother I am. So perhaps I should seek something like that out. I wonder if I can find one that will accept children.

I'm suffering mommy burnout after eleven years of being a work-at-home mom. I'm depleted and exhausted. I have nothing to offer them right now.

The Bible says: "Ask and you shall receive." I ask for money constantly. It's my never-ceasing prayer. To not have money

makes me feel insecure. For instance, I started this year with the intention of saving 10 percent of everything I bring in. It is January 30 and I have only $20 to my name. This causes me anxiety. I did save, but I am late on my sanitation bill to do it. Then one of my subcontractors asked to be paid early because she had an unexpected expense. I wanted to be generous so I paid her what I had saved for the month. Which left me broke, again.

The paradox in this is that I know that I have never, and will never, go without. God has proven this time and time again since I left home at seventeen. Yet, I constantly wish I had more. And it's not as if I'm pulling in $100,000 and wishing I had more. It's me pulling in just under $40,000 last year and wanting things like shoes for my kids, garage door openers, so my tenant doesn't hurt herself, fences to keep the dog in the yard, teeth cleanings, and eye glasses so I can see when I drive. I know with my *knowing self* that I'll achieve these things and more. The wanting and needing becomes an obsession that drives me to distraction sometimes.

I will think of it in my sleep. *If I buy a garage door opener this month, then the next month I can buy a fence. I owe the neighbor for the fence she put up, how am I going to pay for that? I have no idea what I will have to pay in taxes and I want to pay those in full. I am determined to save 10 percent and tithe 10 percent to my church, but I can't see how it's possible to live on only 80 percent of what I make when there are so many needs and the credit card bill is due on the fifth . . .*

This goes on in my brain while meditating, yoga, working out, writing, watching TV, reading books. It's exhausting.

෴

LATE IN 2012, I STARTED TO ask for something else: *relief from the chronic obsession with money. Peace about money. A correction of my thinking about money. A surrender to God and my Soul about money. A* faith, unwavering, about money. Surrendering all beliefs that aren't work-ing for me around money. Now sometimes I achieve this kind of se-renity. It's fleeting.

Oh Soul, must we always be so hand to mouth? I'm tired of it and want to learn other lessons. Like maybe what to do with a million dollars or ten million dollars or one hundred million dollars! Surely there are val-uable lessons to learn about this.

I am chronically in a state where I feel bound by my inability to fully give my gifts because of money.

❧

I HAVE BEEN "REVIRGINIZED." This means I've not had sex in over a year. The thought both repulses me and attracts me. The exchange of bodily fluids is kind of gross when you think about it. Though I was rather sexually adventurous when I was young, now there's the whole spiritual exchange of energy and I'm not very into the yang of sex. I'm much more attracted to the yin of it.

Much of sex in my younger days was masculine: fast, hard, emotionally detached energy. What a turn off now. I was well into my thirties when I realized that I could have an orgasm during intercourse if I was controlling the movement and going slow. Every single lame lover I'd ever had before then was totally into going fast and hard. Boring. Gross. Ineffective.

Will my Soul choose to have sex in 2013? Will she lead me in that direc-tion? Will a man ever turn me on enough for me to want his tongue in my mouth again?

❧

LORD, GRANT ME PEACE OF MIND *about money. I release all negative and misguided beliefs, feelings, thoughts, and behaviors about money and around money from this moment on. I surrender to the fact that I know* nothing about money and its powers, and I open myself to learning how to attract money immediately and permanently. Free me from my obsessive and worrying thoughts about money. Free me from the constant calculating and thinking about money, and what I should and cannot do with it. Free me from any negative and limiting generational, DNA, familial, lineage beliefs, thoughts, and behaviors about money and events around money. I release all beliefs, thoughts, and feelings connected to money and my marriage and wasband, freeing myself from our mutual relationship to money and all of the negative dysfunctional energy around that.

Free me from the idea that how much money I make determines my worth, as defined by my wasband, and the power of money in our marriage. Liberate me from my starving artist beliefs: feelings and thoughts that require poverty and struggle of writers and artists. I release all unworthiness around money and my ability to get it, earn it, and spend it freely and without restriction. Also release me from all religious beliefs that regard mothers as incapable or forbidden from making money and spending money at the risk of becoming a bad mother. Liberate me from Dave Ramsey's Financial Hell and Joy Killing relationship with money, and the lack/debt management habits resulting from it.

Place me in the way of money. Put me in its path and allow me to collect great multitudes of it. Allow money to flow through me abundantly, and to give it freely and with wisdom in whatever places and endeavors I choose. Give me appropriate and right thoughts and feelings about money.

In the name of Jesus Christ and Mary Magdalene, amen.

❧

I WENT TO A HYPNOSIS session I bought on Living Social as a cure to Madigan's fear about sleeping alone. I bought two sessions and she didn't want to go to the second one. I used it to deal with my money anxiety. During the session, I envisioned myself jumping on a trampoline full of money, feeling free and joyous. The trampoline was under a money tree and money rained down on me, never-ending. I frolicked in the unlimited supply of money—jumping and bouncing and flipping and doing tricks.

❧

I ALSO HAVE A LOT OF LAW of Attraction tricks I use to change my beliefs about money. I have a money tree that I stare at and send love to. It makes me happy that it has doubled in size in a year. I have a small globe bank, so that I can say—and believe— that *I have all the money in the world* and *I have unlimited access to the World Bank.* I have a feng shui money corner in my bedroom. I have a drawing of a money tree on poster board hung there. On the limbs and trunk, I have written the things I want money to be and do for me "security, fun, freedom, etc." I've drawn myself under the tree having money fall all over me, easily picked up and stuffed into my pockets. I also have two lucky bamboo plants in that corner. Cash and written checks also frequently appear on my dream boards.

When I say I practice Law of Attraction I mean I *practice* it, the way someone might practice writing to get better at it. I put in the 10,000 hours the way anyone would for any sort of skill or talent.

Money and time are mirrors. You can hold up your relationship with money and immediately tell your values. This is the same with time. They are two barometers of who you're being.

I spend the most money taking care of my family. Housing and feeding them, providing them a certain middle-class lifestyle. My next expense is spiritual growth. I donate 10 percent of my gross income to my church. I also spend money on spiritual growth classes, energy work, bodywork, prayer practitioners, coaching, and spiritual materials, like books and audios. In 2012, I spent a lot of money on visiting with my family. This year I will spend it on spiritually centered travel. These are good priorities.

❧

TIME IS THE NEXT FRONTIER. It acts as a reflection of who we're being. I had a very convoluted relationship with time during my marriage. Money, too. Of course, my wasband's priority was that I spend all my time making money, while managing the children so we didn't pay for childcare and taking care of the house because I wasn't *really* working. Because there are only twenty-four hours in a day and doing all of this felt like too much for me, and because I never could produce enough money to contribute to how he wanted to spend his time and our money—I developed a habit of *rushing*. It was terrible. I was constantly frantic. If I was at the gym, I felt I should be working. If I was watching television at night, I felt like I was lazy for not working at night. If I was spending time with my children, I felt I should have been working. If I was at a lunch meeting, I felt like I should have been home logging billable hours.

This came to a head in 2012. First, as Oprah says, I got a little whisper, *Slow down.* I didn't listen. *Slow down. Slooooooooow doooown.* Because I wasn't dedicated to listening to my Soul, because the voice of my wasband had gotten so loud that it was drowning out the voice of my Soul, she took matters into her own hands.

First, it was a speeding ticket. Then another speeding ticket. Then I fell down some stairs, as I was leaving a massage session, late for another appointment, while listening to a voicemail and answering a text. One minute I'm feeling the rush of rushing, the next I'm at the bottom of some stairs with a very painful ankle and completely disoriented and bewildered. The ankle hurt for months. But I kept working out on it and going at my usual

24

frantic pace. I was constantly thinking about the next thing, never focusing on the thing I was doing in the present. It was also like an addiction that I couldn't stop. I'd always feel better if I accomplished more. More productivity is better!

Then I got another ticket for rolling through a stop sign and not having insurance. I had insurance, but had been too rushed to put the proper insurance card in my car, maybe.

Did I listen to all of these warnings to slow down? I did not. Finally, my Soul forced me to slow down by breaking my clavicle *while rushing on a Barbie pink Razor scooter to the park.*

I had been telling myself, *Give yourself a break, Tracee, you're going through a divorce,* when I was being harsh to myself. I gave myself a break. My Soul had told me to go back and get my phone, which I used to call my neighbor to come pick me up from the side of the road. I felt a huge release in being able to bawl my eyes out about my physical pain in the ambulance. I'd been unable to have this same kind of emotional release while grieving for my marriage. I cried for my pain, for my marriage, for my fear, for my money frustrations, and for the loss of our nuclear family. That release was cathartic and cleansing to my Soul.

Still, not even a motherfucking broken shoulder was enough to make me actually slow down.

⁂

I THOUGHT PERHAPS I'D take a nap the next day and just go about my business. I had never seriously injured myself, so I was caught unaware about the amount of energy a body uses to heal a serious trauma and broken bones. I even went to a meeting *the next day*—one I had scheduled several weeks before—though I was half out of my mind with pain.

Finally, I made a conscious choice to transform my relationship to time. This had become imperative: Slow down or die.

I dedicated myself to rest. I slept. When the co-parent came to get the children, I lay down and slept, I lounged around with books and in front of the television. It was delicious. I made a religion of it. I consciously walked slower, thought slower, moved slower, *drove* slower, and planned little that I *had to* get done.

I finally slowed down to grieve the end of a marriage and a nuclear family dream.

FOUR

JANUARY 31, 2013

There comes a point when you have to ask yourself why you don't have something or haven't done something you want. I have this manuscript titled *The Girl Revolution*. It has been sitting on my desktop in various forms of editing—essentially finished—since 2009. It's a series of essays and rants about topics that concern me about femininity: abortion, waiting until middle age to have children, body image, the media, and culture, lots of parenting girls stuff. It's the kind of thing I used to focus *The Girl Revolution* blog around. It felt fundamentally essential that I write this book. It felt like God demanded it of me. I wrote it in thirteen days, one chapter per day. Charlie was about two at the time and I wrote it with him literally climbing up my back and sitting on my head. Something has stopped me from publishing this manuscript. For a long time I thought it was a fear of mean girls. I assumed that feminists would be angry with me, and that conservative women would take issue with pieces of it. They can be vicious. I felt the book was inspired by Spirit and was writing itself, using me as a conduit. I could publish the book right this very minute if I decided to. But, I don't. I haven't.

I thought it was fear, but maybe it's something else. Maybe it's not something I really want. The book is angry, indignant. What you put out there comes back, right? What place does angry have in the spiritual journey I am on now?

❧

JESUS GOT ANGRY AND threw a table over, at injustice and wrong thinking. The Buddha got angry at the horrible conditions of humanity in general, which incited his path. Roseanne Barr wrote a very thoughtful book in which she talked about her own struggle with the place of anger in her spiritual journey. Her conclusion was that we are *supposed* to be angry, not at people, but at wrong thinking and bad behavior. Gloria Steinem didn't sit back and meditate on the fact that she couldn't get equal rights; she got pissed off and made a big ruckus about it, changing the entire world. God, Himself, is spoken of as angry and wrathful, especially in the Old Testament. Is it possible that God is illustrating to us that anger is part of love?

Add to that the shadow work that the spiritual community is talking about now. The idea being that if you fight or deny the shadow part of yourself, you will turn on yourself destructively. Be it anger, addiction, obsession with a behavior or an unhealthy habit, or whatever it is that's tempting you in your life. To turn away from the shadow ends in self-destruction.

Perhaps the only way to eliminate anger is to express it and let it go? It has occurred to me that if I just published the damned book it would not remain in me, it would be *expressed.* Which might be exactly the right and most healthy thing to do.

I have a thyroid issue and the thyroid is about expression in the mind-body-spirit connection. This means I need to express myself in order to heal my thyroid. But much of what I have to say is angry. I need a productive outlet that will do no harm, but which causes change.

Except . . . generating anger is like an addiction. You can fuel your energy with it, but it comes with a cost.

I began feeling icky and drained when talking about girls' rights. It began to feel like whining and begging to me, so I went back and tried to edit it. But I just. didn't. want. to.

Yet the book plagues me. The unfinishedness of it. It's an energy drain because it's there, on my desktop, and I think about why I'm not publishing it all the time. I feel guilty about it. I feel afraid about it. It's been four freaking years. What the hell is my problem? What is stopping me?

This year, though, is my year of *gentle contentment* and my Year of YES, which means I'm letting myself off the hook for this TGR Manuscript. I will not publish the book unless I can be content about it, and I will not publish the book unless my Soul directs me to. I will not publish the book unless it makes me feel good to do so. I have an urge to move the folder into my desktop trashcan to free myself of it completely. Yet, I don't want to destroy my work. Perhaps I should email myself the manuscript and then ceremoniously toss it in my trashcan. Though this thought occurs to me, I haven't been able to follow through yet.

༄

THE THING ABOUT SOUL whispering is that you have to filter out other voices. I've been cutting off communication with some of my friends because I notice that I care too much what they think about my path, about my life, and so on. My one friend, Charlene, is lovely and fun and wise. But I internalize too much of what she has to say. She is a bit cynical and often negative. If I had any guts at all, I would just tell her it bothers me. I mean, I've told other people that I'm getting still and quiet to hear my Soul speak. It is a long-standing and destructive habit for me to go around taking care of people's feelings. I have done this at the peril of my own Soul many, many times. Not just with my husband, but with my friends as well. I have been called "codependent," a label I take issue with.

❧

HAVE YOU READ THE definitions of Asperger's disease and codependence? (These are from Wikipedia.)

> **Asperger's disease**: *Characterized by significant difficulties in social interaction, difficulty communicating, difficulty establishing intimate relationships, restricted tendencies toward empathy, alongside restricted and repetitive patterns of behavior and interests.*

> **Codependence**: *Taking care of other people's feelings at the peril of one's self. Often projecting assumed feelings on others. Doing things to control other people's feelings, not realizing that one actually has no control over anyone else's feelings.*

The definition of Asperger's describes almost every man I've ever known. The definition of codependence describes almost every woman I've ever known.

We have effectively clinically diagnosed maleness and femaleness as psychologically abnormal conditions.

❧

I AM BURNED OUT ON mothering. I did fucking *everything* for eleven years: work, housework, writing books, and taking care of the children full time. I am depleted. With Alex taking the kids, I have had a tiny taste of silence and peace. And I like it—perhaps too much. It has made my tolerance for my children's bullshit: fighting, arguing, fooling around, making noise, wanting things, sucking me dry, and acting like I should do everything for them seem very, very limited. The thought of spending all damn day with them over the summer makes me want to scream. I don't think I can do an eleventh summer of working from home with their constant presence unless I also take a few trips where I can be in peace and spiritually focused before and during.

For eleven years I have been unable to afford to pay for quality childcare, thus I work from home. I work amid screaming and fighting, the brain-grating sounds of the Disney Channel, constant requests for peanut butter sandwiches, kids' friends running in and out of the house making messes, and demands for attention; and many times I have worked with children literally crawling on me and my workspace. Anyone who doesn't hire a mother who has been working at home with her children is a fucking idiot. Working from home with my children has made me a productivity ninja. The educated work-at-home mother is the most underutilized resource in America.

❧

ALL OF THIS FRUSTRATED, angry negativity, whining, and complaining is biological. It's the PMS of *perimenopause*, a word spell-check doesn't even acknowledge. This happens now. I used to not bat an eye at my period or PMS. But now my life is a cycle of emotional havoc. I have one week of highly creative productivity happiness, optimism, and bliss, one week of angry frustration and bloating (PMS), and one week during my actual period when I am tired and restful and open to intuition. I'm being robbed of the fourth week by the bioidentical hormones I take.

PMS serves as a "codependence corrector." As women, we let shit slide. We let people cross our boundaries, especially our spouses, lovers, and children. Then, once a month, we set things back in their proper order, drawing boundaries and flexing our muscles, forcing people back in line. I sometimes have a vision of myself as a Mama Dog. She allows a lot of mischief and goofing off and boundary pushing from her pups. But then she nips and barks and puts them back in line, restoring the natural order of "I'm alpha and you're my bitch!"

PMS is healthy and necessary. That doesn't make it suck less.

&

SING ME A NEW SONG, I whisper to my Soul.

FIVE

FEBRUARY 4, 2013

A as I said, I've been practicing the Law of Attraction for quite some time. Since I saw *The Secret.*

Sometimes corny things work. In *The Secret,* someone—Bob Proctor, I think—challenges us to see if it works. "Attract a cup of coffee today," he says. *Oh please! I have a coffee machine in my kitchen, so of course I can attract a cup of coffee.*

But I started to play with what I could attract. I started with a pair of pants. I had a vision of a photo taken on the first birthday of my son, Charlie. In it, I wanted to wear a pair of jeans with a red cuff at the ankle. My son would be naked and we'd be walking down the country road of the family house my uncle still lives on in Kelsey, Texas. A red cuff on a pair of jeans. Where was I going to find that? Oh, and I had another stipulation, I wanted it to cost $1, because I didn't have any money.

This image didn't leave me. I just wanted it. I thought about it and wanted it actively. But I wasn't desperate for it. I was curious as to whether this Law of Attraction business would actually bring me a pair of red-cuffed jeans.

One day, I was driving with my mother-in-law and we decided to stop at a garage sale sign we passed. Right there on a folding card table was a pile of denim. There was my red cuffed pair of jeans for $1. And they were *almost* the right size. I think I had to leave the top button undone for the photos. My photo turned out *exactly* the way I had imagined it.

Think of the miracle of that manifestation. When was the last time you saw a red cuff on a pair of jeans? And to find one at an unadvertised garage sale I happened to be passing? And to have them be in the *right size?!?* I mean, think of all of the sizes the jeans could have been; they could have been for a toddler or a 2X. But they weren't; they were MY size. And they were in time for Charlie's first birthday party and photo shoot.

This, and many other miraculous experiences since, has made a believer of me. Still, the Universe is vast and there remain mysteries to experiment with.

I told this story to a small group of Law of Attraction practitioners who were attempting to start a mastermind group of people committed to learning more about how the Universe works so we can manifest what we want. At the end of my story, one of the women asked, "What if you already had that photo in a parallel lifetime and you were remembering the photo?"

This aligns with *Conversations with God*, in which God explains that all time is happening now and that it's like printer paper stacked on a spindle. We move between realities in time during our sleep, and there is some overlap in consciousness.

That is a bit more than I can wrap my brain around. However, I have been told that I am highly psychic.

Now, before you freak out about the word *psychic*, understand *that* I mean it in the completely normal sense. I have a *knowing*. But this knowing was religiously trained into me. I was brought up to listen to the Holy Spirit, and use the still small voice to guide me. Mormons, the religion of my youth, believe in the gifts of the Spirit, of which "promptings from the Spirit," are a mighty force. A great many religions acknowledge this reality.

The question I've come to lately is: *What am I attracting vs. knowing or predicting about the future—or even remembering from my highest self who may have already lived this life elsewhere? Are my experiences coming at me after my thoughts? Or are my experiences coming at me from another direction?*

Perhaps you've heard something inside you *remind* you that you should take a different action—because you want to bring about a *different* outcome than *last time.* And maybe it happened so fast that if you did heed its guidance you might not even know what you avoided: an accident, a blowup with your kids, a divorce. If you didn't listen and you took the action anyway, perhaps you've found yourself kicking yourself for not listening to that little voice that told you to do something else.

My point being that since I've decided to say yes to my Soul, the higher part of me that knows the way already, I wonder what I am attracting and what my Soul is psychically predicting. Where is the line between these two things? Where is the line between *listening* and *choosing?*

The home I live in, for instance. It made a brief appearance on a dream board I created in 2007. I wanted to move and I wanted a house when we moved. But I couldn't find any pictures of houses I desperately wanted in the magazine I was looking at, so I just ripped out the one image of a house that I found—with grey siding, relatively modest. The one intriguing thing about the image was that there was a party on the lawn and a movie was being projected on the house. I was drawn to that image. Soon after, I realized that I didn't really love the house, so I covered it with another image, but never put up an image of a different house.

I live in that house. Simultaneously, there are things on my dream board that have been there for years and years, and my wanting of them is laced with a desperation that, according to all the Law of Attraction teachers, *repels* what you want.

To attract what you want, you have to want it bad enough to institute practices like repeatedly reading vision statements or saying "I am" or "I claim" affirmations many times a day, envisioning yourself already having or being it, and *acting as if* you already have it or are it. But if you want it so badly that your desire tips into desperation, then you're repelling what you want. Of course, if you don't want it badly enough to be desperate for it, why would you spend all of your energy on getting it or being it?

Is it, in fact, your Soul that is crying out for it? Or is it only the things that your Soul wants that actually manifest, while the other things languish on the dream board, fading into obscurity: "Oh, I forgot that I wanted that once?"

Where are the lines? Do things happen from back or front? Is there a magnificent piece about the play between attracting and remembering or predicting that we need to know about to create the lives we want? Or is all the fun in the mystery?

If this shit were easy, Jesus would have been no big deal. Also, I suppose religions wouldn't have made it all mucky with their weird human-loathing issues.

൙

THIS WEEKEND I WAS SO freaking happy not to be around my children. Do you know all men's dating profiles say, "My children are my world." *Uh. Okay.* If that were as true during the marriage as it is after the marriage, then these men likely wouldn't find themselves on dating websites. I imagine my wasband puts a similar sentiment on his profile, but the truth from my end of things is that they became a part of "his world" only when we separated and he got scared of losing them. I suspect this is true for the majority of these men.

Myself, I am basking in alone time because it was so ever-loving rare for eleven years. So this is not something I put on my profile. I love my children, but they are not my life. Sometimes they are, but I really cherish my time when no one is demanding, whining, disobeying, arguing, talking back, ignoring, and crying. My daughter has been particularly trying. I thought I was going to pull this off so much more smoothly than my own mother.

Perimenopause and puberty combine to make a lethal combination in the mother-daughter hormonal soup. Yeah. *That.*

ॐ

THIS WEEKEND MY FRIEND Donna, a forty-three year old woman who has never been married and is an introvert, suddenly realized, *Oh my god, I want to get married and have babies!* Prior to the last few months she has been: "If it happens, it happens. I don't want to settle."

The modern woman amazes me sometimes. Often I think feminism made us think we were supposed to be like men and share their laissez-faire attitudes about love and marriage and our professions. Let me be clear: *Men's priorities don't make us happy! We certainly should not trade ours for theirs! This is one of the primary reasons our planet suffers, and why we suffer. We women aren't in touch with our own femininity anymore.*

Anyway, I tithed my whole Saturday to giving Donna a makeover at Ross and the ARC thrift store. Shopping while poor is one of my super powers. We came back to my house and I took some beautiful photos of her in the new, bolder, more feminine wardrobe. We put on makeup and curled her hair. She looked amazing! Then I put an online dating profile up for her and the dates are already piling in. I hope it's not too late for my friend to find a husband and get pregnant.

I don't want to settle. I heard this sentiment from a fifty-five-year old woman recently as well. But she has settled, and what she's settled for is *being alone.*

My marriage did not see me through to death. But I don't wish I'd spent the last twelve years *alone* instead of being in the marriage and having two great kids. I'm glad I was married for twelve years. And it's not even that I fear being alone. I don't. It is something special to have *tried* for each other to make a marriage work for twelve years and then finally to be kind enough to each other to throw in the towel, and let each other go make a happier life. It's the *trying* for each other that has value.

Alone. It's not a terrible existence, and God, I'm loving it so much right now. I can't even describe how much I love this little window of alone in my life right now. But if you want to be married and you're afraid of settling for someone who's not perfect, here's news for you: All married people are just stumbling idiots who have agreed to be stumbling idiots together. You can be a stumbling idiot alone or with another person.

That's how I feel about my marriage in retrospect. Not all marriages have to end in "Death do us part" for them to have been a successful worthy endeavor; some of them just die. A divorce is not a failure. At least not for me.

❧

ON SUNDAY I FORAGED. I had gotten paid and we live so ridiculously hand to mouth that the children had been complaining that we have no food. *No food* can be translated to mean: "We are out of cereal and bread and snacks." *I didn't even get to eat breakfast because there is no food in the house* translates to: "I chose not to eat eggs, cereal, or yogurt because I am a spoiled American child."

I went to church and then to run boring, necessary errands. In other words, I got paid and immediately went about spending every penny I have. This is how it goes these days. Our needs run ahead of my paychecks. It is the biggest peace destroyer in my life, though my tween is running a close second. And my relationship with time and ambition makes a play, too.

᪢

I HAVE, LATELY, BEEN experiencing a change in my eyesight. I've had perfect vision all of my life, but this summer I realized I was having difficulty reading street signs. I may need glasses.

What is really disturbing my peace is my light sensitivity. My eyes are being strained by public lighting. Too much light is making it difficult for me to concentrate. It's been going on and getting worse for about a year now. At times, I strongly want to wear my sunglasses in Target or at church when the hideous overhead florescent lights are on. I'm very squinty. I don't know if this is eye-related or something else. I just had a blood test this morning to see if it's diabetes. I pray not.

I'm also becoming very sensitive to noises. I think this is why my daughter is grating on my nerves. It's the noise. The whining and complaining, screaming, and arguing is hurting my ears.

Part of me believes that this is part of perimenopause and the development of my psychic awareness and intuition. I think I'm becoming more highly attuned and playing on a new level of awareness and sensitivity. But this weekend, after I had already exerted so much energy with my friend—which was really fun for me, so don't think I'm saying it wasn't—by my errand-running time in the afternoon I was unfocused.

I'm also on my period and I think I get a heightened sensitivity during my time, plus I was under florescent lighting for many hours. I've been told *very clearly* by my Soul to slow down and rest. But I didn't. The effects were quite scary. It made me out-of-this-worldly: half in my body and half out.

I ran a red light turning left, and I'm fairly certain I'll be getting a ticket in the mail because I saw a camera flash. Then I literally ran a red light after church. It was red. I was looking at a green light, but it was one block up. A very short block, and I'm not sure why I was looking at the wrong light, but I was. Halfway through the intersection, I realized I was running a red light. Thank God there was only one car coming and it was far enough off not to be a danger. I don't know what to make of this.

Then I kept losing money. I had put it in envelopes that I kept confusing and losing. By the time I was going to get gas, I abandoned my mission. I had gotten so disoriented that I would get out of the car and be in the store without my Redbox movies I was returning, and I would leave my purse in the car.

Rest. It has been commanded. But I was feeling free and with time on my hands and I had things to do. It feels good to me to knock stuff off my list and help people and be social. But rest has been commanded by my Soul. I think I was overstimulated.

I feel very fragile. Not in the powerless sense. But definitely in the sense that my body, mind, and spirit are going through drastic changes and I need to be cognizant of myself, and step carefully and slowly through them. I mean, running red lights and not paying bills on time is not cool. My marriage was basically like running on empty: chronically stressful. It was exhausting and physically demanding. My Soul is weary from the effort.

Rest. Command. Not Suggestion. While on my period and during PMS there is a distinctly different vibe to my thinking. It is Monday, at the first of the month. Because I didn't rest over the weekend until Sunday, when I meditated for about an hour, I am tired. I have run out of money and I only cashed my check this morning. I am so stressed about money that even the $3 per day it costs me to come to a coffee shop to write is a frustrating experience.

Another part of me sees that all my needs are met. We have the food that I and my children like in the fridge. My gas tank is full. My bills are paid. I have $125 set aside for a Mayan massage I have scheduled this Friday. My Soul has told me that she can help me with my hormones, my belly, and the pain that I store there. I'm pretty sure I store pain that I've been carrying around for my mother in my belly and that there is marriage pain stored there, too, which makes me look chronically pregnant and gives me chronic constipation. I have a full day of training scheduled with a coach that I scored for $20, which will help me step into my coaching business scheduled for March. I'm getting a garage door installed this evening. I lost one assignment only to replace it for double the price. Big picture, things are well. They are falling into place. They are happening in my favor.

We have enough. We are blessed. But the stress it causes to live from hand to mouth is distracting me from my joy. I'm conflicted about tithing. My Soul says this means I should probably contact Tammi, who is running the churches tithing program. I've been tithing for a little over a year, and it's great. Except for the fact that I have not one penny saved. Every time I save a penny something comes up that requires *all* my pennies. In January, I saved 10 percent of my earnings, just as I tithe 10 percent. Every solitary dime vanished by January 31. My savings account sits on empty. One of my checking accounts was down to $-119 from tithing and the other was down to mere dollars.

I'm so weary of living like this and it's causing me so much stress that I fear I'm sabotaging my ability to rest and recuperate. I don't want to stop tithing, but I am very frustrated and I get a little angry when I look at the tax document that says I've donated

$3,880 to the church this year while I have not saved a single penny to protect my family in the future and relieve my own stress.

God, what do I need to know about money in order to have money saved and to feel financially secure? I open myself for God to change my beliefs and thinking about money to achieve this end.

SIX

FEBRUARY 6, 2013

Hi Tammi, I am having conflict about tithing and I should probably talk to you about it and try to clear the conflict, since you're the Thriving by Design lady and all.

I got my end-of-year statement from WLC and feel happy that I was able to keep my commitment to myself and God by giving $3,880, or something like that, last year in spite of everything. What I feel bad about is that I was unable to save one solitary dime. During the same year I had to feed my family from the food bank for several months. I hate living hand to mouth and am in a constant state of fear/obsession about money.

I attempted to tithe 10 percent to the church and 10 percent to myself for January, because that is what my intention is. But in fact, every single dime had to be spent on gas or bills or groceries. I have nothing saved for retirement. By the time I got paid this last week, I was down to $15 in my checking and zero in savings. I was out of gas and groceries and late on the sanitation bill. By the time the check was in my hand, the money was already spent. I'm in debt from my divorce as well, and I am unable to make anything but the minimum payments. The stress is wearing me out.

Part of my conflict is that I am tithing on my GROSS income. I'm a freelancer, so when I get a check I tithe on it in full. This is a problem because it doesn't account for any business expenses, like paying employees, or taxes, or anything else that I have to pay. I feel conflicted about whether or not I should continue to do it this way. In fact, I often use my checking overdraft to pay tithing out of my maintenance and child support check.

I think I need some help working this out.

Tracee

❧

Good Morning Tracee,

Thriving by Design lady; interesting, I mean the lady part!

I apologize for the delay in my response, but honestly, I have been thinking (praying) on this since I read it yesterday and I want to respond as thoughtfully as I can. This isn't an easy philosophy to actually practice; it takes a kind of faith to truthfully believe that the Universe will come through for each and every one of us, to the very degree that we believe.

Having said that, I know, all too well, that the circumstances that we find ourselves in are very real and have an impact on our decisions. Here, Tracee, is where the problem or challenge or opportunity (you, as someone who works and plays with words a lot, will understand the importance of which of these you choose) lies. If we can shift our thinking, intending, daydreaming to be proactive regarding our circumstances (i.e., what we really want) and become the "designer" so to speak, we will become less of a prisoner of our seeming lack or deficiencies and these circumstances will lose their power over our creativity and passion.

The truth is that we will "have" exactly as much as we can receive; that goes for good as well as seeming "bad." I know you "know" all this, but in my opinion, I think your work lies in the movement of that knowing into your heart, where it then becomes possible to trust that as long as you are true to your passion and intention, you will always be provided for. Given what you have told me, it sounds like you are "being provided for." It just isn't enough. I hope that's a fair interpretation; you have traversed an extremely difficult path and have come out the other side in large part because of your courage and passion for living a fuller life and despite

44

your fears. There is a real opportunity here for some serious gratitude and conscious planning for a bigger, louder, and fuller life for you and your family.

Tracee, I believe that you have everything that it takes to create this life. I would suggest relaxing into a feeling that the Universe (God, Buddha, whatever) is truly on your side and wants to give you MORE than you could ever imagine. (But don't let that stop you—imagine away!) Remember, it's the feeling nature that drives all the intention, thoughts, dreams into manifesting into the physical "stuff" that we desire.

This note has gone on longer than I intended, and I know I probably didn't give you the answers that you expected, but I do know that as you ask questions and gain some clarity about how this works, you will be able to become more comfortable with the idea that we don't have to absolutely "know" how everything works; we can just know it does.

About tithing, I'm not an authority of the subject, but I think 10 percent is kind of a guideline, and I suggest that you don't get too hung up on how much and on what to tithe on. Go with your gut; if there are feelings of angst or fear around your tithe, DON'T DO IT! It's all about circulation: giving, as well as receiving. Your tithe may take the form of service or giving time and not so much the money (which is just energy).

Relax, Tracee! You ask great questions and you certainly have Passion! Try not to drown in the details. Know what you want and be grateful for what you have now.

I hope this helps, even a little. Know that you are not alone and that these are valid concerns, lending themselves so that you can learn and grow and expand!

Have a great week!

Love,

Tammi

❧

"YOU DO NOT HAVE TO HAVE money to attract money, but you cannot feel poor and attract money. The key is, you have to find ways of improving the way you feel from right where you stand before things can begin to change: By softening your attention to the things that are going wrong, and by beginning to tell stories that lean more in the direction of what you want instead of in the direction of what you have got, your vibration will shift; your point of attraction will shift—and you will get different results."
—Abraham-Hicks, Money and the Law of Attraction

❧

PHEW. THERE ARE THINGS about Tammi's letter that rankle me. It's not Tammi; it's the teachings of the Science of Mind Church that I go to. It's the supposition that people get what they "allow" or what they "believe" about themselves and their worthiness.

I allow that what she says could be true. But I have issues with it regardless. I've been told by many a practitioner of faith and healing that I feel unworthy of love, money, healthy relationships, and so on. And that's why I'm broke. That unworthiness is the thing that I must heal for things to come flooding into my life. For a long time I just took them at their word. But then I stood back and looked at the evidence. For over a decade, my wasband demanded that I stop being a writer and go get a "practical job" whether or not I liked it because he was utterly convinced of my inevitable failure.

Except. I didn't.

I was dumbfounded by his insistence that I could not do this. It was utterly offensive and foreign to me that that he would believe in my failure as a writer. It was inconceivable to me to even

46

consider quitting and joining cubicle nation, punching a Soul-sucking clock and not being present to mother my children.

Millions of women have given up their paths due to spousal unsupport, and demands that they give up on their dreams to fill the family coffers. Literally millions have abandoned dreams and callings to appease their husbands and "make peace" in the relationship at the cost of their Souls. I did not.

I never even considered it. I stood my ground. In many ways, I sacrificed the marriage to appease my Soul. I participated in twelve years of struggle over whether or not I'd be allowed to pursue my calling and my gift and be able to have a happy marriage. The answer was no; as long as I continued to pursue my calling and my gift, there would be no happy marriage for me.

My punishment came in the form of deep, dark, long excruciating silent treatments, the withholding of love, the withdrawal of affection, the withholding of money to the degree that I went without medical attention and never bought one damn thing, including groceries, without fretting over his approval, I held fast to my dream. In the face of incredible pressure I did. not. give. it. up.

To me that illustrates belief. Worthiness. Allowing.

If I really didn't believe it or allow it, or believe that I was worthy of getting it, then I would have just folded and gotten the teaching certificate Alex wanted me to get. Right now, I'd probably still be stressing out about money, but I'd have a fully invested 503(1)(c)(3) plan, health insurance, and a paycheck that was automatically deposited into my account. But I wouldn't be following my Soul's purpose. I would feel unhappy and suicidal.

I know this because I did betray myself and get jobs for him. Many times. And regardless of what the job was, I was in some degree of misery for having betrayed myself.

The only thing that saves me is the work. The only thing that keeps me from addiction and self-destruction and dangerous anxiety and depression is the writing. This is how my Soul heals itself and creates my life.

I could have surrendered to Alex and his version of "reality," and given up on my own "delusions" of success. I could have. It would have been so much easier. I might still be married. I might even have some measure of contentment around money and finances. It would be the path most traveled. It would have appeased him and it would be inline with the expectations of society. It would be inline with the "realities" of the writing industry—that no one can make money doing it and that artists are starving and bat-shit crazy and tormented.

Except I didn't. Haven't. And will not.

I have pushed forward and remained true to myself, my path, my calling, and my gift. I have believed in my calling and remained faithful to it despite all the evidence that this is a foolish and naive thing to do. I've invested all my emotional energy into it. I haven't wavered. I've been afraid, yes. I've been doubting during certain times. I've wondered if "it" will ever happen for me.

Yet, I continue to make my living, as modest as it currently is, with my pen. Or with my Mac, rather. I have steadily increased my income over the last two years. I continue to increase my income. But unlike all the potential writers who quit, I DO make my living with the Word. That's more than most people can say.

❧

BOY, DO I HAVE ISSUES with the word *worthy*. This can be traced to the Mormons. My religion of origin uses the words *worthy* and *unworthy* to signify if God is going to let you in his temples and if you deserve blessings. If you follow all of the church's many rules—abstain from alcohol, drugs, cigarettes, unwed sex, coffee, caffeinated tea, pay your full 10-percent tithe, confess to believing all of their beliefs without question, tell your personal, spiritual and professional business to your bishop annually, and go to church every Sunday—then you are worthy.

If you don't do these things then you are unworthy.

As much as I logically do not believe this, I became "unworthy" when I was thirteen years old and I really did believe it. I had sex, that's the worst unworthiness possible. Period. I smoked, I did drugs, I drank alcohol and coffee. I was unbelievably unworthy. The very definition of unworthy. I was unworthy to see my siblings get married, unworthy of a special patriarchal blessing from my grandfather as a teenager, unworthy to go into the sacred temple.

Sure, there is repentance in this cultural story, but there's a deep-down part of me that carries this unworthiness as a fact. In the eyes of the church, I am literally "unworthy of all of God's blessings." The only way to remedy this is to go back to the church, suffer disciplinary measures in Church Court, and become a faithful Mormon, following all of their rules and confessing belief in their worldview. I don't believe it or want it. It's an irreconcilable unworthiness that I carry with me. *Ouch!* I've done a tremendous amount of clearing and healing work around this. Yet, a part of me doesn't accept it or want to let it go, evidently.

&

OR MAYBE, JUST MAYBE, all those healing practitioners are full of shit. Except, they don't know each other or my history, and they all report the same thing from my energy. So there must be something to it. I have no idea how to rectify it.

I submit that every person on the planet suffers from feelings of unworthiness. Someone I know just got the word *worthy* tattooed on her forearm where she must read it millions of times per day. She had to get it inked in her skin to begin to believe it.

Then there's this: I read a lot of autobiographical articles and books, and I watch television interviews about wealthy, successful people. Wealthy, successful people do not universally report feeling worthy. A great many of them actually report feeling unworthy of wealth, fame or success. A lot feel actively unworthy.

In fact, a lot of rich and successful people actually are unworthy. Some rich wealthy people do shitty, despicable things. They harm others and are complete assholes. And yet, what? They believe they are worthy, so they get millions or billions of dollars?

I don't buy it. I'm not sure that worthiness has anything to do with money at all. If success and wealth is attached to the "feeling nature of worthiness," as many spiritual teachers say it is, how do you explain the rich motherfuckers who feel like shit about themselves and suffer low self-esteem and actively self-deprecate? There must be another element that I haven't put my finger on.

Perhaps there are people who are wealthy who think, *I am wealthy, so I must be worthy of wealth.* But which comes first, the worthiness or the wealth? In my experience, unworthiness is the human condition. Otherwise, why would religions even have come up with the word *sin* to describe the condition of feeling unworthy? They wouldn't.

I also question the conventional wisdom of the spiritual community that success is directly related to the amount of good you put out there. *Really?* Are the Kardashians *really* doing better work than I have done and continue to do on my empowering girls blog *The Girl Revolution*, which I've written for five or six years? For that matter, is Mastin of *The Daily Love*, a feel-good newsletter, really putting out better energy than I have been putting out for many years on *The Girl Revolution*? Mastin, in fact, is only achieving fame as a great spiritual thinker because Kim Kardashian tweeted about *The Daily Love*.

Don't get me wrong, I am absolutely expressing unveiled jealousy at Mastin's success. I have subscribed to his newsletter and he's frankly not a very good writer. He repeats himself and he's an utter whiner. And I am jealous of his success and I want what he's having. But here's the point I want to make about his success: The guy very obviously does NOT feel worthy. He's doing it anyway and the Universe is aiding him with things he cannot make happen on his own. For whatever reason, it's happening for him. It is not, however, a result of feeling worthy or the amount of positive energy he's putting into the world. In fact, his feeling nature was one of utter despair at the exact same time that Kim published her life-changing tweet.

A correlation does not a cause make. You might correlate two seemingly connected things, like worthiness or positive energy and an outcome of success and wealth, even though they are not related just because you have a cultural belief about money and hard work. You likely believe: *If you work hard, you make money. If you do all the right things, then you meet success.* These are part of our collective consciousness as Americans. That does not make the correlation true. In fact, I'm strongly suspicious that it is not.

I think there is an element of the Universe that we have not yet named that is the controller of the energy of money and the energy of success. Some people have learned to master this element, though they cannot name it. Others struggle with the element and cannot figure out the energy of it. The Law of Attraction is definitely part of it. However, there is something to a predetermined path that pulls you to your destiny.

Abraham, of Abraham-Hicks, is a "group consciousness from another dimension" which is channeled through Esther Hicks, I get the Daily Law of Attraction Quotations in my email. Abraham brings up a solid point: There is a difference between *thinking* poor and *being* poor. Poor people think poor and that's a huge part of the reason they remain poor. They teach their children to think poor and that's a huge part of the reason their children continue the cycle of poverty.

Case in point: my marriage. While my parents saved every dime, scrimping and forgoing dinners out and impractical purchases, they are now sitting pretty in retirement, continuing a pretty comfortable lifestyle. My wasband's parents on the other hand have always lived hand to mouth on the brink of disaster. They think poor and make poor-people decisions. They will buy the cheapest blender at Walmart, rather than finding an exceptional blender on sale for the same price. Then the blender breaks in three months and they have to buy a blender again, and they buy the cheapest one, again. They fix a hole in the bottom of a bathtub with another bathtub with a hole in the bottom because that's what they can "afford." Effectively destroying the foundation of the house.

People don't pay enough attention to their spouses' families of origin. They get all blinded by love and think, *But my lover will be different because he/she doesn't want to be like his/her parents.* Of course, people can't change flawed thinking unless they recognize it and commit to changing it. I'm not saying people can't change; I'm saying it takes persistent, committed effort.

As long as I was married, my husband and I "couldn't afford it." It doesn't matter what the purchase was, we simply couldn't afford it. We couldn't afford to buy a house, until I made us buy a house. We couldn't afford to take vacations or go river rafting. But it was a values problem. There was usually enough money to eat out and buy beer. In fact, we would be on vacation and we couldn't afford river rafting, but we could afford to spend the same exact amount of money on a dinner of chicken wings and beer. We couldn't afford the dresser our son needed, but we could afford to go to a restaurant the second we left Ikea and spend more on meat and beer than the dresser would have cost.

My curiosity about my own money issues lies in the fact that I gave up and allowed my wasband to control the money, probably because he made the money and was in a constant state of anger about my not making enough of it. *What is mine? What is his?*

So now I am finding it to be an exercise in diligence to not default to thinking: *I can't afford it.* I almost caught myself saying that I couldn't afford medical care because I don't have insurance yesterday. The truth is that I do spend money on medical care, but I spend it on holistic practitioners and massage therapists, because I make that the priority. Holistic practitioners are not cheaper than a visit to the doctor. But I scrimp on other things in my life to actively participate in the healing of my body and Soul.

We spend our money on the things we really value. Different people have different values. I value healing and body work right now. I value spiritual growth and following my Soul's purpose. I value Apple products enough to pay more for them. I value good, healthy food. I value experiences and relationships. I value providing for my children. I value a great dress from the thrift store or Ross. I value expensive mascara and a good haircut and color twice a year. I value my skin and pay good money taking care of it. I value living in a good neighborhood in a decent house.

My wasband values eating out, costly daytrips, golf, and beer. I judge that, but that's what he values. There's nothing wrong with that as long as his values aren't trumping my values.

It must follow then that what I do not value is saving money: because it's not fucking happening. I could have stashed away thousands of dollars during my marriage. I could have just taken $20 here and there and hid it away. And I did. But then I spent it on something I valued more, like publishing my book *Love Distortion: Belle, Battered Codependent and Other Love Stories.*

I suppose I could go without the bodywork and healing massages and good haircuts and expensive mascara and thrift store dresses. I guess I could save that money. I could pay off my debt quicker and put it into a retirement account. But I don't. The evidence would suggest that saving money is not the predominant value in my life.

Is this because I don't feel worthy of a fat bank account, but do feel worthy of good haircuts and healing? Or is it that I simply need to make more money to support the lifestyle I intend to grow accustomed to? I mean, last year I brought in $38,000 from all sources. That was my gross income before business expenses. So it's not like I'm rolling in dough and doing blatantly stupid things with it. I'm running a house and supporting a family, and running a business and taking care of my body, and paying my tithing. That pretty much accounts for every dollar—and it's a significant miracle that I'm able to do all of that for $38,000.

Hell, I'm rrrrrich!!! Just think what I'll be able to do for $96,000 or $125,000 or $1 million! I'll be able to do sooo much because of all the money skills I've learned by living on $38,000.

I'm open to the allowing of all God's blessings, including the form and energy of cash and professional success.

As of late, my prayer has become less about making me feel worthy, and more about asking for something different. I'm sick to death of trying to become worthy. It's frustrating and boring. I surrender to my own feelings of unworthiness.

Lord, you say "With God ALL Things are Possible." I feel unworthy. I ask you to give me all of God's blessings anyway. I ask you to SHOW me how worthy YOU believe me to be, so I can learn to feel worthy. YOU show ME how worthy I am of love, happy relationships and money in YOUR eyes. And so it is. This or something better.

SEVEN

FEBRUARY 7, 2013

antam. Dove. Bantam. Dove. Bantam. Dove. Bantam. Dove. This is a message that my Soul whispers to me periodically. Usually it's when I'm about to give up on writing a book. I thought it was connected to the as-of-yet-unfinished *The Girl Revolution* manuscript. But maybe it's connected to another manuscript. I believe it's about a publisher. Bantam is a publisher, to which I would have sent a manuscript, but they only accept writers with agents. I don't have one.

Dove, of course, ran that Real Beauty campaign which really touched me. I thought I would have been a fabulous ambassador for the message to girls. I was, in fact, though, a free one, running posts about the campaign on *The Girl Revolution*. But I wanted Jess Weiner's job. I thought she was very unhealthy to be the poster girl for self-esteem and beauty. She recently came out that she was, in fact, morbidly obese and borderline diabetic with a terrible cholesterol level.

I have long thought that the girl empowerment/body image thing took a wrong turn with the Healthy at Any Weight movement. The glamorization of obesity is not the same as self-acceptance or self-love. Jess wrote an article, "Did Loving Myself

Nearly Kill Me?" to which I responded with a post that basically said, "No, because people who love themselves go to the gym and exercise their bodies because that's what bodies need. Exercise and eating right is an act of self-love."

Then I started to gain weight wildly, without any obvious explanation except that my hormones and thyroid were fucked up—oh, and I broke my clavicle and was doctor-ordered to be inert for about four months. *Touché, Universe.* I wrote a post apologizing and stating that Jess's weight is none of my fucking business and I shouldn't have called her out in public.

The point being that Dove didn't fire Jess and hire me. And now I'm not sure that I even care about girl issues. I think I should top talking about my middle-schooler in public, and I could just about vomit about the incessant whining of girl-empowerment bloggers and activists.

Please, oh please, make it easy for us to like ourselves by putting photos of fatter and uglier women in magazines.

I've asked the Universe to sing me a new song. Still I hear: *Bantam. Dove. Bantam. Dove. Bantam. Dove.* It's been going on for four years. It often happens in yoga or on the elliptical machine.

I've looked up the symbolism. Bantam is a breed of small chicken that is suitable for backyards. The Bantam rooster is aggressive and known to "puff up." The hens are aggressive when their young are threatened; they are very protective mothers. They are believed to be fertility omens in dreams, and the Chinese consider them a symbol of pride. They are the first up in the morning to crow and make the day known.

The secondary symbolism, according to PsychoBabble.net, is that "they are agents of enlightenment in their adulation of dawn," and "when a chicken's head is cut off its body, it refuses to recognize death." Then it gets rather depressing, "The chicken, in the end, is a symbol of the futility of hope. In the end of every day, of every life—night comes."

The dove is the bird of love, peace, and new beginnings, and is considered a messenger. In *Genesis,* God's spirit is represented by the dove. It is the symbol of the Holy Spirit that appeared at Jesus's baptism. It is the symbol that appeared to Noah to signify the presence of land. According to BiblicalArcheology.org, "In the Ancient Near East and Mediterranean, the dove became an iconic symbol of the Mother Goddess." Doves represented fertility and procreation. Doves are used in the Ancient Hebrew tradition as sacrifices, such as when Mary and Joseph sacrificed two doves right before Jesus was born. Jesus, however, became angry at merchants who were exploiting people's guilt, including dove sellers. Doves often appear in religious icons to symbolize the presence of the Holy Spirit. Christians used the symbol of the dove to identify themselves as Christians during periods where being involved in Christianity was a dangerous practice. In other traditions, the dove signifies a call to serenity and peace.

The question of significance remains. One truth I've come to accept: On the spiritual path, you have to get comfortable with the mystery, you have to embrace the mystical and just be in it.

ANOTHER PROPHETIC VOICE I've been hearing just in the last few weeks is that I'll be married in three years. The palm reader said that I will have a wildee time and then I'll meet him, and it will be everything I've ever wanted. What I want is hieros gamos.

Three years feels exactly right. It will allow me time to unmesh my energy from the wasband's energy. When you've been married to someone for a long time, it's difficult to determine what part of the energy is you and which part is him. Families, couples, develop shared habits. For a time after a divorce, you don't really know whether you buy that brand of toothpaste because you like it or because he likes it. Even deeper, you don't really understand which part of the money issues impacting your life are yours and which are his that leaked all over you. If you don't take time to sort these things out and clear the energy that isn't yours, it's like running straight for a cliff to your own demise when you get with another person right away. Then you bring your energy to a new relationship and mix it with the energy of your new mate and your ex-lover's energy together in a goopy stew of mucked up energy—unable to tell which is which and who's is what. This is the proverbial "baggage."

I'm still sorting out what is mine and what is Alex's. Do I really feel pressure to make more money because of my finances or is this residual pressure that he placed on me about not making "enough" money? Do I really feel unworthy of being a successful life coach and writer, or is his left-over negative energy polluting my confidence? Do I really want to do this, or that, or the other thing, or did I do them because he wanted to?

I have had several spiritual advisers tell me that a great deal of energy that we feel isn't even ours. Because "all is one," it is easy for energy to leak out on us and interfere with our energy. For instance, you get depressed after speaking to a negative friend. The negativity isn't yours. You've simply allowed the friend's energy to pollute yours. That's why peer pressure is dangerous. One energy worker I know claims that 95 percent of energy isn't ours. We're just picking it up out of a field of collective consciousness.

I had started to drink a lot for a few months in 2012. I normally don't care much about alcohol, perhaps having a few binge episodes a year, a few too many drinks at book club, for instance. But when we were getting a divorce, and were still living together, I started to drink every day. It made me feel like total shit, it made me depressed and anxious. A practitioner at church told me that she had been through the same thing with her ex-husband and finally had realized that his toxic energy was leaking onto her. Once she differentiated his energy from hers, the urge to drink vanished. Shortly after the finality of the divorce, I stopped drinking all together. I realized that a toxic familial and relationship history of alcoholism had meshed with my energy and caused me to crave alcohol and want to over-drink, when in fact, my Soul never wants to drink again.

My Soul had been giving me prophetic dreams about the danger of me participating in drinking for a while. I would wake up every morning, even after one glass of wine, and feel depressed and anxious. It would lower my spiritual vibration dramatically. I dreamed that I was walking up a steep hill of quicksand while my husband and other friends who drink were able to sprint up the hill. It was clearly connected to me drinking.

At my divorce party I got very drunk and fell asleep in the bathtub. My father is a very sick man, and when I would think about him my Soul warns, *Don't drink. If you continue to drink the price will be very high.* The divorce party was my last drink. I honestly have no urge to drink anymore: no cravings, no temptations in social situations. I just let it go and realized I didn't want it in my life. On dating websites, if I see photos of a man drinking I don't contact him or accept invitations.

I honestly believe that the drinking cravings weren't mine. It was toxic energy leaking into my energy field. This is codependence in the extreme. I've heard other stories about women who were physically ill as long as people they loved were alcoholics. And not just from the devastation of their outward behavior, but as an effect of living in a highly toxic environment. I think perhaps I've become a teetotaler and a throwback Mormon.

❧

THREE YEARS IS A GREAT time to get married again. I can't describe how utterly wonderful it is to make choices based on what I alone want. Not based on some compromise or mitigated, watered-down decision that accounts for his version of reality stamping out my version. To choose what happens to my money without considering how he will judge it or be angry about it. To prioritize my time according to what I feel is valid and important. To do what I want and when I want to do it is delicious.

I want to enjoy this freedom for three years. I'm going to savor every second of it. All the same, I do enjoy being in a significant relationship. I enjoy the stability of marriage, the having of someone to report the mundane to, the physical contact and affection. I remember these things. They were there to a degree in my marriage, but I've had them before in greater quantity and quality with men before. It's comforting.

And hieros gamos? Well, who doesn't want that?

Year 2013 will be the year of healing and building a foundation. This too is comforting. I need so much rest and healing. Honestly, I've been through a twelve-year battle. There wasn't a lot of yelling after the first few years, because he fucking didn't care if I yelled or not and he wasn't invested in the relationship enough to yell. The not-yelling was as painful or more than the yelling. The silent withholding was excruciating. It spoke louder than yelling.

I spent a good ten years of marriage trying not to care what he thought about me or what he felt about me. This did two things, it made me strong and I developed a serious core of emotional self-sufficiency. It also destroyed me, because your husband is supposed to care about you and you should care what he thinks. I felt like a failure for not being able to accomplish a detachment that would allow me not to care what he thought of me.

A marriage where detachment is the goal is a problem. That right there is enough to justify divorce.

EIGHT

FEBRUARY 12, 2013

I am leaving for a week-long individualized retreat in Sedona, Arizona, on Saturday. At first I was thinking I would stay for a few days. But then I thought, *Why? I have childcare, I've got my work assignments handled and I'm a home worker, so I can work in Sedona if I need to. So I'm going from Saturday to Saturday.*

My hosts at SpiritQuest in Sedona are custom-designing a retreat for me and I'm all in. I'm so relieved because I am sick to death of my children. I'm suffering from Mommy Burnout. They are constantly pushing me, and it wears me down. I don't want to ask them to help me clean anything because of the exhausting whining, complaining, screaming, and crying involved. They follow me around, constantly telling me about stuff they need that costs money and things they want to do that cost money, and most especially, the things they want to eat that cost money. I buy $10 worth of strawberries and they vanish in two days. Their very presence makes me feel a sense of lack, like I don't have enough to quench their endless *need.*

I don't particularly feel guilty about not buying my kids everything they want, but I get annoyed by their incessant requests and demands. I often feel like they expect me to do for them what they can do for themselves. I mean, things like waiting on them or inventing shit for them to do, or making them dinner. I fucking hate making my kids dinner. Co-parent feeds them boxed garbage, like chicken nuggets and frozen pizza and nachos. I do not. I feed them healthy food and vegetables not grown in a can, and they complain. They complain. They complain. They complain. This makes me wonder why I even bothered cooking an actual meal when I would be perfectly happy with a cup of yogurt sprinkled with almonds or edamame for dinner. About once a week I make a nice meal, only to regret it because of their refusal to be grateful and eat it; then I go back to the "fend for yourself" model. *Eat a peanut butter sandwich, just shut up about it.*

I love my children. I adore them. They are great beings, sweet and loving, and very pretty. I have built my entire life around being there for them, working from home and ensuring they have stability post divorce. But it's been almost twelve years of me being a SAHM and I am burned the fuck out, and exhausted, by it.

Summer is looming, only four months away, and I don't know if I can do it for another summer. The summers are so fucking hard. During the school year it's great because I can work and go to the gym while my children are at school. I can be here when they come home and that's the end of my workday. But, this year even school breaks have been unproductive, so I've smashed all of my work into the weeks around school breaks. But, summer. Oh my God, it's like a twelve-week exhausting demand fest. It's hours and hours and hours of opportunities for Madigan to defy me and pick fights. It's endless hours of daily fighting over chores, messes, and responsibilities. It's days and days of monitoring squabbles between them. It's *stress*.

My whole entire commitment for 2013 is to alleviate stress. Working from home flies in the face of stress reduction. Something's got to give. Like every other year, I would like to put them in camps and extracurricular activities, except it's so fucking expensive. It runs around $300 to put your kid in a five hour-a-day camp for one week. One week. I can take a pretty decent family vacation for $600.

I'm considering a few options: running away every morning to the free coffee and Wi-Fi at the gym (where I am now before my Tuesday Anusara yoga class) or dumping them at the Boys and Girls Club with all the other poor kids whose parents can't afford childcare either. I've even wondered what the fallout of telling the co-parent that I'm not the summer nanny anymore would be. What would he do with them for half the week?

That's where I'm at. It's not right or wrong, it's just where I'm at. I'm burned out on mothering. I've had a BITCH of a 2012 and I'm left weary. I'm on the rough and jagged edge. So I'm excited about Sedona and the opportunity for me to de-stress and hopefully fill my spiritual cup back up so that I can have the energy and optimism it will take to be the summer WAHM.

❧

I WENT TO A MAYAN abdominal massage therapist last Friday. I've written about her for local magazines and sent people to her numerous times. This must mean that my Soul really wants me to benefit from her healing arts, right?

I scheduled an appointment and against reason paid a whopping $125. *Boom!* That's a lot of money for me. There was a lot more lifestyle counseling than I had bargained for. I mainly wanted to go and get my stomach rubbed so I could get rid of the belly bloat that makes me look chronically pregnant no matter what size I am. I have a sense that this is not hereditary. Although my mother is plagued by belly bloat and she loathes it, it seems more like emotional osmosis.

Emotional osmosis is the way feelings, and how you handle feelings, get passed down through families for generations. It's not that the DNA declares that the women in my family were born with bodies that have belly bloat; it's that the women in my family teach their daughters, "Store your pain here. If your marriage (or whatever circumstance) is terrible and painful, store all that resentment, anger, and hurt in your belly."

In *You Can Heal Your Life,* Louise Hay writes that belly fat is fear and anger, and feeling undernourished. My marriage was a mirror image of my mother's marriage, so it follows that what I did with the hurt and anger emotionally mirrors her methods.

Except I want to let it go. I left the marriage, which is different than what my mother has done with her marriage. I have stood my ground and reclaimed my power, I have developed a very centered foundational sense of self that has value outside of what a husband or lover believes of me. Honestly, I don't actively feel any pain about my marriage. But energy gets stuck in the body if it has no way to release itself. That's why healing modalities like massage, kinesiology, tapping, meditation, and yoga are essential to the healing process—they physically allow for a way for negative energy to escape the body.

Often people will have old feelings trapped inside and they have no way to release them. They may be completely over the trauma of the event, but the energy is still banging around their bodies causing mental dysfunction, emotional outbursts, and physical manifestations of illness. Once the body releases the energy, the imbalance restores itself. This does not require 20 years of sitting in a therapist's chair rehashing the misery of the past, talking over and over about how it makes them feel.

I have released decades of energetic garbage in fifteen-minute visits to an applied kinesiologist who performed neuroemotional technique (NET) on me. It was far more effective and less painful.

Mayan abdominal massage is effective for infertility, hormone balance, fibroids, and other female issues. My hormones are whacked out due to perimenopause and stress. I am chronically constipated, my belly is chronically distended and bloated, and I'm losing my hair and eyesight. The belly is so embarrassing to me that I have stopped taking breath all the way into my abdomen because I am always trying to "suck it in."

Catherine Gregory is a Colorado holistic healer, so automatically she tells me I have to give up gluten. Every healer in Colorado believes gluten is the devil's blood. Eating it causes misery of all sorts. So I am challenged—after I get embarrassingly defensive about my attachment to my salad dressing and having freedom to eat whatever I want—to a two-week gluten fast. She held out her hands like scales, "Do you choose gluten or your belly fat?"

Honestly, I was torn. Then, I committed to the fast.

She also wanted me to go off bioidentical progesterone, pointing out that it is making me have a three-week cycle so it's obviously not doing me any favors while not making my PMS better. She prescribed Chaste Tree Berry tincture. I have to plug my nose to choke down the tiniest little bit twice a day. But she promises this is the natural, gentler way through perimenopause.

❧

TITHE HERE. TITHE TO *this part of God, tithe to your own healing.*

❧

WE DISCUSSED THE spiritual interpretation of my symptoms.

Chronic constipation is: not letting go of shit. Obviously. This is the proverbial "baggage" that people carry around, weighing them down until they let it go. This is in line with my belief that I'm storing my pain in my belly. My "pain body," as Eckhart Tolle refers to it, is physically manifested in a bloated stomach.

I've been getting progressively blurrier vision since the spring. I have a feeling this is more psychosomatic than physical. Mainly because it happened so fast and seems to be somewhat random. It involves a serious need to wear sunglasses in buildings, not just outside. While most people might need reading glasses in their middle age, I'm having difficulty seeing far away.

Catherine, myself, and Louise Hay agree that blurry vision is symptomatic of a fear of seeing the future. Which I need to reconcile. I've put off getting a diagnosis from an optometrist both because of the expense, but also to see if I can reconcile myself about what the future holds for me.

I am doing vision work as a Law of Attraction and spiritual practice, and I've come to notice that I sometimes have difficulty envisioning certain outcomes I'd like to experience. For example, I had a lot of fear connected with visioning *The Girl Revolution* manuscript. When it takes so much effort, it begs the questions: *Do I really want this? Is this vision scaring the crap out of me? Why?* And then some things are envisioned effortlessly, so effortlessly that I find myself daydreaming about them when I'm supposedly doing something else. Perhaps only these things are what I really want?

Words are so powerful that they created the entire Universe. The tracks we replay over and over have great impact on our lives. Case in point, during my divorce I told myself repeatedly to "give yourself a break," when I was being harsh to myself. It didn't take long for me to crash my scooter and break my clavicle. I literally "gave myself a break," which forced me into giving myself a rest.

I realized when meditating on my light sensitivity that I had a, "The Future's so Bright I Gotta Wear Shades" divorce theme party in September. *Uh, yeah, now I actually do gotta wear shades because the whole damned world is so fucking bright that I can't take it.* The Universe can be a very literal trickster.

I replaced this messaging with, "I can see clearly now."

Finally, after I've nearly had a breakdown with all sorts of fidgeting and defending of Caesar salad dressing and all things deliciously gluten, I get on the table for my massage and energy work session. Catherine is an intuitive as well as a massage therapist. Immediately she says she is seeing a very long line of women in my family who have self-acceptance issues. She asks me to breathe in a light of self-acceptance and breathe out any lack of self-acceptance I am carrying. I light up my family lineage from my daughter, through me, back through my grandmother to my great-grandmother and great-great-grandmothers. "This light is healing the generations," she says.

She then sees pink peonies flowing through the light I am inhaling. I had to Google this flower afterward because I was envisioning small blue flowers. I don't know the names of flowers. My womb was a large pink, peony-like flower, and there were many bees swarming to it and then going out into the world. "The bees," she says, "are your coaching clients getting nectar and then spreading it throughout the world." The hard knots in the top of my abdomen represent my withholding of breath, the sun. If I let the sun's rays shine, my flower will flourish and blossom and attract more bees.

Then Catherine gets an image of me shitting flowers. These same pink peonies are the shit I need to release from my bloated belly. *"All choices were the right ones. They are all blessings, they are all flowers,"* she says and I tear up. I choke my tears back though, because I have issues about crying and not "keeping it together," even on the healing table.

My poop turns to flowers as I release the pain I've stored in my belly. Poop to peonies. I like it. *I am blossoming.*

NINE

FEBRUARY 19, 2013

My Soul has kindly and generously manifested me a trip to Sedona. I'm being hosted by SpiritQuest, a spiritual guide company that coordinates personalized spiritual retreats. It is a customized retreat, which incorporates many gifts of the Spirit, such as hands-on healing, prophecy, listening to the Holy Spirit, and opening the heart. These, of course, are not your typical Christian methodologies, though the outcome is the same.

Thus far, I have experienced a range of modalities, including an intention-setting and releasing ceremony on the bank of Oak Creek with a life coach/healer named Barbara, a life coaching/clearing session with Bobbie, a seventy-year old woman who could pass for fifty-five, a chakra-opening massage while lying on a bed of crystals with lovely masseur/horse whisperer Adele, and a hike up a mountain with Ed, co-owner of SpiritQuest.

On the way here, I scored $390 in airplane vouchers through Southwest Airlines by volunteering to take a later flight. The Soul nourishes me with abundance. I have, of course, been anxious about money and whether I could afford this Soul trek.

I can't afford it is a difficult habit to break. Do you know that in the last twelve years I never once heard my husband say, "We can afford it." Even when we could afford it, he would say, "We can't afford it," and I would say, "I can't afford it." How I wish I had never uttered those words! How I wish my children had never heard those words come from my mouth.

The Universe is testing me on this trip. I came with $200, which has to last seven days. I have to pay for food, extra expenses, and travel. Shuttles alone cost $160. Yet my Soul has been instructing me to tip generously. I've been handing out $10 bills. This may sound like a lousy tip for an hour's worth of emotional and spiritual service, yet my worldly self is afraid to give it because I'm afraid to run out of money. I almost revolted from my Soul's instruction to give Adele a $20.

But, I can't afford it! I practically yelled at my inner voice. *I'm going to run out of money!* I tried to reason. Souls are un-reason-able.

Give her $20, my Soul instructed over and over. So I did. Because obeying my Soul is my commitment this year.

I am doing a lot of work with my second chakra. The chakras are energy points within the body that carry special meaning in the Vedic tradition. They correlate with emotions and the manifestation of illness. The second chakra is the womb/stomach area. It is associated with the color orange, which I am drawn to and wear every day of my life. I have been preoccupied with my belly and the fact that I look pregnant regardless of whether I am a size four or a size 12. It embarrasses me. I'm ashamed of it. Having never experienced body image issues before, it is out of alignment for me to be so preoccupied with it.

The second chakra is where nourishment occurs, and digestion. It is where we create: We grow humans there. It is also where we are "pregnant with possibility," as I am. Sexuality also occurs there. The art of creation resides in the second chakra. It's also where we draw breath, if we are healthy and not blocking it.

Breathing has been an issue for me. I have been drawing breath only to the diaphragm area at the bottom of my ribs. I do not allow it all the way into my belly because I'm afraid I look fatter when I do. Especially in public, I "suck it in," as both my mother and every exercise instructor I've had has commanded. Well, sucking it in does not allow the clean, nourishing breath of God to flow through the belly as it is supposed to—which, ironically, stimulates stress hormones, which makes the belly get larger. It is a problem and one that I have been focusing on here: How to let go of the pain that I have stored in my belly—the trapped energy left over from constant stress from being in a marriage in which I was not emotionally nourished or spiritually supported, where I felt creatively and sexually inhibited, and suffered emotional starvation as a blackmail tactic. A marriage in which I was pressured to drown out my Soul's direction and encouraged to give up, because my failure was guaranteed. A marriage in which I was practically forbidden to create my own life in favor of following a more limited and depressing vision.

While I did not submit to his vision for my life and continued to follow my Soul and made every attempt to manifest my purpose without his support, the situation took a tremendous toll on my body, mind, and spirit. My Soul became weary from the stress of it. It took a great deal of energy to resist his resistance.

All of this stress and pain is stored in my second chakra.

❧

AN UNEXPECTED phenomenon has occurred: I am highly eroticized. I'm horny, to put it more bluntly. I am having visions and fantasies about making love during every session. On the massage table, having lunch, glancing around the airport, during meditation, overlooking the Verde Valley on the top of a mountain. Everywhere I am preoccupied with the feeling of a man's hands and lips on my nipples, with a man touching and licking my *yoni* (Hindu word for pussy), with the moment of penetration of a new and exciting penis. There are crystals everywhere, which seem to be intentionally carved into phallic symbols. I envision inserting them into my vagina and collecting their mystical and healing energies.

I am having very clear fantasies about being consecrated with oils in sexual healing rituals. I can practically taste someone's tongue brush against mine. I have visions of a tall, masculine man pressing me against the red, smooth rocks under the Arizona sun and making love to me: kissing me deeply, running his hands under my shirt, slowly taking off my layers, moving his mouth over my vaginal mouth, penetrating me as I feel the hot rock against my back, healing me with his saliva, tongue, hands, and cock. I hear him whispering his desire for me, giving me erotic compliments as he explores my body. My Soul is crying out for sexual healing and release.

Sometimes I have profound gratitude that I chose this body, with its curves and thick blond hair and perfectly bowed lips and blue eyes. I love being beautiful, desirable, and attractive. I have a date tomorrow to go hiking and have lunch with a man I'm calling Sedona Steve. I found him on a dating website and messaged him to ask if he'd like to hang out and have a few laughs. I'm intoxicated with the thought of this stranger exploring my body.

The *spaces between* don't happen very often. At least not to me. I have a *knowing* that I will be blessed with a Sacred Union in around three years. But right now I am in the space between. I am untethered, unattached, at liberty to have experiences only single people are privileged to have. I can allow strangers to touch me and explore my body. I can receive kisses and touches from a variety of people. When you are young you have this, but you don't know you have it. It doesn't feel rare so much as it creates angst. The yearning is to pair up and procreate. But on the precipice of forty, it's different. It's finite. It's temporary. At least for me it is. Which makes it all the more special. Which makes it a holy space of pleasure. Pleasure. Pleasure. Pleasure. Unadulterated pleasure. Pleasure drenching is a spiritual practice.

When I was younger I carried shame and judgment about my promiscuous sexuality and the fact that I loved being desired and touched by many different men, and even a few women. It's different now. I feel *sovereign*. I feel at ease in my skin and trust my judgment. I feel like there really can't be mistakes, only experiences and my judgment of them. For all I know, Sedona Steve might be a bad kisser or have body odor. Or he might be exactly the right person to initiate a sexual healing and seduction of my Soul. He might bring me my first holy orgasm in many years and be a sacred sexual dalliance. He might be delicious and intoxicating.

Speaking of chakras, my next healing session is in twenty minutes. It's with Katherine, co-owner of SpiritQuest. She emanates an open, loving, and accepting energy, and has a fascinating life story of following her own Soul and forming a sacred partnership with her husband, Ed. Together they manifested SpiritQuest to facilitate healing. Very generous people, they hosted me in their home for two nights when there was an issue with my accommodations.

"After months of planning, we decided to launch the company on the new moon and held a ceremony," Ed told me over dinner in their home. "The next morning the phone rang."

"It hasn't stopped since," Kat said.

Remarkable. Thus far in my career, finding work has been more of a struggle than that. Except this experience with the spiritual travel column and The Year of YES! has fallen into place. Pitch an idea, Click. Ask for a place to quest to, Click. Cover the cost of travel, Click. Seek a part-time lover, Click. Seek a spiritual healing, Click.

Oh make love to me, Spirit. Go deeper, deeper, and deeper still.

TEN

FEBRUARY 20, 2013

I have an entire empty day staring me down. My date cancelled in favor of work. Whatever. He's cancelled twice now, so I'm not planning anymore outings. It's disappointing. I don't even have a good book to read. It is snowing in Sedona, which makes me not want to lug my computer into town on foot.

Everyone keeps telling me I look "bright." Which is great. I love looking bright.

Yesterday I had a great deal of sexual energy. I did two sessions. One was a chakra alignment session with Kat. She used vibrational sound and the essential oil of rose to stimulate the senses. We talked about my obsession with orange and blue. Every day of my life I wear orange. I wear an orange scarf and a blue coat, and carry a blue purse. It makes me feel bright and shiny, cheerful and optimistic.

Orange is the second chakra, the one based in the stomach and womb. It is the center of creativity. Blue is the chakra of the throat, the one of expression. We talked about how I always felt inhibited from creative expression in my marriage. Essentially, it came down to his refusal to support my writing as a viable path or career for me. He wanted nothing more than for me to fail, and even sabotaged my career. He did not want me to be a writer. Period. He didn't want me to write about certain things—all kinds of things really. He will disapprove of this book and of the therapies and healing I'm describing seeking.

I manifested a belly full of pain about my inability to express myself creatively, and a thyroid condition due to my inability to express my feelings, beliefs, and experiences. My Soul was silenced in the marriage. The belly and the thyroid imbalance is the physical manifestation of repression. During our session, Kat placed her hands over my heart and stomach while I visualized cords attaching me to others. These were cords I needed or wanted to cut. When relationships end, often physical cords remain, tying them to you. These cords can drain your energy and cause you to react to new events in your life in inauthentic ways. Someone can say something to you and you freak out, not because of what they said, but because of a cord that clings to you.

Cords also must change and shift. My daughter has been acting out with me. She's been moody and defiant. I have been triggered by fear: primarily the fear that she will turn into me and I will turn into my mother. My mother took my adolescence so personally. She constantly refers to my adolescence as the worst thing that's ever happened to her. I am turning forty and she still mentions this every time I see her. "No one should have to go through that!" she declares, as if she's the only mother who had a teenage daughter who didn't do what she wanted. I have accepted this as truth, and carried shame about it, for many years. *I was a terrible daughter.* This is a fact, according to family lore.

Except. Except here are the things that I wanted to do: stay out past dark, which happens in Utah's winter at 4 P.M.; hang out with my friends, although she didn't approve of them; have independent experiences; date boys; and be in theater.

How terrible. How *rebellious* of me.

Having these simple pleasures of adolescence denied me was what led to my rebellion. My God, I was grounded for two years for staying out past dark in my own neighborhood with kids she knew. Then one thing led to another: marijuana, to drinking, to sex with boys, and more. But here's the thing: I didn't get hooked on crack. I wasn't doing heroine. I wasn't selling drugs. When the "right path" is so narrow, there's simply no way to stay on it.

Well, there was no desire in me to stay on it, anyway.

The real issue, of course, was that my mother wanted control of me. *And so did I.* She loved being my parent when I did everything she wanted me to do without question. But when I developed other feelings and intentions for *my life,* it wasn't okay.

Rather than being loving about it, she was cutting and harsh.

The point here is not to go off on my mother for her failings. The point is to acknowledge that I now know how she feels, because I am reacting to my daughter in the same way. I want to maintain authority over her. I want to be able to control her, so that she doesn't "get out of control," like I did. I want her to do and behave and react how I want her to. I want her obedience and deference and respect. And she's not giving it to me.

I feel entitled to it, largely because that's what the 1970s parents who raised me demanded of their children. *"If you don't do what I want, then I won't give you anything!"*

My parents disallowed theater, which I was quite good at. And which, I might add, probably would have kept me hanging out with thespian nerds instead of the drug-using crowd I ended up with. My parents did not pay for me to go to college, though they paid for all of my siblings to go to top private colleges. They did not buy me clothes. They did not expend their resources on me. Why not? I was the *bad child.* And thus I behaved according to their expectations of me. The black sheep. *Unworthy.*

I am afraid of creating a repeat of this un-nurturing and un-loving relationship with my daughter, so I've been acting exactly like my mother did as my daughter exerts her independence. I've been taking it personally.

During my session with Kat, I visualized a cord, dark beige and crusty, between Madigan and me. We stood facing each other, expressing our love. I committed to allowing her room to grow, to experience life, to pursue her own path, and to supporting her in that. I recognized her as the sister of my Soul and thanked her for the opportunity to mother her. I expressed my trust in her judgment and her holiness. Kat then pulled the cord out of my belly button, pulling, pulling, pulling, and then cut it, swept it away.

I then visualized a celestial cord of light running from Madigan's middle to mine, a new cord that allows her more independence and a different kind of love between mother and daughter: one that recognizes her individuality and Soul's purpose.

This ritual and a week of rest, when I am not constantly bombarded with whines, demands, complaints, and screaming, will, I hope, make for a better, more loving, relationship between us.

Following that cord releasing, I also released several other people in my life. One was my mother. I did work in the summer with Radical Forgiveness coach Rena Petty. That work was to forgive my mother. Rena said that one of my purposes on this planet was to carry my mother's pain, because she was not strong enough to do it. However, now I am ready to lay her pain down and stop carrying it, because this is my time and she is now strong enough to handle it herself. This realization came after I dreamed that my mother died of a heart attack three times in one night. I was devastated and terrified that it was real. After the second time, I told myself if it happens three times it is prophetic.

I called my mother and all of my siblings to warn them. They all blew it off. They believe in prophecy, but what . . . not from me? Only from the right people? Rena said that the dream signified the death of a certain kind of relationship with my mother.

To have a healthy and loving relationship with my daughter, I needed to cut the cord between me and my mother. Other cords I cut were with Jake, who is a pest, always appearing when a relationship in my life is ending. He taunts me with his super lame advances, advances in which he gives nothing and attempts to take everything. Ours is a non-romance in which he gets his ego stroked and I romanticize my attraction to someone I don't even hold in high regard.

A major cord cutting was with Viveka Moon, my cohort in my teens and twenties. Our friendship was a dysfunctional marriage between hurt, lost Souls if there ever was one. She is a mean girl who hides behind extreme anorexia, and claims she's perfectly healthy emotionally, spiritually, and physically. She's also someone who appears randomly in my life either to declare her love or threatening to "expose" me as the slutty drug addict that I am, depending on her erratic moods.

The last person I needed to sever my bond with was Dave Lev, the boy I loved when I was thirteen to seventeen years old. I loved him probably more than I've ever loved anyone since. And he used to beat me up and do crystal meth and cocaine, then have rough sex with me all night long. I loved him still, beyond reason. I experimented with every kind of sex act with him. I did much of it because I was pressured to do so and I was extremely submissive. I was not the owner of my Self when with him. Leaving him was one of the hardest things I have ever done in my whole life.

❧

HERE IN SEDONA I'VE BEEN healing my sexuality quite a bit. During every session and during my off hours I have been seeing and feeling a presence, a man without real features; I can feel his hands on my breasts, his tongue on my clit, his tongue in my mouth, his hands on my belly even. He has appeared during meditations, during my chakra session, during my massage, and while I was lying down to go to sleep. He was with me when I cut the cords. Standing next to me, holding my hand. I am often pressed against the red rock as he explores my body, initiating, cleansing, and healing my body, my sexuality.

During the next session I was doing breathwork with a woman from Australia. She was a soft spirit and very accepting. "What is coming up for you during your sessions here?" she asked me.

"A lot of sexual energy," I replied. I explained that I had suffered abuse and experiences that needed healing.

She had me shuffle a deck of storytelling cards. "They are not oracles," she said, "just cards that might symbolize something."

I pulled one card.

And there was the man. There were five of him actually, repeating in a circle, this arms were in a Y so that when each of the men connected at the hands it made a star, there was an aura of yellow around them and the earth in the center of the card where the torsos connected. "What does this card mean to you?" she asked.

"This is the man who has been making love to me in all of my sessions," I said, only half-believing. "The earth is symbolic of how I feel at this point in my life: that the whole world is open to me, that I can do anything I want to, that the world is mine. The star came up in my first session on the bank of the river for my opening ceremony. It symbolized illumination," I noted.

Within the room was the same-shaped five-pointed star, illuminated and hanging from the ceiling. On the wall was an illustration that looked like a feminine version of the man on the card, depicted with a flowering vagina.

"Is it an angel, an archangel, or a spirit guide?" she asked.

"I don't know. He feels like the one I will have my sacred union with," I said.

"He has come to heal you sexually, perhaps?"

"I think so," I said, admitting to the possibility.

I then lay down on a mattress on the floor. She covered me with blankets and asked me to breathe a circular breath through every cell of my body. I drifted deeper into a trance-like state. There was music in the background with which I timed my breathing. During the session, my visions and thoughts and movement would change and shift. I don't remember all of the images; however, I do remember some.

She asked me to imagine myself somewhere, and I was lying against the red rock, hot against my skin, with the sun beating down on my naked breasts, feeling sexual and free, liberated.

"This, perhaps, is the innocent, sexual you, untainted and unharmed," she suggested.

"Yes, that could be so," I consented.

"Perhaps she has come to heal you sexually. Perhaps she makes love to you," she said.

And she did. She kissed me all over, running her tongue and hand over the squishy hallows of my belly. She poured oil over me and then lay down on top of me, slipping her supple body all over mine with sexual abandon, but slow. She kissed my mouth and it felt like her tongue delivered life itself. She inserted a crystal spire inside my vagina, illuminating healing light all the way up through the crown of my head. It was warm and delicious, my vagina pulsating with the energy of it.

Then, I imagined having sex with the being again. He placed his hand over my belly and his other fingers inside my vagina, sending healing light into my sexual organs, healing them with love and light. He anointed my breasts with oils and then his tongue. He kissed my mouth and my neck. He lavishly sucked the nectar of my pussy, playing with his tongue, pressing his fingers into my hole. Then he inserted his penis into my revirginized vagina, and his penis was a phallic rod of healing light running through all of my chakras, shining bright and potent, healing every cell in my body, illuminating my inner body, spiritual body, and outer body, giving me immense pleasure and splashing a baptism of cum deep, deep inside of me, cleansing me completely from the inside out.

I was pregnant with the Earth in my womb. I was Mother Earth, pregnant with all life within me, healing her within my belly, which was distended in a pregnant shape. I was Goddess, Mother Divine, the Sacred Vessel. I kept hearing the words *challis* and *phallus*. Then I saw Jesus anointing me as his lover, myself as Mary Magdalene, and us celebrating our sacred union.

The music shifted and I was dancing, moving my body slowly and rhythmically, baring my midriff without shame or self-consciousness, with goddess sexuality. This, I felt, was where all life was born and it reminded me of the Dance of the Seven Veils when Shalom exposed her whole self before exposing her face.

Then I went so deep that I remember nothing. It was yoga nidra, the yogic sleep, a state when you are lucid, and have access to the subconscious.

ELEVEN

MARCH 8, 2013

Finally, as I boarded the plane in Phoenix, I felt a twinge of missing my children. *Oh good,* I thought. *My mommy muscles aren't broken, they simply needed a rest.*

I feel far more patient with my children than I did before I left. My daughter is grieving and she has every right to. The entire family unit has turned upside down and I shouldn't be taking it personally. It's really not about me anyway. She has issues with her father because she doesn't get what she needs from him emotionally. He gives what he can; that's the truth.

In fact, though feminists would argue otherwise, I'm pretty sure men have limited emotional capacity in general. Certainly, as a mother I've noticed my son isn't as emotional as my daughter and has very little interest, if not outright discomfort, about sharing his feelings. He appears neutral about quite a lot. His expression about the divorce has been long delayed. "You and Dad should get back together," he said the other day.

"That's not going to happen, Charlie, but I can see why you're sad," I said. Better to disillusion him immediately than to pretend that there is even a slight possibility.

"Why did you guys get divorced anyway?" he finally asked

"We were fighting all the time and it wasn't fun for anyone. We are happier apart than we are when we're together. Not everyone stays married forever," I told him.

"What were you fighting about?" he asked.

"Money, how we wanted to live our lives, what I did for a living, how we raised you guys, what church we went to," I said.

"Oh," was his reply as he absorbed this information. "Well, then I want Dad to move close to us so we don't have to drive to his house, we can just ride our bikes over."

"I would love that, but Dad's the one that has to move to make that happen," I explained. "You'll have to talk to him about it."

This is the most in-depth conversation Charlie has had with anyone about the dissolution of our family.

Madigan, however, is a ball of hormones and unscreamed fury. My friend Anna came over to practice her new Healing Touch therapy skills. She's taking a class and needs people to practice on. My children and I are happy volunteers. After an impromptu dance-off to the family theme song "Thrift Shop," during which Charlie broke out his moves like Jagger and won hands down, Anna worked on each of us. It is very relaxing and we all love it.

Madigan's throat chakra, the source of expression is blocked. This was one of the issues that came up when I was in Sedona. She has things to say and I don't like them, put simply. I don't like them mostly because I can't fix them and also because she's screaming all of this anger in my face and it doesn't belong to me. It belongs to her father, but she can't express it to him at all, so she is snide and angry and mean to *me*.

I have this irrational idea that she *shouldn't* be treating me this way and that I deserve to be spoken to with respect. But she is angry and hurt and has no one else to express this to.

I don't want her throat chakra to be blocked and I can see that she's in pain. Now that I've had time to do some clearing and healing work in Sedona, I feel ready to be a witness to hers.

Be a witness. I once heard Goldie Hawn say that much of mothering, girls especially, is simply being a witness to them. You don't have to correct, hover, advise, or demand behaviors. Simply the act of witnessing is a profound function of motherhood.

So I granted Madigan *Amnesty Day.* For tonight, she can say anything she wants to say without retribution or punishment. This will be healthy for her. But I am afraid. I am telling myself that I can take it. But part of me doubts that I can.

No, I can. I can take it. She has a right to her feelings and stopped up, blocked feelings can come to no good. They can only be destructive.

My own throat chakra is the primary motivating force in my life and to be inhibited in my expression is one of the most painful things that can happen to me. Hence the dramatic adolescence and the miserable marriage leading to divorce. If I would just stop expressing myself, then *other people* would be happier. I, however, would quite simply die. And I mean that literally. Every time I have silenced my own expression it leads to severe depression and anxiety, resulting in suicidal tendencies from slow kinds of death like addiction and hanging out with self-destructive losers and lovers to very real suicidal thoughts. These suicidal moments have been rare, but real. Thankfully I maintained enough clarity to know that these thoughts were not normal and got help. I love myself for that.

I have been radiating since my return to Sedona. People have been calling me "bright" since my marriage liberation. Sovereignty looks good on me. It has opened my heart, because it doesn't always have to remain on the defensive. But on Sunday a gentleman named Cash said that he saw me "radiating" from across the room. The kids and I think it's funny that the first boy to flirt with me, have a crush on me, if you will, is named *Cash*.

The following conversation took place between my children and me only days after the divorce was final.

"Mom, are you going to marry a rich man?" Charlie asked over breakfast.

"Heck yeah! I'm totally going to marry a rich man!" I answered.

"I can't wait until we get our rich dad!" Charlie said.

"Yeah, then we can get a bigger house," Madigan chimed in.

"And we could have anything we want. Plus a pool," Charlie said, adding, "I can't wait until we get our rich dad."

"Me either," Madigan piped in.

Both have already mentioned that Cash would make a nice husband and that I should date him.

"He is nice, he's funny, and he's good with Eli (our dog)," Madigan reasoned. "I always wanted a funny dad that likes dogs. Dad is so serious and he hates dogs."

"Hey, I just met the man. I don't know enough about him to decide whether I want to marry him," I said. "I am really enjoying being single for now."

"Then you should date him," said Madigan.

"I'll probably go out with him if he asks me," I admitted.

"He's not handsome," Charlie noted.

"He's not bad looking; he's kind of cute, isn't he?" I asked.

❧

THAT'S THE THING. I've been out of dating for so long that boys turned into men. Men are kind of gross. There is a myth that they become more distinguished as they age. I suppose that's sometimes true. But when you begin dating you realize that there's a lot of forty-year old men who are potbellied and bald, and some have almost entirely abandoned the pretense of hygiene. This makes a man in his forties who cares what he looks like "good looking," even if he's not handsome. I think.

It's hard to tell whether forty-year old men are good looking on first glance. There are always lurking fears, like: *Does he have hair on his back that he's unwilling to wax? What other dirty little hygiene secrets lurk underneath his exterior? Does he sweat profusely and snore loudly at night? Is he a regular bather? Does he expect a blow job after sitting on his balls for twelve hours? Does he drink coffee all day and then expect to kiss you, with tongue?* Forty-year-old men can be repulsive.

When I think back on the boys I dated pre-marriage, they were young and still had baby skin, and hadn't yet turned into hairy beasts. It's hard to be ugly when you're young, simply because youth is so forgiving of bad habits. Age is not so forgiving.

So is Cash cute? Undetermined. Would I go out with Cash? Absolutely. The appeal, of course, is that I met him at church, so he's on the same spiritual path. He is coming to our money club, a Law of Attraction/spiritual prosperity group that I help organize. Being spiritual makes him attractive. Being focused on prosperity makes him attractive. Also being flirted with makes me feel good, though I feel a little shy about it.

I am at once, horny and lusty and hot for the idea of having sex again, and completely shy about the entire idea of being that intimate with a person. It's a sexual paradox.

❧

DURING MY SEDONA retreat I let go of the need for validation around my life coaching business. I had already taken steps in the direction of shifting my focus to life coaching. My website is being redesigned and I've been visualizing how I want it to look and what kind of niche I want to focus on.

The Girl Revolution.

I'm still a tad conflicted. There's something about it that isn't in alignment with me. However, I've built it up already with 940 posts, Google likes me, I have a following and name recognition. I don't want to sacrifice that and start over. Nevertheless, I did discard my need for Martha Beck certification on my trip. Who certified Martha Beck? Martha Beck. Who certified any of the life coaches making big money while helping people? Nobody. They certified themselves. Like them, I am called of God and certified by *The Girl Revolution.* Yes, it takes audacity, but I submit that I'm not short on audacity. I've lived much of my life audaciously. Sure it comes in bursts, but they are big bursts that have impact.

I don't know how to do it. That is true. But coming home from my trip and writing 450 mini-blogs about heating and air conditioning companies was enough to make me say, "I have to make this life coaching work and step into it and attract clients right fucking now, because I can't keep doing this kind of mind-numbing, energy-sucking piecework anymore."

I'm profoundly grateful for the blogging work I've been given because it has allowed me the luxury of not being psychotically stressed out about when the next check is coming. It has given me the peace of mind to relax about money because our primary needs are being met. It has even allowed me the mental rest I needed to regroup during these rough waters.

Yet, I'm over it.

❧

THEN I WENT TO AN accountant because taxes are due in April and it's March. I figured I'd only have to pay a couple of hundred bucks because, you know, I grossed only just under $24,000 in my business last year. It was a hand to mouth existence, very stressful to make ends meet. So I asked the accountant, "If I claim no deductions what am I looking at on $24,000?"

"Three thousand dollars alone in social security and Medicare," he said.

I spent the next twenty-four hours converting into a Paul Ryan style Republican and vowing that I simply *must* make a lot more money.

I am more than happy to pay for little old grannies that don't have any money. It is my pleasure to support people who are *worse off than me and my family*. But that's not how the social security system works. Instead, we send the largest checks to the richest people. My family that scraped by on $24,000 sends $3,000 to millionaires and those who live on six-figure retirement incomes and have paid-off mortgages and big fat 401(k) plans. It is beyond me that Democrats are down with this. That they keep defending this kind of system and claiming it protects the welfare of the poor.

This is what I was thinking, in a bit of a tizzy, to be frank. Because where am I going to get $3,000 in a month? And how, exactly, if I am working as many hours as I can work (or at least that I can work and still maintain a life and fulfill my mothering obligations) am I going to set aside enough money for next year's taxes while I pay off last year's debt to the IRS so rich people can get free money from me?

I'm also investing some energy in hating Baby Boomers. There's this enormous generation, which had 50 million abortions so that the generation that followed shrank so dramatically that now those babies can't pay for the Baby Boomers' social security. *Great choice, dorkwads.*

Then they crashed the economy, long before 2008, by increasing housing prices, and gas and grocery prices so phenomenally that MY generation has to struggle to pay for basic necessities, while they live high on the hog and pad their 401(k)s.

Yeah, I'm forty and have no 401(k) at all. Neither do most of the families I know. We're too stretched to have enough money simply to eat, pay for shelter, shop for clothes at the thrift store, and put gas in our cars. *And NOW we have to pay for you guys to get old and live a great lifestyle and have free medical care while you vote against "socialized" medicine? Awesome.*

Democrats are into this because . . . . ????????

Yes, I know. This is lack consciousness and won't do any good in making me more prosperous. The more effective thing to do is to jump in the game and simply declare and claim the $8,000 a month that my Soul told me I was going to be making in 2013.

I noticed yesterday on my financial spreadsheet that the $4,000 I wrote as my intention in my 2012 Vision Statement has manifested. Four thousand dollars was as big as I could dream during my divorce, while supplementing our grocery budget at the food bank. This seemed like a lot. And it was. It is. I can afford to feed the kids, pay all of our bills, and even put in a garage door opener so my tenant doesn't fall and hurt herself while entering through the garage. I finally felt like I was making headway and could afford to knock out long-term goals, like getting eyeglasses, teeth cleanings, and paying down some credit cards. Then I visited the accountant and it "threw me for a loop," as my mother would say.

I *have to* make more money. While I could try to do that by growing the writing/blogging business and managing a force of other writers, the fact is that it's measly work that sucks my Soul dry. There's no joy in it. Instead, I've been *called* to be a life coach and there's money to be made doing it. I *can* help people. In fact, I help people every day.

I don't know how to make the $100,000 I'll need to make to live on $50,000, but I don't need to know how. What I have to do is take the next step, the next step, and then the next one. My Soul knows the way, that's a fact. God is putting the right people and the clients who I can help in my path.

Since visiting the accountant I've begun offering my coaching services to clients. I have my first paying client this morning. She's in need. I can help her. She's broke-ass poor, so I'm only charging her $25 an hour. As a businesswoman (snicker snicker), I realize there's no way to make $100,000 a year selling my time for $25 an hour. In fact, there's no way to become rich by selling my time at all. I need to think bigger and I'm attending a bunch of free coaching trainings to learn how to do it.

If I had the money, I'd drop $8,000 on coaching for myself from master business coaches. I'd drop a bunch of money on packages and tools. As it stands, I'm going to have to step into my dream with a pocketful of audacity and a sugar bowl of faith, and just start where I'm at and build from there.

At Money Club on Tuesday we are declaring our dream and holding the intention for each other. It's a bold and scary step. Sharing big dreams makes people vulnerable to criticism and doubt. But as Jesus said: *Wherever two or more of you gather in my name, and agree on something, then it must be done unto you.* So we're stepping into that. We're going to declare and hold each other up.

Myself, I'm going to declare my intention: to *become a highly paid life coach that helps people step into their Soul purposes.*

TWELVE

MARCH 15, 2013

ON Tuesday I declared: *"I affirm that with God all things are possible, including these things, which manifest easily and effortlessly now for the highest good.*

"I am a highly successful and profitable life coach and I make $8,000 every month. I attract motivated clients who love to invest generously in themselves and my life coaching services.

"I now claim this or something better. And so it is."

A declaration is a very powerful statement, especially when it's uttered in the present tense and incorporates the most powerful words in the Universe: *I am.*

It was great to get together at Money Club and hash out the optimal wording for our dreams. It's so easy to get caught up in language that doesn't best serve us.

Way back when the wasband and I were struggling financially and taking a course based on Rick Warren's book *The Purpose Driven Life,* I gathered the was-laws: his brothers and their wives, and his parents. We had a prayer meeting in which we begged to "have enough just to get by." At this particular church, there was an underlying message that God wants you to suffer sometimes, because suffering grows you. It's considered somehow good for people to suffer and go through trials.

We got exactly what we asked for: just enough to "get by." We felt this would be less greedy since we weren't asking God for "too much." We were asking for far too little. Scraps. Struggle. Pain. Strain on our marriage. What a terrible thing to ask for.

About six months ago I tuned into my own verbal begging of God. I kept using the words *just* and *only*.

"I just need $10,000."

"If only I had $30,000, I could get by."

What I really wanted was ten grand to fall in my lap, some sort of windfall that would allow me to meet financial goals instantly.

But look at the sentence. If I just have $10,000, then I'm screwed because I have a mortgage that's more than $10,000 annually, and I also have other bills and commitments. I have a $100,000 lifestyle to maintain. Asking for $10,000 is like asking for complete and utter financial ruin. Words created the entire Universe and they create our micro-Universes as well.

❧

OH HOW MY SOUL wants to take a business class. I wrote down "business class" and dropped it in my Paid in Full Box. I have this little gold box with the words *Paid in Full* scribbled in Sharpie on the outside. Into this box goes everything I am surrendering to God. The purpose of the box is to relieve myself of the anxiety of trying to figure out how I am going to meet my financial obligations or wishes every second of every day. Rather than stress out about how I'm going to come up with $1,500 by March 24, I jot it on a scrap of paper and surrender the problem to God.

"This is your problem, not mine," is the message I'm giving to God, to the Universe. I let go of it.

Before going to sleep, I did a brief meditation, asking: *Show me how to make this happen, show me how to get $1,500 for this class.* Then I woke up with a check for $525 sitting on my counter that I had no desperate need for. My intention has been to set it aside for the taxes I expect to pay in April. All very wise and rational, except . . .

Except I can get an extension and make payments, and if this business class is as effective as they say, then it won't be a problem to pay the taxes quickly during the class, I reason.

I have a check from the city for an overcharge for $360 coming. And I can blow off my bills for a month and just double up next month, and that's another $450, and I have a check coming for $150 and another for $200, and there's an overdraft of $165 on my checking account that I could use. I'm sure the rest will appear and they have a payment plan, I thought.

Something has to change, that's the bottom line. If I keep doing what I'm doing, then I'll keep scraping by—and I'm over it. What I want is a thriving business doing something that I love. And this course can teach me everything I need to know to build that. So I'm signing up for it today as soon as my check clears.

"The more money I spend, the more money I make." That's one of my new affirmations, and it is working so far.

❧

I HAVE STARTED TO suspect that the Universe expends available dollars according to needs. I noticed that when Alex and I were married we lived hand to mouth basically the whole time. But our budget always increased proportionately to meet our increasing obligations. When we stopped renting and the mortgage was $500 more, we found $500 more. When we moved to Colorado and our mortgage increased $600 more, we found $600 more.

When both of our cars broke down simultaneously, we found the extra $250 for a car payment. Just like that.

It follows then that our financial set point was "just enough," exactly as we had declared over ourselves at the prayer meeting.

Now, as poor as I am, all my bills are paid all the time and I always have money in my pocket, even if it's just a few bucks. I aim to change that and raise my set point much, much higher.

As I was listening to this one business coach talking about money and creating systems and structures and selling packages and charging top dollar versus lowering rates, I thought, *I think so small. I think in terms of low four figures, not even close to six figures. I need to learn how to think in terms of six figures.*

This is one of the joys of being sovereign. Signing up for a business course would have never, ever happened had I stayed married to Alex. There's no way in the world that it would even be considered. I was not allowed to spend money on my business or professional development. That would have been contradictory to his demand of me to solve all of our money problems by "getting a job."

❧

THE OTHER PREOCCUPATION I'm having these days is sex.

Facebook: What's on your mind?

Me: Sex. Sex. Sex. Sex.

I'm revirginized. I haven't had sex in a year and three months. I'm ready. First there was the whole horny Sedona experience. Now, I'm finding my fantasies are really taking off. I'm masturbating as a hobby.

Cash stayed until 11:30 P.M. on Tuesday, left his phone, and came back on Wednesday. I can't decide if I like him and there are a few problems. Including that one of his intentions is to meet his soul mate by Christmas and my intention is to stay sovereign for at least three years. I'm to have a wildee time before I meet my One. I'm pretty excited about that.

I was sitting on the couch, however, wondering, *Why don't you just lean over and kiss me?* He's a cute boy, like the preppy I might have had a crush on in high school, but one who would not be much interested in me. At least according to my junior high self, who didn't realize how many boys actually were interested in her. I was leaning in, I had intentionally shown a lot of cleavage, I was putting my hands within reach of touching, and Cash just kept talking and flirting. There were plenty of awkward I-want-to-kiss-you moments he could have taken advantage of, but he finally left.

He's tall and fit and believes in the Law of Attraction and I love that. The only thing holding me back is the one thing that I kind of asked for: he attends my church and goes to Money Club. This means that I can't go around kissing him casually. If I do, he'll start holding my hand in church and that will pretty much make him my boyfriend. If it doesn't work out, he might drop out of Money Club and that would mess up the good vibe. I like having men in the group because they bring in a different energy.

Also, he's *waaaaay* too into me. I remember this happening to me when I was younger, too. A boy would fall instantly "in love" with me and propose marriage without so much as a date. Of course, this is weird and boundary crossing . . . and also quite the ego boost. He's crossed a few boundaries, such as texting me: "I like having a girl." *Um, why don't we start with a date and a kiss before you call me your girl.* And on Tuesday he said, "I decided on the way over here to tell you that I love you."

It's awkward. I love the attention and the positive feedback. This means I've still got it. *Why won't he just kiss me?* I keep imagining his mouth on mine and his big hands in my hair and his worshipful look as he enters me for the first time. *Flutter, flutter.*

This weekend I have two dates. It's hard to date as a mom. And it's easy. I get these weekends of freedom, but they only come twice a month, and if I'm out of town for one of them, then a date is rare. But this weekend I lined up two dates with two cute boys. One of them is very, very cute. It's tonight and I'm excited. I've been planning which cleavage-flaunting dress I will wear.

Both men are taking me on the same date, because I met them online and I was scouting for one great date. We are going to get fabulous foot massages and then eat Chinese food. There's no downside to this date. If it's a bad date, then at least we got foot massages and ate Chinese food.

I keep thinking of kissing these men as well. They don't strike me as one-night stand type of guys, but I'm so very horny that I'm hoping to at least get a kiss. *My first kiss from a different man in twelve years! It is going to be so hot!* I hope.

THIRTEEN

MARCH 25, 2013

It strikes me as amazing that so many noteworthy things can happen in a week to change perspective.

Dates: The first date was a great date, except. Except he didn't pay. We went Dutch, which is a total turnoff. I agreed to it because we were on an expensive date. He also admitted that he's a heavy drinker and uses alcohol to self-medicate. We have almost nothing in common. But he's sooo good looking.

The second guy cancelled on me an hour before the date, which pissed me off and speaks volumes about his dependability.

Since I was already prepared to go out, I called Cash, the guy from church who has the hots for me. He said he needed to be frugal, so I suggested a dollar movie . . . WHICH I HAD TO PAY FOR!!! He couldn't afford a $7 date. Fuck that. I'm not dating a poor man. Every single cell in my being is entirely turned off and absolutely unattracted to him.

If you're in your forties and can't afford a $7 date, then get away from me. That's not the kind of energy I'm going to attract or invite into my life.

In fact, Cash mentioned having a discussion at the homeless shelter. When I asked what he was doing there, he said he was serving food and helping out. *Me thinks the man lives in a homeless shelter. No fucking way.*

He's weird, too. During the movie he laughed at inappropriate times and afterward said he felt he had been in the Civil War in a past life. Nobody ever has a boring past life.

❧

MY DAD PASSED ON $6,000 of his inheritance while I was in Utah. It's a life changer. I'm not kidding. I had been asking for a way to unload these terrible 400-something blogs that are time-sucking, Soul-killing tasks of excruciating boredom. I was very grateful to have the work, and more importantly the steady paychecks that come on the same days every month so I could feel financially stable and secure. However, I hate them. I hate having to do them. So I have been hiring writers to write them. Which was great at first. But even entering them is a time-sucking task that takes away from my real work with this book and my own blogs and other writing assignments.

Then there's the bullshit task of managing writers who flake out and don't turn assignments in. Honestly, I've been surprised at how unreliable stay-at-home moms are with their work. They accept assignments and disappear. They do shoddy work. One of them even plagiarized. Another one keeps saying, "Oh I have it done, but I keep forgetting to send it. I'll send it when I get home." *Yeah.* And the economy sucks and these "poor people" are so unfortunately unemployed. It's done a number on my compassion for the unemployed.

I swear to God I am becoming more Republican every day.

Anyway, I want out of those blogs. But I need the income. I am also facing taxes. I don't remember the exact number, but the accountant said a number that frankly terrified me.

Something has to change. I have to do something different. I can't spend all of my time going after low-hanging fruit. I needed it while I was going through my divorce because I had no energy to devote to bigger projects. However, if I don't get more ambitious and make a lot more money, I hate to think of my future. To meet the needs of my lifestyle and my responsibilities a great deal more money is required.

Facing this reality head-on, the week before I left for Utah I registered for that $1,500 Uplevel Your Business (UYB) business class. Because I am the type of person who participates in these types of personal growth programs and actually does the work, I think this is a sound investment. I think I am a sound investment.

I had $360 in my checking account and the down payment was $350. I bought it, but I really had no idea how I'd pay off the rest of it. Then my dad handed me an unexpected $6,000 check and it changed everything. Now I can pay off the class, pay my taxes, quit the loathsome blogging gig, and, gosh, the list of dreams I hope to fulfill with $6,000 is endless.

I've had a great deal of fun playing "I can if I want to." I can build a fence and buy rock and gravel for the backyard, if I want to. I can get my hair cut and colored, if I want to. I can save a few thousand dollars, if I want to. I can pay off one credit card and my Kohl's charge card, if I want to. I can get my car fixed, I can get my phone fixed, and I can buy an Otter Box case. I can throw myself a badass fortieth birthday party! If I want to.

These are delightful possibilities. These possibilities make me feel secure and relaxed and relieve stress. It's so fun to think of the amazing things that I can get done.

It makes me feel confident about my ability to have a successful business. It makes me feel that money will come my way.

The Year of YES!

EVERY SPIRITUAL PERSON, practitioner, palm reader, life coach, and so on, has said that I will be successful and make a fortune.

The fortune card came up in my Soul Mirror reading in Sedona. The palm reader said that I was very lucky and my income would keep going up, and I'd be very lucky in my career. Rena Petty, the Radical Forgiveness coach, said that the money was just waiting for me. I've always known that I will make a great income, achieve some sort of fame, and become a thought leader. That's why it was offensive to me that Alex didn't believe any of these things about me. *How could the person I was married to not know?*

I am ready for it.

2013 will be foundational.
2014 will be huge.

This year is about building the foundation, doing the healing work, and getting the rest. I need to maintain the slowness, the extra pampering of myself, the bodywork, the energy work, the massages, the travel, the spiritual questing. I need to keep going. It's already almost April. Obviously this year will fly by. Before you know it, it will be 2014 and things will change drastically.

I am going to live a large life. I'm going to play on a much larger field, in a much bigger and more public game.

FOURTEEN

MARCH 26, 2013

We went to Utah for spring break and to celebrate the ninetieth birthday of my grandma, Viola. Ninety is a lot of years to live a life. We are so blessed and lucky to have had her presence for so many years. It's difficult for me to talk about her because there simply are no words to describe how I feel about her or who she is. My feelings are too deep and pure.

Pure is the word I would use for her. She loves purely. No matter what I have done in my life or where I've been—regardless of how many thousands of miles away—I've known, without a doubt, that her love for me never wavers and remains true.

What do you know for sure?

Thank you for asking, Oprah. I know for sure that my grandmother loves me.

When I was young I didn't know how special my family is. I thought everyone had big parties with fifty to a hundred people laughing and catching up, joking and hugging, squealing with delight at the simple pleasure of seeing each other again. And by again, I don't mean after twenty years of not speaking. I mean, since the last wedding or Thanksgiving party a season or two ago.

Meeting each others' new babies and marveling at how our babies have grown into little tweens and teens.

My grandmother had six children, thirty-seven grandchildren, and over sixty great-grandchildren, with six more on the way, and one great-great grandchild. And we know each other. We grew up together, were at each other's graduations and weddings, and passed around each other's babies. We have prayed over delicious food, and wished each other well. We have teased each other and scoffed at each other's antics. We have loved each other despite bad choices, wrong choices, mistakes, and misguided whatevers.

My favorite part is the laughter. I don't know how my family is so funny, but I laugh the whole time I am with them. Quick wits all of them. They are also beautiful. My family is very attractive and married other attractive people, making mostly pretty, blond-haired, blue-eyed babies.

Surrounded by ninety-one people who had come to celebrate my grandmother's birthday—many traveling for many hours to do so—I was touched by how much effort this has taken. Many families fall away from each other. They don't make an effort to make one another a part of their lives. They get busy, too busy, to bother. They don't place a high value on knowing what their cousin is majoring in or what a couple names their fourth child.

My family does. That takes significant commitment by six siblings and all their children and grandchildren.

My grandmother continues, at ninety, to make the long arduous drive to Utah. It takes twenty-four hours if you drive straight through. It's difficult for her body to sit so long. It hurts her back. It's uncomfortable. She would fly, but it is frightening to her to attempt to navigate large, complicated airports. She hasn't driven in decades, but her children chauffeur her back and forth to see the family in Utah. We're Mormon people, so Utah is home base.

"Are you having a great party?" I asked her.

"I really am," she said.

"Look at all the people you made!" I said.

She beamed brightly, for the creation of a family has been her life's work.

At one point my cousin sang my grandmother's favorite song, "I Hope You Dance."

"I do hope you dance. I missed a lot of opportunities to dance and I wish I hadn't," my grandmother said afterward, in a short, moving speech.

She continued, "One of the things that mean so much to me is to see that you're so delighted to see each other. I hope you'll continue to meet like this after I'm gone."

She created a family. A big and loving family that shares history and traditions. But most of all, this family shares a big expansive love.

I have a family. What a gift.

FIFTEEN

MARCH 28, 2013

In Law of Attraction circles, they say that you always get what you want. Of course, you'll get it faster if you stop changing your mind, set one course, and never waver.

This is more challenging than it sounds. I've come to realize that it is no harder or easier to build a writing business than a marketing or coaching business. Whatever you spend your time on manifests. If I'm spending my time picking the low-hanging fruit of marketing writing, then that's the part of my business that will grow. If I'm spending my time learning how to build a coaching business and devoting my visioning to that, then it follows that this part of my business will grow.

WOMEN LACK NO SKILLS or talent. What they lack is *witnessing*. Through witnessing, we learn. When someone's father is a doctor, that child might witness the training, the day-to-day challenges, and the dinner table talk about medicine. What did I learn? How to raise babies and keep house. My father was in the military. He flew airplanes and managed a fleet of men and women who did exactly what he told them to do. This is not like business.

I feel my way through my business. The only mentors I've had are those I follow online, learning from their newsletters and blogs. I honestly don't personally *know* a really successful businesswoman. I know many who own businesses, but they're feeling their way, just like me. A step behind, a step ahead, no more.

❧

MY FORTIETH BIRTHDAY IS only five months away. I've been thinking about what I want to do to celebrate. Where to I want to be and how do I want to feel? I realized that I don't want to be alone, I don't want to be disappointed that I've invited forty people and only eight people make time to come, like my thirty-ninth birthday party. And I don't want to go to dinner with my children.

I think I will take a cruise or do a house swap with Neecy. She's fun and she gets me. Maybe we'll invite Alexis Saint to come with us. Maybe we'll invite the whole Texas book club. Resting, relaxing and being stimulated by some exotic foreign location, perhaps on the water, is how I want to construct the beginning of this phase of my life. I want to experience a "moment." Perhaps even an epiphany.

I am impatient for my Soul to tell me what to do with my newfound riches. I suspect the way I'm feeling about it needs to change, because I'm acting as if this is a one-in-a-lifetime amount and it's not even one month of what I want to make. In fact, my current number I'm trying to attract is $8,000 a month. So it signifies a lack mentality to act like the money my dad gave me is the only $6,000 I'm ever going to get all at once so I should be ever so careful to do the "right thing" with it. The truth is I have about $20,000 of "the right things" to spend this money on.

Speak up Soul!

SIXTEEN

APRIL 2, 2013

I am so happy. The difference?

Money.

Perhaps it is true that once you reach $65,000 your happiness quotient doesn't improve. However, I have to say that money *can* buy happiness. And it has.

I'm noticing what I'm feeling and what I'm being urged to spend money on, and it is interesting. The relief I feel when I can decide that a networking event—a masked ball—is something I should attend and am able to buy the ticket is profound.

The anxiety I feel about buying certain other things is also interesting. The thing I'm feeling most urgency about spending money on is maintaining what I already have. Getting the gate on the fence to keep the dog in, so we don't look like the Clampetts, with a piece of wood blocking the way. *So tacky.* Getting my car fixed. It has an oil leak and an antifreeze leak. It may also need brakes. My minivan is *essential.*

Cleaning is a huge one. Did you know that it will cost $352 to get a four-level house, a set of microfiber furniture, and a minivan cleaned? *Wow.* This is why I have lived here for nearly three years and never had the carpets cleaned. And it looks it. So do my couches, which have never been cleaned in five years.

Getting my teeth cleaned is a big one. I think I need a root canal and crown on my right side; the area is sensitive so I don't chew hard things on that side. It makes me feel like an old lady.

My dishwasher leaks and turns on randomly. The other day I was taking a nap and no one else was home. It randomly turned on and flooded my kitchen floor. My floor is wood. If I don't take care of this with a new dishwasher, my kitchen floor will be ruined; water may also leak into the downstairs bathroom.

This is all stuff that has built up which needs attention. It needs some money thrown at it to keep it in good condition. Thousands of dollars of simple maintenance. Yet, it's important to me because I want to live a certain lifestyle.

Clearing, maintaining, and cleaning one's personal and professional space is crucial in the Law of Attraction. It goes to a set of values and character. A jumbled, messy house is a reflection of a jumbled and messy mind. A dirty or poorly maintained car is a symbol of not being able to move on or move forward because leaks and grime are holding you back. Not maintaining one's personal appearance and physical well-being is a sign that one doesn't sufficiently value one's body or personhood.

Yet, these things were not acceptable expenses in my marriage. Nor in my family of origin. My mother has wanted new carpet for twenty years. Yet, she doesn't have it. Her linoleum is shabby and shameful. My dad doesn't want to spend money—though he has it to spend—on the appearance and upkeep of their home.

When I was in my formative years I wanted things like a Guess pair of jeans. My parents were evidently going through financial hardship and they wouldn't buy them for me. These jeans probably cost an enormous price of $40 at the time, but they were the only thing I wanted for Christmas. Surely my mother spent $40 on things she found on sale at Mervin's. The idea is that you can never spend money on what you really want; you have to make due with what is on the sale rack. I wasn't *worth* the Guess jeans was the story I told myself. This is just the way they handle money. It's not a bad way to handle money, I mean, they do have a kickass retirement income because they made sacrifices. But I want something different.

How my home looks, how I present myself, and my overall health and well-being are important to me. They matter both in how I live my lifestyle, and also in my Law of Attraction mastery and my ability to make more money and live a prosperous life. Creating an office space with the necessary tools to build a mini-empire is another thing I want to do with my money.

Act as if you already have it, is a key principle.

Still, the anxiety is big. How can I spend $350 on carpet cleaning and car detailing when I owe money on a credit card? What if I have to spend all my money on taxes? What if my money leaks out and I am once again left with nothing?

It boils down to this:

A lingering mentality that my needs exceed my means.

A gnawing feeling that this is the only $6,000 I'll have access to, like, *ever*.

An anxiety that I will do the wrong things with money, blow it and make bad decisions.

An underlying feeling that I will spend money on things that aren't worthy, namely *things I want*.

A guilty feeling that I will spend money on my business and my business will fail and I won't make my money back. This likely stems from Alex's faith that I would fail inevitably so I should just *"get a job!"* Oh, and also that I have failed before, and in many ways my writing career hasn't manifested what I had hoped it would.

Plus, my dad thinks that me owning a business is the most ludicrous thing he ever heard. So there is an underlying fear of failure with this money.

My dad wants me to pay off my debt. And that would no doubt be a great idea. Except. Except. Here is the real underlying issue: *What if this is my one chance to spend money on my life and my business?*

I don't want to look at my bank balance. For fear that I have spent the money frivolously and that it has leaked away and disappeared. I keep forgetting what I have spent the money on. A life coaching business course, two pairs of shorts, my healing tithe, eyeglasses, fixing my iPhone, buying an OtterBox case to protect my investment, dog grooming, a networking event, some this and that, but not much. All legit. But, I want to keep my money and spend it, too.

I have a window here. In this window of three point two five years remaining on my alimony, my wasband is paying me enough money to cover my mortgage. This was granted to allow me to get on my feet. This was granted by the court to provide me the support that I provided him during our marriage when all our resources and family decisions were made to propel him forward in his career.

If I sit back and waste it being terrified of being a single mother. Or taking shitty jobs like mass blogging, or pursuing something that is not my Soul's purpose—then I will have wasted the window to my future.

If I do that, what awaits me is a life of struggle and just getting by. If I do that, then getting to where I want to go with my business becomes that much harder because I won't have the support any longer.

I will not do that. Instead I will use the money to clear, clean, maintain my lifestyle, yes. And also to propel myself forward and *build* my business.

This year will be foundational. Next year will be huge.

Again, I go back over and over with this money, or any money that comes into my hands, really: *What are my values? What is my purpose? What are my commitments? What is my Soul calling me to do?*

They are these:

This is *The Year of YES!*

This year I obey my Soul.

I tithe to my body, healing, and well-being: *this piece of God.*

This year I build a foundation for my business.

This year I call forth and step forth in faith.

Still my struggles remain anxiety about money and time. Those two creatures of the Earth produce more angst in me than is comfortable. I perpetually feel there is not enough of either.

I am creating a new form of scheduling to organize my time in the business class. This involves blocking out sections of time for my priorities. As I do so, it's interesting to see how full my life is. It's also interesting to see what kinds of conflicting emotions I have about my time and where I choose to spend it, and on what kinds of activities.

Of note is the amount of time I spend exercising and how much I feel like this takes away from my "work time." Also, how I feel like networking is not legit working time. Too, how I feel it takes "too much" work time to do the healing work I've committed to. Once you add in the "kid time" and walking the dog in the evening hours, I have hardly any time left to actually work. Certainly nowhere near forty hours a week. My schedule is jam packed without time to spare, and I have only one client.

Then I remind myself that I don't actually want to work forty hours; I never have. That's the whole reason I want to own my own business: I want to be the boss of my time.

The class puts networking above other activities because they are instant cash makers and should always come first. This includes networking events, following up with potential clients, and pitching potential clients.

Yet, these things tend to come last in my life. I tend to write a newsletter as my priority because it "brings in cash," although it never has, not even once. Or waste time with low-hanging fruit because though the pay sucks ass it still brings in steady income to pay the electricity and put gas in my car. It's shortsighted because what I really want are coaching clients and ways to make money through more meaningful writing and coaching packages. Still I neglect the activities that will get me those things, in favor of menial crap that keeps me in a safe little box in my life.

❧

I HAVE TRADITIONALLY suffered social anxiety. I always felt that people didn't like me. That I was essentially a bad person because I made some serious mistakes as a teenager and thus was unredeemable and no one could really like me. Add to that my sensitivity to criticism due to my parents' sometimes harsh view of the world and my place in it, and I suffered years of social anxiety.

I don't mean a little shyness. I mean taking Xanax for over a decade and rehab for Xanax to control my social anxiety. I mean walking around feeling like I am about to be attacked for having an opinion. I mean fearing the reaction to my work—work which I feel so compelled to do that I can't *not* do it, but which causes me a tremendous amount of stress about people's reaction.

That kind of social anxiety.

I have healed a great deal of that over the last several years. I have let go of so much built-up emotional energy in my body. I have detached from other people's opinion of me to a great degree. I have detached from my wasband's opinion of me, and to an extent my family of origin's opinion of me. The Universe sent me great gifts like mean girls and bullies to confront me and find my center in the face of criticism. It was hard, but I held fast to *who I am* in the face of it. Much to my surprise, having let go of past shame and no longer putting so much stock in the criticism or feedback of others, I find that people like me.

People like me. Isn't that wonderful? And funny?

Turns out the Universe has also been sending me little gifts confirming that people like me and that perhaps they always have. People from my past have shown up and said they like me and they always have liked me: my roommate from college; and most recently, the boy from junior high school that I ran into, who remembered me after twenty years. Twenty years later he saw me in a thrift store and remembered me. I remembered that he had written me poetry. He *liked* me, *liked* me.

I was a girl to whom poetry was written. Boys had crushes on me. One boy I didn't even know made me a mixed tape. Others proposed marriage immediately, they were so smitten with me. Boys thought I was beautiful and charming and funny and bright.

I didn't even see it. I couldn't even hear it. Because I was so busy hanging out with men who thought nothing of me, because I felt I was unworthy, because I thought nothing except horrible things of me. Because I made some mistakes.

How unfair of me.

I am noticing now, however, that I am bright and shiny. That my optimism and my generosity are appreciated by people. That people feel good when they are around me. That people think I am beautiful and funny and worthy of their attention. That people are "attracted" to me.

It shouldn't be such a shock, really. Still, it is.

People like me. They really, really like me. (To borrow a line from Sally Field.)

❧

IN SUMMER 2012, I was having a very rough patch, with hardly any money coming in, a broken shoulder, and a divorce pending. I felt like people didn't appreciate anything I was doing. In my work, on my blog, as a person. I was depleted and broken.

Do I even make a difference? I cried out to God.

Why would you give me this work, this website, this calling, if no one wants it, if I can't succeed at it? It's too much to ask of me if it's not going to succeed. Release me from it or tell me that it's what you want me to do and make it successful, I challenged.

I then thought, *You always receive what you ask for. So maybe God is talking to you through others.* I started scrawling notes of compliments other people would give me and putting them in a box.

"Your book changed the way my brother thought about violence toward women, thank you."

"Your blog post changed the way I see my body, thank you."

"You're an amazing strong woman and I wish I could come to your party."

On and on, I began receiving confirmation that what I do matters. That I am valued for my body of work. That I am making a difference and that people really do like me.

SEVENTEEN

APRIL 9, 2013

MY battle with time continues.

It's crazy making. It's causing me a mild level of anxiety. The same kind I was experiencing before the shoulder crash. Where I'm rushing and racing against time. Putting everything on a calendar to look at it is making me realize how little time I have and how much my time should be worth.

I went to breakfast with my friend Leslie to arrange for our Red Tent screening. It's a launch of my coaching programs. We're going to use it to advertise an upcoming workshop, and I'm going to use it to offer a Year of YES! life coaching package.

She had a meeting directly after with a woman who has a vision of a movement called Women Awaken. Her vision had clarity and organization. But her timeline was way far out. She wanted to fund it with grants, but didn't intend to apply for them until 2015. With a few short sentences I told her she was ready, that she needed to proceed with imperfection and not wait for the perfect circumstances.

That conversation changed her whole paradigm. She immediately scheduled a presentation at the library for Wednesday and asked me to speak. She also asked me for my rates so she could write it into her budget.

Phew. Okay. So I stole numbers and wording from other life coaches who have been offering six-month and one-year-coaching packages and shot if off. She said she intends to work with me. Which is amazing.

But the numbers I ran included $50,000 as my goal. Only, with taxes, I need to count on living on half of what I bring in. Which means I need to make over $100,000. So I need to up my game.

I've also been noticing who is making what kind of money, what people are charging. For instance, my carpet cleaner was charging $400 for three to four hours of work. My hairdresser charges $150 for two hours. My massage therapists charge between $60 and $135 for an hour. These people are no more valuable than I am. AND *they* get tips.

The tip thing is irritating me because they give no better service than I do. Also tips are supposed to be compensation for poorly paid work, such as waitress who makes $3.20 an hour, plus tips. Well, the hairdresser and massage therapists are making good wages and being tipped on top of that.

The real issue, of course is that it's pushing my money buttons. I can't "afford" to tip generously, but I do anyway. So it causes me mild irritation, like an itch during meditation.

Then I remind myself that I simply need to make more money. I need to charge more money for my time and efforts and sell six-month and one-year packages for the security I crave. Also, I enjoy receiving big wads of cash, like $6,000 at once. It makes my life so much more enjoyable.

Interesting pattern with money lately: I finally have money to do things that I need to do, all maintenance, as we discussed. But it's *off*. I keep getting shoddy work that needs to be redone.

I got a pedicure; it smudged and chipped the next day. I didn't have time to go get it redone. I scheduled carpet cleaning, and as soon as they walked in the door their whole attitude was telling me what they were *not* going to do as part of the agreed upon price. They intended to upsell me a few hundred bucks to do basic carpet cleaning chores, like pretreat stains and move furniture. *Fuck that! If I have to do half your job for you then why would I even pay you?* Carpet has furniture on it. *Duh.* I need it cleaned because there are *stains* and I want them clean.

They also were detailing my car and the first thing the woman said was, "You don't want me to do *this* part, do you?" *Seriously?* I want my car detailed, which means I want *all* the parts done.

I include editing as part of my writing services. If the customer wants changes, I do them for no extra charge. I also don't say, "Sure I'll write this blog for you for x amount, but the headline, tagline, and editing are extra." Again, I'm finding it difficult to believe in the poor economy if people can afford to have these lazy and craptastic business practices.

This is making me examine the way I do business and charge for my services. It's also making me examine what thoughts are making people offer me the knock-off craptastic work price.

I believe the problem is that I will settle for less than exceptional work in order to avoid conflict or appear demanding.

Women are often told to suck it up, so as not to hurt anyone's feelings or cause people any inconvenience. Inconvenience, like actually doing their jobs.

I also find this in dating. Men will literally complain about spending more than the price of coffee on a date. *Excuse me?* I don't want to date a cheap man who doesn't value me enough to spend $10 on lunch. I don't need lobster. But if I'm going out with you I do need you to spend more than forty-five minutes and $5 on coffee (if I dare order the great café mocha instead of black coffee). Not to mention how unoriginal and unexciting this kind of date is. I do find myself thinking, "Well, if I have to settle for this. . . I guess I understand why he wouldn't want to pay for me." *Pathetic.*

A girl needs some standards for men to live up to or they will live up to nothing.

The same pattern is showing up in Money Club. I'm happy to have a mastermind group, as I think the Law of Attraction works better in numbers and it's good to keep my head in the game with accountability. I love talking about this stuff and it feeds my Soul. I enjoy the hosting and organizing of it, as well. However, people are noncommittal about it and they are blowing it off. I don't want to run a group and go to the effort in my overscheduled life if people aren't going to make it a priority to be there.

I should change my thinking and turn the "I'll settle for this" thought into something like, "I expect exceptional work for all services paid for." Or "I'm totally worth a perfect pedicure, exceptional writing, an exciting date, and an operational car with an accurate diagnosis at a fair price."

What I'm asking for is not too much to ask. I really need to believe that. I suspect that when I show the Universe and the Law that I am demanding more, then I will get more.

This is a test, like the few months when I had to confront mean girls and bullies in order to show the Universe that I wasn't going to be a scaredy pants anymore.

Dear God, YOU show ME what YOU know I'm worthy of. And I know it's more than this half-good nonsense.

అ

I'M FREAKING OUT ABOUT taking a week off to go to Texas in May. I'm feeling like I rarely get to settle into a routine and get down to work. I take these weeks off and then I spent the rest of the month scrambling to make a few bucks to live on. Still, I feel I have to do it. I want to go. I do.

I'm dreading summer and the bickering and boredom of my children being constantly in my work space.

I have to get a summer plan, it's only weeks away. I have to arrange a way for us to coexist. I have some ideas. Like getting Alex to take more time with them to give me an evening break. Like putting them in enrichment courses. Like dropping them off at the Boys and Girls Club for several hours. Like leaving them home alone while I work at the gym or coffee shop.

They are old enough now that the desperate cry of my Soul, the physical undeniable need to be present for them constantly has vanished. What a relief that is. I swear to God it was biological and unwavering when they were babies to preschoolers. Now, it's gone and I want to do other things than hang out with them all day listening to their bullshit whining and bickering. I'm worn out from being in constant demand and persistently available.

What does my Soul cry out for right now?

Rest. Time.

She is getting harder to hear these days. Probably because I'm so busy. Again, I have to remind myself that this is a year of foundation building. A year of rest. A year of listening to my Soul's whispers and saying YES! To do that I can't be so chronically busy. I have to find another way, one in which I can lean into her instructions.

EIGHTEEN

APRIL 18, 2013

I'm working through the end of my marriage in my dreams. One night I'm dreaming that I'm waiting for Alex to return, whispering kindly and lovingly to myself, *He's not coming back for you, Tracee.* A part of me is still hurt that he didn't love me, that he didn't quit drinking to save our family, that he abandoned the relationship many years ago because he couldn't make me get a job. God, he was obsessed with that.

Last night I dreamed that I was with him, in the form of another male acquaintance who I am not the least bit attracted to. We were divorced, but working together with the logistics of life very well. In fact, this is what we do now. We're flexible with parenting time, we're helpful about responsibilities, etc. It feels good. And in my dream I was wondering, *Why did we get divorced, again?* I thought about getting back together. Then he held my hand and I was repulsed. I didn't want that kind of contact.

Dreaming is an essential part of working out the parts of us that are conflicted. Dreaming is the tool my Soul is using to grieve and accept the loss of something. We could have gone on as we were. Millions of couples go on—becoming roommates, partners in the logistics. It's really comforting to have a partner in the logistics, or as my mother calls it, *maintenance of life.*

Still, my Soul cried out for me. Once Alex disconnected from the relationship, my Soul starved for intimacy and attachment to a lover. To someone who really is into me. I reread a letter he wrote me the other day, in which he meant to be loving. It was after a religious retreat we participated in. The interesting thing, which I noticed even at the time, was that the letter was all about *him.* It was supposed to be a love letter to me, but it really wasn't. It was really about him. He admitted that he was furious with me for not doing what he wanted me to do—get a job—of course. In the letter, he said was going to focus on loving me instead of being so selfish. At the time I didn't believe it for five seconds. I could *feel* that the love was gone and in its place was a deep need to make me submit to him.

Evangelical boys want their cake and tell her what to do, too.

I was playing cards with the kids last night during a snow storm. It was peaceful and beautiful and quiet. It reminded me of how many hours I spent playing cards with Alex's family and friends. I thought it was boring. I thought about how many of the things we did that I didn't want to do.

I did not want to be married to him anymore. Yet, I grieve the idea of a happy marriage that should have been fun and happy and lighthearted and intimate. I know it will still happen for me. But I still grieve this loss of a wish.

I've signed up for online dating and I'm noticing what my deal breakers are. *Religious conservatives are unforgivable.* You can be a Baptist, but I can't date a Baptist. I just can't. It's the "submit to your husband" bit, the "gays are sinners" bit, and the whole fucking punishment/sinner identity. I can't tolerate it in a mate.

Spirituality is essential. I'm just not into someone who is not on a spiritual path in alignment with mine. I craved that so much in my marriage. So did he. It is such a big part of my life that I don't want to sacrifice this part of connection with a mate.

Facial hair is ugly. I can't seem to get over it. I look at goatees and think it looks like men are wearing a pussy on their face. I look at a mustache and it's a deal breaker. I look at a beard and think it's like a woman wearing a veil. *Who knows what kind of hideous beast lurks under there?* It feels like they are hiding something, some essential part of themselves. Why would I need to get a bikini wax or groom my pubic hair if they're going to wear hair on their faces? *Fuck that.* It's counter-indicated. Colorado is full of Grizzly Adams wannabes and hard as I try, I just can't get into it.

Must have shit together. Honestly it's been shocking to realize how many men have done *nothing* in the last forty years to make anything at all of themselves. Or they talk about ridiculous stuff about enjoying life and finding enlightenment, which is why they only have a part-time job. *Fuck that.* I have two children and I'm not about to add the responsibility of a forty-year old man to the things I have to maintain and support. I try really hard to make something of myself. There is no way I'm settling for a loser.

Must be good looking. I have to want to have sex with him and stare at his face for a damn long time. By the time a man is forty he has either taken care of himself or let his hygiene and looks go to hell. He either has active hobbies and hits the gym or he can be found sitting in front of a football game with a beer and chicken wings. *Been there, done that, no thanks.* I have taken care of myself and worked really hard at being attractive and put together. There is no way I'm settling for a lazy slob. *Must wax back, if applicable.*

Must pay for a date. Gimme a break. Whether a man desires to or is able to pay for a date is indicative of whether or not he has a poverty consciousness or a prosperity consciousness. I do not intend to spend the rest of my life fighting over money or resources with an.y.one.

I'm sexy, beautiful, smart, witty and funny, bright and shiny, and I work really, really hard to maintain a lifestyle, grow personally and professionally, be a good parent, be a good friend, and invest in my spiritual growth and relationships, and to have my own company. I will not allow a leach to feed off my ambition or positive energy. If you haven't made something of yourself by the time you're forty you're not going to.

One woman I recently met said she "didn't want to be judgmental" when dating. Are you joking? Dating is the one situation where you should exercise the most judgment. You get to choose ONE person. Out of billions of people on the planet, you pick one. *And you don't want to be judgmental?* The fact is that you will say no to hundreds of thousands of great men when you say yes to one.

There is at least one man who meets my criteria. And he is the only one I need or want.

NINETEEN

APRIL 23, 2013

My Soul keeps demanding that I do scary things. Things I wouldn't have done while married to Alex. Things I would have liked to do, but which I didn't do because it would have been a struggle. I hate to say, "I wouldn't have gotten permission," but essentially, I wouldn't have gotten permission.

I signed up for a business conference in Atlanta in June. It's at a nice hotel and costs money. I was never allowed to invest in my business or in professional development. Then I was accused of "failing" because I didn't magically make millions manifest without training, essential knowledge, tools, and resources. I love having money and making my own financial decisions.

I took the leap of faith. I got a roommate from Canada. Strangers have always been good to me when traveling. I'm excited and nervous about it. I'm nervous about the money spent. *But I have money in my bank account,* I remind myself.

I love having money. Seeing money in my account is giving me such peace of mind. It's changing the choices I see in front of me and the decisions I make regarding my business.

My Soul is also asking me to create a proposal for a comprehensive marketing package for a woman who is interested in hiring me. She is a Hindu teacher, crystal healer, and Goddess coach. My Soul is giving me the number $6,000. The truth is that she has asked me to do a tremendous amount of work. Once I sat down and realized the cost in time, and the fact that it would suck up my time for a month, at least, I realized that I've been *losing* money when I work for people at my current rates. For what I'm willing to do for $6,000, she's getting a bargain.

I believe that if this is of value to her then she will spend the $6,000. I have this "belief" that people can't afford coaching and marketing. But *I* always find the money for what is important to me. Making my website and other marketing materials look professional is important to me, so I spend money on it. Coaching and healing work is crucial to me, and so I spend money on it. Even last year when I grossed $25,000 from all sources, and I donated over $3,800 to the church, I spent every spare penny I could find on taking care of myself with massages, hypnotherapy, and other services.

I always find the money for what is important to me. My career, professional development, self-care, spiritual development, and physical and spiritual healing are priorities for me.

I'm playing with the concept that we should only work with our "ideal" clients. This is basic LOA. The Universe loves clarity.

My ideal client:
- Values my services.
- Places a high priority on coaching.
- Can easily afford my rates.
- Loves to invest money in him/herself.
- Experiences satisfaction and joy when paying me promptly.
- Has resources available to him/her.
- Is open to change.
- Is ready to let go of what no longer serves him/her.

- Is grateful for my energy, enthusiasm, and encouragement.
- Comes to me over and over because he/she makes such incredible progress that it feels like a miracle.
- Is spiritual and in the process of awakening.
- Is strong enough to handle my straight talk and blunt style.

❧

OBVIOUSLY THE DEFINITION of my ideal client is a work in progress. I will continue to hone it.

❧

I NEED SOME SEXUAL HEALING.
How's that for a transition?
I have an appointment with a Tantric healer/coach for Sunday. About one week a month I get extremely horny. I have revirginized. Celibacy has not happened to me since I was twelve years old. Fantasy and masturbation are playing a part in my life. I'm in my sexual prime—without a partner.

❧

MY FIRST SEXUAL experiences were very traumatic. When I was almost fourteen, I got with a boy, Dave Lev, who loved me deeply—and hit me. He was abusive in every way: sexually, emotionally, spiritually, and physically. I stayed with him for two years. Immediately after breaking up with him, I got married to one of his friends, Zeke.
What? Why? How?

Like every story of man, it all goes back to sex. One of the most freeing realizations of the last two years has been the fact that my feeling of "unworthiness" was about my loss of virginity. It wasn't the loss of virginity. It was the circumstances: I betrayed my best friend by sleeping with her ex-boyfriend, Poly Peter, and had sex with someone who didn't love me. This automatically entered me in the category of "unworthy" in my religion of origin. I was only thirteen, but I judged myself a *terrible friend* and *worthless whore.*

It wasn't even the circumstances; it was the extremely harsh judgment against myself as a *terrible friend* and *worthless whore* "in need of *punishment.*" Now that I think about it, allowing the church to punish me with sanctions would have been a gentler path than choosing men to abuse me and mean girls to friend me.

It has been a major block to my feelings of worthiness. Uncovering this underlying belief that has controlled my life for twenty-five years gave me a tremendous sense of liberty. During those years, I developed a false sexual identity that no longer serves me. I was sexually experimental and sometimes quite extreme in trying sexually risky things. I had sex with many men and I only wanted to have sex about half the time, possibly less. The other times I did it so as not to hurt their feelings or appear rude, or because they were pressuring me, because I was wasted or high, because it was convenient for someone else, or because I felt badly about myself and wanted someone else to make me feel good.

I was a "pleaser" in bed with almost no boundaries. I wanted men to think I was a "cool girl" and could hang with their perversions, fetishes, and fantasies. So I happily participated.

Some of these I adopted. Dave Lev used to make me watch pornography. Now I watch pornography. Pornography isn't like it used to be. Now it's got a violent edge that makes me cringe, even as I'm aroused by it. Often my sexual fantasies include me being "used" as a teenager. Which is what happened with Dave Lev. These were my first sexual experiences and they were extreme. But I was madly in love with him, so my attachment is "love includes extreme sexual experiences of a violent nature."

I find it difficult to impossible to become aroused by fantasies of loving sex, romance, tenderness, and spiritual intimacy. I simply have no context for it. The last time I remember having sexually stimulating romantic fantasies was when I was twelve, before I lost my virginity and branded myself a whore, and before my violent relationship with Dave Lev. I would fantasize about simple declarations of love and kisses with a boy who lived around the block. I'd call his house and hope he answered, then hang up.

Wait, now that I think about it, he was too immature to be sexually experimental, so I had a cheap, no-strings-attached relationship in which his older brother used me.

What the fuck? Have I ever had any kind of healthy, loving sexual relationship?

The closest I have come would be my husband, Alex, but he was also very sexually shaming about all of the things I did before he came around. The pandering for his forgiveness for my past sex life gives me almost more shame than the acts themselves.

❧

I ATTEMPTED THERAPY immediately after my abusive relationship with Dave Lev and that ended even worse than the abuse itself. Pop psychology of the '90s was to assume that all abusive relationships could be traced back to molestation by the father, even if we couldn't remember it. Unremembered buried memories were par for the course. We should "have *The Courage to Heal,* confront our fathers, and delve into the pain," soaking there, in the pain, until it went away.

If we had these unworthy feelings, had shitty relationships as adults, and felt violated sexually, then we *knew* we were abused by our fathers or uncles, or another adult male authority figure.

It was all very Freudian in the '90s.

Of course I had these feelings because I had battered woman's syndrome, resulting from my very sexually abusive relationship with Dave Lev, which continued for two years. And I was desperate to relieve myself of these feelings. So I dutifully followed the prescription of the book *The Courage to Heal* by Ellen Bass and Laura Davies—and my graduate student therapist, who gave me the book—confronting my father for "repressed memories" of rapes and sexual abuse, and in the process I created havoc and chaos in my family.

What strikes me most about this now is that my therapist and I never talked about the sexual and physical abuse with the boyfriend. The focus was all on uncovering these supposedly unremembered memories, straight from the first or second session.

For twenty years, my mother has used this against me. Not accepting responsibility for anything in her forty-something-year marriage to a controlling asshole. Blaming me for every bit of poor behavior my father has exhibited. Rather than treating me as the young and vulnerable victim of '90s pop psychology at the hands of an inexperienced psych student after an extremely violent relationship, she claims I "destroyed the family."

To this day there's a part of me that believes it did happen. That my father's drinking is a result of his guilt. That my mother threw me on the altar as a sacrifice to protect her financial security and her "denial" (which is exactly what the thinking was—if a person didn't believe it happened, they were in denial).

Did it happen? Did it not happen?

Yeah, that's all tied into my sexual shame, too.

❧

My recent spiritual sexual fantasies, both in Sedona and of late (which at first I was baffled by), are about sexual consecration—sexual baptism, if you will. A cleansing. An initiation into sexual wholeness. These fantasies are both erotic and soothing for my Soul. We already went into the spiritual being who was making love to me on the red rocks of Sedona.

It has occurred to me that these might not be fetish fantasies at all, but a cry from my Soul to be healed sexually.

There is no context for such a thing in modern Christianity. The only method of sexual resurrection and cleansing is to admit your sin, accept your shame, ask forgiveness, and then wait passively for the shame to vanish.

There is no context for such a thing in modern psychology. The only method of relief from sexual shame and guilt is to soak in your pain, admit your shame, attempt to convince yourself "it's not your fault," and soak in the pain some more.

Having attempted both of the aforementioned methods, I am still left without a context for spiritual, healthy, romantic sexuality. I think the problem with these methods is that they are inherently asexual. There is not a new beautiful experience to replace the previous damaging experience. Rather you're left with a sexual void. You don't want the old sexuality, but there is nothing new to claim the place of your sexuality.

So I am going to see a sexual tantric healer. There will be sexuality involved, actual touching. I have no idea how much touching or what it will be like. But I trust that my Soul is leading me to the sexual healing I'm longing for.

TWENTY

APRIL 28, 2013

I violated my Soul's wisdom and now I'm sitting here feeling like an ass. Worse than an ass. I feel worthless. I feel betrayed. I feel like I've sinned against myself. I feel like God has left me and that I've ruined everything. I feel like I've taken three steps back and tripped on my face. I feel like my light is dimmed and my body is vibrating more slowly. I feel guilty and ashamed. I feel like I've lost everything I'm working toward. I'm angry with myself for not keeping the commitment I made to myself after passing out in the bathtub after my thirty-ninth birthday/divorce party.

I'm scared, too. Really scared. No sooner had I got off the phone with my dad, asking him to go to rehab and telling him there is a Little Liar in His Brain who is going to convince him that he can handle drinking again, I ignored my Soul and listen to the Little Liar in My Brain.

I was on the phone talking to my mother about a terrible, ugly and scary night of drinking my dad had recently had in which he was not in control of his bodily functions. I was highly self-righteous and expressed my frustration with my Mom's submission to a drunken man and her passive ridiculousness and feigned helplessness and obscene inability to take any kind of action about it. Even as it was happening, I could taste the hypocrisy in my mouth. I made her cry.

On the way over to my friend Anna's birthday party, I was already feeling myself weaken. Reminding myself of the "warning dreams" I had about the risks involved with me drinking, I could hear the Little Liar justify. *It's the gluten, just drink something other than beer. I'm going to be tired anyway; it won't really matter if I am hung over. I'll only have one.*

It's not even like I believe the lies. I *know* they're lies. I know that I can't drink one drink, ever. I know that even one drink is poison and makes me feel horrible about betraying myself. I have the alcoholic gene. Just like I have an allergy to gluten.

When I drink, I feel that old evil anxiety I spent my twenties and thirties trying to outrun. All those years of that empty feeling and devastating anxiety—was it the alcohol? There's not a thing in the world to me that is worse than this anxiety in my heart and the hole in my stomach. I hate it so much.

On my own birthday, I passed out in the bathtub, drunk. I slept for twenty-four hours straight afterward and my hangover lasted three days. Prior to that I'd had prophetic dreams about getting stuck in quick sand and being unable to get out—the quick sand was the alcoholism that's chasing me down if I play.

I don't want to play. I want to have the bright and powerful future I'm building. Which means I have to claim that instead of settling for this awful other scenario that ends with my dad's pathetic and depressing life of passing out by afternoon, lashing out at other people randomly to protect his drinking, manipulating his loved ones and the devastating depression that goes with it.

While hung over and self-loathing and hiding under the covers the next day, I prayed for God to enter me and saturate my cells with peace, comfort, wholeness, and oneness. It's amazing how much of that I have normally, that I don't even have to try for. I used to have to try for it constantly. Perhaps because I was drinking or using drugs I had to really reach for any kind of peace.

I feel such sympathy for alcoholics.

They feel like this all the time. Right? Or not. Maybe they don't and that's what makes them susceptible to alcoholism.

I can't handle my liquor. At all. That's a gift. It makes me feel so fucking terrible when I drink that there is not a chance in a million years that I will do this again tonight. In fact, the way it goes, generally, is that it might take me days to get back into my groove and get my spiritual energy to rise again.

Separation. That's what the feeling is. I've been trying to name it. It is separation from God that I feel and it's terrible. I hate it. I feel cut off from God. It's so horrible that I can't figure out how I used to live with it all the time.

Well, I lived in fear and anxiety. I pushed through and practically sleepwalked my whole life, doped up on anxiety meds. Forcing myself to take one step forward. But not loving those steps.

Now I don't. I don't live in fear and anxiety. I live in light. I live in confidence. I live in joy. Optimism and enthusiasm are my middle names. Today has made me realize how precious it is for me to live this way. The sober way. The enlightened way. That's what it feels like, lighter. In light.

I can't go back.

I missed my tantric sex appointment. I woke up and thought that I would never be able to go to the appointment and try to feel sexy while I wanted to barf and have diarrhea.

I felt conflicted about it anyway. I am on my period. I have no real idea about what happens at a Tantric sex session, but I don't feel sexy on my period.

TWENTY-ONE

MAY 31, 2013

Friday night, Madigan had an end-of-year sleepover with eight of her friends. I had been working my ass off. You'll notice the hole in this book where I could have written in May, but I was so busy knocking out deadlines that I hadn't a second to spare. Saturday morning I was going to finish one last newsletter assignment. Then I pushed the power button on my MacBook. Nothing happened.

That damn cord again, Apple's making $1,000 computers with $10 cords, I said to myself.

"Nope," the Apple Genius said. "It's not the cord. It will take us a few days to look at it and at least a week until you get it back."

Great timing, I thought. *At least I finished all of my assignments and had already planned to take a week's vacation.*

The real relief in this is that I wasn't worried. It was a relatively new machine and *I had the money to fix it.*

I'm sorry, did you miss that? What I meant to say was, *I HAD THE MONEY TO FIX IT!!!*

It's hard to describe the feeling of serenity that comes with knowing that I have money in the bank to deal with life's little curveballs. The disparity, the contrast between not having enough to fix my computer and having enough to fix my computer is stark. It's the difference between panic and relief. It's the difference between hysterical and calm. It's the difference between doom and optimism. It's the difference between furious anger and happy anyway. It's the difference between, *I am going to murder my kid* and *accidents happen.*

✍

I HAD BEEN WORKING extra hard to make time for my long-time friend Kristen to come visit for two days. She'd asked me to take her daughter, Jane, to Texas with us so that she could spend the summer with her dad. I had actually put her off and I'm pretty sure I told her "no" in an indirect way, but she persisted. Oh Kristen, she sure loves her favors. She's a "poor single mom" and all that.

"I don't feel comfortable bailing Darrin out and making it so easy for him to be a douche bag, and the car will be super crammed," I think I told her. "I'm not sure how my parents will feel about that, and I'm going with them."

Then she texted and called and gave me the whole *poor Jane* bit. Finally, against my better judgment and my Soul's clear advice, I relented. Kristen was supposed to come Sunday and stay Monday. We would leave Tuesday morning.

Yeah. But she's Kristen, the most unreliable person I know. She's a flake. She's self-centered to the degree that it doesn't bother her one bit to flake out on someone who is a half an hour from her house, driving across the country to see her, and say, "Lunch isn't going to work for me, I have this other really important thing happening."

She's got no problem saying, "I'm in dire distress! Can I come live with you? SAVE me and my children or we will be homeless!" And then the day she's going to move in, she'll call to say, "You're going to be so mad at me. I've changed my mind. I've decided my kid needs to finish second grade here (so I can chase a man who's treating me like shit—again)."

To be honest here, I really was very happy that she had decided not to move in because I hadn't found a way to tell her that, no, she could, in fact, become homeless because I don't want a directionless flake using me as a babysitter and sucking up my resources and going nowhere: which is where Kristen has been going for the eleven or so years that I've known her. No where.

I've known her for such a long time that I've liked to pretend that we were friends, though usually friends make an effort—at least the ones worth having. And I have a savior complex about her, I think. I mean, her childhood was absolutely horrendous.

Have you ever stopped to think about how much traction a bad childhood gives a person? They can ride a bad childhood into their nineties, milking everyone around them for sympathy, favors, and handouts, and sticking them with appalling behavior. It's a trend that I'm about over, myself. Kristen's been milking hers pretty consistently.

I've sent Kristen books to help her change her way of thinking. I sent her an entire course about prosperity that would literally change her life—if she wasn't so helpless that she couldn't find a CD player at the thrift store for $5, or couldn't figure out how to upload it to her computer, or you know, if she wasn't so lazy about her own life that she cared that she was living in a state of depressing poverty and actually wanted to do something about it.

I even gave her a paid job writing simple assignments, which—surprise!—she totally flaked out on. She couldn't find the time or resources to finish and completely fucked me up. But that was my own fault, because to expect anything but failure and flake from Kristen only makes *me* the fool.

I just kept pretending she is not who she is. But she is who she is. Every. Time. And my Soul knows this. Every single time I would change my travel plans to accommodate her for a visit, my Soul would roll her eyes. When I invited her to live off me in the basement, my Soul practically revolted and drew in all of her Law of Attraction powers to repel Kristen and her aura of poverty and depression from our little slice of paradise here.

My Soul told me not to volunteer to take Kristen's kid across the country, but I let Kristen, with her victimized nonsense, persuade me to go against my better knowing.

Can you guess how this story turns out?

Right. I got a text message on Sunday about an hour before I she was supposed to be here, which red: SORRY, NOT COMING 'TIL TOMORROW.

That was it for me. Friendship. Over.

A man once said, "friendship over," to me after he had behaved deplorably, and I dumbly did not terminate that friendship, which did cost me quite considerably in the end.

Finally the *next* morning, she called to make yet more plans. Just in time to collect her big favor, see? *Gimme. Gimme. Gimme.*

"Listen Kristen," I said, "I've had enough of this friendship. This relationship, with your flaking out on me, your inconsiderate behavior, your using up my resources and my favors, and investing absolutely nothing in the relationship, is not working for me. I'm over this friendship. No one was surprised that you flaked out, because that's how you are. This is how you run your life, a complete mess. I changed around my life to make this happen and you text me right before you're supposed to be here?!?! What the fuck!?! I've had enough of this.

"I'm done with this friendship. I'm not doing this anymore. Don't even explain why you did it, because I don't give a shit why. The reason is that you can't get your shit together and manage your life. You had plenty of notice to handle this shit and take care of working out the details. And you didn't.

"Don't pull the 'single mom card' or the 'I have a job card.' I'm running a business here, and I'm a single mom, and I worked it out. You don't take care of your shit; it's how you run your whole life. My parents are coming and as soon as they get here we are leaving. If you're not here when they get here, we're leaving. I. will. not. wait. one. single. minute. for. you."

Of course, she really wanted her big favor, the one that would save her Baby Daddy a few hundred bucks. So she gets here. It is uncomfortable and awkward. Then she says she's going out to dinner with Alex. *Great. Getouttahere.*

"Should I just leave Leslie here?"

"I'm not babysitting your toddler! No way are you leaving that kid here. Those days are over for me."

Yes, she has that kind of nerve, wanting to ditch her toddler on me so she could go off and have a good time drinking with my ex-husband. She's a taker and a user and I've been giving, giving, giving for a decade in the hopes that I could make her life better by bringing her into the light with me. But she wants the dark. On some level it's working for her. She sure is getting a lot of mileage out of it.

Why is this person even in my life? I asked myself. *Like attracts like, so how am I like her?*

Upon reflection, I realized that I had become friends with her in the depths of postpartum depression and Xanax addiction, post-traumatic stress from witnessing 9/11 while I was eight months pregnant, when Alex and I were in a lot of financial trouble and declaring bankruptcy and living in a shack infested with mold that was making me chronically ill. I was *being flaky* at the time because I just couldn't work and Alex was pressuring me tremendously, so I kept flaking out on the jobs I had that I didn't want to have. That's when I attracted Kristen.

Then I never ended my friendship with her, though I'm no longer "like" her. Which is likely why nothing can work out between us: my Soul's way of saying, *Get the hell away from her.*

I used to think we shouldn't judge and that we could let shit slide and be friends with—*how shall I say it without sounding like a stuck-up bitch?*—low-quality people. People who make bad choices, worse choices, and terrible choices repeatedly. People who are stuck in unconsciousness and have terrible thought habits about money, love, right and wrong and their lifestyle. *How is that for putting it nicely?*

Now, I disagree with my former self. I now believe absolutely that we are like those we are around, that energy is contagious, that negativity and poverty thinking are like viruses, and if we hang around stuck people, we get stuck. This is why it's beneficial to sever relationships with people who are living lives that we don't want to live.

Thinking myself totally done with this nonsense, we drove Jane to Texas without incident. The girl is darling and sweet and causes no trouble. But she keeps asking for cough drops.

The day after we turn her over to her stepmother we get a call. "Jane has a bacterial infection in her lungs and ears, and pink eye." *Awesome.*

Now the Hancocks have a great excuse to be the Hancocks. "Our kids can't hang out with your kids because they might be sick," Alex's brothers say.

They *might* be sick. After three years of not seeing their cousins, having driven across the country, my kids *might* be sick, so they should be quarantined and can't see their cousins. *Right.*

The kid next to your kid in school *might* be sick, the kids at church *might* be sick, the people in Walmart *might* be sick.

My kids weren't sick. My kids never got sick. But they did get abandoned after having traveled quite far with high expectations of cousin-bonding and fun and love. Thank God their aunts and uncles withheld their love in order to prevent getting a snotty nose. I mean, think of the alternative: Your kid *might* get sick. How devastating would it be to have a sick kid? Sick kids are so inconvenient and annoying. Sickness must be prevented at all costs. *Right?* Who cares if they don't create a relationship with their family? At least they didn't get sick. Getting sick is the worst thing in the world that can happen to a kid.

Oh, that's right. My kids weren't sick!

It's pretty difficult to describe the hurt this caused both me and my kids, and I'm guessing my wasband. I want to cavalierly write my was-laws off as douche bags, and act as if I don't care that much. But it brought back a lot of painful stuff. After all, we moved to Texas to create a familial support system with my wasband's brothers and their families. We forgot to ask if either of his brothers wanted anything to do with this type of family support. They did not. They refused invitations to hang out with us repeatedly. They objected to every type of babysitting exchange. They never invited our children over. They refused even to allow their children to come to our house.

They wanted nothing to do with us aside from some random cousin-time at Nana's house, and the usual family get-togethers at holidays or when an out-of-town relative came to visit. This was quite hurtful for us as a couple, as a family.

Their sequestering my children away as lepers after a three-year absence was painful because it brought up all the hurt feelings we experienced during the seven years of living in Texas.

Oh, I remember, I thought, *you don't love us. You don't love my kids. I kinda forgot.*

Finally, one of his brothers relented and the cousins had a great time together. His other brother, the hardcore evangelical one, and incidentally the one related to Kristen, allowed his children to have a quick pizza dinner at a public place and made my children sit *across* the table from his children.

My best guess is that, in reality, he didn't want my children's differing religious training to be contagious. Lord knows that only *his* church of 200 people has found the *real truth* about God, and to listen to another perspective could be a disaster. Sanity sometimes leaks through the cracks of fundamentalism, especially in proximity to young minds. *Can't have that.*

My kids are totally buying the "sick" bit for now. But they will NOT be going back to Texas in June, as was the plan. I'm not taking bets on what their big legitimate excuse for not wanting their children to have a relationship with my children will be then. I wonder if Madigan will buy it again? They pulled this the time we sent her back to Texas on spring break, too, a few years ago. One of their kids had pink eye. Of course.

The Hancocks are the Hancocks. I had forgotten.

Byron Katie asks four questions to bring us back to sanity, and one of them I pass through my brain when I get my feelings hurt or when someone shows me who they are. I ask: *Can I accept that this is who they are?*

Absolutely. I can. And I should. It is a reminder to stop pretending that certain people are loving, or reliable, kind, rational, or interested in creating relationships and bonds with me and my kids. I can accept Hancocks and also release myself from the painful belief that there will be a relationship between them and my kids that will be more loving than painful.

❦

IN THE MEANTIME, I'M not away from my email for fifteen hours when I get weird frantic texts from a writer I hired to finish one of my assignments. My regular writer had emailed and explained that she had a "hole in her spine and must be rushed to surgery immediately." *More weird writer/SAHM excuses, anyone? Uh. Okay.*

Crushed for time, I had put an ad on Craigslist, hoping for the best. A man named Charles, who seemed to be able to spell and put periods in the right places, responded. I hired him, gave him the assignment sheet, and was happy to know that this was getting done in spite of my broken computer and my vacation.

By the time we reach Amarillo, I am getting strange texts from this Charles who is upset about an ad he saw on Craigslist. An ad he's convinced is me trying to replace him. And now he's convinced that I'm a fake person who is trying to screw him. So now he's *emailing my clients* to try to confirm my identity. Mind you, I communicated with this person at 10 P.M. the previous evening and I'm now getting this crazyness via text at 10 A.M. the next morning. WTF?!?

It's turning into a mess with my clients that I have to deal with. They have hired me to serve *their* clients and they are really pissed that this guy is attempting to email those people directly.

Obviously, I fired Charles. His behavior was unpredictably weird and came out of left field. But then my client offered to release me from my obligation and I took the opportunity on faith that I would replace the income in a more gratifying way. I knew the trouble it was causing could be energy and resources that would better serve me in building my life coaching business.

It was so weird and random that I figured my desire not to do these assignments and my clarity on knowing that I would have to release it to make my time and energy work for the coaching, was my Soul giving me a message. When I didn't take action, the Universe took action for me.

◈

EAST TEXAS IS STILL East Texas. And my Dad is still my Dad. Meaning Fox News blared the whole time in the living room at my grandmother's house. My father enjoys screaming about politics and quoting the wisdom of Fox News and telling everyone who doesn't see it as credible or fair and balanced how stupid and idiotic they are. Well, actually, I think he mostly enjoys screaming at me, in particular. He had a great time calling me out on all kinds of stuff that I don't pay attention to or care about. He kept having an argument although I wasn't arguing back. It's super fun because there is no way to win. Ever.

During another weird episode, he proceeded to tell me my mother was a terrible person because she saw an ex-boyfriend in Texas once. Their entire marriage was a betrayal, he says, and that's why he perpetually behaves like a douchebag and has gotten wasted at home, in her face, daily, and is being verbally, spiritually, and emotionally abusive to her. She deserves it because she came to Texas once eight years ago in response to an ex-boyfriend's threat to kill himself if she didn't. She says it was the right thing to do because she felt inspired by God to help him.

I told him to get over it, it's not as though she had an affair. That he was being a baby. She didn't marry that guy, she didn't want him back, and he's a total loser. I told my Dad that he was using this brief visit, which took place in public at her mother's house, as a free pass to drink and be a dick, when he had already been drinking for at least a decade and probably four.

My parents are Mormons, so drinking is a big deal. They were married in the Temple and drinking goes against the marriage vows and literally puts my mother's eternal life in jeopardy. So, yeah, it's a very serious issue between them and *God*.

❧

"HEY, TRACEE."

"Yes, Dad?"

"I still love you even though you're a liberal. I still love Jason, too, even though he's a liberal."

"Thanks Dad."

For the record, my brother Jason is a Mormon bishop, a Navy chaplain, and a Republican.

This is how Dad bonds with me, in particular. I wish it were more fun for me. But mostly it just hurts my feelings. A lot.

❧

WHEN MY YOUNGEST BROTHER and his family arrived, my Dad hopped off the couch at the first request from his kids, "Grandpa, will you play with us?"

"Well, of course I will," Dad said in a real sweet, Grandpa-of-the-Year voice.

Charlie had been asking him to play with him for several days. He wouldn't go outside and toss a football with him, wouldn't swing him on the tire swing, didn't want anything to do with him. I tried to not get my feelings hurt about that either. But I did.

It hurts my feelings. In fact, I can't remember a time when I was around my Dad that I didn't feel attacked or have my feelings hurt at least once. He can be generous, helping me financially here and there. But he can also be very cruel, mean, and hurtful.

He's a problem. I don't want him to be a problem. I want to have an ideal relationship with my parents, where Grandma and Grandpa come to visit and we have a bonding and loving time. I see other girls and women feeling protected and adored and supported by their dads. I did an article for *Style* magazine about father-daughter bonds and that, too, hurt my feelings, because I don't have anything resembling that sweet "protect and provide" thing that men do for their girls.

The fact is, my Dad is volatile and he doesn't like me very much. He's aggressive and mean, and frankly, he's becoming downright dangerous.

❧

MY SOUL TOLD ME NOT TO allow him to drive, but I went against my judgment. He got in the car for the trip home, after having disappeared for twenty minutes to air up the tires—and came back with a long, cockeyed story. An addict always has a *story*. I did ask him if he'd been drinking. He was offended and said he'd been sober for nine days. *Uh huh.*

Something inside me didn't believe him. But I let him drive anyway because I'm afraid of him and confrontation with him can get really ugly really fast. It's like poking a poisonous snake with a stick.

In Dallas, smack in the middle of real traffic, he played chicken with a diesel that was trying to move into his lane. Rather than slowing down, as someone sane who was concerned with the safety of his family might do, he sped up and held his ground. I got terrified and then I got pissed off. "What the fuck is wrong with you? This is my van and my children are in the car!" I yelled.

Everyone else in the car played their assigned roles and just stayed silent, peeing their pants. I did not, I yelled and then when it was over I told him, "PULL OVER! PULL OVER RIGHT NOW! YOU'RE NOT DRIVING ANYMORE! YOU DON'T GET TO DRIVE MY VAN!"

Of course, he did no such thing. *My penis is bigger than your penis* was the maturity level of it.

Your penis is a mini-van, Dad!

Of course, I was at fault for not trusting his self-described "great driving skills" and we were "never in any danger," and "You did the same thing on the way there."

A diesel had merged way too close to my lane earlier in the trip and I had put on the brakes as fast as I could to avoid an accident, not instigate one. Obviously the same thing.

"I just wanted to show him my displeasure at him moving into my lane. I was right. I had the right of way."

"Oh awesome. You were right. We'll etch that on your tombstone. 'I had the right of way! I was right!' Awesome. You played chicken with a sixteen-wheeler with my children in the car!"

When he finally did pull over, I took the wheel and we promptly had a blowout. Middle of the night, on the side of the road, it took us a little while to figure out how the jack worked. In the meantime two diesels pulled over to help. Of course, my parents and my cousin were convinced that these truckers were out to murder and rape us. It is so foreign to me to be terrified of the Good Samaritan all the time. Turns out my cousin was carrying two guns and my dad felt much more confident about this. *What?*

This is what comes of a steady diet of Fox News. Everyone, even those pulling over to help someone who broke down 170 miles outside the nearest town, is out to do you harm. They don't even believe in goodness anymore.

146

Hours later my dad reamed me out about my audacity to get upset at him for playing chicken with my van, and he informed me that he would never allow me to travel with him again. *Geez, I've been looking for a great reason to never, ever get in a car with that maniac behind the wheel again for as long as I live.* Wish granted.

I then drove 170 miles at 45 miles per hour for five hours. We arrived at the nearest Sams Club ten minutes before they opened. I was beyond tired.

❧

WITH A NEW TIRE, somewhere in the panhandle of Oklahoma, my cousin's radar detector completely failed and he was pulled over and given a ticket. Major bummer. Except when it's the best thing that could have happened.

Turns out, five minutes before we got to the train tracks, ten miles up the road, the safety arm of a railroad crossing failed and a train plowed into a diesel truck. The driver was alive, with only bruises and scrapes. I doubt, however, that a minivan would have made out so well. I can only call this God's timing.

❧

THE BEST PART ABOUT MY visit to Texas was my book club ladies. When I first became a practitioner of the Law of Attraction, one of the first things I attracted was a book club. I was socially starving. My social interaction was entirely made up of evangelical submissive wives and Kristen, because I couldn't find anyone else to interact with.

I prayed for a tribe of "only the right women," to join my book club and I was gifted generously. When a woman would tell me no, I would know that she was not the right woman. That was the deal I struck with the Universe. The way things played out was quite interesting. Through various unlikely interactions a group of seven women gathered monthly.

It was a life saver for me. And for Neecy and some of the other women, I think. It was the only fulfilling social interaction I had for the seven years we spent in Texas. The whole rest of it was horrible for me. The Between the Covers book club met once a month for three years and it was soothing to my Soul.

Coming back to Texas, everyone rearranged their schedules for me and it felt delightful. These women are still my people. They are kind and loving. They are smart and ambitious and exciting. They are good moms. They are professionals. And they love me. I felt loved. I really did. That was what was missing always in Texas. I never felt loved when I lived there.

Here in Fort Collins, Colorado, I do feel loved and appreciated for who I am. I don't have to tiptoe around weird Southern rules that don't make any sense and aren't grounded in Love.

❧

BEING AT MY GRANDMA'S house was hard for me. I knew it was probably the last time I would visit while she was still living. I tried to breathe in the air, take in the green, lush property, feel the cold hardwood floors beneath my feet, absorb the knickknacks that have sat on the same shelves for decades. I wanted to memorize the details and really appreciate it. But it was hard.

I didn't feel connected to it, in a strange way. I felt outside of most of it for the trip. I participated, but all of my grandmother's children were there. I was the only grandchild staying there and I kept wondering, *Why am I even here?* I felt out of place and discombobulated.

I hate the idea of my grandmother not being in the woods with her door open to me anytime I might need it. I also can't tolerate the idea of ever going back to Texas for anything other than her funeral.

It is not *my place.*

HOW DID I GET IN THIS FAMILY? I have asked myself over and over. Never more so than this trip. Listening to them is simply foreign. I simply think and believe so differently that I can't figure out what my place with them is. *Is it just so my Dad has someone to shout at? Just so my mother can blame me for the demise of her wonderful {{scoff}} marriage?*

Upon returning home, I was thrilled to get back to my normal, which feels sane and stable. In which I feel like a powerful woman, not some teenager with radical beliefs who is just there to be bullied and attacked out of boredom. Still all that energy was ON me, in my skin, absorbing into my brain, inhibiting me from getting grounded and feeling myself. So I went to see C.J.

C.J. worked on me for an hour and said that I was carrying a lot of energy that wasn't mine, specifically and heavily, my dad's very intense energy. I was also carrying other stuff. And some of it was my own stuff riled up by the other stuff. She cleared energy out and did "repairs." Among other things, she worked on generational spiritual agreements, such as alcoholism, cut some cords to some people that need to not be in my life anymore (Kristen and the Hancocks, for example). She did say, however that my heart is more open now than it has been in a long time. Too, my *hara* line (some technical energy term which determines my purpose and path) was stronger than ever.

This was such a relief, because when I got home I was unclear about what I was meant to do or how to proceed with my life.

❧

I HAVE A DATE TONIGHT. I'm calling it a date. The truth is I answered an ad on Craigslist about a Tantric sex partnership and I'm meeting the guy tonight at a classy restaurant. *Deep breath and sigh.* I called this forth, I realize.

When I was in Sedona, I was beyond sexually stimulated. I was crazy horny and all of my meditations and massages were highly sexually charged for me. Not that the practitioners were doing anything differently. But, my energy and what kept coming up for me was highly charged sexual energy. A craving for sexual healing has come up over and over.

As you know, I've been trying to set up Tantric sex counseling for a while now. Something keeps coming up and interfering.

"Wouldn't it be cool to attract a healing Tantric sex partner?" one of the SpiritQuest counselors asked.

"Yes, that would be amazing!" I agreed.

I answered an ad on Craigslist looking for a Tantric sex partner to learn the skills of Tantra. I'm meeting him tonight.

I admit to having conflicted feelings about this. Essentially it feels weird to be meeting a stranger with sex on the top of the agenda. However, I really am craving sexual healing, and it feels like my Soul is putting the pressure on to walk me into forty having resolved it, or at least some of it.

I need a sexual reinvention, a new kind of sexual experience. I want to walk into forty having worked out my sexual issues having to do with my past. Not only the abuses, but the self-sexualization and my identity as a twenty-something sexuality. I need a forty-something sexuality that feels powerful and authentic to me. I want to learn how to stay present during sex.

At the same time, I'm not really interested in pairing off with someone right now. I'm fucking loving my autonomy. That's the truth of it. I like making my own choices without considering another person, aside from considering how something will effect my children, which is a given.

I have attracted this. That doesn't mean I'm going through with it necessarily, but the idea of it is stimulating. The guy sent me photos and he's okay looking. He might be cute in person. It's hard to say. He's doesn't believe in "jobism" (*read:* unemployed) which would make him a lousy husband, I'm sure. But I'm not looking for a husband. He does believe in the Law of Attraction and travels a lot, which is the life he wants to design and create. So that's all good.

My one concern is that we might become emotionally involved. Let's face it: women have a release of oxytocin that masks itself as love when they have sex. It's not the same for men.

Further, we are intending on having a highly intimate sexual experience together. Our intention is not a one-night stand; it's not a commitment either. It's a sexual experience that involves spiritual presence and really intimate interaction.

I'm not sure if this is something that should occur between strangers. I'm not sure that it shouldn't either. I don't know how it is going to go.

I am going to have dessert and coffee and see how I feel in this man's presence though. It could be the spiritually sexual medicine my Soul is thirsty for

Or it could just be gross.

I'm going in open to the possibility, but not yet committed.

TWENTY-TWO

JUNE 7, 2013

The business conference was better than promised. Highlights include the fact that my thirty-year old bestie, Anna, came with me. I always trip out that one of my best friends is a decade younger than me. It makes me feel very cool and hip. She wants to grow up and be me, which is amazingly flattering. She is hiring me as her coach. KILLER NEWS!!!

One of my big revelations at the conference was that I have the unwritten rule: *No one is going to pay me to be her friend, as you can't charge friends money. Everyone is my friend.* This is an unsustainable business model, which leaves me drained and often resentful. Resentful because I'm giving way more value than I am receiving in my friendships. Drained because I'm depleting my energy resources to coach people who aren't paying me. I'm doing crappy writing/marketing work to feed my family and put gas in the car, which leaves little energy left over to market my coaching services to "strangers," whom I allow myself to charge; except I don't, because I immediately put everyone in the "friend" category.

I meet a new person—say at church—and introduce myself. Immediately, I befriend her. She tells me, "Oh, I love your speech about conscious motherhood, could you send it to me?"

I say, "Why, of course, and if you'd like to go to lunch and get to know each other better, that would be wonderful." I never follow through with an offering of my coaching services.

Or she will say, "Gosh you're a good dresser, can you take me shopping and show me how?"

"Oh yes!" I say. Then I spend an entire Saturday shopping with her and giving her a makeover. I take photos. I launch and write an online profile that is sure to get her a man. She sends me a $25 gift card to Chili's and never hangs out with me again.

What the fuck am I doing?

Anna was totally calling me on this bad habit all over the place. I meet people, give up all my skills, insight, brilliance, tips, and life-changing perspectives in a conversation rather than telling them that I am a coach—and could we schedule a "get to know you conversation" later in the week?

We went out to the pool in Atlanta right after the conference and a woman there was asking me all about the Law of Attraction, raising her daughter, and growing her business. I coached her for two-and-a-half hours and gave her resources about love and men that didn't even include MY book!

WHAT THE FUCK?!?!

I've been coaching for seven years without getting paid because I didn't have a script for how to sell my services. And believing that everyone is my "friend," and that as a friend my job is to: change their life, give great advice, push them in a better direction, and do all sorts of time-sucking services for them . . . and then they don't return my favors and they don't pay me.

A friend commiserates, but the advice is not one-sided. In fact, a friend is on the same level. This means that I should be getting equal advice, coaching, and support from friends.

My big epiphany was that I need to put my foot forward as a coach, not a friend, when I first meet someone. But it's a fucking compulsion to automatically coach strangers because they really, really *are* interested in what I can give them. Now, I need to promote that I can help them as a coach.

To date, being my friend has been extremely good for *their* bottom line, but excruciatingly destructive to *my* bottom line.

This has to stop if I am ever going to be able to move forward, make a good living, provide well for my family, and achieve my dreams. I have to get some one-on-one clients to pay the bills so that I can stop the marketing writing piecework that saps my time and sucks my energy. This is the only way to grow my business. The conference gave me a tremendous number of tools to use to proceed in that direction.

One exceptionally awesome piece of news is that I coached Anna for the entire trip. When we were going through security in Denver she was telling me that she had agreed to work for someone we know who is launching a non-profit . . . for free, for up to, like, three years! She would be the director and keep her day job. The *I've got three jobs syndrome.* She would do this to manifest her original dream of running an innovative health center, which would serve the client, and also teach practitioners how to market and grow their businesses. She likes "collaboration," which is why she is willing to do her dream for someone else. It's *like* owning her own business because *she would be her own boss.*

I told her that was bat-shit crazy. In nicer language.

By the end of Day 1 of the conference, Anna had realized her flawed thinking and felt like she really, really could do her health center right now and that she should obviously do it for herself. By the end of the conference she had a million ideas popping in her brain for innovative structures and solutions to what she believed to be impossible. Yes, the conference was instrumental in making her believe this is possible, but *I* was also vital to the process and gave her a million coaching tools to manifest it.

I am drawing up a coaching package for her and will work out the details to work with her on a professional level. It's very exciting. She's so ready for an enormous transformation and growing a business that I would really like to sell her a $6,000 package for one year of one-on-one coaching. By the end of the year, I envision her having a real business, quitting or preparing to quit her day job, and having her relationship transformed. Honestly, I think she'll end up breaking up with her current boyfriend, I'm not witnessing him bringing a lot to the relationship, and they are having serious relationship issues. I simply don't see it going anywhere—not where she would like it to go anyway.

So, of course, the conference was a marketing tool in itself to promote the coach's annual coaching opportunities. These are high-priced packages amounting to about $10,000 or more, with additional costs for travel to mastermind retreats and the expenses that go with that. They are also huge time commitments.

Because I believe that I need coaching to push my business forward and would consider it like getting an MBA, but more practical and useful, I was ready to sign up on the faith that I could conjure up the $1,000 monthly payments using the skills I was learning there. I made a list of fifteen fabulous reasons why this program is something that I should definitely do. I even called my credit card company to ask for a credit limit increase so that I could pay the "right now" price of $7,500.

Then Anna suggested we ask the pendulum. She's been taking an energy class, and asking the pendulum has been one of her favorite tools. We asked and the answer was clearly NO. The pendulum even said I wouldn't be able to keep up with the minimum payments.

I took a step back and thought about what my priorities would be if I signed up for the course. Obviously, if I was spending $10,000, my priority would be to get the most value out of the program and make the course and growing my business—so I can pay off the debt—my number one priority. But then I flashed to my dream board. Going balls to the wall on my business is not on this year's dream board. That was intentional. I intended to remove the high-success expectation for this year and build a firm foundation for a new life in 2013.

Healing work, like going for massages, pampering myself, meditation, spiritual growth, REST, my spiritual travel column, *Soul Trek*, fixing up my backyard, writing this book, and experiencing what happens when you say YES to everything your Soul tells you to do, and growing a tribe are my priorities. My business is on the dream board in the form of a blue butterfly I associate with life coaching. Money is on the dream board in the form of dollar signs. But going full out on my business was not my intention for this year. I realized if I started the program it would interfere and actively wreck my resting, spiritual growth, healing process.

Here's what I know to be true: I cannot effectively manage, grow, and sustain a business long term at the high level I want to if I am not healed of things that have held me back. My marriage and the stress and constraints of it are primary things I am healing from. The first thirty-nine years of psychic garbage is something I have committed to clearing and healing. I have intended, since I was thirty-seven, to walk into forty clean and free of the shit I've been collecting and carrying around. I intend to be a clear, crisp, clean, and free empty vessel as I embark on my Second Act. Or is it my Third? Either way, it's a new and exciting beginning and I want to do it in a specific way. This way does not include investing all of my time and energy building my business as fast and as intensely as possible. This way does include experiencing healing transformation and rest. I intended to take the pressure of success off, not put a rocket launcher under it and intensify it exponentially.

I did not sign up for the program and it made me feel unbelievably rich! For one thing I felt $10,000 richer for having not spent seven to ten grand that I do not yet have. For another, I realized that I CAN conjure up $10,000 if I want to, and that possibility is waiting for me in the future. Suddenly, the $4,400 cash I had seemed like a fortune, enabling me to go to IKEA and get the office stuff I've been needing and not buying. It also felt like I would be able to fix up the backyard and take my fortieth birthday vacation, something that I had figured would be lost to me if I signed up for the course.

Healing, for 2013, is my One Thing.

I know me. My business will become my One Thing for 2014. Unless my Soul gives me different instructions.

৵

Headline: Orgasmic Meditation Ruins My Political Career

About my date with the potential Tantric sex partner, Carl. This guy is not someone I want to kiss, let alone carry on a tremendously intimate spiritual-sexual meditation with. *Uh, uh. No way.* I knew instantly the second I met him that it was a no. I even almost said, "I already know this won't work for me," and walked out of the date before we even sat down to dinner. I did not like his energy and I did not like his looks at all.

He was short, which is a huge turnoff for me. He was decidedly unattractive to me. Further lack of attraction entered when he revealed that he has no job, no purpose, and no ambition. He's got a rental income and makes like $500 doing God Knows What. So unattractive. *Bleck.*

I did not care for the way he talked to me either. First, he was aggressive about how stupid marriage is, which is fine, but he was saying the usual trite things that people say about the state and the piece of paper, as if anyone who gets married is just a sucker and an idiot. Finally, I told him, "I'm not the seller of marriage."

Then he proceeded to argue that there is no such thing as choice and free will, but only the illusion of such things. That because there is only One and that the Universe has already happened and existed in real time and is now over—what happens happens and there's nothing we can do about it. Which is entirely contrary to my belief system.

He used some analogy about Super Mario. We're the player—God/Creator—and we're also Mario. When I pointed out that the player makes different choices for every game and that there are hundreds of thousands of ways to get to the Princess (and die a million times before you do), and that every second of the game is about choice, he said the whole of life was based on one turn.

Uh, okay.

"You're not a real non-dualist then," he informed me.

Uh. Okay. As if a five-minute meeting with me means that you get to dictate the category of spirituality I fall into. It's rather like a Christian saying, "You're not a real Christian because you don't believe in _____." As if they are the decider of how God and the Universe works.

The date was not lost, however. He told me about a group that focuses on Orgasmic Meditation (OM). Isn't that hysterical? The orgasm is the center of the meditative practice. A Meetup group gets together around the female orgasm as a spiritual meditation practice. In a room, men and women partner up—strangers or couples or friends—and the women take off their pants.

They take off their pants.

But not their shirts.

I guess that would be too intimate.

The men remain fully clothed. Then they follow very specific steps to OM. Their bodies are arranged in specific configurations. The timer is set for fifteen minutes, when the meditation—regardless of desire—will be completed.

Then the man spreads the woman's vulva and "strokes" the left side of the upper quadrant of a woman's clitoris in pre-calculated movements that have been determined to bring a woman to the highest ecstasy. When the meditation is complete, the woman puts on her pants and gives the man . . . nothing.

For her it is a meditation in receiving and surrendering to her own pleasure. The spiritual practice is to stay present to her own sexuality, her own pleasure. Also, it's about asking for what she wants. For men, too, it is to stay present to their own sexuality and their partners' sexuality. For the man, it is about giving, and being truly intimate, also.

Wow, this might be exactly what I'm looking for, I thought.

Since Sedona, I've realized that I need to do some healing work in my sexuality. I don't think I have all this stored up pain from prior abuses with Dave Lev or from being date raped or from other less-than-my-favorite sexual experiences. I might have a little shame around some of it. But those same occurrences have paradoxically been the focus of my fantasy life for many years. The thing I want to heal is my ability to feel pleasure and stay present during sex. The truth is that I was not present during my sex with Alex. In fact, I was living in past sexual experiences.

My sexuality in my twenties was very experimental. I posed for photographs at the Bunny Ranch, a decade before it became famous. I sold the photos to *Swank* magazine with an accompanying article. I was a stripper for about two weeks right before I met Alex, until I realized it didn't make me feel good, and also that the hours were deplorable and the money was terrible. I had sex with quite a few people and if you count the number of times a finger or tongue was in my vagina the number of my partners skyrockets. I had sex with men and women. I had sex with two men. I had sex with two women. I took nude photographs of myself when I drove cross-country from California to Texas.

The thing I resent most about dipping my toe in evangelicalism is the fit of shame and self-loathing I was driven to, which caused me to burn those photos. I'm sort of disgusted that Alex let me do it. God, I wish I had those photos today. I even burned my copy of the issue of *Swank* I appeared in.

I had a lot of fun in my teens and twenties with sexual experimentation. Still, it brought a lot of shame and humiliation, too. At least one-third of the time I had sex when I didn't really want to. Many times—I can think of several people right now—I wasn't even attracted to them. Sometimes I had sex because I didn't want to hurt the guy's feelings. Sometimes I did things during sex that were a turnoff because I didn't know how to say no, or because I felt an odd sense of "owing" him that is hard to understand today. Quite a large portion of the experimental sex I had was due to being totally drunk and not thinking clearly. I'd wake up in the morning and be ashamed of myself, and wish I could disappear. Still a huge portion of it was highly exciting, fun, and liberating.

The thing about where I'm at right now, on the verge of forty, having been celibate for a year and a half, is that I want to reinvent my sexuality. I realize that for the last decade I haven't been present for sex, but I have been actively living in the porno movie of my teens and twenties. I watch pornhub.com, specifically searching for the videos that make me the exploited teenager that I was during my first sexual experiences. I seek out scenes of drunken parties in which I relive my sexual past—the past where I'm not fully in touch with myself. Where I'm wasted or confused or feeling half-violated and half-turned on. Where I don't feel as much *myself* or *in possession of myself* as I do now, outside of my sexuality.

When I masturbate to porn, I'm not present to how my finger feels on my clitoris. What I'm present to is the porn movie of yesterday in which I am the star. It's a rather shallow sexuality.

I want to *feel* erotic and turned on and highly charged in the present moment. I want to feel the touch, the movement, the breath, the fingers and tongues and dicks when I have sex again. I want to feel the heat and the desire and the dripping pussy clench against a finger or penis. I want my vagina to be a source of power and energy that moves me to ecstasy.

I realize that attending the upcoming workshop about Orgasm Meditation might not cost me any political ambitions that I harbor. But lifting up my sundress, wearing no panties, and inviting a stranger to meticulously massage the left side of my clit for fifteen minutes in a room full of other orgasming women probably will.

It's totally worth it.

TWENTY-THREE

JULY 1, 2013

My pussy has been stroked. By a stranger named Super Carl. I've also been kissed. And kissed. And kissed. And eaten out and fingered! I gave a hand job.

It was all very . . . surreal. Not as erotic as you might think. More surreal and intense. Highly intense. I've come to realize this about much of what I do. It's about the adrenaline rush.

One Taste, the name of the organization that trains people in Orgasmic Meditation, calls it "turn on" and being "ignited." To feel alive. Present and fully there.

I went to a workshop from 9:30 A.M. until 6:30 P.M. During which sexuality was discussed openly. The good, the bad, the yada yada. Then a woman got on a massage table and a sexy New York Jew, about my age, with a really open and direct presence, stroked her clit for fifteen minutes in front of a room full of people.

I'd had fantasies about this event for weeks, since I had signed up for the course. My fantasies were more erotic than the real, live, onstage event. The real event was rather clinical; pussies are kind of boring, really. Sex is oddly commonplace, so that it's lost an essential mystery that creates the eroticism, I think.

My biggest reaction when watching Rob stroke Lianna's clit was that when she was moaning I was briefly embarrassed and humiliated for her. I had to remind myself that she was feeling pleasure, in a self-declared appropriate place.

It was oddly anticlimactic for me. I wondered why I wasn't feeling aroused, really. I suppose that would be called "turned off." But I wasn't. I was turned on in a new sort of way that I'm still trying to work out. It was like being awake and alive and present, but not being sexually aroused.

Then came the actual stroking. After lunch, they went over some more logistical details about etiquette, and there were some games involving rejection and acceptance. As the time for the "lab," as they called it, neared, I became more anxious, and it was the kind of anxious that also doubles as excitement. It was more about choosing and being chosen as a lab partner than the actual act of having my pussy stroked.

I was also preoccupied with the hygienic properties of my pussy. I had oiled it with coconut oil, I went pee about twenty times in twenty minutes, I washed it down with a paper towel in the bathroom.

The men I had wanted to stroke with paired up with other partners within seconds. Some of the women beat me to the punch. A boy, twenty-four year old Peter, was sitting next to me, and I wanted to stroke with him because we'd had lunch and developed a rapport and he felt safe. But he jumped up and said, "I'm not ready for this," as soon as the middle-school dance of choosing had started.

I said, "Yes, you are and you're doing it with me."

He declared that, in fact, he was not.

"I can't believe I've been rejected for my first OM," I said.

"It's not you, I'm just not ready for this," he said.

It occurs to me that to that boy I am now a MILF, a Mom I'd Like to Fuck, instead of a hot chick. Though perhaps, a cougar is not something he is interested in. I find that I end up in dressing rooms with a form of body dysmorphia in which I still believe I have a nineteen-year old thin body and I end up being surprised in a room full of women that I am a middle-aged woman, rather than the hot young blond one. As problems go, I suppose this is a great problem to have because it gives me confidence and, frankly, very few men have not wanted to have sex with me.

I was asked by one man and told him no. He was unattractive. Super Carl asked me and I said yes. He was a kind-looking man, who was nervous as I was. He was age-appropriate, maybe a tad older. He built a "nest." The man building the nest for a woman is one of the things I like about this practice. They call it a practice, just as yoga is a practice. You never do achieve it, you just take pleasure—or pain, chaos, resistance, fear, anxiety, boredom—in the practice and where you're at is where you're at. The learning and joy of it is in surrender and staying on the journey. There is no getting there.

I enjoy meditation and yoga for this aspect of it, especially in our accomplishment-oriented society. If you can accept that it's a journey without an end result, things flow better. This is their approach to sexuality and the practice of OMing.

The man building the nest is rather nurturing of the feminine, which is, I believe becoming a lost art. And both women and men miss it. It makes us more hostile than we need to be. The man building the nest is like a man paying for dinner, opening a car door, leading on a dance floor, or being on top. It's also like helping her across a river and pulling her up onto the next ledge on a hike. It's nice. I enjoy, and do miss, this form of masculine honoring of the feminine. Stupid feminism made it "weak" to allow men to perform certain "caretaking" of women and the result is sad.

The nest is built to make the woman comfortable while the man strokes her clit. They are very specific in how the man places his fingers. He strokes with his left index finger and places his right thumb just inside the introitus, the entry to the vagina. For me, the thumb being in the vagina opening is a huge turn on. It's a "grounding" force, they say, and I've always found that I am more stimulated with both pressure in the vagina and stimulation to the clitoris. Without the vagina pressure, my clitoris gets over-stimulated quite easily.

The man also keeps his clothes on. While this may sound misogynistic at first, it's really not. I suppose if your heart was set on it, you could get your panties in a bunch about how the man keeps his clothes on and objectifies the woman's body to get his rocks off while the woman exposes herself, and so on. One woman admitted to struggling with this viewpoint.

However, it really feels to me that our social definition of sex is very male-centric and focuses primarily on *his* pleasure and getting *his* rocks off in a masculine sort of "as long as he cums, it's a success" way. There is an objectification of women's bodies in media and marketing, which both genders are consenting to.

This practice is all about the woman's orgasm. All about bringing her pleasure. To me it feels, from this vantage point, to be the masculine honoring the feminine. Sure, it's arousing to the man, but his penis is out of the equation. Completely. There is no, "I got you off, now you give me a blow job." It's not commerce, as the instructor pointed out. There is not an exchange of sexual favors, as there usually is in our culture.

No one is getting a blow job in exchange for dinner or cleaning the house. No one is negotiating a dirty task in the household in exchange for sex. No one is paying back a debt of gratitude with anal sex. There is no commerce involved. Men stroke women. Women enjoy it. Relationship defined.

So we set up and they set a timer, and Super Carl begins to fondle my vag. It was very surreal. Did I mention that we are in a room full of paired off people that we have known only since 10 A.M.? All of the women have their pants off. There are "coaches" wandering the room checking form and finger placement, and ensuring that nests are built properly. The instructor is giving direction such as, "Take your index finger and spread the lips until it's just over the introitus, and then pull directly upward until you're at the clit."

This is a crazy cum cult, I thought at the beginning of this exercise. I honestly was vibrating in my body so fast that I kept having to pull my Soul back into my body to feel what I was feeling. I wasn't at all sure *what* I was feeling during most of the exercise.

An instructor came over, squatting to scrutinize Super Carl's form, hand placement, and pressure, and directed him to where my clit actually was. Super Carl was timid and that was a turnoff. I like a decisive lover.

A primary objective of the practice is to encourage women to give direction, clear, uncaged direction to their lover or stroker.

Up.

Slower.

To the left a little.

No, too far, to the right.

Right there.

It's probably not surprising that women are pretty bad at this. We live in a culture where women cage their opinions behind wishy-washy nonsense to protect themselves from criticism for having an opinion at all. Those who don't, often teeter into the radical feminism of bitchtastic. It's a learned skill to be direct without being confrontational and condescending. With much intention and sustained practice, I have become quite good at it.

In my teens and twenties, I often did things I didn't really want to do because I was afraid of refusing or hurting a man's feelings by criticizing him. It was an epiphany in my mid-thirties that slower, micro-movements were the key to my vaginal orgasm, and that hard and fast sex, while appealing for it's vigor and intensity, was not going to bring me to orgasm. This is terribly difficult for men to accept, having been trained in sexuality by hardcore porn, which is always full of hard, fast, intense sex, weird positions and lots of loud moaning and screaming on the woman's part. In other words, full of performing. I used to be invested in giving a good performance if only to get them off faster so they would stop being annoying in bed. However, I gave that tendency up in my thirties and really began to enjoy sex with the wasband. I realized that porno-sex is about the voyeur, not the lovers.

With OM, I didn't fake it. I tuned in to what I was feeling, and what I was feeling wasn't really sexually turned on. Right at the beginning it felt more like a gynecological exam than a sexual experience. I tried to get turned on and reach my orgasm, but then I stopped trying. The whole point of doing this, for me, is that I want to stop "trying" to climax and start *feeling* my body.

With my current sexuality, I've become used to the crutch of making myself cum with fantasy in the brain rather than actually feeling my body. I *imagine* feeling rather than *experiencing* feeling.

As I've matured and come to acceptance about myself and my enoughness, my right to be on the planet and experience pleasure and joy, I have come to want to inhabit my body in the fullest ways. I feel particularly lucky to have chosen mine to be born in. We get these fantastic bodies and have them for a finite amount of time before we once again become Spirit and leave them. So often we forget how amazingly awesome this is. So often we're obsessed with how they look and what other people think of them that we don't even truly inhabit them and experience what it feels like to be *in* them.

It's tragic really.

This year as I've focused on healing touch and gotten many massages and taken hot detox baths, and exercised and lay in the sun at the pool, and even gotten a bikini wax. I have truly enjoyed being in my body. It has really helped me, been pivotal even, to treat myself to feeling good in my body; it's made me more present in my life and made me feel more worthy of feeling good.

Except not so far in my sexuality. I haven't had a partner, by choice, and my masturbatory experiences have nothing to do with feeling my finger on my vagina, or my crystal wand; they have to do with seeking mental, outside stimulatory experiences and getting my body to orgasm. Which is unsatisfying, really. It's a very shallow sexuality in which it's not even about feeling good. It's more like taking a Xanax or an Ambien and getting stress relief. It's about releasing pent-up energy. Which, I suppose, has its place. But I'm really starving for more.

That's how I find myself, legs spread, vagina open to the world with one stranger's finger on my clit, thumb in my pussy hole, and another stranger peering at my vagina with clinical observation directing my stroker to move higher and to the left.

In the background, I'm hearing women moan and coaches direct. One woman was having a *When Harry Met Sally* diner moment, and I had to restrain myself from calling out, "I'll have what she's having!"

Then it was over and we sat in a circle and shared our bodily feelings. Which is interesting because it's all about being in the body and feeling what you're feeling and tuning in to that. They don't want to hear, "It felt like waves of the ocean washing over me." They want to hear, "At one point my feet were burning and the burning feeling traveled up my throat."

I'm going to do it again on Wednesday and really tune in and see what happens. I feel like I've been "off" sexually for a very long time. Possibly since Dave and his crazy abusive, weird sexual proclivities. It was traumatic and way too intense for someone with my total lack of maturity and limited sexual exploration. Pornography was introduced and I became dependent on imagery and fantasy to achieve climax.

The feelings in my body with Dave were often painful and bruising; many, many times I desperately wanted the sex to end so I could go to sleep and not have my vagina banged to bruising for hours while he was on coke or too drunk to cum. That's how I have often been during sex: completely out of my body.

I don't want to make it sound like I haven't had a fun sexuality. I've had a LOT of fun with partners and during sexual experiences. But also, I've been somewhat detached and not inside myself.

❧

I HAD SCHEDULED A DATE via online dating with a man in Boulder, because of convenience, for right after this workshop. By the time I sat down to dinner with him, I was on sensory overload and feeling entirely too open. We spoke immediately of spiritual sexuality. He is attractive and direct and open. Which I like. Also gainfully employed and upwardly mobile. Slightly neurotic with health issues, which is a turnoff, but not a deal breaker. He immediately picked up the check—unlike the pussies who act like they don't know that men are supposed to pick up the check and so give you a weird and awkward quizzical look like, *Gee, I'm not sure what proper etiquette is here.*

Feminists can suck it on this one. The bottom line is not whether it's fair. The bottom line is whether it's *sexy*. Men who don't have the balls to pick up a check on a date are not sexy. They are the opposite of sexy. They are cheap. Men who don't pick up the check are pretty much telling you right up front: "I have scarcity issues around money and don't feel you're worthy of my generosity. Buckle up, Sister, because if you're in a relationship with me, get ready for a lifetime of arguments and power struggles around money."

No, thank you. I plan never to have that experience with money again.

It's not about whether or not a man can "take care" of me. It's about whether he will be *generous* with me. And not just about money, like I'm a twenty-something who wants a man to buy her a bunch of labeled clothes or something. Money is indicative of your consciousness, of whether you're in lack or abundance. An abundance consciousness doesn't hesitate when the bill comes. An abundance consciousness is generous. Not only in money, but in attention, joy, time, presence, and all the other things women want from men.

Boulder Brad decisively picked up the check and it was *sexy* that he is gainfully employed and masculine enough to simply do it. Then we walked around and there was no difficulty in having a conversation. I found a pair of shoes I wanted to buy at the Croc store. I wore them on Pearl Street and decided they hurt my feet and I wanted to take them back. But we were eight minutes too late. So he offered to return them and then PayPal me the money. Very sweet. Very practical.

At the car, he kissed me. It was a nice kiss. We fit together. He said, "Do you notice that we kiss the same?" I was on complete overwhelm with my sexual workshop and getting my clit stroked, but I was enjoying it and tuning in to the bodily feelings of it.

"Do you want to come over to my house, it's only a few blocks away. I'm just throwing it out there," he said.

I laughed. I do a lot of laughing during awkward moments. Kind laughing. Just releasing overwhelmed energy, really. I thought about it. *Do I want to go back to his place?* I decided that I kind of did. "I'm supposed to be at my friend's house in half an hour. I'll text her and come over for an hour, but no sex," I said. So I did. I went over and we made out. He touched me everywhere, even my stomach, which I'm self-conscious about. It feels more intimate to allow a man to touch my belly than it does to allow him to touch my vagina. It was intense and overwhelming. Which is how my day was going. *Feast.*

He went down on me. I directed him openly. We dry fucked. We practically fucked through his underwear.

Right before he went down on me, he said these words: "I want to taste your sweetness."

I was considering this, asking myself, *Was him saying that sexy? Do I want him to go down on me?*

Then he said, "I need to know whether you have any STDs."

I burst out laughing. *Wow.* I just hadn't gotten there yet mentally, having not been single for thirteen years. I totally understand the reality of STDs and safe sex; I just hadn't emotionally considered this until he said it. He then went over his sexual history, admitting to having HPV in college, informed me of the frequency of his STD testing, and told me he was sterile because he had been snipped.

Holy shit, I hadn't even thought of pregnancy as a possibility. I wasn't intending to have sex with him and assumed we would be wearing a condom, but I hadn't consciously had the conversation with myself about what happens when I became sexually active and what forms of birth control I would be using.

"This isn't the '90s anymore," I joked.

"We have to talk about it. It's a conversation that has to happen if we're adults who will be having multiple partners," he said.

"Of course we do," I said. "I totally get it."

No one is drinking, we're not naive children, we're adults with adult responsibilities, so of course we needed to have this conversation. I explained that, yes, I had been tested and I'd been monogamous for thirteen years. Then he did go down on me.

I enjoyed it. I enjoyed him touching me. I enjoyed the kissing and heavy breathing. It wasn't arousing in the way of my twenties. But it was nice. I was far too overstimulated to cum. So I asked him to stop, and gave him a hand job.

"Do you want to feel your lips around my hard cock?" he asked.

I found his attempts to be sexy by talking about his hard cock and tasting my sweetness amusing and not quite sexy. Perhaps it's my age and that I've heard men say really hot things in bed with more force back when it was new and therefore hot. Perhaps he was just missing the Jake slightly.

I thought about it for a few seconds. I could just do it because now I "owed" him because he went down on me. But no one really wants to deep throat a dick. Some women claim to. An old friend of mine used to claim that it made her feel powerful. *Whatever.* There's nothing really great about a dick in your mouth. And this guy was a stranger. Why would I want a stranger's dick in my mouth? *I don't,* I realized. "No, I really don't want to," I told him directly and yet kindly. "I really don't like to."

"Why not?" he asked.

"What's great about it?" I asked.

"I mean, those lips," he explained, meaning my pussy.

"Oh," I said. "Part of me does, of course, but the bigger part of me knows that I'm already overstimulated; I've had a very intense day and I think I'll stop here. I need time to process."

Then I gave him a hand job and he got too stimulated to cum. Then he started "trying." With grimaces and concentration.

How silly, I thought. "Here's what's going to happen," I said. "I'm going to the bathroom and then I'm going to come back and we'll see what happens."

"I'll finish," he said. "Worst-case scenario, I finish myself."

While peeing I decided that I was done with sex for the day. Too much. Enough. It stopped being fun when it started being about trying. I went back to the bedroom. "Today at my sexuality seminar we talked about how westernized sex is focused around the goal of climax. But sexuality is deeper than that and there's no reason we should be trying to reach climax. I had a good time. You had a good time. We're going to stop here," I told him. "We're trying too hard at this point and that's not any fun."

He expressed that, yes, he did feel like he needed to cum and maybe that's not all it's cracked up to be. "I have a rule that I don't kiss on the first date," he said. "I broke my rule."

"I have a ninety-day rule," I said, though only minutes before I had been lying in his bed with a sundress pulled up to my waist and my breasts exposed, having let him eat me out. "No intercourse for ninety days."

"Ninety days is a really long time," he said.

"The most erotic sex I've ever had," I told him, "was when I was a teenager and we were exploring but not actually having sex yet. It was play. I suspect that if we quit here we'll want each other more tomorrow. We'll maintain a feeling of erotic excitement that will make us want it more. Half the fun is in wanting it."

He conceded that this was possible.

I went to Neecy's and talked until 4:30 A.M., catching up, telling her about my sexual adventures of the day and my trip to Texas, and she told me about her latest breakup with

Tom and how much her mom was driving her crazy, and how hard school was. Then we woke up in the morning and talked for hours more. I love her and miss her and I try not to get my feelings hurt that she doesn't call and doesn't see me. She's busy with college and motherhood.

❧

I'VE BEEN WRITING MY *Badass Magic & Fierce Miracles: How to Make a Dream Board that Really Works* ebook, and managing marketing campaigns and pitching coaching services to people, and it's going great. I've semi-sold two more six-month coaching packages, though both clients have delayed starting due to money issues, so those packages aren't *really* sold. I'm going to start asking for deposits and getting better at emphasizing why it's important to make the change when you don't have the money.

It works. That's why. It adds additional intensity to the process and is a huge act of faith to invest in creating your dream life when you're strapped for time and money. I should know.

The other day I was on a Vision Check Call, explaining my packages to Anne-Marie, the director and creator of Women Awaken, a women's empowerment organization. In one conversation I've already changed her life, so she was already sold on my value. She is probably more sold on my value than I am. I expected to sell her a six-month package, which is the longest term I am currently selling. Once finished with my presentation she offered something unexpected. She offered a one-year contract for me to teach her board of directors Law of Attraction principles, including a retreat to establish a baseline belief for the process and to get everyone on the same page. Totally unexpected.

She also asked me to present several two-hour trainings at another nonprofit in Crestone at a retreat she's planning for fall.

Excellent. I have this week to draw up a curriculum and a package and set my price. Setting my price with a package feels like throwing a dart at numbers. I don't honestly know my value. In my business course they keep saying, "Charge what you're really worth." *Which is what, exactly? How is that determined?*

They'll go through the process of outlining the value and the offerings and then putting a "true value" price on the package. After a few of these coaching sessions, I've realized that it feels like throwing darts because it *is* throwing darts.

I took to the pendulum to determine the number I want to charge for a one-year package in which I have to design a curriculum for a whole board of directors. It's advocacy work, which is tricky for the Law of Attraction because advocates focus on the problem. No one solves a problem by focusing on the problem. But advocates can't resist the problem and get upset when you want them to shut the fuck up about it. So it will be challenging to change their mindset about it.

Twelve thousand dollars was the price the pendulum says I should ask. I feel timid about asking for that amount, though I think it will be a good value for them. It will take a substantial amount of time to construct a curriculum. It will be good though, because I will intentionally construct the curriculum so that I can repeat it with other groups. I think the Law of Attraction for advocacy work is a huge untapped market that I am uniquely qualified to do because of my advocacy work with *The Girl Revolution*.

❧

THE MORE I PRACTICE THE Art of Saying Yes to my Soul, the more confident I am in her ability to lead me to the best places. It is scary to create a package and pitch it. It feels like uncharted territory—because it is. Also it's bringing me a new level of faith in my Soul and her promise to lead me to my purpose and make it easy for me to fulfill that purpose.

I'm gaining such confidence in her direction that it didn't occur to me to be afraid that I would do something I didn't want to do at the OM workshop. I trusted myself to say yes or no to any proposition according to how it felt to me. It also didn't occur to me to be wary of going to Boulder Brad's house, without telling anyone where I was. He was a stranger and a horny one at that. I suppose that was a bit foolish. I should have texted the address to Neecy and I'm sure that a great many people would think I fucking deserved being raped and murdered for being so stupid as to go there. Yet, it didn't even occur to me. I trusted my intuition that it was safe and I had the ability to say yes or no to any proposition.

I'm making confident choices about money because I'm tuning in and listening to my Soul's assurance that there is no need to hoard or worry. *Make this easy for me* is a prayer that I've adopted and repeat frequently.

Yes, I will follow my purpose into coaching others to their dreams. But I don't know how to make it happen. I'll do it, but you have to make it easy for me and point me in the right direction, I have told God and the Universe and my Soul and my team of angels, who are going before me and making the way clear.

Make it easy for me.

TWENTY-FOUR

JULY 22, 2013

I have a crush and now I'm totally fucked. Worse yet, I threw an event—months in the planning—and the people I hoped would show up to support me didn't. Still worse, I had all of this I-don't-dare-be-seen stuff come up and I choked on my speech.

I wrote a lovely speech:

Thank you for coming. Welcome to the Red Tent. My name is Tracee Sioux and I'm a Law of Attraction coach, I help people manifest magic and attract miracles so they can live on purpose. Way before the commercialization of the period from Always and Tampax, way before our menstrual flow became "dirty" and shameful, women gathered in the Red Tent to celebrate the rites of womanhood. During her period, breastfeeding, birth, and transition into a menopausal wise woman, she retreated to the Red Tent. Among the other women of the tribe: Maiden, Mother, Crone, she celebrated her cycle and tracked it by the moon. The tent was a sacred space where feminine knowledge was passed down, Crone to Mother, Mother to Maiden. Powerful healing arts, visioning, intuition, prophecy—women's natural gifts were practiced in this sacred space.

Women are the most powerful beings on Earth. Like God, we can whip up a whole human being in an organ the size of our fist in nine months, then we can spend the next eighteen years filling its head—with consciousness, or unconsciousness, as we choose. Think of how often your own mother's voice fills your mind, welcome or not. People spend thousands of dollars in therapy trying to eradicate their mother's scolding. That's power.

For one week—according to our menstrual cycle—the men of the planet walk on eggshells, afraid of our unpredictable wrath. The leader of the free world even spends one week per month being very, very . . . careful. It's not terrorism that makes him tip toe around, it is Michelle's PMS. That is power.

The Dalai Lama says, "The western woman will save the world." I'm an advocate for women's power, a form of power that I call feminine feminism. *When we chase the masculine version of power, we rob the world of the Divine Feminine, which is the very powerful healing force that will save the world.*

Everyone comes here to live her purpose. You have a purpose, one that is unique to you, that only you can fill. It's calling forth from within you. You have the power to live this purpose. Some words that have been spoken over me about my purpose are that I am a way-shower to the way-showers. My purpose is to help others manifest theirs: to stand behind and lift women up so they can accept and manifest what they came here to do.

As a coach, I believe, that the biggest enemy of women living their purpose is busyness. Charged with doing everything for everyone, too many of us are denying our purposes. Only if enough people live their purpose can we save the world.

This is where the modern Red Tent comes in. The Red Tent is any place where women are affirmed in their purpose: This church, the Whole Life Center for Spiritual Living, is a space where the sacred feminine is powerfully honored, a book club, a mommy group, a knitting circle, a neighborhood posse, a study group, these are all Red Tents. The value of a Red Tent in today's world can't be overestimated because the power of many women together is an undeniable force.

You are the way-showers. You have all the power you need to fulfill your purpose. For us it is only a matter of having the courage to step into our power, manifesting our callings. For those interested in exploring how to have a happy and productive cycle, my cohost, Leslie, and I are putting on a workshop.

It was just under five minutes. The whole time I was writing it and thinking of things to say, I felt like I was "taking too much time." *Before* I wrote the speech I felt unworthy of people's time and attention. *Why would they want to hear what I have to say? They didn't come here to hear me speak, right? They want to go home as soon as possible and I don't want to take up too much of their time.*

So I got up and started with my little notes. I looked at the entire *four* people who came out to support me *and I choked.* There were about thirty people in the crowd and the only people who came out to support me were the same people who came to my Pure Romance party. My tribe is small. My network—the people I work with and help in business—appears large, but I guess my actual, you-can-count-on-me tribe is small.

Who am I to speak of my own purpose, my own importance? Who am I to be taking up air and standing *in front* and declaring myself an expert or declaring myself worthy of their attention. I totally choked. I was soaked in unworthiness, surrounded by a beautiful Red Tent in the church that I view as my own Red Tent. Even from the church—where we have been making announcements for a month—only four of *my* people came out in support.

Instead of giving my speech, I blurted out something like this.

Every person comes to this planet to live her purpose. You have a purpose. My purpose is to help people find their purpose and help them manifest it. You are the way-showers. The enemy of purpose is busyness. We're so busy doing everything for everyone that we don't live our purpose. The Dali Lama said, "The Western woman will save the world." But we can't do that if we're stuck in busyness. You might think that you've never been in a Red Tent, I haven't been in a Red Tent, I've never been in an actual Red Tent. But, the modern Red Tent could be a book club, mommy group, knitting circle or any place where other women are holding you up in your purpose.

Now let me introduce Leslie Carol Botha and talk about how awesome she is and light a candle for her sixtieth birthday! Voila. I can stop wasting your two seconds and you can get to the important stuff: this film and Leslie. Oh and Leslie brought a soul portrait artist—without clearing it with me—who put her amazing art all over the place and that woman got way more attention than I did. She sold all sorts of wares while I didn't even sell one book. We gathered eight email addresses for our lists. I made $20.

I really thought this event was going to be huge. People had expressed interest. But I didn't feel *alive*. I didn't feel excited. I didn't feel like I was stepping into my power. What I felt was: *I am nothing of any importance.*

I hurt my own feelings and ruined my own night by taking everything personally and choking in front of the four whole people who came out to support me. I'm so terrified of my own importance. Wait, didn't I carry around that damned quote by Marianne Williamson in my purse for, like, four years?

Our deepest fear is not that we are inadequate. Our deepest fear is that we are powerful beyond measure. It is our light, not our darkness that most frightens us. We ask ourselves, 'Who am I to be brilliant, gorgeous, talented, fabulous?' Actually, who are you not to be? You are a child of God. Your playing small does not serve the world. There is nothing enlightened about shrinking so that other people won't feel insecure around you. We are all meant to shine, as children do. We were born to make manifest the glory of God that is within us. It's not just in some of us; it's in everyone. And as we let our own light shine, we unconsciously give other people permission to do the same. As we are liberated from our own fear, our presence automatically liberates others.

—Marianne Williamson, *A Return to Love*

My deepest fear *is* that I am powerful. I feel unworthy of being seen. This is why I've been struggling to put out my newsletter; it's always why I've been resistant to putting out my newsletter. *Why would anyone want to hear from me? What the fuck do I have to say that is of any importance?* That's what Alex felt about me—and my family for that matter.

I'm playing small because I'm terrified of playing big. I haven't called back Kelly, a client who wanted to start her coaching in August. Because I feel like she's going to back out and I'm going to be disappointed. I haven't been able to land a client, because I play small instead of talking up how much I can help them. I feel insignificant, like I'm spinning my wheels. I know that I help people with my work. I know I even change their lives. But who am I to charge people money for that? Aren't they just entitled to my energy and when I prove I have changed their lives *then* they will see my value? Oh they see my value, but then their lives have already been changed. So now there is not a reason to pay me.

I'm a shitty salesman. A salesman who doesn't value her own product enough to brag about it. The product is me. And I feel insignificant. It's so embarrassing.

❧

SPEAKING OF INSIGNIFICANT. . .

I have a crazy hot crush on Boulder Brad. He's successful, which is super sexy. He's fun, which is fun. He's open minded. He's other things, too, like "high need" and neurotic, and sometimes a sniveling sick person (being sick is the only time he allows himself to rest, and he's burned out, so he gets sick a lot). He's a newbie on the spiritual path, but he's on it, which is a big deal for me. He's adorable in a social Tourette's syndrome kind of way, which I can relate to. He can't stop talking about it. I like direct communication and he's a very direct communicator.

We got comfortable with each other immediately, which led to a heightened level of instant intimacy, both sexually and emotionally. We haven't had sex because the tumescence is so hot that we're not having sex for ninety days—thanks, Steve Harvey—but we're doing everything but sex. Being in bed with him, I was at ease. It wasn't awkward. It was just easy and fun, and I am totally turned on by him. I mean, I'm walking around horny all the time and having fantasies about making love with him all day.

He's taking up mind share. He's distracting me from my work, my life. And it feels really, really good. Refreshing. After you've stared down your bleak future with a man you don't love for twelve years, this feels fucking fantastic. I called forth a fun summer romance. A part-time lover. I called forth a "real" boyfriend for the fall and it's only July, though I can feel fall's breath on my neck.

"This is just fun!" I've told myself and Sarah and Neecy. "This is my rebound boy. My fun summer fling. This isn't anything. He's fun, he's not the One. I don't want the One right now. I want to date around and have some fun. This is my wildee time, like the palm reader said. It's going to be my last one so I'm going to enjoy it. This man is way too neurotic to be the One. It's a turnoff."

I've called forth hieros gamos. For later. Not for now. I want it. It's the ultimate goal. But I don't want it to show up so quickly and rob me of my last wildee time. (Hopefully my last.)

Right, Tracee? Right?!

Boulder Brad is into me and that feels so good. He's kind of naturally critical, but I'm overlooking it and not taking it personally. He's calling, texting, arranging to see me as much as possible. With two separate parenting schedules and two careers, it does take effort to date someone who lives over an hour away.

Then I realized: *I am totally fucked.*

We had gone to some effort to arrange a hiking date at Carter Lake, very early so as not to interfere too much with our parenting schedules, last Saturday because he was going out of town for a week. We were having a great time. Great conversation. He's very inquisitive. He gave me shit about my social media branding—which I've told him several times is part of my master plan—but which he's still fixated on. (And it does make me feel bad because, no, my products are not online, because, yes, once again, I'm afraid of being seen and putting myself out there, so I'm making excuses like that I have to have my website up and rebranded and this takes time, but it's going to happen, *yada yada* and please stop pointing this out to me because it's embarrassing that I don't want to be seen as selling something as insignificant as *me*.)

Then he asked about the Orgasmic Meditation cult. How is it going? What am I getting out of it? Is it always the same men?

I'm answering his questions. Then I'm asking him questions about his feelings about some of the things in my life. Such as the phrase *Amazing Men* on my dream board. Which is something he brought to my attention immediately when he saw the board.

"*Amazing* Men is plural. I'm only one man," he said. I thought it might have hurt his feelings, or made him feel like I'm not interested in him, or even that I've entirely ruled out a committed relationship with him. I backpedaled a little bit, saying that it's healthy for me to see Amazing Men in my life, in all kinds of aspects, such as healers, because I've had experiences that have not been healthy and I don't want to believe that all men are like my wasband or my dad.

He brought it up again, "Are these men you're doing this with part of the *Amazing Men?*"

"Are you teasing me about wanting amazing men in my life?" I asked. He said that he was. I explained that yes, these are part of the amazing men component I had called forth.

It's healthy for me to see these men, because they are vulnerable. They are kind. They are on a spiritual path. That's healthy for me because I haven't seen evidence of that in a long time.

As we're walking, I bring it out in the open. "Do you have any feelings about the word *men* in *Amazing Men?*"

"Oh, I think it's healthy," he says. "People don't find their relationship in the first person they date—or it's rare anyway—so I think it's really healthy that it's plural."

We talk about it for a while. His "rebound" relationship had lasted three years. "Isn't everyone a rebound from someone else?" I ask. At this point I'm not having any feelings about our status. Maybe I haven't quite connected the dots that he's completely ruling out any potential for us, or maybe in that moment I'm thinking, *Hey, he's on the same page with this.* Either way, I'm keeping my cool and my emotions are in check. I'm Cool Girl.

Then, I'm asking him how he feels about my OMing with other men. He says he thinks it's great if it's getting me what I need. I say something like, "Some men might have feelings about their . . . person . . . letting other men rub their clit," I point out. (Please note here that I intentionally didn't put a label on myself such as girlfriend, lover, summer fling, woman, significant other, or any other definition of our relationship.)

"YOU'RE NOT MY GIRLFRIEND," he blurts out.

"Filter! Fucking filter," I say. Heart wounded.

The way he said it *stung*. All these feelings came over me. I felt insignificant. It was like he had said, "You don't matter to me, so why should I care?" I felt like I didn't matter to him and I wasn't cool with that. At all.

I don't want to be his fucking wife, but I do like to think that I matter to someone who I'm getting naked with—physically and emotionally. I felt overwhelmed with being vulnerable.

He backtracked. "We're just getting to know each other."

"You said it so harshly," I said, completely embarrassed that I had an emotional reaction to his fierce declaration about my non-status in his life. I was embarrassed to have my feelings hurt.

I was also backed into a corner. How do I declare, "I didn't fucking ask to be your girlfriend?" without sounded like a defensive, wounded twelve-year old girl getting her heart broken because the boy she loves doesn't love her back? How do you assert, "Don't flatter yourself, YOU'RE not MY boyfriend!" without sounding like a defensive bitch who's had her feelings hurt?

You don't.

I went with the truth. "That stung. You said that so harshly."

"I didn't mean it like that, I'm sorry, we . . ."

"I'm not your girlfriend. You're not my boyfriend. Got it. We've established that. I get it and I agree. We're on the same page. But it was harsh and it hurt my feelings. You said it like that would be the worst thing in the world," I explained, unable to hide my hurt feelings, completely embarrassed to be having them at all, and even more embarrassed to be showing them to him.

Why can't I hold it in and just go cry on my way home like a normal girl? I thought. That's what Cool Girl does to please her man. She pretends that everything he says to her is totally cool. She pretends that whatever he wants is what she wants. *No pressure, baby. You can totally be light and uncommitted to me and I can take it.*

I can take it? As if this is a healthy requirement for me to have in a blooming romance. I can take it. Like getting a pap smear or having a broken clavicle reset, or getting criticism from an editor, or being screamed at by my father. I can take it.

The shame of not being able to take it was excruciating.

"What are you afraid of? Why won't you let yourself have this?" my friend had asked me, when I had insisted that this was just going to be a summer tryst. Fun. Nothing more.

"I'm afraid of Instant Boyfriend. That's how I ended up married. It's how *you* ended up married," I said.

But when Boulder Brad so adamantly expressed his lack of desire for me to be his girlfriend I was wounded. Bad Cool Girl. The harsh, raw way he said it was clear confirmation that he meant it.

We've come to an agreement: This isn't going to be a "relationship." We're fortyish, so we've had our hearts broken and we've had "failed" relationships and we're carrying those beliefs about what we did wrong and how we're going to do it differently next time. What is tragic is that none of that is true.

So we're on the same page. It's exactly what I called forth and what I wanted. *Right? Right?!? RIGHT?!?!?*

Why then did it sting so much? Why did it sting on my drive home? Why did it make my heart a little sore? Bruised?

On the drive home I realized something: *I'm vulnerable.* I'm playing a dangerous game here. I'm living my life by my heart. Which means my heart is open. That's fucking *risky.* It's not the same as being numb, which is what I finally became to my wasband's callousness toward my heart for him. Numb is protective. It means that I can always be Cool Girl and never display inconvenient, inexplicable, and unpredictable emotions. That's safe.

But hormones are flowing. As much as we modern thinkers want to believe that we can control our hormones and decide rationally who we're going to fall in love with, we underestimate the power of hormones and we completely devalue the heart as a beating force that is sometimes at odds with the rational mind.

The heart wants what the heart wants. Hormones set off sparks in irrational, unpredictable, and sometimes terrifying ways. When you meet someone and you click quickly and things get so intimate and comfortable instantly, you're kind of fucked. It's going to go where it's going to go. You can rational-brain it to death, but it doesn't stop the sting of a harsh dismissal. It doesn't stop you from wanting to frolic in the sheets with your beloved at every opportunity. But when you give into the frolic in the sheets, you put your heart on display. Exposed. Naked.

The best and worst part of it is that Boulder Brad is in my Soular System—someone who your Soul has known before. The phenomenon when you meet someone and it's more than attraction; it's instant intimacy. It's synchronicity that is more than mere coincidence. It's finally seeing a long distant loved one again to see someone you've been intimate with in other lifetimes.

We have the exact same headboard; we both have children named Charlie, both of who had Mohawks when they were babies . . . when he pulled out his matching Hitachi Magic Wand, I couldn't help but giggle at the synchronicity of it. On a Soul level, it was not just like meeting someone I had never met before.

Then what do you do with that? When it feels like you're picking up where you left off in another lifetime? When you've reconnected with someone with whom you've made a spiritual contract? We don't know how it would have turned out if we had trusted our *knowing* of each other on a Soular System level.

All signs point to NO. When I had energy work done with C.J. last time, she said there was a man coming into my life *that was not this man* in the next few months, and that it would be good, really good, if I decided to allow it in. Which is great. And it should make me feel better. It should make me completely okay with that fact that a long-term relationship with Boulder Brad is off the table. Which should make Boulder Brad more precious, and more fun. Shouldn't it? But when you meet someone who is in your Soular System and you know he isn't staying through the next act of the play, then how do you not be sad? How do you not miss him again before he is already gone? How do you not, on a deeper Soul level, grieve the loss of him again?

When you're living your life heart open, as a conscious choice, and you're being intimate with someone you've known in this human experience for a short period of time, but you've missed terribly on a Soul Level, how are you supposed to play Cool Girl?

I've got a mad crush on Boulder Brad. I'm still playing with him. I'm living my life heart open. I'm totally fucked.

❧

HERE'S INFORMATION confirmed at my energy session with C.J., who channels my God team, guides, angels, God, my Soul:

I haven't been with Boulder Brad for only a few dates. I've been with him for seven lifetimes. Every lifetime we've been in love. During two lifetimes, we've been lovers. Three lifetimes, we've been married. We've had children together during three lifetimes. We've had seven children during all our lifetimes. In previous lifetimes, our two Charlies were our children together. Not our other current children, Madigan or Austin, though.

This probably explains my disapproval of him allowing fifteen-year old Zachary to have slumber parties with his girlfriend. It also might explain why when Brad saw a photo of Charlie with a Mohawk he recognized him in some way. He even mentioned that it feels like we might have been together in parallel lives. Which, did sound true at the time.

We have a spiritual contract. In our last life together, he betrayed me: He broke a commitment and left me. Somehow the memory of the pain is still present. That's why my reaction to his dismissive, minimizing, and belittling comment was so intense. I've been in love with this man seven times, which is why we immediately dove into intimacy together and why his harsh comment hit a raw nerve.

The unhealed wound had been created three times in this lifetime. Once by my mother, during a shoving episode when I was around eleven, in which she wanted me to play small and I insisted that I was not small. Two other traumas involved me being belittled, both from Alex. He never thought I was significant enough to do my work as a coach or writer, or to fulfill my purpose during this lifetime. I had two beliefs. One was: *He doesn't care enough about me.* The other was: *He doesn't believe in me.*

Boulder Brad brought his own issues to the incident. He *was* harsh. I didn't just receive it that way. Oh, he regretted it. But he meant it, too. He meant it with a fierce intensity that I matched in my response. Likely, we were both baffled by the intensity of it.

He is here to repay his karmic debt to me for breaking his commitment. It's happening right now to help me heal from my marital wounds. Which means this could be less fun than it sounds. I am here to push him to the next level of consciousness, as I have made more growth in that area in this lifetime. Which I should do by being very direct with him and giving him lots of feedback. Which he will take to heart and use to bring him further into consciousness. This will minimize the pain I experience as a result of this very important healing work we'll do together. This can last for however long I want it to. My intuition tells me three months. The pendulum tells me three months.

Now that I know we are playing out a spiritual contract, C.J. says I'll be more in control of my emotions—because I can *see* the way things will play out and I can trust my intuition.

❧

WHAT I VISION—what I have been visioning for some time now—is a reunion in Cabo San Lucas: a reunion between two Souls who have been in love in several previous lifetimes and are so happy to be together again. I see sex and passion. I see fun. I see him spoiling me with lavishness. I see us having a beautiful week, unburdened by parenting or work responsibilities. I see us experimenting with each other's bodies and our spirit bodies, mingling our energies together in new and exciting ways. Specifically, I see us making love under a cabana on the beach. I see deep looks into each other's eyes. I feel kisses. I feel him penetrating me again—for the first time—and it feeling exquisite.

I asked if I was seeing this because it is there for us or if I was attracting it and the guides said I was seeing it. It is the most likely outcome for my Cabo vacation. I love Neecy, but this week of love is calling me.

I feel crazy for saying this, but I remember loving Brad and I remember *missing* him. It makes me sad that we won't see each other after this interlude when we play out our spiritual promises because his energy is something I crave. Like craving chocolate.

You know those dreams where you dream of eating chocolate and you want to find more and more and more? Like that.

What I don't feel like doing anymore is pretending that we've just met. It feels totally false to me. I want to go with what is true. That we *know* each other. That we *love* each other on a very deep Soul energy level. I want him to repay his karmic debt by spoiling me like crazy. By treating me to fabulous dates, dinners out, attention, affection and love. By spoiling me sexually.

I would be very happy if his service to me was to awaken my kundalini, allowing me to manifest the spiritual sexuality that I am craving. I would love to have him put his fingers on my g-spot and his tongue on my clitoris and be able to cum in five minutes. I want to be able to slide him in me while I'm on top of him and have mind-altering, Soul-quivering orgasms during penetration. I want to feel deeply and intimately connected to him—as I know that we have been many, many times before.

Our energy is perfectly matched, C.J. said. I miss his energy when I'm away from him. I ground him, which he needs so desperately. He uplifts me, which I enjoy. We keep reconnecting because our energy is matched up well. It is a delicious treat to see him again. Such a delightful joy to feel him touch me again.

Oh Soul, thank you for guiding me back to him, even if it's only for a short while. I call forth that this will be an enormous, joyous reunion with him. With him I will drop all pretenses and live heart open.

TWENTY-FIVE

JULY 24, 2013

Since learning that Brad and I are Soul mates with a spiritual contract and an intimate history of hundreds of years during seven past lives, I've been looking at what I've been calling forth for myself since Sedona. The words from the Marvin Gaye song "Sexual Healing" come to mind.

The words *healing touch* are on my dream board, in addition to the words *amazing men*. Miraculous results are displayed prominently. *Spiritually open* is another phrase listed.

How good God is to bring Brad, a lover from many lives, someone with whom I feel instantly and inexplicably connected on a deep Soul level, to deliver the sexual healing I crave. How lovely to have him be the one to heal me with his touch, his kisses, his energy, as he plays on me like I'm a familiar jungle gym.

Just when you think something is going to be hard, awkward, painful, or traumatic, God sends a wave of deliciousness, ease, and delight. To be reunited with a lover who will allow me to be vulnerable is pure delight. To be reunited with someone who has loved me well over many lifetimes feels like a sacred and holy golden ticket. It feels like a sweet, succulent gift of the Divine.

Universal good karma is what it is. How delightful that Brad is called to me to heal a karmic debt for betraying a commitment to me in a previous lifetime, but that it gets to be such a sweet and meaningful good time for both of us. I have slight twinges of fear about how it's going to end. I just want to hold on to this feeling of love and pleasure.

It is hard to explain the expansiveness of how I feel as a human these days. The things I'm being grateful for are of a physical experience from an expansive and eternal spiritual mind.

Exquisite is what the gift of being reunited with Brad feels like. I can taste the expansiveness of my spiritual cosmic existence and Brad is an exquisite, tiny part that tastes delicious in its intensity, that feels very at-home to me, as if he has come home from work to me and I've pulled off his boots and served him tea by the fire in our cabin. A true love connection in the midst of an everyday life. When I close my eyes I can see it. This time, it will be a brief and intense true love connection, very grounded in sexual healing, but it will not incorporate the day-to-day, long-term marriage/commitment element. Which makes me feel two ways simultaneously. One, it makes me miss him already. My bones ache to make this last longer so that I can soak in his familiar and much loved healing energy for as long as possible. It is painful to see a loved one go. The other, more expansive part of me wants to shout in glee that this is the most wonderful part of being a goddess having a human experience.

This serendipitous connection with a long-loved lover in the earthly experience is an example of perfect timing! Perfect timing! Perfect timing! Perfect timing! We're both single, we're both in transitory places in our relationships and work lives, we're both craving something. He is craving an up-leveling of his consciousness and I am craving sexual healing. He needs to become softer and I need to become freer with my feelings.

We meet. We instantly connect sexually and emotionally, and it is divine intervention at its best and most precious. As a Soul, I say bravo to the Universe, the Law of Attraction, to God. With the greatest gratitude that I can muster up! Hurray for us! We are so lucky! What an abundant Universe, full of delicious and delightful surprises and glory and orgasms.

Mixing orgasms heavily into the mix is just the best treat ever! What a wonderful gluten-free organic dessert!

Oh Soul! Oh Soul! Thank you for leading me to this! I'm so glad I said yes when he asked me to come to his house on our first date! How strange that it didn't feel risky, awkward, or dangerous. How delightful that it felt like falling into a familiar lover's arms. How delightful that it was falling into a familiar lover's arms. I am so lucky. Abundant.

I wish I could spend more time with him. I crave his presence now. I want his breath in my open mouth. I want the pressure of his body on my naked, surrendered body.

OMG, I want to surrender to him. Even though he hurt me. Even though he might yet hurt me. I want to *surrender* to him. An act of sexual vulnerability.

I have visions. I do. I haven't known what quite to make of them. There is a huge distinction between *trying* to vision something and attract it, and these effortless and deeply pleasurable visions. I had pondered the idea that my Soul wants one of the visions more than another vision. While on the table my guides told me, via C.J., that I should trust my visions more, that I'm *seeing* myself in Cabo with Brad, not just fantasizing or attracting it. That I should trust those visions as what will be, or what already is in another dimension. That it's more like ESP.

Oprah, I have these visions about our interview all of the time, in effortless and delicious detail, right down to the Louboutin heel. *Oh Soul, oh Soul! This, too, please!*

TWENTY-SIX

AUGUST 3, 2013

I had sex with Boulder Brad after his trip to Canada. It was passionate and sort of wonderful. First, it was an unconscious slipping it in during a very heated make out session. Very, very hot and very, very sexy. I won't go into details, but things got lost in the mix and it was amazing. We decided it was an accident and didn't count. Then he took a nap and I poured my energy into him, a healing power. It was amazing for him and later very draining for me. I didn't protect myself well. In any way. Hours later we were heavily making out—or as they used to say in church "heavy petting"—and I told him I wanted him inside. So he thrust it in and we made love.

It felt like losing my virginity. His penis was hard and much bigger than I thought it would be. It was downright pokey. It hurt. I was sore. *Oh baby, make it hurt so good.* Then we did it again in the morning. That was Sunday.

Brad has HPV. We didn't use a condom. My love-high brain justified this because he had been rubbing his penis over every inch of my vagina for weeks already, I figured that if I was going to get something then I would get something from the making out as easily as from the sex. I understand that this is a load of crap because there are eighty-something strains of HPV, but it's the load of crap that I wanted to believe because I wanted loving physical contact—*intimacy.* I wanted to connect, and connection is so much lovelier when it's skin to skin.

The next day I processed what had happened and it made me weirdly weepy. Am I about casual sex? It didn't feel casual to me. I wanted it to not be casual to him. I messaged him about it and he called. He assured me both that I am *not* his girlfriend and that he cares about me. I told him that honestly, I didn't even think I was made for casual sex. "I'm not all about casual sex either," he said, "I'm about the connecting with someone."

At one point in the conversation—when I had accused myself of having something wrong with me to make me a choice for casual sex—he listed attributes such as smart, spiritual, attractive, and ideal. I wish he has slowed down so I could remember the sweet things he'd said about me. Because he honestly doesn't compliment me often. You know what else he doesn't do? He doesn't call me by name. The only time I've heard him say my name is when he introduced me to a friend we met on the street, and when he saw my name on a sign in a bookstore, and once when he was instructing me to create an Evernote list, *Brad & Tracee's Epiphanies,* which consisted of random "stuff" that we epiphanied for him, not for me. Otherwise, he doesn't say my name.

We had a delightful date on Wednesday and over dinner (a dry rice and pesto concoction that meets my liver cleanse dietary needs, but lacked taste), he reminded me of his HPV and said he felt people should use condoms until they are exclusive. When he drops these things into everyday conversation, it puts me off kilter. We rode bikes to Band on the Bricks and danced. He dances like an engineer.

One minute he's professing that he feels so completely connected to me that he can say anything, like, "I really want to have a prostate massage and climax that way, have you ever done that?" or "Can I put it in your ass?"

You know sexy things like that, which make me ask questions like, "What vibe am I putting off that screams, 'I'll let you fuck me in the ass' and 'I'll play with your ass?'"

"No vibe," he promises. "I just feel so completely comfortable and connected to you that these things come out."

I know it sounds crazy that this is okay with me. The truth is that I don't even know what to do with it. Yes, I could be talked into a prostate massage, if I felt special enough. And when he's kissing me, I almost feel special enough.

When I'm with him, I feel special and connected. When I'm not with him, I review the messages he's giving me and feelings come up. *What did he mean until we're exclusive? Why, exactly, would he not want me to mention our date on Facebook?*

Brad is obviously fucking other people. I have feelings about this. They are coming in waves and they conflict with each other.

Is this dating in the 2010s? Because it feels awfully similar to dating in the 1990s. There were a few boys who withheld themselves while attempting to give themselves and take others. One was a boy named Paul who was visiting for the summer. He made it clear that he was seeing another girl, that we were a summer fling and not exclusive. I pretended to be okay with it, but I wasn't. Another was a "fuck friend" who ended up sleeping with my best friend in my bedroom only an hour after he had his dick in me. Several years later he date raped me by fucking me while I was drunk and *unconscious.*

Yet another was Nathan, who not coincidentally I had been remembering and romanticizing at the same time I met Brad. I might have even called a "relationship like Nathan" forth out of the ether. He lived in L.A. and I lived in Utah. We met in Park City, Utah, on New Year's Eve 1998. We had a long-distance romance via email and phone calls that we had to time to keep our long distance charges in check. The wordplay was such a turn on. His dick was huge and he was so much fun.

I moved to California—still several hours away from him—to pursue the relationship about a year into it. Like Brad, he insisted on keeping our back door open. Until I walked through it and slept with the delightful Mr. Benchley.

Mr. Benchley is one of the good guys and I wish I had liked him as much as he deserved to be liked. But I was hung up on Nathan who insisted on the back door. Then he didn't like it when I used the back door. He got all hurt and upset, and only then did he grudgingly call me his girlfriend.

These are my experiences with men who want the back door open. It never did feel very good. It always felt disrespectful. It feels disrespectful with Brad.

I'm confused though. He's calling this "dating" and "not jumping into a relationship." There's a huge emotional energy charge attached to his version of "not jumping into a relationship." Which means it's not just dating. It's avoidance of real intimacy. It's fear. I've only been seeing him for a month. What kind of exclusivity can a girl expect after a month? Honestly, had he not been so passive-aggressively honest about his non-exclusivity clause, I would not have thought much about it. He'd been so attentive during our ninety-day rule. Wanting me must have driven him mad for me. He was texting, calling, Google+ hangout video sexing, emailing, and otherwise cyber-chasing me. That kind of attention was fucking awesome. So I felt pretty secure in the fact that he was into me. *Where would he find the time to sleep with other people?* I thought.

Still, tonight I got feelings that were inconvenient about his little hints about sleeping with other people. After we had sex, I also felt a drop off of *desire*. On his end, as well as mine. The texts stopped coming as frequently. The flirting waned. I know it has only been less than a week, but I'm tapped into energy and I could feel it. So I texted: "I miss tumescence."

This led to a series of texts that finally included my disclosure that I am feeling jealous and my question: "Are you sleeping with other women?"

"Yes."

Zing.

"How have you even found the time?"

"I'm a very driven, high-energy person."

Zing. (Who can't cum because he's having sex every day, though he blames the inability on medication.)

It's fascinating to me that because a man doesn't expressly say something like, "Will you go steady with me?" he feels women should not have feelings about sharing him.

Cool Girl doesn't have feelings about this. Well, really she does, but she pretends it's okay, just as I did with Paul and just as I allowed with Nathan. Cool Girl acknowledges, *Of course we're not exclusive,* and keeps right on seeing him, all the while trying to get him to fall for her.

That's not what I felt like doing. It's not what I did. I confessed to having feelings about this. For one thing, I feel like his positioning on this has always put me on the defensive. Right from the beginning, since he declared, "You're not my girlfriend," I have felt like his assumption was that I wanted to be his girlfriend, which I didn't think was fair to establish on our fourth date. It put me in a position where I wanted to be, due to the sheer fact that he felt so adamantly. It doesn't make sense.

I'm reeling a little bit and wishing I'd never had a jealous feeling and never brought it up. Because the other complexity about my feelings is that I don't want to stop having sex with him. I have been celibate for a year and a half. I haven't had sex with another person in thirteen years and my married sex life left something to be desired in creativity and passion. Not just because we were married, but because my wasband didn't care very much about the art of sex. Brad does care, though he's a little more proud of his penis and "what he can do with it" than is justifiable.

Honestly a penis does few creative things. It thrusts in and out. It goes harder and faster, often at the wrong times; it goes slow or deep or in a twirl. But it's just a penis. A one-trick pony.

The truth is that it was more fun not having sex with Brad than it is having sex with Brad. For one thing, it allowed me the luxury of being far more casual about our relationship because I was still revirginized, and we were just making out and fooling around. Also the art of desire was the turn on. The *not* doing it created this very powerful tumescence, the buildup of wanting, which only increased in intensity. It took up all sorts of mindshare. It created creative and sexual energy that felt really good.

It was all kinds of hot to be walking through the grocery store completely preoccupied with what it would feel like to have him thrust inside of me. It was also really fun to romanticize it.

I can't tell you how vivid those visions of him and me in Cabo were. And my pendulum has told me for weeks that Brad would come to Cabo with me. I had planned to surprise him with intercourse on our first night. Then I went and ruined it by having sex. I leave Monday and Neecy is still in. I'm having issues with how the pendulum works and whether it can be trusted. Anna has been showing me how to do it, because for her it said that Brad would not be coming to Cabo with me. He only would come with me on an *emotional* level.

Here are the emotions I've gone through tonight. I feel:

Hurt.

Sad.

A sense of loss.

Foolish for romanticizing the relationship.

Indignant that he would assume I wanted him exclusively.

Awe that he can actually pour this much effort and energy into more than one relationship.

Sad that he is unable to be okay alone.

Righteous in the knowledge that I am way too good for this.

Pandering in the sense that I want to take my question back, at least until I can sleep over on Sunday and soak in the pretend love some more.

Like playing Cool Girl because I'm horny and I love, love, love kissing Brad. (Seriously, he's one of the best kissers I've ever kissed. We match completely in the kissing. It's intoxicating.)

Like closing my heart in order to casually see him until my Real Guy comes along.

Slutty, like thinking, "Well, since we're not exclusive . . . let's take this ballgame into the big leagues before my boyfriend enters the picture: swing club in Denver, Ménage à trois, role playing and just getting so dirty horny."

I KNEW BRAD WASN'T the Real Boyfriend that I've called forth to show up in the fall. But here's the emotional surprise: *I love him in a weird way.* I miss him already. I feel sad not to see him anymore. I want to kiss him some more. I feel sad that he's on a date with someone right now, and probably she's in his bed at 5:12 A.M. and his arms are wrapped around her, and that makes me feel jealous that I'm not the one in his bed.

I already know that I don't want to be his Real Girlfriend. Because he's a neurotic hypochondriac and I'm pretty certain (and I have experience in this matter, so let's just call it absolutely certainty) that he has a substance abuse problem with pain medications and marijuana, and who knows what else, probably Xanax. He has migraines and allergies. He's so "driven" that he's making himself sick. Sicklings aren't sexy, not really. It's something that I have to intentionally overlook, all the whining and pandering for sympathy is rather nauseating.

Brad's also got social Tourette's syndrome, which he justifies as "honesty," but probably has its roots in Asperger's. I love words, which means I don't want someone to use them as weapons and I suspect, I'm pretty sure, that in a relationship he fights ugly with his version of "truth" and his complete lack of a filter. I mean, he's totally into me now and numerous times in the last month I've had to address inappropriate and sometimes hurtful shit that comes out of his mouth. "My mouth always gets me in trouble," he says. *Uh, yeah. 'Cause you allow it to run off on its own without regard to who might be on the receiving end of it.*

His mouth has been interesting. In many ways he's been a good mirror for me to see myself, as the receiver of some of my communication methods. It has made me realize both how cutting I probably am sometimes when I'm indulging myself in "truth telling" and feeling all bold and brave and invested in the rightness of it. Simultaneously, it has made me realize that I really do filter my words based on not hurting another person's feelings—even if I don't like them. Honestly, Alex and I exchanged very few hurtful words at the end of our marriage. My intention was not to hurt him. My intention was to get out of the marriage with as much integrity and as little pain as possible.

Even in the face of Brad's bald-faced truth telling, I have held back from saying biting things so as not to hurt his feelings. It's made me realize that when I do walk through the world my intention is to be kind, even to those I have just met, and those that I actively dislike. Even when I'm being intentionally provocative for an emotional response, I try not to hurt people.

I don't believe that is Brad's intention. So, no, I don't want to be his Real Girlfriend. I think that job would ultimately be pretty painful to the woman. I'm sure if I asked his ex-wife and his "rebound woman" (who he spent three committed years with), they would report that they have mouth scarring. Certainly, I don't have the desire to keep my balls of steel and my armor wall up to protect myself from the random shit slinging that is sure to fly out of his mouth. But I also don't like imagining him saying, "I feel so connected to you," to another woman either.

I want him.

I don't want him.

I want him to want me.

I don't want him to hurt me.

I want to cut ties and walk away before I get hurt.

I want to see him again.

I want him to care whether he sees me again.

I want him to pursue me.

I want to take care of him.

Much of our interaction has been about me coaching him on how to handle his feelings and chronic thinking. I've offered all sorts of solutions and skills, and new ways to think. He appears to want such things, but I don't think he's followed through on them. An indicator that he has no intention of changing. This dynamic has sometimes drained me. I felt totally depleted for two days after the Sunday in which I infused him with my energy.

Another question that begs to be asked is a crucial one: *Where is my self-preservation?*

Why did I pretend that I didn't hear him clearly state numerous times that he's sleeping with other women? Why did I pretend that wasn't true, to the extent that I thought it was safe to have unprotected sex with a man whore? Why did I attempt to open my heart and be vulnerable to a man who really isn't interested in real connection, but who is playing at intimacy because he's afraid to spend one minute alone with himself?

Now we come to: *How did I attract this?*

Easy. Simple. Obvious.

I called forth *a summer fling* and *a part-time lover.* Literally, those words. I also had called forth *the essence of my relationship with Nathan,* having selectively forgotten the parts that hurt my feelings and made me feel insignificant. The Nathan-essence came complete with the inconvenient logistics of being able to see each other, which in a way is comforting now that I won't have to run into Brad all over town because he lives in Boulder. I called forth something casual and fun, not something real and serious.

I made a conscious choice to call forth a summer fling and then *a Real Boyfriend for fall.*

I also have this dirty little secret in my personal masturbation life in which men degrade me, such as demanding that I do inappropriate things for them, and having absolutely no boundaries in the bedroom. Brad asking for a prostate massage and to fuck me in the ass is quite tame compared to the fantasies I entertain when I'm pleasing myself. I will go on the casual encounters pages of Craigslist and arouse myself with men's dirty fantasies of what they want to do to women. This is everything from gang bangs, to visiting the swingers club in Denver, double penetration, and playing daughter to his daddy. Sexual energy is powerful attraction energy, so I'm lucky that Brad has simply made inappropriate requests rather than doing more degrading things.

I'm getting exactly what I asked for, which is how the Law of Attraction works.

Oddly, just because you ask for something doesn't mean you don't have unexpected feelings come up as a result. I'm quite sad that Brad isn't the Real Boyfriend, precisely because I do feel such a connection to him. I'm also quite offended that he believes that I'm not amazing enough to distract him from his other lovers. *Does he not know who I am?*

Mostly I wish I hadn't had sex with him and that we could go back to the wanting and playing. It was ever so much fun. Should I see him again? Can I do it without closing my heart down? Can I do it and just have some more sexual experimentation? I'm single so rarely that a little sexual experimentation is refreshing. Maybe he's a perfect partner to do it with? Because I am connected with him, it might be a safe place for such things.

I leave for Cabo very, very early on Monday. I had hoped to spend the night with him on Sunday. I still want to.

❧

BRAD EMAILED ME AT 3 A.M. expressing that he does not feel we're the Ones for each other.

Tracee,

Here it is, 3 A.M., and I have all these thoughts spinning through my head about us. I think we have reached a plateau. I believe we both have realized this.

Once you begin to engage in sex, you begin to form deeper connections, and deeper feelings for each other. The question is, were we really ready to go there? Yes, we both really wanted to go there. And it was amazing. But now the true question is, where do we go from here? Things ARE different now. The ex-

ploration has turned into connection. This is where things turn complex and why we need to address things now.

We have choices in how we define what relationship we want to have going forward. Of course, each of us has formed our own idea of what we might want. Possible choices include, business as usual, a committed relationship, friends with benefits, friends, acquaintances, parting ways, etc.

Business as usual has been: a fun time together, a very physically connected relationship. Lots of learning from each other. Lots of grounding experiences.

In the time that I have gotten to know you, I care a lot about you, I like you, I connect with you, I really enjoy intimacy with you. My intuition has not raised a flag and said she's the One for you. This is why I never stopped dating.

I can't explain this very well, but my intuition is telling me that we just aren't compatible enough, or there is some reason that wouldn't allow us to be in an easy relationship together. Perhaps I don't know you well enough yet, I don't know. But since we are at this plateau, it sounds as if we may need to decide on our next steps. We may need to define what relationship we are going to have.

I've told myself to listen to my intuition a lot more going forward, this is what I am doing. Hopefully this is what I am doing. Does this make sense?

Brad

❧

BRAD THANKS FOR YOUR NOTE. I just wrote 3,000 words about us in my book, exploring this very question. I never write in the middle of the night, but I wasn't sleeping very well and writing helps me process. I think we're cowards for doing this digitally instead of in person. It's chicken shit, really. Texting about it and then emailing it. It's the anti-intimacy solution to emotional intimacy.

I came to a lot of conclusions and no conclusions. Mostly, I've arrived at an emotional paradox. The not-having sex was more fun than having sex. The wanting and being wanted felt more intimate and exciting than plain old sex. Sex is weirdly boring and not as intimate as what we were doing in a lot of ways. I guess because we've been having it for 20 years already.

The change we both feel is that we're not wanting anymore, we're having. We were high on desire; it was quenched. I wish we were still on day 35, so we were still on the high with fifty-five days to go. I really loved walking around the grocery store being horny out of my mind. You don't get that every day. What a   delight.

I have 5,000 different feelings about the whole "girlfriend" thing. Straight from the beginning it's felt like you're refusing an invitation that wasn't being offered to you. Which, of course, both made me want to be your girlfriend to prove myself worthy of it and made me adamantly oppose being your girlfriend on sheer principle. I think your definition of "girlfriend" and mine are different. I think you see it as high commitment and I see it as low commitment.

Frankly, I think being your girlfriend is probably a painful job. I suspect you fight mean and dirty with your "truth telling," and I'm afraid I'd always have my guard up and that's not how I want to live. I don't even know what to say about your definition of "dating."

We're not the Ones for each other. You ruled it out on our first date when you realized you would be my rebound. And that makes me: sad, hurt, disappointed, and bummed out. Because I care about you, and love being intimate with you and love having your attention focused on me and love having your mouth on mine and love sharing what I know with you and love getting texts from you and really enjoy knowing you as a person.

I called forth a summer fling/part-time lover and a Real Boyfriend in the fall. I guess you're the summer fling. I didn't expect to care this much for, or feel so connected to, a summer fling, so I got some emotional surprises. That said, there's a lascivious part of me that wants to have even more, naughtier adventures with you before our time is up. There are so few moments in one's life when you're connected enough to trust someone sexually and emotionally, but where you're not so committed to them that sexual experimentation is not an infraction on the relationship.

It's such a shame to waste such a rare opportunity. And there's a part of me that thinks I should back away from that statement and keep my wits about me because I'm just full of emotional surprises these days, exploring what it means to be single in my forties.

We could spend Sunday night together and I'll get up and go to Cabo and you'll go on your Keystone trip and we can reconsider our feelings about each other and what we want with each other when we get back?

Tracee

P.S. I hate us for communicating all of this via digital media instead of having the guts to be vulnerable in person or on a phone call. So disappointed in us. Brad don't email me back, Fucking call me on the phone.

❧

HE CALLED AND WE HAD an open and honest discussion in which it was determined that there is no long-term future for us. He was getting ready for a date.

It still hurts my feelings. It still feels like loss. It still feels sad.

It feels so fucking *good.* The pain is delicious. It's jagged and deep; it's dull with sharp twinges.

It feels good to be allowed to have those feelings simultaneously and tell him about them. And have him acknowledge them—all—the good the bad and the painful and the happy as legitimate. In so many ways I love him. My Soul loves his Soul. We have a very deep connection that is hard to describe and that I've already said is completely romanticized: It's not meant to be.

He is my Rebound Man. Which he very poignantly described as someone you're supposed to have a lot of fun with, a lot of sex with. They help with the transition between being married and being single. But you're not supposed to fall in love with them. It would be easier if I didn't already feel like I've been in love with him for many eternities. If I could just blow off the fact that I feel incredibly connected to him or that he, too, feels this amazing energy between us. We're in sync.

Oh how badly I wish I hadn't cut this short by violating the ninety-day rule and having sex with him. I wish that I hadn't sent him the text that said, "I find myself feeling jealous," which started us down the path of discussing our relationship. If I hadn't, I'd still have my cake and the promise of eating it, too. I'd still be riding the high from tumescence.

What a gift this relationship has been. Being Brad's not-girlfriend has been such a joy. I wanted to bask in the joy longer. I know the Real Boyfriend is just around the corner, within months even. I love being single, so it's not that I don't want to be alone. It's that I miss Brad and I miss the joy he's brought to my life for the last month. I miss the "wanting high."

The door to a future relationship with Brad is closed as a result of our conversation. The door to our being "business as usual" as he calls it is open. I want to be able to walk in that door without being hurt. But sex is a dangerous game. When you have sex with people you allow them to enter your field of energy in a very intimate way. You increase the likelihood that you will have love feelings instead of casual dating feelings, and Brad is clear about himself not seeing that happening. I'm clear about it, too, but it hurts my feelings that he is clear about it. It doesn't have to make sense; it doesn't have to be fair. It just is.

If I walk through this open door, I will have established a primary ground rule: I don't want to hear about his women. I wish I was emotionally detached enough to be all Modern-day Progressive Cool Girl, but I'm not. I have feelings of jealousy and longing when he talks about other women.

Actually, consider that statement: "I wish I was emotionally detached" is a fucked-up statement. The whole joy of Brad is that I am emotionally connected to him. If I were emotionally detached it would just be fucking. And it's not *just* fucking. It's complex, as he says. So I'm wishing for a lack of feeling. So anticlimactic.

It feels good to have access to the full gamut of my emotions, even the painful ones. It's a joy just to be able to feel my feelings and not have them kill me or shut me down. It is a joy to be able to ride the high of wanting and sit quietly in the afterglow and to sink into the sadness of loss without feeling like any of it will drown me. Feelings are so delicious and I shut them off from myself for so very long.

Thank you, God, for granting me access to ALL the emotions and for giving me the skills to use them to my advantage.

TWENTY-SEVEN

AUGUST 14, 2013

I am forty. I went to Cabo San Lucas with my Sister Wife (a nod to my polygamous Mormon ancestry), Neecy, and it was wonderful to spend so much time with her.

We are unabashedly inappropriate together. There's so much to say about this eventful trip that I'm a little overwhelmed with where to start.

Boulder Brad, Boulder Brad, Boulder Brad on the brain.

I was uncomfortably lovesick over Brad the entire time. I spent the day before I left for Cabo with Boulder Brad. We made love twice, once in the afternoon and once in the evening. He was so intense and present with me that evening that I could barely contain my joy mixed with sadness that the moment would end.

I know what I know. I know that he's emotionally invested in me, inexplicably in love with me even, and that he doesn't want to be. We're not the Ones. It's a simple truth. But: I am in love with him and he's in love with me. When he's making love to me I can feel its intensity. When he's away from me, I can feel him energetically pull back and it hurts me.

The whole trip, Neecy obsessed over her new crush and I obsessed over Brad and how lovesick I am.

He touches on a deep, deep feeling of insignificance in me. He's seeing other people and dating incessantly and it makes me crazy that he won't just sink into our romance. He fucks with my narrative. After I left, he was inattentive and energetically pulled back and got all rational and in his head about our relationship and didn't answer a few of my texts that were obviously meant to provoke an emotional response from him.

I had taken painkillers, tapping into my pain body and addiction issues, for some oral surgery I had. My Soul told me to get all of the mercury fillings out of my mouth and I had a root canal. Happy Fortieth Birthday! Actually, I had a complete oral makeover, an impulse purchase that cleaned out my bank account. I was really upset about being lovesick, so I unfriended him on Facebook and then blew up all over him, splashing my pain body of insignificance in his face, pinging all of his old marriage shit.

❦

HOW TO BLOW UP YOUR summer fling on Facebook in only a few short hours . . .

Boulder Brad: Happy birthday, Tracee! You are a truly amazing woman and greatly appreciated!

Tracee Sioux: Thank you, Brad. I miss you on this trip. More than I wish I did. Still going to Keystone before I get back? My flight lands at 9 P.M. tomorrow. (This is me NOT sending you nude photos taken on the beach today.)

Boulder Brad: Yep, leaving in the morning.

Boulder Brad: I refined my "authentic" note to: 4. Attract authentic people into your life. These are people who share their life story. They do not hide behind a fear or cover something up. They embrace vulnerability and imperfection. They often are seen as "what you see is what you get" because they are original.

Tracee Sioux: Be it if you want to attract it. I don't know how authentic you're being with me right now. And I'm pretty sure "what you see is what you get" is not in alignment with how this went down. What the fuck? You Steve Harveyed me: being super attentive until you got laid. Then your interest gets diverted by the newest pussy distracting you from the demons in your head.

I am pretty mad at you and your stupid fear about being in this with me even though this is not the One for us, it could've been fucking epic. I'm hurt about you diverting your attention in a million directions with incessant dating and sending me a kaleidoscope of mixed messages. "I'm so connected to you . . . Now, let me tell you about all the other women I'm fucking. And, oh, by the way I just made this policy right before you walked into my life. Yay for me."

How you are with me in bed is not in alignment with how you are when you compartmentalize me and withhold to protect yourself from relationship failure. Failure is being unwilling to put yourself in the game, even if it's not permanent, and even if you might get hurt. (I know what you feel for me when you let yourself go there is real and powerful, or I'm a naive divorcee who romanticized this ridiculously).

I've been vulnerable and open and authentic, and I'm not feeling that from you, except when we're physically intimate. I feel vulnerable, emotionally naked, laid bare, and I'm out here alone. This does not feel good to me. I'll send you my price sheet and you can hire me to help you find the girl of your dreams.

Boulder Brad: Tracee, your previous message was "I miss you on this trip more than I wanted to." Then I get this unloading message, and I can't find Steve Harveyed on *Urban Dictionary*, so I am lost with that implication . . . What has transpired to create the catalyst for change?

If you are not the One for me, there is a valid reason I am not allowing myself to fall in love with you. This is my protection mechanism to not invest in you, since I've determined, or made the conscious decision, that you are not the One for me, and we are not going to enter into a long-term relationship. Is it wrong of me to do that? To not fully invest and allow myself to fall in love with a woman I've determined is not the One for me?

We have each brought something very special into each other's lives. Time, aligned energy frequencies, emotional and physical connection, fun, adventure, learning, knowledge, communication, desire, fantasy, want, and so on. Do you value that? Did you value that?

Boulder Brad: I want to keep you in my life, in whatever relationship we define, whatever boundaries we define. But if you keep pulling out the "I'm going to start billing you and invoicing you" card. That's not going to happen.

Tracee Sioux: Steve Harvey has the ninety-day rule: Don't give up "the cookie" for ninety days or he will lose interest. I fucking hate that rule.

You didn't respond to my miss you message or my reference to nude photos and it hurts my feelings. It's super uncomfortable to put yourself out there with someone who isn't being equally vulnerable. Super uncomfortable. When you're not in bed with me (since you got the cookie) you make me feel like I don't matter to you and I hate how that feels.

Boulder Brad: You are more than a contractor I hire. I understand your feelings. I am not the fall boyfriend. I spent over an hour last night talking to a friend about vulnerability and who to be vulnerable to. Ask yourself the question, who should you be vulnerable to? The summer fling or the fall boyfriend?

Tracee Sioux: What the fuck do you want from me? My vagina is connected to my heart. I live my whole life heart open. I'm vulnerable right now, in this. Are you telling me now that I'm making a bad choice?

Boulder Brad: I told you I've had no expectations from you, except fun, adventure, learning, experience.

Tracee Sioux: You're intellectualizing and not talking about your feelings at all. I think you're scared.

Boulder Brad: Choices are yours. I have difficulties talking from my emotions, I know that about myself.

Tracee Sioux: Yes I know, "Be Cool Girl" because "I told you." Talk about your feelings. Mine are laid bare and it's only fair.

Boulder Brad: 1. Do not create expectations for yourself, otherwise you are setting yourself up for letdowns, disappointment, and/or that you didn't succeed in something you've set out to enjoy and/or accomplish. If you go into something with no expectations, you'll enjoy and feel good about whatever comes about.

We are not a failure.

Tracee Sioux: You had SERIOUS expectations and set up a bunch of rules to guard yourself.

Boulder Brad: Do you want to keep me in your life in some form of relationship?

Tracee Sioux: Here's what I know. I care about you. I value you. I want to have sex with you pretty badly. (Right now this pisses me off.) And this current dynamic feels bad to me. I was hoping our summer fling would involve a lot more romance, way more good feelings than hurt feelings, and way less fucking other women.

I deserve to captivate a man's attention because I'm fucking awesome. I'm hot, smart, conscious, and have my shit together. There's no reason for me to settle for being a disconnected fuck buddy.

Tracee Sioux: Dear Universe, do better. Way better. I deserve it. Love, Tracee.

Tracee Sioux: Dear Brad, talk about your feelings. Or stop talking. I don't give a shit what you "think" right now. I care only what you're feeling for ME.

<u>*Tracee Sioux:*</u> Dear Neecy, I think I'm breaking up with my not-boyfriend because he's emotionally retarded and he can't even have a decent summer fling.

Boulder Brad: Are you on the plane? Why are you being hurtful and degrading to me?

Tracee Sioux: I'm sorry. That was harsh. I apologize. I feel hurt by you. Here's the thing. A summer fling is supposed to make me feel amazing about myself. It should make me feel sexy and attractive and captivating and smart and interesting. It should make me feel confident and lovable. It should make me feel really special. That's the whole point of a summer fling. That's the whole point. There's supposed to be an exchange of feelings. Not just me sharing mine with you while you guard yours.

But this is making me feel not good enough, like a conquest: insignificant and disposable. The opposite of what I want to feel from any kind of not-relationship or relationship I'm in. Your new dating strategy is totally backfiring. At least it's not working for me. I feel like you've rubbed my nose in this whole fucking other-women thing and it's painful. You're better than this. I don't think this is authentically you. Step up your game.

Boulder Brad: No. You're putting a bunch of complex expectations on me that I never asked for. This was supposed to be fun, adventurous, lighthearted, and easygoing. I thought we had gotten there. I had a lot of fun with you dancing on Pearl Street. I will not be present with someone again who makes me feel that I cannot live up to their expectations. I did that for eighteen years.

Tracee Sioux: I have every right, obligation even, to expect the best of himself out of a man. I don't even know what I'm wanting here. I'd like you to say soothing things, with terms of endearments. A sweet nothing wouldn't hurt, an expression of affection, a compelling reason to sleep with you again, a sweet lie, an expression of your feelings for me, a confession of desire . . . This entire conversation, you've said not one word about your feelings.

Boulder Brad: You completed unloaded hurtful things to me. This dynamic tonight is reminiscent of my marriage, and we aren't even dating.

Tracee Sioux: Okay then. We aren't even dating.

Boulder Brad: That was supposed to be "in a relationship." My mistake.

❧

I AM SO EMBARRASSED. I sabotaged my own happiness. I should have just kept my cool and maintained my distance. The next day I apologized over the phone. I am sorry that I lost my shit and exposed my pathetic insecurities. They're really not his problem.

So embarrassing. So painful, really. Being lovesick sucks ass.

When I got home, I went to see C.J. and the guides, angels, and light workers—my God team—who she channels to help heal my wounds and give me direction when I'm facing choices. They shared the root of my insignificance. I had casually mentioned before the session that I felt like a desperate thirteen-year-old girl. Therein lies the root.

When I was thirteen years old I got stoned (I think, it may have just been Peach Schnapps, I honestly don't recall the details of my "out of mind-ness.") But I was out-of-mind, making out with my best friend's ex-boyfriend. We were in a sleeping bag on the back porch of his mother's house. I was only there because my friend Melinda was sleeping with his brother. At the time, I usually just made out with the extra boy. The extra boy that night was Poly Peter. A polygamous kid (he had eighteen brothers and sisters from a man who married two sisters), who was very cool and good looking, and I had a crush on him from afar. Had I not been out-of-mind I would not have been with him, though, because he was my best friend Jenna's ex-boyfriend and I knew she loved him.

But I *was* out-of-mind, feeling aroused and floating outside of myself. Then he said, *Let yourself cum,* and I jolted back into my body and thought, *Do girls do that?* And I realized I was having sex.

I was thirteen.

I was a "good" Mormon girl.

I was having sex.

With a boy to whom I was completely insignificant.

With my best friend's ex-boyfriend, a girl I loved dearly and never would want to hurt.

I was no longer a virgin.

I was ruined.

I was ashamed.

I was humiliated.

I was insignificant.

I made harsh, very harsh judgments about myself: *I am a horrible friend. I am a worthless whore.*

I did not let myself off the hook.

My entire group of friends dumped me.

My best friend was critically hurt.

I lost my best friend.

I was unworthy of friendship.

I lost my connection to the Church.

I lost my purity.

I lost my worthiness in the eyes of the Church.

I lost my worthiness in the eyes of God.

I had sex with a boy who didn't care about me at all.

I immediately found a man/boy, Dave Lev, who would punish me as harshly as I felt I needed to be punished for my terrible and horrible mistake. He beat me. He "consensually raped" me for hours and hours. I consented to being harmed, fucked harshly until I was bruised and sometimes bleeding. I allowed him to call me all the names I felt about myself, including "used meat." He agreed with my belief, *No one will ever want you now,* and said those words to me over and over, especially when I tried to leave. "You're a used piece of meat, no one will ever want you now!"

Brad brought this old pain-body stuff to the surface with his "fucking other people" pronouncements. It is irrational and silly, nevertheless so painful and real for me. The feeling of being love-sick dates back to me being thirteen and is phenomenally painful.

❧

ONE OF THE HARDEST THINGS I've ever done for myself was de-cide that I was done punishing myself by being beaten and date raped by my boyfriend. It will seem strange to people to hear how difficult it is to give up such an intense love. But it was love. It was intense. I know people say that love doesn't hurt. And that's true: Healthy love does not hurt. Nonetheless having someone pay such extreme attention to you, and being so obsessed with you and feeling so intensely about you, is a form of love. Damag-ing. Painful. Harmful. Self-worth destroying. But still love.

There were many times during my marriage when I would re-flect that it was better to be loved by Dave so violently than it was to be ignored and dismissed as insignificant by Alex. Crazy, I know. But Alex's apathy toward me was excruciating. I used to marvel at the concept that violent attention was better than no attention. I used to think, *Why can't you just lie to me, like Dave?*

There was always a payoff to Dave's violent episodes. He would go ape-shit violent when he was drinking and doing coke or crystal meth. The next day he was intensely repentant. He showered love all over me. He rained compliments and cherishment and adoration all over me. He expressed how significant I was to him. How vital and important. He begged forgiveness and pleaded with me not to leave him or he would die. It was intensely emotional. A roller-coaster of highs and lows. Never average. Never boring. Never apathetic.

Fucking Alex would just go on being apathetic about my emotional pain. That was painful without the highs. It was painful without the intensity and passion. It was painful beyond the pain that Dave caused me. For I was sure of Dave's love. It was a wild, violent, chaotic love, but it was mine and it felt phenomenal much of the time. The other times it was wild, violent, chaotic, and excruciatingly painful.

That night with Poly Peter changed the trajectory of my life. I was on a path that had been slightly to the left of the "straight and narrow." Sure I was fooling around with boys, making out with quite a number of them. It was fun and I adored being touched and complimented and wanted. I loved the sensation of kissing and touching. But the night I lost my virginity was like a hard left turn onto a completely different path. There is no "sorta" virgin in the Mormon Church. There is only Worthy and Unworthy. I was irrevocably Unworthy in that instant. Which put me in the position of struggling to redeem myself ever since.

Every choice I made from there forward came from a place of Unworthiness and Insignificance. I didn't apply to the journalism program. I didn't apply to the Peace Corps. I didn't apply to prestigious colleges. I didn't hold out for better romances. I didn't expect enough from my romantic partners. I married poorly, twice. I married incompatible men who were not on my level of consciousness or ability or ambition. I didn't hold out for a burning passionate love, instead taking what was offered from a fear of never being offered more.

Oh and my friendships. I damned myself to horrible friendships. I scooped from the bottom of the barrel, taking whatever I could find. Accepting completely shitty behavior from friends much of the time.

Boulder Brad brought all of this insignificance and unworthiness to the surface with his harsh, *You're not my girlfriend* declaration, his proclamations of fucking other people and his conscious choice not to fall in love with me.

So I could heal it all.

❧

ON THE TABLE, I ASKED C.J. to ask my spiritual guides for guidance. "Where should I go for my fortieth birthday?"

"Cabo San Lucas or San Luis Obispo," they said.

Weirdly, San Luis Obispo immediately brought to mind my relationship with Nathan, which I had been romanticizing. I lived in Morro Bay, about ten miles away from San Luis Obispo and spent many wonderful weekends with Nathan there.

I had called forth Brad because I had been thinking about and reminiscing on the good times with Nathan. Ours was a carefree and light sort of love. I enjoyed him immensely. He was a playboy in his mid-thirties, and I thought he might be on the verge of settling down. I took his eventual rejection—after two years—pretty roughly. But I had forgotten how painful it was to be lovesick over him and not get what I wanted in terms of commitment from him. That's how I feel with Brad. And I don't like it.

The lesson here?

DON'T CALL FORTH THE ENERGY OF PAST LOVERS!

Because then you get the energy of past lovers. They weren't the right lovers, which is why you're not together any more. There were painful things about past lovers that you're not remembering when you romanticize these relationships.

CALL FORTH A MAN LIKE YOU'VE NEVER KNOWN BEFORE. A MAN SO AMAZING THAT YOU NEVER EVEN THOUGHT TO WISH FOR HIM. A MAN SO PHENOMENAL THAT YOU NEVER EVEN THOUGHT YOU HAD A RIGHT TO HAVE HIM.

Lesson learned. Since dating Brad, my prayer has gone from a few sexy paragraphs of generalities to an extended list of desires of characteristics and feelings. One of the tools I use for attraction is to write what you want *as if you already have it.* Like this:

My Man

MY MAN SEDUCES ME with words. He is witty, clever, and creative with language. He makes me laugh with his use of witty banter. He does not rely on sarcasm; he is genuinely funny. He is a wordsmith. He says all the right things to me, praising me often for my physical attributes, praising me often on my personhood and womanhood and power. My man is verbally seductive and even when I'm angry he uses words to diffuse, apologize, authentically communicate, and seduce until I'm weak in the knees and fall into his arms. My man is not afraid of my tears.

My man is wonderful kisser with a big dick, who is talented at pleasing a woman and making love, who wants to make me cum over and over, who is very powerful in his divine masculine. He loves, loves, loves to eat my pussy. We make love five times a week for the sheer pleasure if it. He's very commanding and masculine in bed. He makes me squirt and he loves it.

My man encourages me to express myself and wants me to develop feelings for him. He rains praise on me about all aspects of me. He buys me sexy and meaningful gifts. He only has eyes, heart, mind, body, and Soul for me. We reach the ecstasy of God together.

My man is super healthy and smells good. He always pays, is extraordinarily generous, makes well over $100,000 per year, is financially established, and has a very, very powerful abundance consciousness. This elevates my income dramatically, as well. He loves to take me out and show me a good time, he loves to shower me with gifts and takes me on trips and adventures.

He lives and works in Fort Collins. He has children and is involved with them, but we don't co-parent, and he has plenty of free time.

My boyfriend is incredibly grounded in his divine masculine: over six feet tall, sexy, fit, attractive, powerful, assertive, and respectful, who I am very, very proud to introduce to people.

My boyfriend is sober and clean, a healthy living, health-conscious man who is spiritually centered, attends WLC with me, and who loves to have sacred sex and worship my divine feminine with his powerful divine masculine. He is a touch further than I am in his spiritual path, so I learn from him. He is able to lead me because he is masculine and powerful, and I trust him implicitly because he knows me better than I know myself and he's easily able to hold a bigger vision for me than I can myself. I never doubt that he wants the best for me. He pursues me in the most delightful ways, something that continues for the duration of our relationship.

My man has impeccable hygiene with smooth skin. He has a vasectomy. He has a great sense of humor and is very clever with words. I date a man who can fix stuff and build stuff and wants to do the man chores because it makes him feel powerful.

My man enjoys my children and honors my parenting. My children love to be around him and we easily allow him into our family.

I am pursued by this man. He always calls me for more dates and our relationship deepens in perfect timing. I feel brilliant, creative, beautiful, smart, sexy, rrrrrich, lucky, generous, and loved in his presence. He adores me and compliments me often and genuinely. We are deeply, intimately connected with each other. We are exceptionally open, honest, communicative, and affectionate with each other.

My man elevates me in every way, including intimacy, communication, physically, professionally, sexually, and consciously.

Hieros gamos!

This or something much better!

❧

I OPTED OUT OF SAN LUIS OBISPO because it seemed like a visit to the past and it felt too Nathan, and Nathan is married with children and isn't likely to come have great sex with me at this point.

So . . . Cabo San Lucas. I kept asking my Soul if this is what she really wanted and she said, YES!

Honestly I wasn't that sold on the idea because there are absolutely no spiritual attractions in Cabo. But, this is The Year of YES! So YES! is what I said. I booked the trip and Neecy let me bully her into coming with me.

In Cabo, we figured I was meant to see a Mexican healer of some sort. We began asking around whether someone knew a medicine woman, shaman, spiritual healer, or Mexican witch. The bike taxi driver took us to the home of a curandera in Cabo. The neighbor said she was on vacation.

The "tourist desk" (*read:* Time Share Sharks) were interested in helping us. One man at the counter told us of a curandera—very skilled and powerful—in Todos Santos. We would have to rent a car and drive up the Baja coastline about sixty to seventy-five kilometers to meet her. "How do we know she'll be there, can we call her?" Neecy asked.

"She is always there. She doesn't use the Internet and phones," he said.

The next morning, August 8, the day before my fortieth birth-day, we rented a car and drove to Todos Santos. We had been told to visit Hotel Todos Santos and they would know where to find Maria Tarot. "Be sure to have the breakfast at the Hotel California," they had said.

We found a lovely boutique hotel with the name Todos Santos in it. The woman in the office was very kind and sweet, she looked everywhere she could think of, calling friends and colleagues in the town. Dead. The curandera had died.

We sat down in the Hotel California, of the famed Eagles' song, we were told, to eat the "best breakfast in Mexico." We opened the menu on the beautiful patio.

"I'm not feeling this," I said.

"Me either," Neecy agreed.

"Let's go somewhere else," I said.

"Let's go eat at that taco stand we parked by," she suggested.

We walked over to a taco food truck. Fish tacos were the only thing on the menu. There were cheap plastic patio sets to eat on. A pretty Mexican woman who looked like Rosie Perez, a thirteen-year old girl, and a gringo ex-patriot from L.A. named Patrick.

We began a casual chat with Patrick. "We are looking for a Mexican spiritual healer, a Mexican witch," I finally said. "We were told to come to Todos Santos. Do you know of one?"

Patrick and his wife chatted in Spanish, obviously trying to decide what to make of our request. "We do know a woman," Patrick said. "But she is in La Pez, the next town over, about thirty miles from here. What do you want to see her for?"

"Cleansing. Healing," we answered. "We were led here."

"You'll need someone to go with you to show you the way and to translate. She doesn't speak any English," Patrick said. "Do you have a car?"

"Yes, we have a car. Would you know anyone who would be willing to come with us?" I asked. He said he would.

They called the curandera to make arrangements.

"Two hundred dollars each," they said.

"Uh, we don't have two hundred dollars with us," we said.

"One hundred dollars each," they said, and we agreed to the price, having brought that much money with us on our adventure into the Mexican desert.

"She will do a cleansing and read an egg, and read cards," they said.

We shrugged. "This is meant for us," we thought. "We're up for anything."

"Angelina has been very good to our family," Patrick said. "She's a wonderful woman. I'm doing this for her."

La Pez is a dingy industrial-like town. Unattractive, dirty, and carrying a dark energy. We drove into a ghettoish neighborhood and entered a concrete box where the curandera lived. She was in her sixties and not particularly pleasant. She had a grimace on her face most of the time. She wasn't very open or very "light."

We asked to use the restroom and she wasn't delighted about it. She resentfully led us into an outhouse with a toilet you had to dump a bucket of water in. There were chickens and pretty birds, and feral cats and dogs roaming around the dirty courtyard.

Around the studio apartment were Catholic icons and symbols, all cheap and impersonal. Our Lady of Guadalupe—which is prominently featured in this area of the world—was pinned to the wall, as were images of Jesus. There was a rosary. The furniture consisted of a bed, a dresser, a bookshelf to divide the living area and the bedroom area, a couch, a love seat, and an altar/shelf where she kept her divination tools.

She handed each of us an egg to hold. While we held it, she and Patrick caught up on each other's comings and goings in Spanish. I went into a meditation. The apartment was like a hot box, at one point I was deep in trance and felt like I might be starting to hallucinate.

She had Neecy stand and rubbed the egg all over her body, especially on her womb. She cracked Neecy's egg into a glass and held it up to the light to examine it. "You make your own fences and sabotage yourself," the curandera told Neecy.

"Do you see this person?" she asked, pointing to a white string of egg floating upward in the clear glass she had cracked the egg into. "This is a light woman, a blond woman, who has put a curse on you. She is jealous and she sabotages you."

She then rubbed the egg on my body and cracked it into a glass. Holding it up to the light she pronounced that I had two people in my egg, holding hands.

Oh, a lover, I thought. *How wonderful.*

"There is a 'dark,' red-haired woman and a light woman, with blond hair, who are working together to curse you."

She pulled out a deck of cards, not like the tarot I've seen before—much like playing cards, but different. For my reading, she said:

"It is a terrible curse. The red-haired woman has spent a great deal of money and energy to put a terrible curse on you. She has spent a lot of time and money to wish harm on you. She feels you did her harm and she wants to hurt you. She works with a blond-haired woman. She is very pissed off with you. Her eyes are on you and these two are working against you. She works with a photo of you. The blond-haired woman is sad and sick, with tears.

"There is a dark-haired man who thinks about you a lot, who is sad, because he cares very much for you.

"Your ex-husband suffered. The dark, red-haired woman did both of you a lot of harm. He loved you very much, but this red-haired woman broke up the sentiments of love and took away the love. The dark woman was responsible for the dissolution of your marriage. Your ex-husband was worked on a little bit by her and so were you.

"This person who is doing this bad stuff against you, it's going to come back on her. These relationships that are stormy are still active.

"There is a bad surprise coming with money and some kind of document.

"All of this is negative. You are stuck in a trap with this curse. You need to get cured and then all this stuff will come to the surface and you will see things more clearly. You have a lot of potential, you are a strong person, very intelligent, but you are contaminated by a deliberate black energy. This curse is a very serious problem.

"The work that's been done against you is very strong, but you can heal from it. Then you need to put up protection around you to forge ahead and prevent this dark cloud from further attack and penetration."

WORST BIRTHDAY BLESSING EVER!

Fucking Viveka Moon. I knew immediately who she was talking about: Viveka Fucking Moon. Frenemy of the first order. Jealous and horrible to me since I was sixteen years old.

Neecy's reading was much more positive and light. "A blond-haired man thinks about you all the time and cares for you." A marriage. Money and fortune. Joy. Happiness. Success.

"HER dark energy is messing with your reading," the currandera accused me.

WORST BIRTHDAY BLESSING EVER!

Obviously, this put me into a funk. I was deeply upset on the drive home. So much to process. Such a terrible and awkward ride to drop off Patrick. I was in a daze. Bewildered. And still hung up on thinking about Brad as the dark-haired man who cares for me. That fucker was sucking up mindshare that I could have been using to obsess about a curse from a Mexican witch and a bitchtastic stalker frenemy who had cursed my life for twenty-four years. WHAT. THE. FUCK?!

Brad thinks about me! Brad thinks about me! Brad thinks about me because he cares for me! Brad cares for me and it makes him sad that he's not going to be my Real Boyfriend.

It's embarrassing, but that's completely what was going through my head. In between thoughts of: *Fucking Viveka. How do I get rid of her? I can't believe this terrible birthday present from the Universe. I was high on forty! Yesterday I was parasailing—literally flying through the air with my bestie, singing* Wind Beneath My Wings— *high on life and excited and hopeful about my exciting and promising future. Now I've got a black, dark curse on me! What the fuck!!!!!!!!*

Brad Brad Brad

Fucking Viveka Fucking Viveka Fucking Viveka

Fucking Mexican Witch Put a Curse on Me on my Fucking Birthday!
Cursed by a Mexican Witch.
Fuck You Universe!

❧

ON THE DRIVE BACK TO Cabo, I shared my deepest, darkest, most shameful secrets with Neecy, attempting to process this dark and terrible curse.

Did Viveka have something to do with the end of my marriage?

Yes, she did. Only months before we decided to divorce, she had been angry about a blog I posted (evidently she reads my blog posts) and sent me a heinous, threatening email demanding that I take it down. In the blog I had talked about how mean jealous women had been to me when I was thin and I was trying to let that shit go. She knew I had referenced her and she was furious.

She threatened to have an Internet war with me. "I will tell everyone about . . ." oh the list chronicling all the sins I committed since I was sixteen-years old went on and on. But, it was distorted and completely insane. She had rewritten history in her mind. Calling her drunken indiscretions "date rape," accusing me of hating Jews and having email proof of it, etc. I forwarded the email to Alex immediately, hoping he would support me. His only response was, "Did you cheat on me?" This was one of the accusations she made that I hadn't paid attention to because it simply wasn't true.

There were two indiscretions that she might have been referring to. One was a minor French kiss in the back of a cab with Mr. Benchley. It was a goodbye kiss from an old friend. I would hardly call that cheating. It's not as if I went up to his hotel room and had a goodbye fuck. It was innocent. We were fond of each other. We kissed goodbye. I can't remember if this was right before or right after I was married.

The other was a more serious offense. I got completely wasted at the work Christmas party at the Tavern on the Green with a coworker. We made out on a bench in Central Park, I went to his apartment and then came home. He touched my boobs. Is this "cheating?" I guess it is. It wasn't cool. I honestly am not even sure that I told Viveka about this indiscretion. I felt awful about it and years later, during my recovery from Xanax addition and dipping my toe into evangelicalism, I "repented" and "confessed" at a retreat I attended. I was advised that admitting such a thing to Alex would likely ruin our marriage. It wasn't a big deal. That's what I wanted to believe.

Still the email I forwarded to Alex set him off. "Did you cheat on me? She says you cheated on me."

"Most of that email is complete bullshit. No, I didn't cheat on you," I told him.

But, yeah, the email contributed to our already damaged and suffering marriage. A crippled marriage with an accusation of an affair. Yeah, damaging. In the early part of our marriage she would do fucked up shit like that, too. In fact, when I began looking at all the ways Viveka has cursed my life I realized that she interfered with and damaged a great many of my romantic and familial relationships. She had phone sex with Jake, knowing I was in love with him. She fucked Doug Denton in my house about an hour after I had been fucking him. She gossiped and criticized and caused trouble in my relationships with my first husband, Zeke and Walter Dumberg.

Now that I think about it she encouraged me to make out with Walter Dumberg when I was married to Zeke. I had forgotten about that. I don't remember if I kissed him, but I do remember that he took me on a motorcycle ride and for a ride in his sports car. Many years later I got with him, even living with him in a short destructive romance that ended in him stalking me so severely that I was fired from my job because he wouldn't stop making harassing phone calls. Eventually Walter (an ex-convict on parole) was ordered to go back to prison or leave the state of Utah for no less than three years. (Oh my God, I'm rolling in laughter that this is my life).

Viveka meddled repeatedly, whispering criticisms to me about my boyfriends from Zeke Stevens, to Walter Dumberg and Nathan. "He has a giant head, he's stupid, he's gross . . ." She fucked my date, at least once.

Viveka wanted to match me man for man. All of her betraying conquests contained one message: *See, men want me too, you're not so special.*

The lesson I learned there is that men are not really that picky. They mostly want to stick their dicks in vaginas. And they don't care all that much which vaginas they get into. They wouldn't marry Viveka, but they fucked her or wanted her to talk about fucking them—I'm looking at you Jake—with her sultry phone voice.

When Madigan was two or three I went to Viveka's house on a visit to Utah. Viveka pulled out her old Barbies. She then reenacted a violent fight she and I had had in L.A. during my move to California. The Barbies were hitting and screaming at each other. The Barbies were screaming, "You slept with my husband!" (her) and "Give me back my Xanax!" (me). It was so uncool, passive-aggressive, and inappropriate to do around my kid.

Viveka didn't spend time with Madigan after that.

She also wrote a book, or at least started a book, about a daughter who hated her mother as a teenager so she went to her mother's best friend's house to live and she loved the friend/auntie more than the mom because she was so much cooler than the mother. "It's not about you," she claimed. Except for the physical description, the characteristics of the character, and the events that made up her life, it wasn't about me.

Fuck that noise.

❧

VIVEKA WAS ALSO INFLUENTIAL in the destruction of my family of origin's bonds.

I met Viveka coming out of my relationship with Dave, when I was hiding behind Zeke so Dave didn't murder me. This is not an exaggeration. When I say that Dave was going to kill me I mean that he thought of me as his property and chased me around town, demanding that I not leave him. He would get physical in front of other people: pushing and shoving me and calling me a "used meat whore." He would show up at my job. He would call my house. He would come to my window in the middle of the night. I was hiding behind Zeke—I even married Zeke—because I knew Dave could never see me as an autonomous person, but only as another man's property. There were other reasons, too, but that was an important one. Zeke adored me and he was harmless, so he was a safe person to hide behind.

This is where the story convolutes into too many personal dynamics from a small town with a particular group of kids. Zeke was friends with Keith. Keith was Jenna's sister. Jenna was the friend I lost when I slept with her ex-boyfriend, Poly Pete. Zeke and Keith were both weird-friends with Dave. Viveka had been in love with Keith for many, many years and they were living together at the time. Social incest. Zeke took me to Keith's house to smoke weed and hang out and I didn't really want to go. I was still bearing so much shame about sleeping with Pete and betraying Jenna. I literally had ZERO female friends. Dave had isolated me completely from any social life at all with his jealousy and I honestly didn't feel that I deserved any friends because I had betrayed one that I truly loved. Viveka jumped right into that hole in my Soul. She was six years older than me and was carrying her own pain to match mine.

"I don't know why everyone hates you," she told me. "I think you're awesome!"

I was desperate for someone to think I was awesome. I had battered-woman's syndrome pretty severely and was very vulnerable. Viveka and I fell together in an intense way in our friendship; it was almost like a marriage. I was terribly grateful to her for being my friend. After all, I was so unworthy of friendship.

❧

SHORTLY AFTER MY whirlwind dating/marriage to Zeke and my friendship with Viveka, I went to therapy. I had been beaten and sexually violated, sometimes consensually, sometimes not, for two years by a man who claimed he loved me. I was fucked up. I was emotionally unstable. I felt inherently wrong. I was broken, weakened, and depleted. I didn't even have a "self." And I knew it.

I wanted help.

So I started going to this grad student doing an internship, Kelly Fisher. After one or two visits she did a visualization-hypnosis thing and had me imagine myself in our old house in Shreveport, Louisiana. I was about four or five and I envisioned myself in a hula hoop. I also had a memory of my parents bringing me a birthday cake while I was in bed on the morning of my fifth? birthday. (I have no idea if that really happened.) That's all I remember from the hypnosis session.

When I came out of it, Kelly handed me a copy of *The Courage to Heal*, the Bible of healing from sexual abuse. Kelly indicated it was about my father. I don't remember exactly how, but rather than dealing with my boyfriend who beat and raped me, our focus shifted to my father sexually abusing me.

This was 1991. At the time, pop psychology held that if women or girls put themselves in abusive relationships it was because the father fucked the daughter. It sounds crazy now, but that was the thinking of the time. *Everyone* was remembering sexual abuse. It seemed that every dad was suspect. Every dad, grandfather, uncle, or brother had his hand in a daughter, niece, or granddaughter's panties. It was extreme. Celebrities from Oprah to Roseanne were *coming out* as sexual abuse survivors.

We never worked on Dave or what he did to me in two years of therapy. We worked on my dad sexually abusing me.

In *The Courage to Heal,* it says that if you have "these" feelings—then it lists common feelings associated with victims of abuse like sadness, fury, like something is wrong with you, violated—then *you have been sexually abused by a father/grandfather/uncle.*

And I *did* have those feelings. Intensely. *Why?* Because I *had* been being sexually abused by a boyfriend. Repeatedly, between the formidable ages of thirteen and sixteen.

Kelly had a whole gaggle of clients who were sexually abused and formed a therapy group for us. I sat in a room full of women who were having flashbacks and uncovering repressed memories of all kinds of crazy shit. Possibly many of them are true. Probably some of them weren't. They kept getting bigger and bigger. We formed "enmeshed" relationships with each other, several of which turned sexual.

Including a love affair that I had with a woman named Lisa who had being diagnosed with a buncha mental health disorders, had a rap sheet a mile long, a prison history, a convoluted story about her father and an illegitimate son, and a scary "wife" that I should have been more afraid of. I was deeply in love with her.

She was my first same-sex sexual experience. She was overweight, crass, and dangerous; she even had whiskers and was a squirter (I did not know what this was, I thought she'd peed). But I loved her. LOL. She was batshit crazy, too. She had a job working as a bounty hunter under a fake name, though she herself was on probation. She taught me how to get a fake identity by getting social security numbers from the graves of babies and I got into some minor trouble with the law over some stolen parking passes and a fake ID. I talked in my sleep one night and said, "I love you, Lisa," with Zeke lying next to me. He once saw us kissing in a parking lot. When I asked him with he wanted for our second anniversary he said, "*A divorce.*" She told me later that as soon as she met me she thought, "I could fuck her." Very romantic.

Anyway, my life had this kind of crazy going on during my friendship with Viveka. She is the first person I came home and told that I had been sexually abused by my father.

Oh boy did she get into it. She jumped right on that train, telling me of her own abuse with her grandfather and all the pain and damage it had caused her. She encouraged me to remember more stuff and then she and my therapist were encouraging me to write a letter of accusation to my parents demanding my due.

Family collapse. I can't even describe the amount of damage that letter did to my family. For twenty-two years, my mother blamed me for every single bad thing done/not done. I "ruined" the family. The therapist ruined our lives. For twenty-two years.

It amuses me in a morbid kind of way that my father is a known liar, but "liar" is the label she immediately put on me. Immediately. She didn't even consider that I might be telling the truth. Her fangs came out and she was hot for blood.

My father has been a secret alcoholic for the majority of her marriage. He chewed tobacco and she pretended not to know. He, very likely, had affairs and flings through his trips with the military. He is cruel to her, withholding all love and affection and approval to get what he wants. He screams in her face if she doesn't obey him immediately. He towers over her threateningly to ensure that she is afraid of him constantly. He is mean to everyone around him, gruff and frightening, cold and angry.

But *I* ruined her marriage.

Several years after I "destroyed the family" with my accusatory letter, I was so exhausted from the battle with my mother that I rescinded the accusation. My mother insisted that it be in writing, just as the accusation letter was. I complied, only to find that twenty-two years later she still blamed me for the ruination of her marriage and the family because I failed to recant in person. My accusation letter, according to her, is the reason he's a mean alcoholic. Of course. I mean, we couldn't actually hold him responsible being an asshole. Men are not held responsible for their own behavior, after all.

False memory syndrome (FMS) was the new diagnosis, as diagnosed by my mother. It was decided in academia and media that the whole world could not be being fucked by fathers, uncles, granddads, and neighbors. There was a public battle over whether repressed memories were legit, or bullshit caused by suspect and unethical therapeutic practice.

Did he do it? I don't honestly know. My dad and I never—not once—spoke to each other about it. All communication happened between my mother and me. That is, until I complied with my mother's demands twenty-two years later that I apologize to him in person, so as to fix his alcoholism.

At some point I decided that whether or not my dad did abuse me didn't matter. If he did it, I had to move on. If he didn't, I had to move on. I had to forgive and ask forgiveness of myself and him and my mom and my poor siblings and extended family—who did suffer—for the whole sad, tragic episode.

Sometimes I catch myself having thoughts about making sure my dad isn't alone with my children or his favorite granddaughter. Other times I have flashes of memory or weird Freudian sexual fantasy. It's hard to say which. Every now and then I'll have a flash of a smell and I can feel myself in a bed with his hands on me. At times I'll remember awkward sexual moments when he allowed me to watch inappropriate television with him, involving sexuality and nudity. I will flash on a time when I had my shoulders bare and was feeling sexual at about eight-years old and my dad made a comment, "I can see you," which both titillated and shamed me.

False memories?

Repressed memories?

I don't know and I couldn't begin to trust any memories I have of that dark and terrible time. I was mind-fucked either way. I was mind-fucked by therapy and mind-fucked by my family and mind-fucked by Dave Lev and mind-fucked by myself and mind-fucked by my Church and it's standard of worthiness. I was mind-fucked completely and utterly and totally. I was mind-fucked by others who are attracted to those who are mind-fucked, including Lisa, Viveka, and Zeke and all the other people I hung out with.

This period of my life—and that letter—has been the deepest shame that I have carried in my life.

≈

IT IS ALSO THE ONE THING that Viveka has been able to hold over my head and use against me. I have feared her because I wanted no one—ever—to hear about my awfulness. The other things I've done that she knew about—while embarrassing, are not soaked in such a core shame. When she threatened to "out me" on her blog, I outted myself to take my power back. I did not out myself on this because the shame is too deep and unbearable.

Except I don't want it anymore, which is why I share it here.

Of course, this is the root story, the causal story, the back story. Viveka's not responsible for it. The part she played was typical of the day. She murmured in my ear about my mother being in denial. She ranted about my father. She was supporting me, as good friends do. She spoke as if she actually knew my parents, my family, and it was venomous. I was a willing listener because she was my only friend, I felt she knew me better than anyone and I was all fucked up from years of mind manipulation, bad choices, and boyfriend rape and battery.

Don't let me run away with my victim stance here. Because that's not how it was. I wasn't just sitting on the sidelines of my life being barreled over by events out of my control. I was the active leader of my own life sabotage. I was the punisher of me more than anyone.

Viveka hates me because I repeated exactly the same behavior that changed the trajectory of my life to begin with, birthed from the same underlying belief: *terrible friend, worthless whore.*

I first cheated on my best friend with her ex-boyfriend—destroying myself in the process—and then I cheated on Viveka, my best friend with her ex-husband.

☙

WE MUST ALWAYS REINFORCE our fucked up beliefs about ourselves by providing more evidence of the facts: *I am a horrible friend and a worthless whore.* Otherwise we might go around feeling good about ourselves and making positive choices and letting old shit go. That's the tactic I take at forty, but it was not my tendency in my early twenties, which is where the story had brought us.

Of course, *she* slept with *my* date, Doug, about an hour after he had been fucking me, at an impromptu party, in a very passive-aggressive, self- and marriage-destructive, and embarrassing way.

So I had every right.

Except I didn't love the man she slept with. He was a wiener and I knew it. We had a fuck-friend arrangement. He was my friend, and not a good one. I'm not even sure why I was sleeping with him to begin with. I wasn't hurt over him, per se; I was hurt *at* them. I was furious with her and deeply hurt she would do it.

Her husband, Keith, was there that night. Though separated, they were on a date, and both he and I tried to stop her from sleeping with Doug. It was a bad choice. It was hurtful to our relationship, her own fractured marriage, and ultimately herself. She now claims that it was a date rape—a delusional rewrite that fits into her attachment to being a total victim of everything.

Afterwards, her husband and I slept together. We didn't just sleep together, over the course of several months we had an affair. We touched and kissed when she wasn't looking. We made out. I went to his house when she wouldn't be there and we made love. We stayed in a hotel to make love once. We planned a surprise birthday party for her together and made love before, kissed during. We had strong feelings toward each other, but I wasn't in love with him.

Viveka found out. I can't recall how. It was devastating to her. It hurt her heart deeply. It was not the first time that Keith had cheated on her, having done so with our mutual friend Virginia many years before. Viveka chose to marry him anyway. Viveka wanted to divorce Keith because he was a disconnected alcoholic. A good reason. But she'd been in love with him since she was sixteen and was afraid to leave him. Who would she be without him?

Thus, our cycle of pain and hurt and destruction.

Actually, it wasn't really a cycle, because after I had played my part, I was done hurting Viveka.

She was out for blood, however, hiding under the guise of forgiveness. She exacted her revenge in a multitude of ways including having phone sex with Jake, a man I was inappropriately in love with (he was still married); having sex with my date after I had fallen asleep on the couch (I woke to him petting my hair, not knowing she had fucked him that night); meddling in my relationships with other boyfriends and husbands; criticizing my boyfriends; abandoning me in bars with no way home; starting big, huge physical fights in public places; constantly bringing my betrayal up over and over, holding it over my head and making sure I was always the bad guy in her mental scenario; and eventually trying to wedge her way between me and my daughter, me, and my husband.

Still, we loved each other. Fiercely.

❧

I NEEDED HER. I HAD NO other real female friends. I didn't want to go this life alone. Eventually, though, I was exhausted by her.

Viveka was all-consuming. I couldn't seem to get away without being suffocated by her endless need for emotional support. I used to think to myself that if she ever had children she would suffocate them with her endless need.

I called her my emotional vampire.

Eventually, I got a job in California and never returned to the state of Utah, where all of this crazy took place. Still, she remained my primary means of emotional support and connection. We had a very tight bond, as horrible as we had been to each other. But some things cannot be undone.

My relationship with Viveka was often laced with her encouraging me to do things I normally wouldn't have done. Usually sexual things. I think she lived vicariously through my curvy, blond body in a multitude of ways. Being anorexic and red-haired, she would always say, "If I was a blond, I would marry a millionaire." I have been a complete failure at marrying millionaires. Instead I bought into the nonsense that when in love money doesn't matter. I now realize that if you date millionaires instead of losers, you're more likely to marry a millionaire than a loser.

I had a baby. She screamed with jealousy. She meddled. She stopped speaking to me because I no longer devoted my primary emotional support to her endless vacuum of need. *She dumped me.*

"Nobody loves me!" was the sorrowful lament that always dragged me back into her life. My Mormon upbringing brought with it a distortion of what forgiveness and love means when you have dysfunctional people in your life. Back then, I thought it meant that I still had to be her best friend in order to forgive her.

In dire straights after a year or three, she called with her *Nobody loves me!* refrain and hooked me briefly again. This time it was her defense of her anorexia, in the guise of offering me parenting advice that I found intolerable. I unfriended her on Facebook and stopped talking to her.

She resurfaced again after reading a blog about my attractiveness and her being a big fat meany. She threatened to "out" me all over the Internet.

"Take the blog down, I didn't mean it, I was just feeling threatened," she wrote in another email after I "outted" myself. Viveka is always threatened.

"Too late. Don't ever contact me again," I wrote back. The feeling of freedom was liberating. I had made a powerful move in Emotional Chess by claiming my own past in public. It was cathartic to simply state my sins and flaws and boldly stand in my own power as someone who has lived and made both good and bad choices.

❧

HOWEVER, I HELD THINGS BACK. In service to others' feelings and in service to my own shame and my well-cherished identity as *Horrible Friend* and *Unworthy Whore.* I did not disclose the two men I kissed right after I married Alex (or maybe it was while we were dating—I honestly can't remember that detail). I felt it would damage our already weakened and shaky marriage to confess to a decade-old indiscretion.

Obviously, I was right, because her email threatening to "out" me on that front worked its dark magic, planting enough seed of doubt that he refused to get in the game of his own marriage and months later confessed that he no longer wanted to be married. Much to my own mixture of relief and terror of financial ruin.

I also did not disclose my major sin against my family. The episode of repressed sexual abuse memories, FMS, the ripples of which still reverberate within my family to this day. My family is so terribly embarrassed by the entire thing. While I believe that my father was, and would have continued to be, a domineering, mean, and miserable drunk, because he was already on that path, it is a certainty that my accusations of rape and sexual abuse exacerbated the problem tremendously.

How does a family come back from that?

The whole family dynamic is "Dad Management." How do we ensure that an unpredictable and volatile head of household doesn't blow up? We don't. But my mother can't seem to understand that. Everyone, myself included, walks around like there is a landmine about to blow. Because there is. The familial belief is

243

that this is *my* fault, because of my lie. My malicious lie. My intention to destroy the family.

I didn't confess this on my blog, in part because of my deep shame, and in part because of my remorse for my family. I had spent one summer in Utah with my two children, nineteen years after the accusations. I was determined to hash it out with my mother and father. After nineteen years I was tired of the burden of having "ruined the family" and being held responsible for my father's deplorable and inexcusable behavior. In my mother's eyes, the root of the problem was that I had turned fourteen and it was a very terrible experience to mother *me* as a fourteen-year-old. That's when I had started destroying her happiness.

"A million choices have been made in the last twenty-six years, Mom. I can't bear this burden forever. You sure are giving a lot of power to a fourteen-year old girl. Your marriage is not my responsibility."

"You ruined our lives."

"I didn't. Your life is not ruined."

"I know you were a victim of that therapy as much as anyone."

"You don't treat me like that. You treat me as though I did this with intention and malice."

"I know."

"Mom, I had been beaten and emotionally abused for two years. You knew. Why didn't you help me? Why didn't you get me help?"

"Therapy ruined our lives!"

"Our lives aren't ruined. Look around your life! You live in a prosperous home, in a prosperous neighborhood. You have a great family. You have friends and a Church that brings you peace. Your life isn't ruined. Our family isn't ruined!"

"I tried to help you. I sat outside your door once and you wouldn't let me in."

"Once? One time?"

"You have to apologize to your father's face. That letter wasn't enough."

"YOU insisted on the letter. Now you insist on an in-person apology twenty years later? It's not going to make him stop drinking and it's not going to make him kind."

"Yes. Maybe it will."

"Okay. Mom, I'll do this for you. But this is the last time I do penance for this. I'm done with this. I'm done playing this role for you."

The next day I found my dad in his garden. "Dad, I am sorry I said you sexually abused me," I said.

"I am, too."

"I hope this isn't why you're drinking."

"It's not. I just like to drink."

"It's not an excuse, but I was messed up. Dave had been beating me and sexually assaulting me for two years. I was confused and broken. I love you."

"I love you, too."

I walked back into the kitchen. "I did as you asked, Mom."

"What did he say?"

"He said that he drinks because he likes it. I'm done with this."

❧

WHEN I WROTE MY confessions of all of the edgy things I'd done, including appearing in *Swank* magazine, dancing at a strip club, having sex with lots of people, having sex with girls, doing drugs, stealing prescriptions from friends and family, and sleeping with Viveka's husband, I was aware that my family reads my blog.

They said nothing about my blog. Which is how they roll. They read it, they absorb it, and say nothing. Mostly, they talk about it with each other, not with me.

The next time I saw my mother I told her that Viveka had blackmailed me into confessing all my sins. But that I withheld the accusation of sexual abuse to protect the family. "She still has this power over me. Eventually, she'll use it," I warned my mother.

So here, in *The Year of YES*, I liberate myself from the last secret that steals power from me like Voldemort steals people's Souls. It has robbed me for more than two decades. The *secret* of it has held me back in a million ways.

The fear of being "outed" as a liar who did the worst thing imaginable to my family has kept me playing small professionally. It has kept me hiding in a corner—knowing that I am being called to a bigger stage, a more visible spotlight in the world—but also knowing that doing so risks exposure. It has taken me many years of healing work and much letting go of my ensconced identity as *horrible friend* and *worthless whore* and *terrible daughter* to be able to write about this episode.

❧

ON THE DRIVE HOME FROM the curandera I confessed the power that Viveka held over me to Neecy. It was cathartic and cleansing. Neecy loves me just the same. I am not *horrible friend* with her. The Universe has generously and kindly blessed me with wonderful friends. The Universe also sent several people from my past back into my life to tell me that I *am* a wonderful friend.

Viveka feels I wronged her. Because I did. She is morbidly anorexic, mentally unstable, angry, destructive, and jealous. I know that she has invested great energy into exacting her revenge for my affair with her husband. But I did hurt her, devastatingly.

I've been pondering who the blond woman might be that works with her. It's possible that she has a friend who is helping her hurt me. I don't know who she has relationships with now. It don't recall a blond woman who we both knew who also has revenge in her heart.

Possibly the blond woman is *me*.

I have exacted revenge on myself, punishing myself ever so harshly, for the last twenty-six years of mistakes I've made. I've placed excruciating judgment on myself and never let myself off the hook for that night in a sleeping bag and my betrayal of a friend. I've placed the tightest bonds of judgment on myself for destroying my family, when I was broken, weak, and fragile.

I gave myself no compassion or forgiveness. I have been exacting and punitive toward that little thirteen-year-old who made one tiny, terrible mistake: She had sex with her best friend's boyfriend.

I can now see her, beaten, broken, scared, ashamed, and so very fragile and young, and I can forgive and love her. She was in deep and serious trouble. No one helped her. My parents didn't help her, though that was arguably their job, because they were angry at her for her rebellious disobedience.

She was so isolated by her original sin and her abusive boyfriend that there was no one else to help her.

When she tried to help herself, she fell victim to pop psychology and well-meaning, but misdirected, forms of therapy that caused more damage than the original traumas.

The consequences were extreme.

But that poor child had no malice in her, except for herself.

❧

WHEN I RETURNED HOME from Cabo—cursed and having sabotaged my not-relationship with Boulder Brad—I immediately went to see C.J., to get the curse lifted.

This came of the session:

"You still have some karma to balance with Boulder Brad. Your connection with him—the reason he pains you so, is that he is reminding you of an old trauma in the second and first chakra/pelvic floor from thirteen, from first your sexual experiences.

"We had to bring this part of you back and tell it, 'You are safe,' 'You can enjoy sex,' 'You can use sex as a tool for spiritual development,' 'It is okay to want more,' and 'It's okay to demand more.'

"You had some nine curses, two hexes, and two vows to clear up—most from this woman and her white-blond friend—through several lifetimes. These correlated with crown chakra, second chakra, and root chakra.

"You have been bringing back many of your missing Soul parts on your own, but not integrating them fully."

❧

IT'S ALL TIED TOGETHER. Girl loses virginity to a boy to whom she is utterly insignificant while betraying her best friend. Girl punishes self for twenty-six years. Girl repeats pattern with best friend. Best friend curses her. New man makes girl feel insignificant by informing her, rather tactlessly, she's "not his girlfriend," he's fucking other women, he's consciously choosing not to fall in love with her, and she's an idiot for having expectations of him. Girl sabotages relationship with man by finally taking the opportunity to say what she long wanted to say to the virginity-taker.

"I deserve to captivate a man's attention. Because I'm fucking awesome. I'm hot, smart, conscious, and I have my shit together.

248

There's no reason for me to settle for being a disconnected fuck buddy."

Beautifully, I had the opportunity to say it to a man who was treating me as insignificant to him—or at least it felt like he was. It touched all my buttons. Love, insignificance. Intimacy. Withdrawal. He was pinging that which needed healing, desperately. Without that old, raw wound healed I would have walked into my next real relationship and likely sabotaged it with my feelings of insignificance.

"This is as important to you as it is to him," C.J. promised during our session. This means that whatever he had to examine, deal with, and heal was also brought up for his own healing. I pinged him as much as he pinged me.

I still hope that we can get together before my wildee time is over, and that I can be with him as a healed woman who has the precious gift of uniting with an Eternal Lover for a snapshot of time during this lifetime. Perhaps that's not meant to be. Perhaps he came only to bring me this gift of healing and that was our spiritual contract fulfilled. C.J. says though that we have more to do together.

I sure hope it's more fun than it has been so far. He's in my Soular System, and I love him. Or maybe I just love the narrative.

❧

THE CURANDERA CAME JUST in the nick of time. It's all connected: the virginity episode and Viveka and the curse. One thing led to another. The feelings of the one incident and the harsh judgment laid down as a powerful I AM statement fed the entire relationship with Viveka, including the pain I caused her, which led to the Curse.

I had declared that I would walk into forty healed. I wanted to be clean and empty of shame, relieved of the burdens of my past mistakes, and unbound by my secrets. I've been working toward this vision of myself with dedication and persistence for the last three or four years. I've been seeking healers and processing past pain. I've been working through and letting go of forty years of psychic garbage. The Universe left me bread crumbs to follow: a passionate and intimate night with a lover, bike taxi drivers, drives down the Baja Coast while jamming Eminem with my loyal and loving friend, Neecy (a friend who I am worthy of), an ex-patriot named Patrick, a drive into the barrios of the Mexican desert, and a curandera named Angelina were brought to tell me that there was one last assignment on the evening before my fortieth birthday.

Heal *this*.

Forgiving that little girl who made that pivotal mistake—literally altering the path she was on with a hard left—is the process by which I will heal and integrate her back into my being.

I forgive you darling, Tracee. You sweet and lovable girl.

You can't understand yet how significant you will be in the world, and the Universe, when you grow up. Right now you don't understand that your mistake led to all of the experiences that followed. It is precisely these experiences that will allow you to help people heal their own pain and have the courage to stand in their power to heal the world. You're a light bringer and you don't know it yet.

Do you remember sitting on the hood of your car at Utah Lake, conversing with the moon, swimming in pain, vowing that you would grow up and help people who were in pain?

You're manifesting that in a powerful way.

You can come back now and stand in your own power. You've developed audacity and resilience. You've been through the fires.

I forgive you utterly and completely. I thank you for your mistake, pain to power. I invite you back into the womb space, allowing you to flourish fully and completely. I honor your sacrifice for the world, for me. I see your vulnerability and I honor it. I invite that vulnerability to be incorporated back into us fully, allowing us to experience the authentic breadth and depth of our emotional capacity.

You are my darling. I love you. I honor you. I forgive you. I cherish you. Welcome home.

❧

ON THE MORNING BEFORE we left Cabo, I went to the ocean.

I went down to the ocean to baptize myself in the womb of Mother Earth, rid myself of the Curse, review the last four decades of my life and call forth what I'm claiming for my next chapter. I was addressing Mother Earth, the Universe, God, and my Soul. And I was being pretty bossy.

I released, I claimed, I demanded, I vowed, I declared what I expect from the Universe, God, and my Soul for the next chapter in my life. I addressed the ocean. Remembering the words spoken over me last year by a prayer group: "You are like the Orca: powerful, enormous, resilient, and unique. God has *traced* (notice the root word of Tracee) your life for you, and it has breadth and depth. You will go many places and do many things; it is not a straight line, but a powerful, complex picture. You are in a tunnel, but you are very close to bright white light and you are very powerful."

I claimed ease. I claimed professional success. I claimed hieros gamos with My Man.

I baptize myself in the salty womb of Mother Earth by my own authority as a Daughter of God, made of God stuff, a Holy Being of Light and Love and Unlimited Power.

TWENTY-EIGHT

AUGUST 20, 2013

'm in grief. A sweet grief to be sure. The kind where you're relieved to find that you can feel the full spectrum of emotion. The kind where it's not so overwhelming that you need to get wasted or consider killing yourself.

Just grief.

Last night, I wept. I was thinking about the concept of meeting a lover from past lives and then losing him so very quickly. *Can't I just have him for a few more weeks?* I asked the Goddess tarot deck I bought at the Red Tent event I put on a few weeks ago. *Just a few more weeks? Couldn't I just go away with him and have him all to myself for a long weekend?*

I drew the two of Earth: Cycles.

The ancient Ouroboros, Goddess Nehushtan, a snake, my phobia and also a universal symbol of transformation and change, symbolizes rebirth, transmutation, change and transformation. Release what's not working to make room for the new.

I then drew the *Patience* card.

Every card I draw is about rebirth, regeneration, renewal, complete transformation, resurrection, death, and illumination, insight, reflection, and following my Soul.

I am on the brink of something.

To get there, I am grieving.

Grieving what?

A poor thirteen-year old girl who accidentally had sex?

A sweet, sweet darling who was so devastated that she punished herself as harshly as possible with a boyfriend who beat her? And then chose friends based on the "fact" that she was a *terrible friend?*

Do I grieve twenty-six years of choices made, based on the fact that I was an insignificant virgin to my first lover?

Am I grieving the end of a twelve-year marriage in which my husband knew me to be so insignificant as to be a sure failure? So sure was he, that he would bet our marriage on it.

Do I grieve the loss of a brief love affair because he was a delicious kisser? Or do I grieve him because I love him and I miss him? Is that even possible or is it a hormone cocktail going to my head? Can one ever be sure?

❧

I'M HAVING PATTI STICKLER, my local favorite artist, paint a very sexy and intimate photo of me with my man in a hieros gamos embrace. I intend to hang it over my bed.

One would think that knowing that My Man is coming right around the corner I would feel less sad about Brad. I don't.

One might also think that having a coffee date with Law of Attraction silly guru Andy Dooley might dull the pain, too. It hasn't.

Neither have the other three dates I have lined up. Well, they might. I haven't been on them yet. The idea of them hasn't set me free from my minor heartbreak though.

Major or minor, I hadn't remembered what heartbreak felt like.

No, there was no heartbreak at the end of my marriage. A million times during the marriage my heart was broken, but by the end I had no heart left for him anymore. It had been deadened by the fact that he felt me insignificant to him and to the world in general. I'm really struggling with the insignificance issue. It's touched a painful nerve.

Stupid Brad.

It's making me struggle with my work. To do my thing, serve my purpose, I have to tell people what I can do and how I can help them in a way that makes them want to work with me and pay me money. To do that, I have to explain my significance.

Explain my significance.

People, truly, can't believe that I am a person with a confidence or self-esteem problem. It baffles them entirely. And I suppose I don't have that issue in the way that other people do. I mean, I feel good about myself and who I am most of the time. I carry myself in a confident way. I feel confident about my skills and my influence. I feel confident in my Zone of Excellence, as Gay Hendricks, author of *The Big Leap*, would call it.

Yet, I find it painfully difficult to step into my Zone of Genius. The Zone of Genius is where I declare my value as a coach and step into my power. The Zone of Genius is where I send off soft letters telling my friends what I do and asking them to pay me for the services I've given away for years.

What if they think me insignificant?

What if they think I'm charging too much money? What if I'm not good enough? What if I'm not important?

This whole thing is JACKING with me. Brad is. The Curse is. My lack of clients is.

Once you start on this spiral, you end up proving yourself right: *I am insignificant* leads to more evidence of it.

That's why I have another appointment with C.J. tomorrow. Then a healing touch session with Anna and a hypnotherapy appointment on Saturday.

I don't know what I'm processing.

Honestly, it feels so big. Like it's the key to this whole insignificance/unworthy thing I've been carrying around my whole life. But I have no idea how to unravel it on my own. None   whatsoever.

What I want to do is to sit in my orange chair silently and sadly. Just being sad for the time being. I don't want to make phone calls, write copy, fix the Internet, or take any action beyond writing this page. I want to sit quietly and grieve.

Whatever this is, it feels grief-worthy.

∾

I WISH I COULD CRY MORE easily. After weeping last night, I did feel better. It felt like a release of something important.

I want to be able to cry. I shut that off so many years ago. During my relationship with Dave Lev, I cried so hard and for so long that I ran out of tears and hardened my heart.

I drew the Kali card yesterday. Kali is the fierce goddess. She is a kickass bitch who gets things done by drawing fierce boundaries and letting old shit go. Kali is a fierce energy that has served me well. Kali energy is the energy I used to get away from Dave Lev in the end.

People don't understand what it takes to leave a lover who hurts you so deeply and completely that your psyche, your insides, your Soul, your selfhood is literally broken. To finally have the courage to leave him—and not go back to him despite his promises of reformation—I had to call forth a fierce, hard core of power within myself. It was a hard energy. One that eliminated softness and vulnerability, out of necessity. This hardness formed around me like a shell. I carried it for so long I thought it was me.

But now I am letting it go. I'm being vulnerable all the time. I'm putting myself in situations where the emotional risks are intoxicating.

Like when I was with Dave, I find that the pain feels good. Again, you might cringe reading this; certainly Oprah might cringe when I try to explain how the pain felt good when Dave was being abusive, physically, emotionally, and sexually. Or maybe she would totally get it. The pain was high-intensity emotion. The belief was that the higher intensity emotion, the stronger the love.

All fucked up.

For sure.

This kind of pain reminds me of that. Grief reminds me that I'm alive. Feeling heartbroken over a man is a signal that I've awakened to my own feelings again. Perhaps Brad is the Prince and I am Sleeping Beauty, and he has awakened me. But I'll go have happily ever after with someone else.

It's such a pleasure to know that I have feelings that weren't permanently deadened by feeling all the things I've felt that I couldn't previously deal with.

Funny that. Pain is better than a dull nothing. Therapists working with abuse victims should understand that dynamic. We'd make much more progress with the problem.

TWENTY-NINE

AUGUST 23, 2013

Just like that, the Boulder Brad hormone cocktail wore off. Well, I'm getting a new perspective on it anyway.

Besides acting like a total lunatic on the way back from Cabo, I also started reading *The Big Leap* on the plane. Seriously. Not even joking about the total lunatic part. I alternated between crazy ranting, in which I was upset with Brad for being inauthentic and pulling away from his feelings for me, and reading. Then I read Gay's explanation about a happiness set-point and self-sabotage.

We only allow ourselves a certain amount of happiness and when we exceed our self-prescribed allotment, which he calls our Upper Limit, we sabotage an area of our lives to return to our comfortable happiness zone. We do this for various reasons, such as not wanting to outshine others, feeling inherently flawed or unworthy, not wanting to leave friends and family behind in the success meter, and wrongly believing that success is burdensome.

With Brad I felt that the Universe had offered me a precious gift that I would have to return fairly quickly. I knew I had to let it go—we both did—but I didn't expect how intensely I would feel for him, nor did I expect how much the hormone cocktail would fuck with my head.

Brad was scared. I got scared. Me. I was trying to be all rational and *I can handle it* and be vulnerable while in this (even though it's not going to last). Then *we* sabotaged it. Since I'm not responsible for his behavior or feelings, the only thing to do is to accept and take responsibility for my part in sabotaging it.

For weeks I've been being a *victim* about it. I thought, *He did this to me. He chickened out. He cheated us out of at least a few more weeks of something amazing.*

Except . . . I realized last night that in the journal I took to Cabo I wrote out an affirmative prayer releasing him from me emotionally and spiritually. I physically "cut spiritual cords" with him. It was the first thing I did when I got into the hotel room. I spiritually cut him off . . . and I never saw him again.

I chose.

Not to be with him was *my* choice.

Even if it broke my heart.

THIRTY

AUGUST 25, 2013

ost-secret Confession: I fall in love with every man I have sex with. Untrue. I tested this hypothesis and it is completely, unequivocally untrue.

It is highly inconvenient—painful even—to be in love with Boulder Brad. I've been heartbroken, truly. I've been telling myself, *It's just because we had sex. Just a hormone cocktail. If I have sex with someone else, the feelings will transfer and I'll know they are not really for Boulder Brad.*

Wrong. I now know that the feelings are completely for Boulder Brad and only Boulder Brad. I know the only way one can find this out: Bad Sex.

❧

THE MARINE IS HYPER-masculine. He was in the Special Ops and he's built like a Marine. He carries himself like a Marine. He has a total Marine vibe. Very, very masculine. He had messaged me several times on Plenty of Fish, the dating website I'm on, and I had ignored his messages because he's just not my type.

But . . . I've been having fantasies about being aggressively taken and ravished in bed. I guess I've always had them, but I've been observing them and judging them for the last little while. I notice that I like dominance pornography, when I do look at porn. Not beating or anything overt like that. But power dominance, such as me being the babysitter or younger girl in a situation where a powerful man has dominance over me and coerces me. I've felt totally guilty and ashamed of these types of fantasies   at times.

I've been OMing with Robert, a local author who is sixty-five and very respectful. OMing is getting better and better. We meet every Tuesday. I'm able to experience the most delightful orgasms, followed by a bubbling up of gleeful laughter, but only if I fantasize about being doubly penetrated by two big, hard, masculine men, or being shoved up against the wall and lifted right off my feet while being fucked madly, or being bent over a very masculine man's knee in doggy style position while he finger fucks my pussy and my asshole, pinching my nipples hard with one hand and talking to me like a slut.

This is the type of fantasy that is making me cum.

I've been concerned with that, because sexual energy is a very powerful energy and I don't want to attract an abusive relationship. Obviously. I want to attract a deeply holy and sacred spiritual union. But where are all of these fantasies coming from and what do I do with them?

I've been exploring the work of David Deida, a teacher of spiritual sexuality. His book *Finding God Through Sex* put my fantasies into context for me. It is my Divine Feminine's craving for a strong Divine Masculine. My very *Soul* is crying out to be taken and ravished by the Divine Masculine. I was married to a very passive and unimaginative lover; he was often apathetic about sex. I have not been properly fucked, manhandled, ravished, and   *con-*

sumed for many, many years. Probably not since Nathan. He was such fun in bed: not at all abusive, but he did ravish me well.

If the Divine Feminine does not get the masculine ravishment she craves, she ends up making terrible choices and accepting abuse from men to get something that resembles powerful masculine sexuality.

If the Divine Masculine does not get to ravish and "take" a woman, as he needs, then he will act out his masculinity in ways that are damaging and harmful: through rape, aggression, and violence. Deida says that if men and women are paired in masculine-feminine relationships where ravishing sex is taking place in a safe, sacred environment, then both male and female are spiritually and sexually satisfied, and neither goes to the dark places of both polarities.

Reading this was like a light going on inside of me. It felt true. It made me feel much better about my fantasies.

I was fantasizing about a spiritual craving for the Divine Masculine to ravish me. It was a relief, really. This means my fantasies are not necessarily going to attract a gang bang, but a spiritually-centered sexual life with a man of my dreams, and it's a clear signal that this man needs to have a strong, masculine presence.

In other words, I'm not fantasizing about double penetration from two big, hulking men, I'm fantasizing about being ravished by my masculine lover in a divine way; the two big, hulking men are just filling space in my brain until he gets here. *I'm fantasizing about being filled up, being fuller, being full-filled.*

So I accepted a date with the Marine. He's a gentleman, a good man, a man who is looking for love and a committed relationship. And he is genuinely into me. After our first date, a lunch, I started thinking that he'd be a man capable of shoving me against a wall and pulling my hair as he fucked my brains out. I fantasized about him putting me on all fours and finger fucking me in both holes. My mind started tricking me into thinking that I could roll with casual sex, just because the fantasy was good. I started thinking, *Hey, this is my wildee time. I should have some fun before my Soul Match gets here.*

So I brought him home and basically asked him to manhandle me. First of all, kissing other men has brought to light just how *wonderful* Brad and I kissed together. We *matched* completely and utterly. Kissing him was blissful. Kissing the three other men I have kissed has been slightly disappointing, full on disgusting and *okay, fine, whatever.*

The Marine is the okay-fine-whatever kisser. It wasn't good. There were parts that started getting me excited. I got on all fours and he spanked me, which I loved because it didn't hurt so much as make a loud noise and feel exciting, while he finger-fucked my ass and pussy. That was really exciting. But he said he couldn't truly ravish me unless he was fucking me.

Inside myself I'm thinking, *Brad ravished me for an entire month with no lack of imagination before fucking me.* I honestly was hoping that fucking the Marine would be as amazing as fucking Brad and would help me get over Brad.

No.

It was actually pretty horrible. His dick was too thin.

Women care. That whole "size doesn't matter" thing's bullshit that works for twenty-year-olds. By the time a woman is in her forties and she's had big cock, it fucking matters. I don't care much whether it's long, because frankly I don't enjoy having my cervix slammed into, but I care whether it's thick and fat. I want thick and fat. The whole entire point of sex is to feel filled up.

The Marine did not fill me up.

Then he just started slamming it into me from behind. *Bam bam bam bam bam bam.* Uttering some nonsense like, "You like that, baby?" And he couldn't keep his dick hard because of medication he was taking for pain. What's with forty-something men and their smooshy dick medications? Come on, science, get it together.

This is his idea of *ravishing*.

My idea of ravishing is a lot more energetic and a lot less banging around wildly.

I was *bored*. Almost immediately.

Then my dog ate my $200 vibrator and I flipped out, and I was over it.

He knew I was over it, because while forty-year old men can't keep it hard and they experience "anorgasmia," forty-year old women are done faking it. I've never faked an orgasm, but I have faked enjoyment of sex. "Oooh. Ahh. Yeah, baby! Cum! Cum! Cum!"

I can't even muster up the faux enthusiasm anymore.

We stopped in the middle of it. I told him it was an energetic thing. "I'm just not feeling it." I thought I could have casual ravishment, but it turns out that it's not a turn on.

The poor man really wanted to wait and develop a real relationship with me. I just wasn't into it. He wanted to snuggle. I didn't even want that. He could tell that I wanted him to leave.

"I know how women feel. Women want to use me for my body," he said. He meant it and it is kind of sad. I guess I feel a little bit bad about it. But not bad enough to pretend that I want to date him or be his girlfriend. I just don't.

It's a spiritual paradox.

I love Boulder Brad. Boulder Brad is bad for me.

I'm heartbroken.

❦

NEECY AND I TOOK the kids to City Park Pool and I was telling her about my heartbreak over Boulder Brad.

"There's a little voice inside me telling me, 'He will not elevate you, Tracee,'" I told her, listing again the reasons why it wouldn't work: *"He's a neurotic whiner who needs coaching, blah blah blah."*

"Tracee! He has YOUR addiction! He will Drag. You. Down! That's the number one reason you should not be with him. You went to REHAB for pills!! Rehab!! Eventually, you'll give in and take something. Do. Not. Go. Backwards! It's not just any old addiction; it's YOUR addiction," Neecy eloquently pointed out.

"Oh my God. I forgot. I forgot about the painkiller, pill, substance abuse thing," I said, jolted into reality. I had told her about the codeine cough syrup he had in his refrigerator, his use of alcohol as a calming agent, his use of marijuana and psyche meds for anxiety. My addiction red flags had gone off. And my higher self was self-preserving enough to tell Neecy about it, so she could throw down if it came to it. I had gone to rehab for Xanax addiction after 9/11 and severe postpartum depression; I hadn't been able to turn off my physiological terror response for five years after witnessing the second plane hit Tower 2. I gave birth three weeks later.

I'd flirted with pain killer addiction in my twenties and my dance with alcohol has come to a head this year.

"You wanted to forget!" Neecy said.

Oh Ego, you sly fuck. Universe, this is a hell of a curve ball. I'm not going down that easily. Throw me a doomed romance with a pill popper who can't control his mind or his anxiety? I'll toss it back.

Brad is for me: who I *was.* A proxy for the boy who devirginized me. A Universal temptation to revert to old ways. An asshole. A mirror for my own filter/non-filter communication style, and an opportunity to reassess how that's working for me. The Rebound Man. A past-life lover come to make love to me between my real relationships—and how sweet that bitter fruit was. A love that spans the space of the Universe, defying time. A spiritual contract come to complete my feelings of insignificance and my fear of being "seen," so I can release them once and for all. Brad is a metaphor.

Brad could have been My Ruin.

THIRTY-ONE

AUGUST 28, 2013

Peaple are invested in my outcome. Though they believe that they mean well—because, of course, *they* know what's best for me—they are invested in a particular outcome that would equate to failure for me if it came about.

I've been taking shit for the painting I commissioned from Patti Stickler. I want a hieros gamos love, a sacred marriage like the marriage of Mary Magdalene and Jesus. A marriage of twin Souls, it's also a marriage with sacred sex. It's a highly charged, passionate romance between two Souls intertwined in bliss and ecstasy. Therefore, the painting is a portrait of me all blissed out with my arms and legs wrapped passionately around a tall, dark-haired man whose face is buried in my neck.

There are red sheets and spiritual symbols of unity in the portrait. It's huge and it hangs over my bed. Art is a highly charged Law of Attraction tool. I posted this exquisite, one-of-a-kind painting on Facebook, both because I am proud of it and because I want to give Patti, a wonderful, unsung artist on a spiritual path, public props. But oh heavens, I offended the Mormons.

Oh, the Mormons! How much of my life have I spent adjusting my behavior, filtering my expression, and dancing around the truth of my life so as not to upset the Mormons. The very same Mormons who would follow a raging alcoholic off a cliff.

The very same Mormons whose sex lives I do not envy.

A Mormon relative chastised me on my Facebook page for exposing my children to inappropriate material by hanging my painting over my bed. Children in this day and age are exposed to very, very damaging sexual imagery every day of their lives, regardless of whether you're insulating them in a Mormon bubble. Sex is everywhere nowadays.

But whatever . . . the point is that it's MY bedroom. I'm an adult woman. I want a spiritual sexuality in my life, and there's no reason I shouldn't have a painting that attracts that hanging over my bed. I talk to my children about sex and I don't do it shamefully or to terrorize them with the evils of it.

I pointed out the fact that I will have sex again, unmarried sex, and that "I will likely do a great many things that she doesn't approve of during our remaining fifty years as family on this planet—let alone eternity—so buckle your seatbelt."

❧

ANOTHER SHAMEFUL SECRET: I voted for Mitt Romney.

It was an attempt to win my father's approval and make him stop screaming at me like he's Bill O'Reilly and stop blaming everything he doesn't like about politics on me. Specifically, I have come to terms with the fact that my family will never, ever approve of me. Voting for Mitt Romney has not curbed my father's vehement hatred for my "women's lib" or my inexcusable "liberal" leanings. Hell, my brother, Jason, is a Mormon bishop and a Navy chaplain and my father recently screamed that he too is a liberal.

In other words, my dad likes placing me in the role of his political adversary, though I, myself, would prefer to never fucking talk about it again.

They disapprove of me, in general. The only way to win their approval is to jump into their "Reformed Mormon Girl" box and stay there chastised and "taught a lesson" by life about the right way to live and the wrong way to live. To be a good girl, submitting to my husband, making stay-at-home mothering the focus of my life, and keeping my fucking embarrassing mouth shut.

I realize that I lived in an unfulfilling marriage for years to appease them. Alex wasn't Mormon, but I may as well have been a Mormon housewife for my lifestyle and the conservative rants I posted on my blog about protecting kids from media. Those made me so much more palatable and easy to stomach than my current situation of "outspoken divorced single mom."

I hated it. I hated that lifestyle and that life and that marriage, and also the fact that I chose it, in great part, to appease the Mormons in my life. And I stayed in it for many years after I wanted the fuck out to appease the Mormons in my life.

❧

TO BE FAIR, the couple in my portrait could simply be embracing and not having sex, but that's beside the point. I realize my family is invested in my playing small. They want me to keep my mouth shut because it let's them project whatever image they want about who I am. They get to keep me in the "poor divorced single mom" box and not acknowledge that I'm fucking happy being divorced and liberated from that god-awful marriage.

They are invested in my being poor because it lends validity to the rightness of women staying married—and staying home— no matter what. They are invested in my playing small in my career because then I not only get to maintain my victim, divorced mom status, but also can give up on my particular career as a "women's libber." My role as an empowerer of other women threatens their perception of the "right" role of women. They are invested in my becoming married again because then they can feel good about my not being promiscuous—rather than being embarrassed yet again about me having a life of what they consider immorality.

They are highly invested in shutting me up. Because when I write and speak I often share beliefs and values that are different from theirs. They live in an insular world where they are "right" and everyone else who has a more expanded view about religion and spirituality are "wrong."

I can respect their life choices because they work for them. Well, with varying results, honestly. As rule followers, having all of their choices premade is good for them, as it grounds them. It makes them happy—well, it makes them focused on a united goal anyway. Awesome.

I don't know why I expect the same courtesy from them, or any of my other Mormon relatives. I really shouldn't. It's an unrealistic expectation because their very belief system *has to* make me *wrong*. There can be no other outcome for them. They can love me. But only in the "wrong" box. They can pray for me and try to shove me back in the "right" box. They can feel sorry for me. They can *tsk-tsk* me. They can judge me. They can try not to judge me, as good Christians must, while shaking their head in dismay. They can love me anyway. They can be scandalized by me.

What they can never do is *approve* of me.

Yet I've been like a naive girl attempting to gain their approval in every way except by actually going back to the Church. I've filtered, I've adjusted my mothering, I've adjusted my marriage, I've adjusted my career, I've adjusted my behavior, I've adjusted my freedom of expression in a desperate attempt to get them to approve of me. They cannot. It would violate their belief system to *approve* of me.

I now realize that this is an unattainable goal and I hope it liberates me to live the life I really want to live, by my own God-inspired value system. I do not betray my own values. I listen to God's words to *me*, for *me*.

❧

ROB BELL, THE EVANGELICAL pastor, wrote in one of his books, I think *Velvet Elvis*, that he came to realize that his calling was in the creative life and *for him* all else was sin. *For him.*

We come here with a purpose that is only for us. Mine is not to live a Mormon life and win my parents' or my family's approval. Mine is for expression and exploration and, yes, sex.

I feel that part of what I'm here on this planet to experience is sexual. I love, love, love for men to play with my pussy. I love to be touched by men. I love kissing. I love to submit during sex. I love the whole messy business. It has really come home to me that I'm supposed to unite physically with certain Souls, while with others I am not. The sex that Brad and I had was something amazing and special, and it really was a spiritual union of two Souls who are temporarily lost to each other. The sex I had with the Marine to test the theory "I fall in love with every man I have sex with" absolutely was *not* sacred sex. It was horrible.

The point I'm making here is that I hope I can allow myself to be liberated by the fact that my Mormon family and community will *never ever* approve of me and so I am relieved from trying.

I JUST HAD A SESSION WITH C.J.

I really am dealing with something big. Bigger than Boulder Brad. Except Boulder Brad really is big for me.

The #2 lesson that I came into this incarnation to learn is "how to love myself so much that a man can't hurt me."

The original trauma was Brad leaving me for another woman in a previous life. That trauma brought shame to me and a feeling of not being good enough for him to stay. This explains my intensity of feelings and deep sense of loss since he stopped talking to me. It also explains why phrases like "Don't go," and "Stay" run through my head as pleas whenever I think about him.

The spiritual team has said that his leaving wasn't about me. *Can you love yourself enough to let him go?* Was the question presented when I asked whether I could spend the next few weeks in bed with him, having healing sex and being engulfed in his wonderful energy, and experiencing his energetically perfect kisses.

They stated the obvious: that in this incarnation he's not playing at my level. Which really is obvious. But in the Spiritual Realm, when we aren't incarnated as humans, we work together as a spiritual team; that's why he means so much to me. We have a spiritual contract for this incarnation since he had a spiritual debt to pay to me, and the terms of that contract have been completed.

His job was to come bring up my traumatic feelings of not being worthy of love—be it God's, a man's, or my own love—and then to help me get over it by making me confront it.

Oh dear God, why can't you give me gentler ways to learn lessons?

How about so much love running over and coursing through myself that I can't deny the love. Rather than having one of my Soul Mates leave me again?

The spiritual team did promise that my lessons will be bite-sized from now on. They will be more manageable than they have been in my life so far.

Geez, it's about time.

❧

DO I LOVE MYSELF ENOUGH to let Brad go?

Yes. That's the simple answer. I was planning to anyway, because as we've discussed, he is a *terrible* choice for me and I'm forty and much better at making choices. And he's already gone.

I did want to sneak in another few weeks of lovemaking with him because it was so intensely loving, intimate, and delightful. But, yes, I love myself enough to let Brad go now.

The team mentioned that the Big One (those were the words they used) is coming in three to four weeks and he would be here when I was able to love myself in spite of losing Brad.

I deleted Brad's number from my cell phone, hid his presence on my Gmail account, and unfriended him on Facebook. I suppose I should "uncircle" him on Google+ too.

We have a strong spiritual cord, C.J. said, but it looks like a withered vine right now. When she said it, I had an image of a pumpkin vine after the plant has been harvested; it's dead and will slough off. C.J. did some work around it.

There was a connection between my work and my fear of being "seen" tied to this idea of loving myself.

There was also a connection between my first sexual experiences with Junior High Eric. Huh, I just wrote that and never connected him to what I'm going through. I wanted him to love me, but he was too young and immature to do it. I loved him. But I fooled around with his older brother, Shawn. I didn't want to hurt Eric, but I did enjoy the attention and the experimentation of my sexuality with Shawn. For at least a decade after I last saw him, I would smell Eric in my dreams. His smell was intoxicating to me. I felt ashamed of my experimentation with Shawn and unworthy of Eric's love. One night at church camp at a local lake, Eric and I snuck out of our tents and met each other to kiss, make out, and *almost* have sex in the sand. I would've preferred him to be my first, because I truly was in love with him. I never saw him again. He moved to Las Vegas. I suppose he was my first love.

Gosh, I guess there really has been a lot of shame around sexuality and being unlovable in my life: unlovable by God because I'm unworthy due to my sexuality. Unlovable by Eric because I experimented with his brother, which I was ashamed of. For that matter, I was ashamed that I didn't expect more from my partner; he was in love with another girl who wouldn't fool around with him. Unlovable by Poly Pete, because he was too cool for me and I was so ashamed of having sex with him and hurting my best friend by doing so. Unlovable by Dave because of my shame about having sex with Joe. Zeke loved me. Period. No shame there, except I didn't love him in that way really, so shame about marrying a man I wasn't in love with. Shamed about Walter Dumberg, because what a fucking loser, and such a sweaty mess in bed.

Shamed, yes, I guess I felt ashamed that the neurotic guy in California that I dated after Nathan dumped me flat—and who then called the cops on me when I went over to his house one day. Shamed that I had sex with people. Shamed that Nathan didn't really want to be with me. Shamed that I posed nude at the Bunny Ranch and shamed that I wrote about it in *Swank* magazine. Shamed that I danced at a strip club for two weeks. Shamed that I had a three-some, well two of them actually. Shamed by my husband for even having a sexuality, or a sexual past. And shamed that I deeply enjoyed most of these experiences. I really did.

Shame. Sex. Love.

For me they are all tied together and they are all unearthed by Boulder Brad. Is that even *possible?* Doesn't that give more credence to Boulder Brad than he justifies? I have no idea. Evidently in the Spiritual Realm it does not. In the Spiritual Realm, it would appear that he is crucial to my growth and has played a highly significant part in me fulfilling my spiritual purpose.

I asked about sex as well. I've been having the dark fantasies of being "taken" and "ravished" by men, sometimes more than one simultaneously. I've been a consenting submitter. I've been craving aggressive-dominant masculinity. I've been masturbating a great deal.

The spiritual team said not to worry about it. That I am really *in control* in these fantasies and I am choosing to heal myself with self-love that isn't shame-based. In these fantasies, I am wanton and shameless. I'm fully making a conscious choice about being overpowered and positively drenched in masculinity.

It's also my craving for a masculine partner who can match my power and intensity. I am a powerful woman and it will take a unique and very special man to match me in every way. I am craving that, not just in the bed, but in my life as well.

They also said that the extra weight I carry around is protection to prevent myself from being hurt by others. But gladly, I don't need it anymore. I'm letting it go. I'm ready to do it rapidly.

The mantra for me now is this: *They can't hurt me, I am love.*

This information ties into everything I've been going through. My fear of being seen lest I be hurt, my fear of playing big in my business, my unworthiness issues, my curse with Viveka and my fear of being exposed, my fear of not having my family's approval, and my shame for having a sexuality that many won't approve of.

All is well. We did a ton of work today and now I need to integrate it and experience the relief of healing it. Two significant parts of myself are integrating—one part in my pelvic floor (hopefully this will eliminate that incontinence problem and make my pussy orgasm multiple times within five minutes) and one part in my heart. These are big pieces of me, too.

I am preparing the way for the Big One to come into my life. The spiritual team said he will come to me in my dreams. That I have a stronger and deeper connection to him than I do to Boulder Brad. That he will be amazing! That we will have even better chemistry and energy between us. He's coming in three to four weeks, and this work I've been doing lately, all this grieving and letting go and healing, has been preparing me for being able to receive him and have an open heart ready for him.

THIRTY-TWO

SEPTEMBER 5, 2013

I n bare feet I stand on the worn dirt, holding a wooden water basin on my left hip, next to a brick well. I have a luxurious, wavy brown mane and I am quite stunning. I am wearing a farm dress with a white apron. The bump of my belly confirms my pregnancy of only a few months.

I look toward our wood cabin to see our children playing happily on the large front porch. There are ranch fences containing cattle, chickens, and pigs. A large garden supplies our table. When I look at our land, I am confident and happy. This is our domain. We run this place like a well-oiled machine. I feel blessed by this land, by our home, by our children, and most of all—by our love.

I enter the cabin to see Brad sitting in a wooden chair looking forlorn and contemplative as he takes off his work boots. He brightens on seeing me. I set the water basin on the table and sit at his feet, laying my head in his lap, clinging to his legs. He pets my hair, playing with the locks. We are sad. He is leaving and we know we will never see each other again.

That night he takes me to our bed. We have made love in this bed every night for many years. He takes my face in his hands and holds my gaze as he enters me. A thrill of electricity shoots from my pussy to my heart, running up and out my brain. It's a whole-body orgasm. As he thrusts in and out of me, our lovemaking is mixed with glory and grief. We move in time together, our breath exactly matched. We kiss very intimately as we make love. It thrills me now as much as every other time since I married him. Our tongues and lips move in such synchronicity that it feels like a holy experience. I weep, knowing he will leave me soon.

His heart melts into mine, opening my heart completely to his. Our Souls mingle and dance together, energies so intertwined that there is no separation between us.

The next morning I sob as he gets in the wagon to leave. I will never see him again. It is a betrayal. I am devastated, completely and utterly. I am desperate to make him stay.

Don't Go! I reach for him.

{{{{{{{{{{Stop, *you don't have to relive this moment. When the baby is born, what do you see there?*}}}}}}}}}}

I am on our bed. There is a midwife and another woman next to me, encouraging me. He is not here. He is not coming back. I grieve and sob during labor.

{{{{{{{{{{*Rewind back to the moment when you knew he would leave*}}}}}}}}}}

I am slamming things around the kitchen. I am furious and shouting. He has told me he is leaving, maybe for a war or some kind of duty. I know he will never come back, if he goes.

"What if you never come back? We need you! You can't go! I won't allow it. You can't abandon your family. What kind of man abandons his family? You said you'd always take care of us, always be there for me! What about that? Don't do this! Don't go!"

{{{{{{{{{{*Now rewind to your everyday life before he said he was leaving, what was that like?*}}}}}}}}}}

We are making love. We stare into each other's eyes. His are pools of adoration and never leave mine. We are connecting deeply; our love is intimate. There is no fear, embarrassment, or inhibition between us. We are home when we are in each other's arms, especially when we're in this bed. This oak bed is our love altar, our lovemaking is communion. No matter what happens during the day, we come together in this bed at night to play and enjoy the depth of our love for each other. Our love is so deep it fills every part of us.

He buries his hands in my hair, giving it the perfect tug as his tongue enters my mouth, his penis thrusting deeply inside my wet, open pussy. It makes me whimper. The pleasure makes me submit to him in the most erotic and delightful way. My hips move in time with his thrusting. We are synchronous in our breath and movement. We are so comfortable with each other that we are one when we make love. Our Souls blend to such a degree that we can't tell self from other. We have been doing this every night of our marriage with as much joy and intimacy as could ever be imagined.

I am not an inhibited lover with him. I roll over on top of him, pulling him deep inside of me. I lift my body enough so that he can see me from pubic bone to my eyes, which never shift from his own. We make eye contact as I move him inside of me while I stroke my clitoris with my left hand, and hold myself up on his chest with my right hand. His hands grasp at my breasts, pulling at the nipples. I feel seen by him and it makes me feel sexy, loved, and insurmountably valued by him. The way he sees me when we make love is an ecstasy unmatched. I quiver and shake in orgasm after orgasm. When he cums deep inside of me, we lay entangled together, satiated and contented.

We love each other deeply and open our hearts to each other without reservation. Our trust is absolute. We love our farm and we love our children. We work side by side enjoying each other's company, laughter, and conversation. We are husband and wife, and enjoy our roles immensely.

{{{{{{{{{{{{Rewind to the moment when you met.}}}}}}}}}}}}

I am leaning against a ranch fence. I am young and beautiful, and wearing the biggest grin as I flirt with him. He's young and strong and funny, with a wide, infectious grin.

I am going to marry this man. I will have this man's babies. We will love each other deeply. Our connection is instant.

{{{{{{{{{{{{Okay, now I want you to fast forward through your life with him. I want you to see yourself get married and have his babies and live on your farm and have great sex. But this time he doesn't leave. This time you see your whole life with him all the way to old age when your children are grown and you have grandbabies.}}}}}}}}}}}}

Scenes of joy flash through me. A moment laughing. A birth. Snuggling a little one. Watching him bounce a baby. The smell of baby hair. His kiss. His teases. He coming up behind me in the kitchen for a little nudge and snuggle. He whispering that he loves me in my ear. Me declaring my love for him passionately. He lifting me off my feet in an embrace. Our children running under our feet. Working in the fields and bringing in cows from the pasture. Our children grown up. Our daughter as a teenager. Our daughter bringing home her baby to see us, walking up the porch, us bright with joy. Our children moving away. Coming home with their own spouses and babies. Us making love night after night in complete joyful union, never tiring of the pleasure of it.

I see us old and wrinkled, in matching rockers on the front porch of our well-lived-in farm house. Our family, robust now, surrounds us. We are happy. He reaches for my left hand and pulls it to his lips for a gentle kiss, as he has done a million times before during our long, long love affair.

I see him pass, I know I will soon follow and we'll be together again in the blink of an eye. Our love is eternal: timeless and without form. Oh what a beautiful, great love we have had!

{{{{{{{{{{{*I want you to go to your deathbed. You are ready to leave this human body. It is not a scary or sad occasion, as you know the spirit world awaits.*}}}}}}}}}}}

"Oh what a beautiful Great Love Life I have had!" I say as I leave my body.

I leave my body and shoot—like a shooting star—up through the void into the light, higher, higher! I am free! I am liberated. I am energy and joy and light and delighted to feel this way again. He waits for me and our energies smoosh together, mingled in one Spirit for a time; it is ecstasy to be with him in this way again. I have a joyful reunion with others.

{{{{{{{{{{{*All of your Spiritual Team is with you; your guides, angels, loved ones, and Soul Partners are there. They are telling you something. What do they say?*}}}}}}}}}}}

"Oh! What a beautiful great love I have had!" I rejoice.

"What a wonderful life that was," Brad and I marvel.

"You are love," I hear. "You ARE love."

I am love.

I am love.

I am love.

I AM LOVE!

Patsy Dollar, the past-life regression therapist, pulls me out of the trance over the electronic waves of Skype.

"You have a Soul contract with this man. But it needs an expiration date. There is someone else for you, but that life with him was so beautiful and wonderful that you want to cling to it, to get it back. You are love and you can have that kind of love anytime you want. But someone else is coming who is waiting for you to let go of this. He will just keep circling until you let Brad go,"

Patsy explains. Her plan is to guide me through a short meditation where we will have a contract signing ceremony, and we will put an expiration date on the Soul Contract when we sign it.

I walk through a garden until I come to a stairwell going down. At the bottom, there is a door—always a red door. I open it and find myself in a well-appointed office with a red, velvet settee and walls lined with expensive, leather-bound books. I giggle as I watch myself assume a position behind my executive desk. It strikes me as amusing that I've chosen an office of importance, learning, and power as my contract-signing headquarters.

Brad comes and we embrace. We hold each other and kiss. It is less passionate than our earthly joining; we are more like very intimate friends: deeply connected, but the passion we had in that incarnation and this one is missing. It feels normal, not tragic.

Patsy invites all our spiritual guides and angels and the rest of the God team to witness our contract. We excitedly exchange information about our agreement—none of which I can hear—and then we scribble it down in the contract. We are excited about this; doing this feels really sweet to us. It is like a fun game that we have agreed to play together during our next incarnation. We know no one can get hurt and we understand the outcome, so we aren't the least bit afraid or sad about our agreement. I am particularly excited about getting down to this lifetime.

We bend over the contract and sign our names and very intently add the expiration date of our Spiritual Contract.

Tracee Sioux, September 5, 2013

Today.

There is a party to celebrate. We do a little dancing. There is glitter confetti. I am joyous. I hug Brad and tell him I will see him soon. We kiss briefly. I think: *Yay, I get to go be Tracee Sioux now! What a fun incarnation, I love being Tracee. She's such a fun person to be. So much life, such interesting things to learn, such a big stage.*

I come out of the trance feeling peaceful and euphoric. Through the reflection of Skype I look glowy and relieved.

"When you think about Brad from here on out, you remind yourself that the contract is now complete," Patsy says in her singsong Tennessee twang. "You are love and you can access that love anytime you want with anyone you want. He's coming, you're ready."

I had a Great Love. How wonderful it is. Best still, I have been promised another for this lifetime and I'm on the brink of it.

I *am* love.

I can feel it now.

THIRTY-THREE

SEPTEMBER 11, 2013

Random bits.

I'm having orgasms while OMing with Robert, every Tuesday at 6 P.M. Each orgasm is followed by joyous laughter. This happened a few times with Brad, too.

Orgasmic laughter. It's is like a bright energy bubbles out of me, like popping a cork of champagne. It feels like riding a roller coaster or that scary-ass swing at the Adventure Park in Glenwood Springs. It comes straight from my vagina, or maybe my kundalini energy. It is a de-light-ful release. Robert says his late wife experienced the same phenomenon and he finds it glorious. When it happened with Brad, he was confused by it.

Bursts of laughter are also happening at other times. I'll be driving along and think about how I blew up my summer romance and I will burst out into laughter at the absurdity of it.

I am getting a great deal of attention from men. They are flocking to my online profile. All day long I get notifications of people "liking" me and wanting to "meet me." Several messages a day pop into my inbox with men telling me how wonderful I am.

When I go out dancing, the most attractive men come to make out with me. It's fun. I enjoy the attention.

Concurrently, I'm weary of it. I'm no longer satisfied by flings or lackluster kisses from intoxicated men who aren't My Man.

Kissing Brad first—and experiencing our electric energy and synchronistic kissing—ruined me for average energy and unmatched or even gross kissing. Within a kiss or a date, I know without a doubt that these men are not My Man. They are nothing special. They are attractive and successful. But they are not my *match*.

I was explaining to Robert what I was looking for, and I said, *I am done dragging men up the hill like boulders. My Man has to be on the mountain of enlightenment of his own accord. He has to elevate me.*

"Boulder" Brad. Connection made. Every time I draw from my Goddess Tarot Deck, cards such as *Failure, Manipulation,* and *Depletion* come up in connection to him.

I've been asking my Soul to do healing work in my Dreamtime, and to speak clear messages that I need while I sleep.

"Move as solidly as possible through time," I heard, almost audibly, yesterday morning in my waking sleep. Over and over, I heard it, until I wrote it down, *"Move as solidly as possible through time."*

I took this advice to mean that I should not leave my body completely, but stay a solid mass, rather than pure energy when I'm time traveling. It was advice.

I'm getting used to the idea that I am time traveling—both in my Dreamtime and also in the past-life regression and hypnosis. In *Conversations with God,* God describes time as parallel: All things are happening at once and we live simultaneously on different planes of time. We are choosing to experience one lifetime when we want to, or when it is most beneficial to us. This is a hard concept to grasp, but I think I am starting to get it. This means that in a parallel Universe Brad and I are deeply in love and contented, which is why he pulls me in; but in this lifetime, someone else is meant for me.

Tomorrow I will do another past-life regression, and I'm excitedly curious. This one will be different from the last one. I *knew* what I was going to experience in the last one because I had already had flashes of myself in that life pleading, "Don't go!" laying my head in his lap in our cabin with him stroking my hair; and the intimacy and beauty of our lovemaking in our oak bed. Tomorrow I have no idea what I'll experience, but I will remember to stay a solid mass. I hope it has something to do with work. I want to be able to be free in my work.

I asked God, "What is the one thing I should do to get more clients?" and I drew the fool card. Lest you think this is bad, the fool card in the Goddess deck signifies allowing the Wild Woman to express herself freely, rejecting conventionality.

Do I remember how to do this? I can't, right now, think how I should go about rejecting conventionality and allowing myself to dance through life. I feel too introspective and grounded. I am trying to shake it up a little and get out of my patterns of habit. I'm putting myself in the way of My Man. I'm working in coffee shops, which I rarely do. I am doing Crossfit training, which many men do. I am going out dancing, which I love, but which also attracts drinkers—and that's a deal breaker for me.

Deal Breakers

Substance use
Tobacco use
Under employment
Spiritually asleep
Boring
Can't talk
Unemotive
Unattractive

❧

LET'S TALK ABOUT BEING attractive. In my twenties, I was attractive. I had plenty of interest from men. So much, in fact, that I avoided interest from men in a lot of ways, like dancing all night at gay clubs where the men were only interested in each other.

Now I am forty and I've moved into the "top tier" of attractiveness. By the time you're forty, if you're not putting in the work and taking care of yourself, the body goes downhill. I put in the work. The fake weight of forced immobility breaking my shoulder, and high-stress fat is vanishing quickly. I'm back in a size 8 and expect to hit a 4 by January. I work out daily, doing kickboxing, yoga, and Crossfit. I spend money on looking stylish and having good skin and great haircuts. I get my vag hair lasered off. I meditate, get enough sleep, and take care of myself emotionally.

My Man cannot be an average-looking man. I want one that tries as hard as I do. I want a man who makes me want to do gymnastics all over his body. I want a man that I love looking at day in and day out. My Man is HOT! And tall. I want a man who can pick me up and make me feel tiny. Yes, yes I do.

❧

MY WEBSITE MADE *The Today Show*. I was quoted on a piece about styling children's hair. Fun, it produced no clients.

I am energetically holding clients off because I want to—or need to—build a structure in which to catch clients and funnel them through a system. I foresee a flood of clients in 2014. I feel my business will really take off at the beginning of the year. I feel it in my bones. Which gives me less than five months to get all of my structures and systems in place.

I want worksheets and programs and packages and calendars and workflow systems in place, so that I don't have to reinvent the wheel every time I get a new client. I also would like to have a passive income, online courses to sell both as an entryway to my services, and also to collect cash while I'm sleeping. And I need time and space to develop these tools and structures.

I have quit my menial marketing work because it was time- and energy-sucking and keeping me from having the space to do the genius work of developing programs and structures.

Quitting was Cliff Leaping—but that doesn't scare me any-more. I even went out and bought the exact Cole Haan, Nike Air black leather boots that I wanted last year. Without batting an eye. Those boots are mine!

Money will come. I've developed faith about it. I don't know why exactly, but the Universe requires release and cliff jumping before it grants new and exciting things.

Want better work and more clients? Release the crappy work and bad clients.

Simple formula.

It only takes a bit of courage—courage that is developed through practice and repeated cliff jumping.

THIRTY-FOUR

SEPTEMBER 17, 2013

*B*ring to me what you want me to have,
Bring to me what you want for me.

That was my half-asleep mantra during my meditation this morning. I felt too tired to meditate in my orange meditation chair. Sleep was grabbing hold of me. I didn't have to take Madigan to school, so I lay back down in the bed, placing crystals (sent to me by Patsy, the past-life regressionist) on my womb, my belly, and my throat. Then sank into a deep waking sleep.

For some reason, I remembered that I am surrendering to my Soul, as that's the point of the Year of YES! I've been resisting how compelling I found Brad. I have been creating mantras during meditation, like, "Bring me clients and My Man." I've been doing all the right things. What I haven't been doing is surrendering to what my Soul wants.

That was one of the primary lessons of my divorce. Resisting my Soul's desire for a divorce was like paddling upstream. It was exhausting and painful—and ultimately futile.

Surrender to it, I remembered this morning.
Bring me the work and clients you want me to have.
Bring me the lovers you want me to have.

Bring me the experiences you want me to have.

I've been in a mental and emotional state between wanting to be deeply meditative and introspective, and coming into a phase of restlessness and feeling like shaking up my energy a little.

I've been buying high heels and going dancing and having sex with Hottie Hank, man candy extraordinaire. Fun, but not spiritually enlightening or connected. He's not present with me, but his body is like a sculpture. He's intellectually boring and immature, and so not my guy—but oh, my goodness, his body is amazing and his cock is delightful. I'm just going with it.

I'm fighting with the Upper Limit Problem that Gay Hendricks describes. I'm torn between wanting to work all the time and "get out there" and just wanting to wait quietly. Something is building in me and for me. I feel I'm quietly waiting for something HUGE to manifest and I'm conserving my energy right now.

I have some opportunities cropping up. For one, I met someone in a coffee shop who began to talk to me, and when I told him what I did, he wanted a meeting with me. Immediately. I'm preparing a proposal to work with a real-estate investment partnership. I quoted them a twelve-month contract with three trainings per month for twelve grand. On the spot. Just like that. Now I have to actually prepare a proposal for this servive.

Is this work I want to do? Is this work my Soul wants to do?

Telling this story on a Facebook group, a contact referred me to an interview opportunity with Forbes.com.

#Yesthankyoumoreplease

We had a miscommunication about the time for our call and how to connect. Hopefully it happens. We've rescheduled for tomorrow.

There's a strange grief that overtakes me suddenly and sporadically. I really don't know what it's about. I feel anxious to get somewhere, but I'm not entirely sure where.

Part of me suspects that my path is more about this book, than about building a coaching business. Writing here pulls me in. It's the easiest, most natural book I've ever written. Dare I hope? Dare I dream?

I can't help myself.

↵

WHAT I'VE NOTICED IS THAT there are certain fantasies that come so easily you know that they are meant to be. Whether it's making love to someone, or an interview with Oprah, or receiving an email with an offer of a book deal from a publisher—or even visualizing writing itself (yes, even when not writing, I visualize it), or having conversations with Boulder Brad (get out of my hea(rt)d).

Some things are just meant for you.

Then there are things that you "want," but they are so hard to visualize. For instance, you might want to attract a certain type of person, because you've made a Dream Man list. Or the Perfect Job list. But it's hard to visualize so you have to try too "hard" for it.

I think I've realized that the things your Soul wants, the things that are meant for you, are so easily visualized that they are practically real. I'm having a spiritual and emotional affair with Brad in my head. But it's not my head; it's like my heart/head/etheric/Spiritual Realm space. It's frustrating and irritating that this is happening, but resisting it and trying to convince myself that he wasn't relevant to me or I'm just being silly and he's not a good man for me to love simply. isn't. working. In fact, I am unbelievably disappointed that I have written so much about him here and that his name has appeared once again.

I'm dating other people and they just aren't having this effect on me. What the fuck is going on? Show up Soul Match. Free me from this preoccupation with what he called my "rebound."

❧

I HAD ANOTHER PAST-LIFE regression session with Patsy. I had no inkling where this one was going to go. There were so many layers and elements that I've been resistant to write about it.

Patsy had me go down a hall full of misty dreamtime energy, and open one of many doors—I opened the red door, as I always do. At the bottom of the staircase I found on the other side of that door, she said there was a guide with me, who was going to help me. "Who is the guide?" she asked.

It's funny, because at this point I had to make a choice. The name Mary Magdalene came to me immediately. But it sounded crazy. It was such a serious leap. The choice then was whether to go with it and trust my own Soul's experience, or to question it and resist it.

I chose to go with it.

Then I experienced a blending with the body and mind of Jesus. For half a second, it was as if Jesus was me and I was looking at Mary Magdalene. But then I didn't allow myself that experience. I removed myself and stood outside of Jesus and observed the intensely intimate flow of energy between him and Mary Magdalene: hieros gamos, the sacred marriage.

It is my belief that Jesus and Mary Magdalene were joined in a sacred marriage of Twin Souls, that the intimacy was "complete," the sex was deeply sacred and their love spanned across the space of time throughout the Universe. I. want. that. It is my romantic ideal. It is the type of love that I shared in the other life with Brad and I want it again. I experienced the energy between them: It was visible and tangible, like a sound wave force or a tunnel of magnetic pull. It was blue and purple, and very power-ful. It was like the power that propels the entire Universe.

Patsy had me go with Mary Magdalene. I found myself in Je-rusalem, a bustling dusty town in the desert, filled with barren homes with cut-out windows. Everything was beige and built of natural clay/dirt. It wasn't a beautiful place, but it was a place of energy and commerce. I was wearing golden sandals and a beige, belted robe. My throat started to hurt and feel scratchy, like I had been screaming with grief.

I saw myself reaching out for a baby, who was being taken from me, a son. The entire city was screaming in devastation, like me. Mary Magdalene was with me and it was comforting. With her presence, it felt as though I knew this pain was only temporal, temporary, and ultimately inconsequential.

Again, I had to make a choice. This was surreal and obviously a story I knew before from the Bible: Male babies were all killed at the order of King Herod to prevent the Jewish King, the Messiah, from reigning. The story is paradoxical, because we are to rejoice that God protected Jesus from the infant slaughter, but what are we do to about the fact that all the other babies were ripped from their mothers' breasts and brutally murdered?

Is it possible that I experienced being one of the mothers of this biblical tale? Again, I had to choose whether to go with the experience my Soul was presenting me or reject it and use my logical mind to declare it improbable, if not impossible.

I chose to go with it again.

When Mary Magdalene brought me back from it, I asked her to heal this grief and pain. It eased almost immediately and I once again found myself soaked in the energy tunnel of the great, vast love of Jesus and Mary Magdalene. I was standing in the middle of it, allowing it to flow through me and heal me of grief and wounds that I've carried for who knows how long, but definitely through many lives. Soaking in that love was luxurious and peaceful, euphoric.

⁂

THERE WAS AN EMBRYONIC child self stuck in my throat, full of grief and shame. Several years ago, I saw her trapped in my womb, curled in the fetal position, during a meditation in an Art of Feminine Presence meditation I did. She is the girl who had sex when she was only thirteen years old, the girl who bore intense shame about being "unworthy" in the eyes of family, friends, God, and self. She is the girl who betrayed her friend and had sex with a boy to whom she was entirely insignificant. She is the girl who came back to her body and to her mind—after floating in the ether in sexual bliss—to the words of the boy, which have reverberated through her body a million times during sex ever since, "Let yourself cum." Oh what a struggle it's been to "let her cum."

This is the girl whose shame led her to the harsh and unrelenting judgment that altered the course of her path for over twenty years. This is the girl I've been trying to heal for three years. This poor, sweet thirteen-year old girl. She moved from my womb to my throat.

All tangled up in her shame is the fact that she's sexual and loves being sexual and wants to be sexual. The fact is that during the pivotal moment of her life—the loss of her virginity—she was extremely sexual. She was, for the only time, completely "out of her mind" with sexual inhibition and sensuality. When he invited her to cum, it shocked her back to reality and created a moment of shame. She wants to be free to experience her sexuality again.

Mary Magdalene understood that. She soothed and invited the girl to feel sexual and to enjoy her body. There was a definitive sense that sex was one of the gifts that her Soul had come to experience. That her joy about it was part of the fun that the embodiment Tracee Sioux gets to play with. That her body is the playground that she's allowed to . . . no . . . that she's *supposed to* experiment and play with. Mary Magdalene invited her to enjoy sex and to be in it and to stop holding back. I soothed and invited that little wounded girl as best I could.

❧

I FELT HANDS AROUND my neck, a sexuality that was dominating in nature. I wanted the experience of sharing sex with a powerful man, but I had no context for that when a man isn't dominating and violent. I was feeling a man behind me, overpowering me, dominating me, and being aggressive with me.

Patsy asked me to take this feeling off like a scarf or a wrap around my neck and burn it. I did it like a proper witch—with magic. I took it off and tossed it into the fire and it burst into flames. I quite enjoyed the magic of it. *Poof!* I enjoyed the powerfulness of it too. *Poof!*

She then said she felt there was more, there was something that is DNA deep and she wanted me to take it off and heal it.

❧

I HAD A DISTINCT visualization of me unzipping and stepping out of an entire layer of body, like a human suit I was taking off. I left it on the ground and walked away from it. No remorse there.

Patsy asked me if there was anything else in my throat to heal. I told her there was still a tiny piece of grief there. Like an acorn. Before Patsy could tell me to do anything with the acorn, I had opened my palm, and it instantly popped into a giant, beautiful, full oak tree that sat in my palm. Magical and powerful again. *Pop!* Instant manifestation from seed to full-bloomed bounty.

Patsy said I could ask Mary Magdalene for a gift to take back. I chose multiple orgasms in under five minutes. Truly, I am woman in my sexual prime and I want to experience this delightful body of mine fully and with the utmost pleasure and inhibition.

I also asked for a website logo.

"Is there anything you still need to do here?" Patsy asked.

I wanted to soak some more in the hieros gamos energy of Mary Magdalene and Jesus. I had insights that the pussy is the portal for the entire Universe—the creative mechanism of joy. That's why men want to go inside of it. It's also why I want to experience the spiritual sexuality I crave so deeply.

I then saw myself on the mountain.

Meet me on the mountain, I told my Soul Match—My Man— who is about to find me. *Meet me on the mountain.*

I then saw us both holding hands and looking up the mountain of our spiritual path, both eager to go up, eager to enjoy the journey together, joined in unity for the ride and experiencing hieros gamos. I know he heard me through the spiritual ether of time and space. In fact, I wouldn't be surprised if he saw the vision of us holding hands on the mountain during a dream or a flash of visualization.

❧

YES, I THINK THERE are some things that are meant to be ours. Some things that are so easy to visualize that it is as if they have already happened. And maybe they *have* already happened.

Find me! Find me!

I have said this inside myself quite a few times since meeting My Man on the mountain. I keep looking at men's faces online and on the street and a thought comes to me, *Are you my lover?* It's a reference to P.D. Eastman's children's book *Are You My Mother?* It just comes from somewhere deep inside of me.

Find me!

I have just been allowing the experience to seep into my psyche, Soul, body. Just resting in it, trying not to deconstruct it or "make sense" of it. I'm growing impatient though.

❧

THE OTHER DAY I WAS having a conversation with Brad in my head, and I had this thought: *What if I'm not talking to Brad at all? What if I'm really talking to My Man, who I haven't met yet, but who I am already deeply psychically connected to?*

It's a fascinating thought, isn't it, that I want to tell him about my day already? That I am deeply connected to him because he is so close to me that I can already feel his presence and I am already making him part of my life. I can see us waking together on Christmas morning. I can see us making love intensely and passionately and presently. I can see us experimenting. I'm so ready to have the whole thrill of it.

I have had a thought, not a warning, but a nice piece of advice from my Soul: *Don't rob yourself of all the good stuff, Tracee.*

The good stuff is the getting to know each other, the ascending in love, the dating, the making out, the anticipation of when he'll call me, the vibration of excitement and adrenaline, and the feeling of letting it grow naturally.

I realize that there are delicious, wildly delicious experiences that we get from being human and I'm feeling rather blessed to be gifted another wildee time and ascension into love experience. These earthly experiences are exciting and delightful and they bring such joy. They are some of my favorite things.

THIRTY-FIVE

SEPTEMBER 19, 2013

When I got to my energy work appointment with C.J. yesterday, she had downloaded a ton of information that my God team needed to work on with me.

Driving up to the building, I felt deep grief wash over me. It's hard to describe having feelings just wash over you. I suppose everyone has such feelings and we've been trained to write them off, or as I do, to look for something in the present circumstances to explain the feelings so we can justify them. What many of us don't realize is that they aren't even "of this world."

They could be another person's feelings that have leaked onto us, like residue from an oil spill; they could be feelings floating around in the collective consciousness (or unconsciousness), and if you're open enough, you just pick them up. Or they could be issues from another of your Soul's lifetimes needing attention, fucking with your present circumstances. But if you're not taking a journey into Crazytown of the Soul, you'll just keep recycling those feelings for eternity, never pinning down their cause, never sifting through them enough to move on.

You'll just be driving in your car, as I was, and have a wave of intense grief come over you and it will be about someone or something that doesn't match your grief; or maybe it will be completely out of place and you'll think, *Is this depression? Maybe I should see a doctor?* Or it could be anxiety or a lack of confidence that seems to bop you on the head from out of nowhere.

When I went into C.J.'s office, I was irritated and frustrated that I was still thinking about Boulder Brad. I mean, I dated the guy for the month of July and he wasn't even that nice to me really. He gave me a lot of attention when he wasn't getting sex, then he immediately felt like I wasn't the One, he hurt my feelings pretty seriously once, he was hypercritical and picked me apart in minute ways, and he rubbed in my face that he was fucking other people (chronically talking about other women when he could have just been kindly discrete, *like normal people*), and repeatedly told me how connected and in sync we were, and dove deep into intimacy with me, while creating a weird "you're not my girlfriend" dynamic as a disconnect. I never did figure out what I was supposed to do with that. What's to love here?

It is frustrating to me because I am being pursued by other attractive, successful men who don't have social Tourette's syndrome and don't pick me apart, but instead flatter and praise me—but I'm not hung up on them. I vowed not to even talk about Brad when I got in the office.

C.J. started reading from notes, explaining that this is a very deep Soul Wound that needed to be healed, that I had been so affected by this experience in a past life that it's taken me several past lives to try to work it out and get over it.

My guides said: *You ran away with a man, defying convention, that your family disapproved of, against their orders. You did it to escape from your family and to escape convention. But when you were with this man he belittled you and became emotionally and verbally abusive. He did not like it when you let your light shine. So you pushed your light down into your belly, your womb space, your sacral chakra, where you have been having all of this blocked energy.*

Your belief is that you will be punished if you defy convention. You will be punished if you let your light shine. You will be punished if you allow people to see who you are.

You've been repeating this pattern, and you've been repeating this pattern with Brad; he's helping you see that.

Does this resonate with you?

Does it resonate with me? It's a mirror image of my life with Dave, especially the part about me defying my family and their convention and him hating my light and trying to squash it. I did feel terribly punished for defying my parents' convention—because I *was punished.* They did not pay for me to go to college, while they *did* pay for my siblings, because I defied convention, and, as my mother has reminded me for twenty-six years, "You *left!*" I ran off with Zeke to defy convention and get away from my parents. I ran off over and over again.

Never has a man been okay with me expressing my full light. Forget Alex. I defied convention by marrying him and he did everything he could to sabotage my dreams and deny my light. He punished me and punished me and punished me for wanting to dream big. He told me over and over that I would fail, and encouraged me to—no he demanded—that I quit writing, that I quit having "ridiculous" dreams about making it as a writer or a life coach. He was threatened beyond reason by my big, bright light. He put me down, he withheld love and affection, he punished me with silence and disapproval and harshness. Brad, too, was threatened by me "exuding power," because it made him feel vulnerable. Only this time, I didn't shrink myself much.

Run away with man, defy convention, be punished by him for letting my light shine.

Repeat.

Repeat.

Repeat.

As I got on the table I was once again overwhelmed with grief. I didn't have many flashes of the life she had been speaking about. But I was back in that square, sparse house with Mary Magdalene standing just behind me, and I was grief stricken about my baby being taken and killed. I started to cry as C.J. worked on me and tuned in to my God team.

I hardly ever cry; it's been something I block, I suppose.

As tears streamed down my face and I was racked with sobs of grief—all too familiar grief lately—she said, "Oh wow, guess who the baby is? Brad. Your baby is Brad and you feel responsible for saving him."

Oh, how I have sent him healing energy this past month and a half. I have felt like I wanted to help him, heal him, save him from his own internal demons. I was chastising myself for being too invested in someone I barely knew.

My lost baby in one life, my deeply intimate lover and husband in another. Both sources of deep grief for me.

I shook with sobs of grief, and C.J. had me work on bringing my light from my sacrum up to my heart and my throat. I imagined kissing and holding my baby.

Mary was with me the whole time, comforting me with a great energy of love. Mary says: *"Your baby boy is okay, he's in God's hands."*

"You knew Mary, she was very important to you, she changed your life," C.J. said.

"I know," I said. "I don't know how I know, but I know." I had the feeling of being in on a Revolution with her. The birth of Christianity. I also knew/know that she is the female In-Body-Meant of God, as Jesus is the male In-Body-Meant of God. Both equal in the divine marriage they came to teach of, and illustrate so that we can experience it.

Mary Magdalene was In Spirit. She had to have been, because the mass killing of babies happened around the time she was born. She is on my God team and has been since before her In-Body-Meant as Mary Magdalene and this life of mine.

My God team also said that the conversations I've been having across time and space haven't been with Brad. They have been with My Man, who is showing up within the next couple of days. C.J. says she never gets definitive answers from anyone else's God team, and would be uncomfortable giving such answers because free will can change outcomes.

But I can feel him coming.

Stop punishing yourself for being unconventional. Stop dimming your light for men. Stop your self-abuse. Stop punishing yourself in your work for having an unconventional career.

Stop punishing yourself.

Stop punishing yourself.

C.J. had told me to scream and shout the blocked energy of my womb space sacral chakra to get it to move upward toward my heart, and I had shouted and screamed in my car while running to the grocery store, and back and forth to sports.

When I finally got home—seriously I have to stop going to see her in the mornings on a workday because I was so emotionally drained and shook up—she had sent me homework to integrate the parts of myself that are returning to my body-Soul.

"These are all the statements I am guided to share with you," she said. "The intent is to align your Soul, especially those pieces that have recently reconnected, with all other aspects of self including your physical body. The intent is also to bring to your conscious mind new belief systems to override any remaining belief systems you may still have subconsciously.

"Say them in order. Say them out loud in a quiet space. Say them loud enough to FEEL THEM resonate throughout your whole body/being and OWN EVERY STATEMENT. Feel the power that increases as you go down the list.

"Feel free to make as many noises out loud as you are prompted to:

1. I am not a victim of convention.
2. I once chose to punish myself for my choices.
3. I no longer view my choices with regret.
4. I am proud (feel it when you say it) of my decisions, as they have led me to where I stand today.
5. I affirm that I will no longer suppress or hide my LIGHT.
6. I affirm that I am making choices worthy of my Soul and in its FULLNESS.
7. My fullness and light are no longer served through men who want less than ALL that I truly AM.
8. I stop punishing myself now.
9. My choices are only for the expression of my HIGHEST LIGHT.
10. My spiritual contracts with Brad are complete.
11. I ask my God team to dissolve all remaining unresolved energies between us NOW. (You may get some visuals on this, so allow for a few minutes of them working on you).
12. I will grieve for you (Brad) once more now, then never again. (Scream this out and use words that flow up. Take your time and be sure to grieve for the lost child.)
13. I bring my power, my presence, my light up (from my sacral chakra) through my body now, and I shine it through my heart.
14. Add any other affirmations you have to attract the new love here."

I grieved heartily. Grief just poured out of me as I mourned the loss deep in my Soul and the tragedy of my baby. I spoke candidly to Brad across time and space. I sent him healing energy one last time, pouring my love into him and giving him peace in his scattered mind, whispering, *Shhhh, shhhh* as a mother would for her son, snuggling his little baby self to my neck; and expressing love and adoration and loyalty to him as a wife would to a husband, thanking him for such a beautiful and great love. I wished him well and said goodbye as a not-girlfriend would to a summer fling who had the deeply satisfying pleasure of being made love to in such a spiritual and present union.

I sobbed and sobbed, whimpered and moaned, guttural sounds pouring out of my sacral chakra through my throat. I writhed around the room and danced to Eminem to move the energy out of my sacrum and through my body.

Jake has presented himself to me again these past few days. I broke it off with him again. I dim my light for him. Nathan also had presented himself to me, then he vanished. These are men who did not appreciate my light.

"Let your light so shine before men, that they may see your good works and glorify your Father in Heaven," so says the Bible.

My light is frightening to some people. But I have to let it shine forth regardless of that.

"This is getting crazy," I said to C.J.

When I began the Year of YES! in January, I couldn't have predicted the thin veil between the many dimensions or Kingdoms of Heaven opening themselves up to me. I would not have guessed time travel to be something I would be venturing into. I would not have predicted being healed across time and space, nor being so effected by a summer fling.

Yes, this is a trip into Crazytown. I'm choosing to roll with it because it has something important to offer me.

THIRTY-SIX

SEPTEMBER 23, 2013

I went to the holistic fair yesterday for my annual reading from the palmist Myrna Lou. My progress over the last few years can be tracked through my visits with Myrna Lou. When Alex and I were getting a divorce in spring 2012, I was traumatized. Myrna Lou, during a palm reading, told me that I would have a Soul Match, that I would spend my weekends with my perfect mate running naked through the house. That he would be a full partner for me. He would be successful and bring something to show to the table like I bring something to show to the table. She also told me that I'd be very lucky in my career and that I'd just go up and up. "Don't worry about money," she said.

During that same holistic fair I also visited an unmarked booth of pray-ers. They received inspiration from God and shared it with me. Among the visualizations was an Orca whale—me—vastly powerful being and the ocean being vast and enormous and both representing me. Also a light at the end of the tunnel. One woman reported that she saw that God had "traced" my life out for me, like a child's coloring page, and it isn't a straight line, but has depth and breadth, width and dimension.

I hung on to those readings for dear life over the next year and a half.

Last year for my The Future's So Bright party, I invited Myrna Lou to give readings to all of my guests. During my reading she told me that I would have a wildee time, very brief, where anyone in pants would look good to me. Then I would meet my Soul Match, and he would be the perfect match for me. We would be very happy and he would be a true support to me. He would, she promised, take me away from my wildee time.

On my way to my palm reading, I stopped at the pray-ers booth again. Within minutes, they had me crying. Such beautiful prayers they had for me. All together they said:

"I see you as a wave. You are like a wave that brings refreshment to people around you, you engulf them with your positivity. You work hard at positivity. You don't see things half-empty; you see them full and running over. You are strong in who you are, like the wave. You're not going wishy-washy, you're carrying strength. You make others feel wonderful.

"You are coming into a deep healing time. You're about to find yourself in a meadow, having crested the mountain, and God will stitch your heart back together. All of the broken pieces, where others have used you are coming back together and I can see God taking needle and thread to them.

"You're coming into a period where God will give you a deep sense of peace and you won't have to worry about anything. You'll just be in the meadow and things will be taken care of. You're coming into a time of deep healing and restoration.

"God is sending new people into your life, people who will support you and hold you up. God loves you so much, you are his favorite daughter. I see you with your arms spread, digging your feet in the sand or standing on a cliff. You're ready to have God swoop in and fly you; it's a deep feeling of joy that you can do anything.

"I see you riding a surf board. You paddled out in optimism and joy, but when you got out there the water was stormy and choppy and it was hard. Now God is going to bring you in and it's going to be an amazing ride! You're going to get on that board and God will hold you in perfect balance and you're going to love the ride, it's going to be amazing! God will be standing on shore watching you come in holding a big, high score: A perfect 10!"

My face just ran with tears. I'm not sure why, but this group of people and their praying brings me such peace and makes me feel broken open and put back together again. It felt like God was telling me that he's seen what I've been through, and what I'm going through, and now will make all things easy for me, finally.

Myrna Lou had wonderful information as well. I will marry my Soul Match at forty-two and I'll live happily, in sync, in communication heaven, sexual bliss, joy, and support for fifty years. That will put me at ninety-two years old. She says I could live until I'm 130 years old, so not sure what happens to my Soul Match after fifty years, but I'll take it. I have known him in a past life.

"You'll live," she said. "Other fools will be saying, 'Oh you can't drink the water or eat the food!' but you'll eat it and drink it because you're the type that perseveres and you'll live."

He will have a full head of hair, be buff, a real hunk, be thirty-eight (two years younger than me), live near me, maybe in Loveland or Windsor, not too far, but not on top of me either, have a college degree and a stable job.

He will be financially established, not someone who expects me to pay off a bunch of debt and live off me; be divorced, so I won't be a home wrecker; be healthy, not someone who is sick and thinks I'm going to take care of him.

He'll be very proud to have me on his arm and to show me off as his woman, not like a trophy, but because of who I am.

We'll meet, become friends, date, live together, and get married. My kids will love him. Dating will be easy, marriage will be easy. It will be very good.

He'll help around the kitchen, pick up his stuff, be a real support to me, be good with my kids, and it will be a like-like relationship. We'll react the same way, think the same way, hold the same beliefs, communicate the same way. It will be great for us.

"Your wildee time is over, he's going to come bring stability now," she said.

❧

As I was leaving I realized I was tired. Bone-dog, drag-my-ass-to-bed tired.

The idea of hanging out in a meadow allowing God to do everything for me—without my struggle—sounds like a peaceful and lovely experience. Myrna's description of my relationship sounds so peaceful and sweet. It reminds me of my Great Love Lifetime with Brad, actually. One of the things that stood out for me about that lifetime and that love was that there was no striving or struggle at all. We were content, in joy with each other, full of gratitude, and it was such an easy experience—full of love and happiness.

Everything in my life so far has felt like struggle or striving. Striving has been the positive side of struggle. Nothing has really come easily. I've invested a lot of energy in persevering and achieving in the face of obstacles. There's been a lot of sweat, blood, and tears to get where I am at today.

❧

C.J. HAD TOLD ME THAT I WAS worried I would have nothing to strive for if things came easier.

I realized I hadn't really done the work around that, and that I kind of need money right now. And I'm tired of running. I'd like to just sit in the meadow and meditate with my Soul Match and write about it right now. I think I'm due for a chill. A time of a peaceful healing, not a heart-wrenching tenacious healing. Just a . . . *gentle contentment* (as posted on my dream board).

So let's work it out.

Query: What is keeping me from success?

Answer: I'll have nothing to strive for.

What am I getting out of striving?

I get to feel like a badass. Striving makes a great narrative. People admire striving, I like when people admire me for striving.

I believe there is more spiritual growth to be had if it involves striving. I'm buying into the collective belief about striving being necessary for single mothers.

Striving makes for excellent content when talking about coaching on blog and newsletters.

Striving makes me relatable to other people.

Struggling and striving brings me to my knees and forces me to surrender to God, and I love being close to God. *How will I make it to my knees if I'm not forced there by striving?*

Striving makes me feel like I'm really "working hard," and we all know that's the only fair way to get rich in America.

People feel my success is "fair" if I've strived for it, and I guess I don't want people to think I am unfairly successful.

I get to romanticize the difficulty of my accomplishments, as in: *Do you know how hard it is to get clients, get press, get a job, get every- thing done in five hours?*

People like that I'm a striver; they admire it, and I like being admired.

Striving keeps it interesting, when you work out you have to try really hard to get maximum benefits. *What if having things come easily is boring?*

Things that come easy are boring, there's a striverly belief!

Here's another: *The amount of money you get should correlate with the amount of work, striving, and trying you do.*

Without striving, I won't have a purpose or a direction; and without that, I won't know what to do with myself.

What will I do all day if I'm not spinning my wheels at my computer?

What will I even do with my brain if I'm not worried about where my next dollar is coming from or worried about how to meet my next client or finish my next project?

Aren't relationships a lot of work? Don't you have to try really, really hard and strive to make them good?

There's a great many ways that striving is serving me. I've become such a great striver that I'm not sure who I am if I were to give up striving. Striving has become part of my identity.

But I'm so tired.

Fall is officially here and my energy is winding down and I'm ready to be in the meadow with my lover and have just have God bring stuff to me for a while.

Bring me clients.

Bring me curriculum content for my coaching clients.

Bring me an agent.

Bring me a publisher.

Bring me money to pay the bills and buy what I want.

Bring me the money I need to make shit happen.

And do it without me putting a lot of energy into it. Just voila—manifest.

I'm broke. I'm bored with my wildee time. My psyche is plunged.

Am I willing to give up all of the gifts that I'm getting out of striving?

What am I afraid of?

Worst-case scenario is this: I go sit on my orange meditation chair and meditate/relax and turn everything over to God, refusing to move unless directed otherwise by my Soul or a very clear voice of inspiration saying something like, *Tracee, here is the name of your agent, write, accept offer.* But nothing ever happens and I just sit there, angsty, depressed, embattled. No money ever comes because I didn't go out there and hustle for clients. No one ever publishes my book because I didn't spend every waking minute sending query letters. No one ever reads my website because I don't post on it enough and I don't *blah blah blah*. I get no checks, because, *Who do I think I am, calling myself a life coach?* And I don't meet the man of my dreams because I'm not out there in coffee shops and in dance clubs putting myself in the way of men.

If I were to give up striving how would my life be different?

Things I want would just come to me. I wouldn't have to try to make anything happen. I would never feel time pressure. I'd never feel like I wasn't doing enough. I'd never feel like I should be doing something different than I should be doing (like right now I'm feeling like I should be writing a newsletter about a fortress interlock, and writing a newsletter and writing blogs for the tat removal shop, and writing query letters to agents, and writing a curriculum, and figuring out how I'm going to get a client right fucking now because I'm out of money, and creating a workshop curriculum—right now, in this moment).

If God was bringing me stuff, I'd never feel pressured to do anything I don't want to do, because I'd know that God would do everything for me and I'd have the money to hire someone to do what I don't have time to do and what I don't want to do. I would be able to sit and meditate or nap any time I wanted to (and I want to so badly right now).

I'd wake up in the morning with clients to see and it would be effortless to know exactly how I can serve them. I would have people working for me to do all the busy work and the marketing and I wouldn't be handling that at all. People would respond to my newsletter and press and blogs by *hiring* me. I'd be on radio and television talk shows without my having to go out and search for it.

I'd get everything done faster because I'd have insta-inspiration.

God! I just realized how it would be. I'd be able to give my gift freely. I'd have all the energy I needed to give my gift to people without expending my energy trying to find the people I want to give my gift to.

What would I do if I could do anything I wanted?

I would meet with clients, helping them, encouraging them, and giving them the tools they need to get what they want.

I would write this book.

I would get interviewed by media.

I would have an agent find me and work out an amazing book deal on my behalf.

I would buy what I want when I want.

God, make this easy for me. I'm weary. I'm tired. I want to serve without striving. I surrender my striving nature to you and all of the beliefs that go with them. Make this easy for me.

I've been seeing 111 and 222 and 333 and 444.

And then I saw the brightest, greenest, lowest shooting star imaginable. It was so low I saw it go behind the house in the next neighborhood. It had a sparkler-y tail. I waited a minute to see if one of the houses would burst into flame when the star hit it, that's how big and close it was.

I wish for more clients and my man and an agent and a book deal.

These are all auspicious signs that things are about to manifest for me, and that the angels are looking out for me.

THIRTY-SEVEN

SEPTEMBER 30, 2013

I grabbed \$2 million and stuffed it in a gold clutch on my way out of heaven on Thursday. I was in a Past-Life Regression session with Patsy via Skype and my Soul was feisty.

She got all up in the God team's face and drew some lines in the sand. She was resistant to more psyche plunging. To be fair, she has been plunging her psyche diligently for nine months now, and the poor dear is tired and probably just needs to percolate and process. I knew that, but I didn't want to reschedule the appointment. I went ahead with it, promising my Soul a good break to process and rest as soon as it was over.

She had some concerns that she needed to address with the Universal Mind, the God team, God. Patsy kept trying to direct her this way and that, but she wasn't having it. She stalked into a garden with her Man and sat on a bench, putting her feet in his lap. When a "guide" walked up, my spirit self got off of the bench and started demanding certain characteristics in a man.

This is born of my nagging fear that the Universe isn't going to do me right in the way of My Man. That the Universe is going to make me settle for an unattractive, unsuccessful man, a man not worthy of me. A man who I will be embarrassed to stand next to. A man who I won't be attracted to. You know the story: Woman *not attracted to man, but they become friends and eventually she falls in love with him even though he's an average loser.*

Fuck that. I'm not down with that narrative.

I was embarrassed by both of my husbands and I'd been feeling like the Universe delivered me sub-par goods. Not only were they incompatible men, but they were embarrassing to be associated with in their own way. Zeke, for example, was a fucking drug addict loser who couldn't keep a job or a syringe out of his arm.

I could go on, listing the various embarrassing things about my previous men: not attractive enough, too short, loser, not smart enough, Asbergery, unsuccessful, etc.

NOT. Good. Enough. For. Me.

That was essentially the issue that my Soul wanted to travel to the other side to discuss and she wasn't doing any more psyche plunging until she had her say, listing her requirements one by one. She had been made more nervous by C.J. channeling the message: *"Stay open, because he might show up in unexpected form."* Which I interpret as a Universal trick to get me to fall in love with an unattractive loser, but I'll be so overwhelmed with his energy and lovesick that it "won't matter." *FUCK THAT!*

To further complicate matters, C.J. said two Souls are coming in to vie for my heart. That I asked for something different.

This is true. I have been thinking about the qualities of the men I have had in my life previously, and listing what kinds of energy about them I loved, and what kinds I didn't. I loved Nathan's wordplay, his body, his phenomenal cock, and that he was fun, I didn't love that he wasn't that into me. I loved Jake's wordplay banter, but he was a pussy. I loved Alex's groundedness, but I didn't love Alex's lack of imagination and creativity, his low joy factor, or his resistance to change and risk—and his vision for my life was insulting. I loved how much Zeke adored me; I didn't love much else. I loved how much I was devoted to Dave; I hated how he treated me and exploited my devotion. I loved Walter's bad-boy energy; I loathed everything else about him. I loved my sexual and spiritual energy with Brad, and I liked that he would keep me guessing on my toes forever, but I hated his wimpy neurosis and his tendency toward unfiltered unkindness.

At the end of this list making, I decided that I didn't want any of these energies, so I directed the Universe: *Bring me a man with entirely new and different energy.*

It appears I may have altered the course of the Universal flow with this statement. Now there are two men who will bring me potential lifelong Soul Mate love, and neither is here yet. Perhaps my path is polyamory?

Because C.J. had said that he was going to come in in the next few days, I've been on guard. It's admittedly a strange response. I could be excited and anticipating that a truly beautiful man will walk into my life and change it forever (followed by another truly beautiful man). Instead I'm getting these dating website messages and my Soul is revolting with adamant verbal refusals. *NO! No Way! Fuck that. No fucking way!* has been her response to most of these men.

Part of me is wondering which of my requirements and requests I will have to sacrifice to get my Soul Mate. Not one of the deal breakers: poor, smoker, drinker, druggy, unsuccessful, ugly, non-spiritual, and inconveniently located. I'm just not having it.

When I went into the spirit realm with Patsy, my Soul was ready to revolt against these jokers the Universe is dishing up.

For one thing, most of them drink and my Soul just can't have that—because my Ego likes to drink too much, and has a history of marrying and dating alcoholics and addicts. The rule of no drinking or drugging is the only way to prevent my Ego from grabbing hold of this human experience and driving it off a fucking cliff into self-sabotage oblivion.

Let's just be honest about the pitfalls we face in this human form. Mine is addiction all the way around. My partners' and my own. My soirée with Brad was a warning signal from my Soul and the Universe. I was on board with overlooking his addiction red flags, and my Ego had already started gnawing away at my vows of sobriety, *It would be kind of fun to get stoned with him and have sex, right?* Neecy is right. It was only a matter of time. NO.

My Man has to be completely sober by his own choice that has been made pre-me. It's a deal-breaker. Which eliminates seven-eighths of the men who contact me via dating websites.

Another deal breaker is looks. I spend money and time looking good. I go to huge amounts of effort to buy nice clothes, use the right creams and potions, get a great haircut and color, work out four to five times a week to be fit and healthy, and curvy in all the right places, get laser hair removal for my vag, shave my legs, pluck my eyebrows, put on makeup, get my teeth remodeled. If I'm putting in the work, he should be putting in the work.

I want a man as attractive as me, one that I can be proud of when I stand next to him and introduce him to people. And dear God, please let him own something other than a blue plaid or striped golf shirt. Do not try to shame me for this. I want to be *attracted* to my lover and at forty if men aren't trying it shows.

He has to be playing in the Spiritual Realm. That's where I spend all my time. Oh how I want a man to spend hours with me in bed exploring God, a man to sit next to me in church, a man who shares a spiritual practice with me, a man who can attract things with me, a man who I can discuss the nature of the Universe with endlessly, a man who can uplift me spiritually. I need it. I want it. I deserve it. I'm not settling for the atrocity of nonbelief and non-spiritual alignment.

He must be successful at whatever he does. He absolutely, un-equivocally must have an abundance consciousness and that has to manifest with cash in his pocket. I need a man to elevate me in this area. Someone who will elevate my own earning potential. If he's poor, I will be poor, and I don't want to be fucking poor. I want to be wealthy. I want to have freedom to buy what I want when I want, accept the experiences that I want when I want them, and never, ever, fight with my lover over money. Period.

These are the major requirements my Soul demanded:

He has to be successful!
He has to be smart!
He has to be spiritual!
He has to adore me!
He has to be sober!
He has to be good looking—totally hot!
He has to have a thick cock!
He has to be a great lover!
He has to be a wonderful kisser!
He has to be emotionally open!

At the end of my journey into the Spiritual Realm, I went into a room, the Having Room, this time behind a blue door, and the room was full of gold light. I was in a totally sexy body, with phe-nomenal breasts and a tiny little waist. I was holding a gold clutch. I felt very sensual there. I flitted around the room. There were objects that I wanted that were available to me. There was money, shoes, representations of things I want, essences of them. I danced and danced in the delightful glow of this room. Then Patsy suggested it was time to leave.

On my way out the door, I grabbed $1 million, then I thought better of it and went back to grab another million—$2 million in two bundles of cash—and stuffed it in my gold clutch.

"I'm taking this. And don't you act like you don't know that this matters down there!" I shouted to the Universe.

Patsy had me throw the clutch over a wall back into the physical realm.

She then asked me to look toward a screen and see my past lives flash by and stop at one if there was one that I needed to heal or release.

I held out my palm, in this gesture I make when I'm performing magic, and I said, "You fix it, heal it, release it. Do whatever you need to do with those lives, God. I'm ready for the living. I'm ready for the having. I'm done with the preparing and the healing and the re-living and the fixing. I'm living now. You take care of it, if it needs taking care of; I know that's within your power. I'm moving on to the living."

That gold clutch, not a natural choice for me, sits on my desk now. I walked into the thrift store and it was exactly where I knew it would be. The $2 million is in the form of a check I have written myself and placed in an envelope in my money corner, along with $300 cash. It is written to Tracee Sioux, Law of Attraction Coach and Author, dated 01-01-2016, and the note reads: "From Heaven."

For several days, I marveled at my audacity in Heaven.

It felt like completing a phase for me. Like I made a choice that will carry power and punch.

Bring me my man.
Bring me clients.
Bring me money.
Bring me an agent.
Bring me a book deal.

❧

I'M LIVING NOW.

It's about the *having* not the getting. I'm ready for the having and the living. I've been residing in the trying and the striving and the getting. Now. I'm Having. I'm Living. It's a completely different energy.

This is a new beginning.

❧

I FINALLY REALIZED THAT I did get exactly what I needed when I got with these other men. When I got with Dave I needed someone to punish me for being a *worthless whore* and a *terrible friend*, he did that impeccably. When I married Zeke, I needed someone who would let me have the power and control, who would adore me unconditionally, who would get me away from Dave and my parents. He was superb at all of it.

When I married Alex, I had been having a minor breakdown and was taking risks. I was essentially homeless and directionless. I was flying through the wind and getting battered. I desperately needed grounding. I wanted babies and I needed a good dad. Alex is as grounded as a boulder stuck to the ground that will never ever move. It was perfect. He's now a good dad, so that was a good call.

Brad's sexual energy was pure delight, and he brought up stuff in me that needed healing; he did that exceptionally well.

When I was trapped in Texas, I tried many methods to get out. First I put "California Coastal Town" on my dream board. Next, I put "Portland, Oregon." But I got stuck. Finally, in exasperation I threw up my hands and prayed, *God! I don't know where the best place for us is because I have not been everywhere on the planet. But, I know you know where the best place for us is—take us there NOW!*

This is the art of surrender. Realizing that the Universe really has brought me exactly the perfect man for what I needed at the time I was finally able to turn to the art of surrender.

I prayed this recently.

Universe! I concede, based on the evidence of my Man Past, that I do not know who the best man for me is. I have not met them all. I have not chosen the best ones. I do not know exactly what I need in a man right now. But I know YOU do. I know you know exactly the man, and all of his characteristics and gifts that I need. I trust you to know exactly the man who will make me happy and who will be compatible with me and who will bring me the perfect energy. Bring him to me NOW.

While I was at it, I confessed the same of my clients.

Universe, I do not know who the perfect clients are for me, as I've had limited experience in coaching different kinds of people and companies. But I know that you know the perfect clients for me who will appreciate all of my gifts and talents. Bring those clients to me. And hurry! You don't have to wait until I have $2 in my bank account every time, you know.

❧

I'M FEELING AWKWARD about OMing. And sleeping with other people. It's such a poor substitute for heart-open love sex. That's what I really want. That's really what my Soul craves. I crave My Man. The dates that I have accepted have cancelled and vanished due to my spell: *Bring me My Man and repel all others.* It's definitely working. One man's daughter had appendicitis, another had a flood, another just couldn't make it out of Denver.

Just as well, I've given myself a nasty chemical burn trying to Nair the fuzzy lady beard off my face for when I do finally get to meet My Man. It kept me up all night applying ice packs to the swelling. What am I supposed to do? I can't date a hottie, marry him and then grow a lady beard. No.

THIRTY-EIGHT

OCTOBER 9, 2013

Stop. Cancel. Clear.

I call a complete stop to the "Bring me My Man and repel all others" spell. I get plenty of interest that doesn't materialize into dates. Something comes up.

This is no fun. There's not even a smidgen of mystery about who he could be.

I'm having a very, very hard time surrendering to this process.

Isn't he supposed to be here already? There is one man that I really want to meet, Buddhist Matthew, but he's so busy that he's not pursuing me and I can't get him to meet me for a date. In fact, all my dates have cancelled. Except for the ones I've cancelled.

New spell: *I pull True Love in all its forms to me. Send me wonderful men—fun, exciting, and attractive—to make connections with, including My Man.*

Tracee: *You have permission to have fun until your Man (or Men) arrive. Doors are open for fun and exciting experiences.*

I am not having as much fun as I should be having. Things are manifesting really well. My rebrand and website are coming together. I got a new coaching client who is really excited about working with me.

I'm going to a conference—Emerging Women—with Eve Ensler, Elizabeth Gilbert, Alanis Morissette, and Brené Brown. I even get to go to a private VIP reception with the speakers and only about fifty other people. This is going to be a huge opportunity for me. *Dear God I wish I had my website up and running right now!*

I'm having a difficult time with "all in good time." In God's perfect timing. All signs point to prosperity, love, and wonderfulness. And yet, I'm restless and frustrated.

I contacted Brad. Told him I think about making love to him all the time. I'm frustrated and pissed off that my Soul isn't letting go of him. I've resisted and . . . what you resist persists.

Love attracts love and I'm resisting love by trying to vanquish Brad from my thoughts. Then I'm caving into these beautiful and delicious fantasies of him making love to me. Then I get mad at myself for caving into them. Then I find myself wanting to tell him about something that happened today. Then I get upset and try to focus on who is coming—but I don't know who is coming, so it's hard for me to conjure up an image and feel a connection to him.

Who is he?

Isn't he supposed to be here by now?

I feel I've lost a measure of pride by contacting Brad and telling him how I feel. I feel that he'll be too flattered, that he'll have the upper hand, that he'll have an opportunity to reject me. That he'll be so much better at resistance because of his detachment Asperger-y thing. And all of that is true.

But the Soul wants what the Soul wants. If she were done with him, he wouldn't keep coming up for me on my dating profile and in my thoughts when I'm having sex or when something good happens to me. I want to tell him things that I want to tell my boyfriend.

I just got invited to a VIP reception with some of our favorite authors!
I just landed a new client!
I totally got locked out of the church before my workshop and my attendees had to sit in the car until a key arrived; and to make it worse, I hadn't made copies the night before! It was terrible and still I pulled that shit off.

I want to talk to my boyfriend about all of this. I want him to cheer me on and console me and tell me I can do it.

For whatever reason, my Soul is putting Brad in the boyfriend slot in my head. He's the person I imagine telling.

It pisses me off. But there it is. Resistance is not working for me. I've tried my best to resist having any feelings for him. But I do have feelings for him. I just do. It's just the truth.

We had such a great and beautiful love once upon a Universe. He and I both opened our hearts wide and unfiltered and unguarded to each other. It was magical hieros gamos. I've had it before and I want it again. Whoever this boyfriend—My Man—is, he hasn't presented himself to me and I can't imagine who he is and I'm frustrated about that.

I can't imagine him, so it's hard to get that titillated, fluttering in my stomach about him. Feelings propel what we want toward us. I'm frankly feeling ambivalent. What *is* the Universe going to send me and am I going to like it? Where should I go to meet him? How many men should I date to find him? How will I know it's him? Will I love having sex with him as much as I loved having sex with Brad?

There's a part of me that knows that the Universe is creating an Open Space in my life for My Man to fit. I message Brad and he's "conveniently" flying back East today—so I can't go make love to him during my conference stay. I try to set up a date with Buddhist Matthew and he's going to be in Copper Mountain. I ask another man out on the Plenty of Fish dating website and he's busy—and then he doesn't message me back.

I have six days to myself next week. What the fuck am I going to do with them? I need to find a place to go for my spiritual travel column. But where?

I feel sad and frustrated and antsy and ridiculously horny in the midst of the Open Space.

Be drawn to me already, My Man!!!!

I'm so freaking ready!

The cards I'm pulling are all *Resurrection* and and *Rebirth*. I am being reborn. I'm in a processing phase. I am processing all of the work I've done on myself this last year. I've made enormous strides. My Soul is doing Universe-changing work, especially while I'm sleeping.

Everything I've been working on in my business is about to manifest. This conference should be a HUGE turning point for me. I'm mingling in the circles I want to mingle in. I will be rubbing shoulders with some of my idols, quite a number of who rub shoulders with Oprah herself. I can feel an enormous shift coming. I feel it in my bones. This book is something that's going to manifest and it's going to be a phenomenal success. I am drawing an agent to me at this conference. I'm drawing a book deal to me.

Wouldn't it be delightful if I could draw a book deal without having to write a book proposal? How magnificent would that be?

Things are going my way. I'm just in an *almost-there* place and I'm anxious to *be there*. I know Abraham-Hicks says you never really get there. And I agree with that.

By *be there*, I mean: My website is done and looks amazing, my packages are solid and sell well, my ecourses make money for me while I sleep, My Man is in my life (and it soothes and nourishes and excites me), and I have a book deal for *The Year of YES!*

I've been in a stage of *becoming,* and now I'm anxious to be in a stage of *being.* I'm ready for all of this so I am craving all of this with an intensity that I wasn't craving it with before.

I draw love to me. I draw success to me. I draw creativity, inspiration, opportunity, and money to me.

THIRTY-NINE

OCTOBER 10, 2013

'm having an Upper Limit Problem. I'm getting so close to everything I want that I'm closing up my heart and bracing myself for collision.

Amazing things are happening to me.

I'm developing a solid, kickass coaching business and getting clients. I'm delivering well-received workshops. I'm crossing things off my to-do list. I'm jumping hurdles galore.

I've been getting a tremendous amount of emotional and spiritual healing work done. I feel 180 degrees from how I felt at the beginning of the year.

I was *literally* the muse for a painting in an art show, painted by a soon-to-be famous, break-out artist, Clint Eccher. He painted a portrait of me. I was the only woman he painted for the show. How flattering is that?

I've been interviewed for Today.com and Forbes.com in the last month or two.

I'm friendly with Andy Dooley, whose family is LOA-famous. I've invited him to my church, Whole Life Center for Spiritual Living, and to have lunch with me today.

I'm on the verge of going to Iowa to learn Transcendental Meditation. Staying at a luxury resort. I scored press passes for Emerging Women. That gives me one degree of separation from Oprah Winfrey.

I'm lining up the stars to take the kids to NYC for the week before Christmas with Neecy and her family.

Is it possible that I am so happy and things are going so well that I am sabotaging the Big Leap into the next level by opening the door to rejection and heartache by contacting Boulder Brad?

Possible?

Practically guaranteed!

Is it possible I'm blocking my heart and obsessing on *where is he?* right in the middle of all of these AMAZING miraculous things in my life because I'm terrified of getting everything I want? Terrified of shining too brightly? Terrified of change? Terrified of so much happiness that I will explode? I'm not going to give in to the Upper Limit Problem. I will keep breathing and opening my heart and filling my body and face with light.

I am a *muse!* Literally a muse. A man—one I have a minor crush on, by the way—painted a portrait of me and then put it in his art show. Who gets to say that? I mean, *really?*

But everything feels somewhat outside of me. I'm afraid it will vanish if I get too close to it or open my heart up to it.

Upper. Limit. Problem.

The fears are: that I will outshine people and they'll be jealous or I'll make them feel bad, and I'm not allowed to succeed to the level of that I want to because I'm a single mom. *Although I don't think I have this one anymore. I've worked through it, and my children are older, which resolves the agreement I made with myself about not working when they were young.*

I also fear leaving people behind. *I don't think this one is an issue either, as I've already left those I'm leaving, or they have left me.*

The core people in my life are core. *Period.* I have a great network of people who want me to shine as bright as the sun, including my children, my friends, and even my FB page and blog fans.

No, this is a shining problem. How brightly dare I shine? As bright as the lights on an Oprah set? As bright as the flash of the DSL camera in the hands of paparazzi?

Yes, I think I'm getting over this one finally.

The brighter I shine, the more people I can help, and the more others around me will be able to shine. *Shine! Shine! Shine!*

I'm interested in being the one invited to give the keynote speech. I'm interested in long lines at my book signing. I'm interested in having zero degrees of separation between me and Oprah. (*Hi Oprah!!!*)

This right now, this second, these last thirteen weeks in 2013 are the Big Leap for me. It's the moment when I start playing a whole new game. When my website and rebranding goes live and I really start putting myself out there. All signs point to serious manifestation. I just gotta hang onto my happiness and not self-sabotage because of the Upper Limit.

On the massage table yesterday, I decided several things that are true: I deserve to be in the VIP room as much as anyone with hundreds of bylines to my name and my bright light and powerful energy; I'm as good or better as a writer and a thought-leader and inspirer as any woman in that room. I'm as good a writer as Elizabeth Gilbert and this memoir is as compelling or more (not to mention self-indulgent) than *Eat, Pray, Love.* I'm a better writer than Brené Brown. I'm building the platform that will catch the millions of fans that will follow me after my book hits the big time and I appear on Super Soul Sunday with Oprah.

It's all about to manifest and I'm overwhelmed, excited, scared, proud, and exhilarated.

❧

MY WHOLE ENTIRE SOUL is reorganizing herself. I can practically feel her pushing buttons and pulling wheelies and re-filling folders and reassigning jobs and shifting the furniture—opening and closing doors, smashing through windows, and taking down glass ceilings. She's sweeping out closets and throwing shit out of the basement and putting the oversized clothes in the thrift store bin. She's shaking out the rugs and scalding the sheets and hanging them to dry. She's buying the updated hardware and installing the new software for the completely new and more powerful Tracee Sioux. She's kicked out many demons, she's shooed away some feral animals, she's mended entire chunks of heart, she's blown out some old pipes and gaskets, she's shining silver and breaking out the gold. She's experimenting with some new styles and fresh substance. There's a "less than" feeling that has vanished and an "of course I am" that's taken its place. But she's still got a few more weeks to restructure herself.

I have done sooooo much internal work this year. This is the part where I process. I have this feeling. . . that My Man will get here when she's done rearranging the office of my psyche and I've made the Big Leap into the next level of becoming. I have this feeling that the My Man I'm looking for has already made the Big Leap and he's waiting for me there on the next level.

We'll make the next big leaps together.

I'm in the elevator. Martha Beck has this analogy about going to the next level of being. You ride the elevator up and often you're alone in the elevator and you're thinking, *Crap, I'm alone!* but then the elevator door opens and you're surrounded by amazing people who are also resonating at that new level. My Man's on the new level.

❧

WHEN I WAS PRAYED over at the health fair, they said that I was coming into a deep healing period in which God would completely take over and I wouldn't have to worry about anything and my heart would be mended and stitched back together until it was better than new.

I'm getting tired. I'm depleted. I like Realm Traveling. I want to do more of it. I like when other healers help me, but I also want to be able to Realm Hop by myself whenever I need to.

I want to take the Universal White Time Healing class with Bina Mehta next month, and that's $400. Universal White Time is an energy healing modality in which healing takes place where there is no past, present, or future, I don't claim to understand it, but as soon as she told me about the class my Soul said YES!

I want to take the kids to New York City for Christmas with the Leas, and I'm thinking that's going to run $2,000 to $3,000.

I need some new clients, a one-year business development and coaching client should help. Maybe throw in a few three-month contracts, too. I want abundance amounts of money to live the life I want to live. I just do.

❧ Deep Breath ❧

I HAVE TO GO INTO a crowd of badass women and network now. Which means walking up to strangers who might be cooler than me and saying, "Hello! My name is Tracee and I'm a Big Deal." Literally terrifying. *Terrifying.* I'm feeling butterflies and shortness of breath, head spinning. I'm gonna be alright. I'm going to be present and a big ball of light and smile my face off.

FORTY

OCTOBER 11, 2013

In her speech, Brené Brown said that the most terrifying emotion for us is Joy. Things start going so right and we instinctively brace ourselves for something bad to happen. I can't be this happy can I? I'm really feeling the impact of this right now.

The very first person I met in the lobby pre-conference was someone who works at Sounds True publishing house. She listened to me talk about my experiences for forty-five minutes. She took my card and promised to visit my website.

I have been gifted by the Universe with a VIP pass, which is allowing me to sit in the first rows and literally rub shoulders with the presenters. I've been invited to a VIP reception. Neecy is the best hostess ever, providing me free lodging and love.

Other things in other areas of my life are lining up—manifesting after a year's worth of really deep, hard work. One of the most profound is this incredible feeling that I *deserve* to be in the VIP section and that very soon I'll be the one on the stage. That it's simply *meant for me*. Feeling deserving is new to me.

It's taking everything I have to let it in and open my heart to it and believe that it's getting better and better. Everything I want and that I've been manifesting feels within my reach. I can feel the joy pushing on my heart and I'm intentionally breathing into it and pulling back my shoulders to open my heart to it. But it is rather terrifying, too.

❧

MY BANK ACCOUNT IS a pitiful sight right now. This is less of a concern for me than it would have been a year ago. A year ago I was downright terrified out of my mind.

❧

I FEEL LIKE WEEPING AFTER the two days of amazing I've just experienced. I feel like weeping. I really don't know what to do with everything I'm trying to process.

As I sat in Elizabeth Gilbert's talk, I had goose bumps and chills the entire time. *This is for me,* I said to myself. I could just feel it in my bones. *I will be up there with my book. This is meant for me. I finally feel worthy of this. Because this is meant for me.*

When Elizabeth Gilbert speaks about creativity, it touches me deep within my Soul. So few writers give credence to the fairies of creativity. When she talks about it, I want to weep for my gift, for this precious inspiration, and for the bravery and vulnerability it takes to even write the word *by* and then have the audacity of putting my name behind it.

One of my visions is to have Elizabeth Gilbert write a blurb for the back of my book that says: *The most self-indulgent book ever written.* That would just delight my Soul: sort of flipping the finger to those women who resent other women's success and trash their work from the cheap seats.

❧

BRENÉ'S TALK WAS FAR more compelling than I thought it would be. I've been kicking myself and being very angry and frustrated with my Soul. How dare she tell me I love Boulder Brad when obviously that's patently untrue and it makes me feel unnecessarily vulnerable? How dare I contact him again and write that I think a lot about having sex with him? An admission that exposed me to rejection—almost a sure thing based on his having rejected me more than once. But I did it anyway and his response was no response. How dare I keep feeling in love with someone who doesn't deserve it and with whom I don't even want to be.

Then I was giving myself shit for telling him it was about sex, which felt vulnerable, although it's far less vulnerable than saying what I would have said if I were braver. "I love you. I don't know why, I can't explain it or reason it out. But I do. You're different and unpredictable, and you got into my heart."

During and after the talk I contemplated telling him. I have nothing to lose. He's already rejected me. It hurts my pride. But, what's good for pride?

Brené says vulnerability is reserved for people who have earned our trust. I trust Brad. To reject me. To ignore me (how like Alex). To be able to turn off and shut down every bit of vulnerability that might leak out of him for me.

Which brings Brad's question back to me. *Should I let myself be vulnerable with someone I've consciously decided not to fall in love with?*

I suppose not. But I've been thinking about him for months now and it hasn't gone away. I'm looking for an out. I'm looking for a way to satisfy my Soul on this one and resisting my feelings for him has been an utter failure. Accepting that we're not going to happen is easy enough, I'm pretty sure I don't even want that anyway. So what is my Soul doing to me here? Does she just want to express love to someone? Does she miss him from her past life? Do all my feelings for him on a Soul level have nothing to do with him in this lifetime? And what do I then expect him to do with that?

Brené talks about getting into the arena and going back in.

I got in the arena. I went back in.

If I sent him another message saying, *"I love you. That is all,"* then what? What outcome is my Soul expecting to come of that? Will it provide me the relief I'm looking for? Does she need to say that directly to him? Will she then stop torturing me with thoughts of him, and let me move on to My Man?

❧

I AM RESISTING THIS. I've been putting tons of energy into re-sisting Brad and my feelings for him. I've spent hundreds of dol-lars with healers trying to get him to go away—to get out of my heart and my mind.

Is my Soul going to just keep torturing me until she gets to say this?

❧

DEAR BRAD,

I love you.

I've spent a great deal of energy trying to banish my feelings for you, but my Soul is torturing me.

I did past-life regression therapy and I experienced one of our lives together; it was a profoundly beautiful and contented Love Life. Sexually it was phenomenal and the depth of our connection was Holy and Sacred. Every night we came together and leisurely loved each other deeply and satisfyingly and it never got boring or rote, it got more intimate. Outside the bedroom was just as beautiful, we raised a wonderful family and

336

worked contentedly together, our home was full of affection and laughter. We ran a thriving ranch and we were very proud of it. Our love lacked nothing. There was no striving, no trying, no anger or jealousy, nor resentment or score keeping. There was nothing but a deep, vast, loving, joyous connection. It was a sacred marriage in every way. I felt profoundly loved and seen by you, and you me. Words can't convey how beautiful a Love Life it was.

Here's who I know you are: a generous and expansive lover, brilliant and unique and warm, kind, and loving, and so completely capable of meeting a woman's expectations. Just because of who you are, as a Soul.

I think my Soul wanted me to see that lifetime so I would know that I am capable of that kind of love, which is what I've been calling forth for myself. Perhaps my Soul won't give me peace about you until you've been told that too, because you really need to know that about yourself.

I heard Brené Brown speak last night and I felt like an asshole for sending you that note, making it about sex. That felt vulnerable, but nowhere near the level of vulnerability involved in telling you the truth: I love you. That is all. I feel like this will cost me something: Pride. But we both know pride is a fierce opponent to vulnerability and the enemy of Love. My Soul wants you to know this. This is my Year of YES, so I'm telling you this, knowing rejection is my most likely fate. I won't die.

The other thing I was reminded of last night is that you have to put Love out into the world if you want to find Love. I've been trying my damnedest to repress and withhold the Love I feel for you, because I can't make rational sense of it and it's inconvenient and messy. But I know withholding and repressing Love, of any kind, is not going to get me the Love I want in my life. That's not living Heart Open.

I don't expect you to do anything about this. I'm hoping that putting Love out there will release my Soul to open to more Love in my life.

You are Loved, Loving, and Lovable.

Love, Tracee

❧

"TRACEE, THIS IS YOUR DAD, call me back, bye."

My dad called and left a message on my phone.

My dad hasn't called me one single time—ever. I left home twenty-two years ago and he has never once called me. Something is up. Has my mom had a heart attack?

❧

I SENT BOULDER BRAD the email. It was an odd experience of exhilaration and peace. Outcome? I don't know. That's up to him. Desired outcome? I don't know.

True: My Soul wanted him to know how I feel. And who I know he is. And what I believe him capable of.

Please Soul, release me from him now. Give me peace and open the door to a new Love, or Loves, to My Man. Open the door to hieros gamos in my present. Leave Brad be. He will do with the information what he will. He'll respect it. Toss it. Ignore me. Reject me. Whatever he does. I will be okay and I stopped repressing Love.

I stopped repressing Love!

That's huge. I opened myself up to Love, knowing that pain was involved. HUGE! FUCKING HUGE!!!

It does beg the question.

Is Love really Love if it's not expressed?

Is that what Love seeks: to express itself?

Elizabeth Gilbert talks about how ideas are floating around looking for a home. They are looking for an open space to land. Someone who is willing to birth them and manifest them.

Ideas want to manifest.

If you are ready, they come to you and you manifest them. You are the conduit for the ideas that are seeking to be birthed into the light of the world to do their work. If you are not ready, they leave and go find a new home.

What if Love works the same way? What if when Love comes to us and we reject it or withhold it or run from it or refuse it, it simply goes to find a new home? What if all it wants is for us to express it?

I love you.

What if Love demands no other outcome? It just is, it found a home and it wants to be birthed into the light of the world.

Did what I just did with Boulder Brad fulfill Love's obligation? Is the act of saying to him "I love you" the only thing Love wanted from me?

Did Brad's God team *need* me to deliver that message? Was that our spiritual contract? I know he's in a place in his life where he really needs to hear from his God team about his capacity to love. Perhaps that was the requirement of this completely bonkers attraction to him.

I love you. Your Soul needs reminding that you are loved.

When you think about it, what good does Love do if you're stuffing it inside and you refuse to let it out because it's going to cost you something?

What kind of ridiculous notion is that anyway? That to express Love—*I love you*—will cost you something?

Love's desire is to be expressed. What if my Soul just did something really pivotal in Boulder Brad's life? What if hearing that he is loved, lovable, and loving is what he needs to open himself to Love? My Soul desperately wanted him to know. I have to trust that she knows.

And what is it that I think I'm going to lose by saying it to him? What kind of terrible idea of Love do I have to think that expressing Love will restrict, reduce me or cause me pain? Where did I get that idea? That if I love someone and it doesn't turn into a forever marriage, that it's painful? That expressing Love to someone who probably isn't going to express it back to me is a devastating event?

Is it?

Oddly, I am finding it exhilarating and freeing. It's liberating.

I love you. I don't expect you to do anything about this.

You're going to reject me. I still want you to know I love you.

What if Love is everywhere around us and it's looking for a home, any expression, any opening to be born—any attraction, any happenstance meeting, any exchange between two living things—and most of us just look the other way or ignore it or reject it because it's scary to express it and not have it returned?

What if Love is just desperate to land and be expressed? What if we're surrounded by copious and generous amounts of it constantly and we're too afraid to say it, receive it, or express it—so it just wanders around not serving Love's purpose?

It feels so obvious now.

Love wanted to tell Brad of his worthiness of Love.

I've been fighting being the conduit for that for several miserable months. I've been heartbroken and sad and grief stricken about having to withhold and repress and reject my feelings of love. Love wanted to find Brad and it needed a messenger, a deliverer of it's message: You are loved, loving, and lovable.

It's not the *loving* of Brad that has made me miserable. It's the withholding of the expression of loving Brad that has made me miserable.

I love him. I don't need a "good reason." My Soul has loved him forever. My Soul recognizes the capacity for Love in him and my Soul knows he has forgotten about his capacity for Love.

What if I was chosen because of our past-life history together and my *Year of YES!* What if Love has been looking for a way into him and my willingness to follow my Soul's direction is the opening that Love needed? And I have been resistant and stubborn and guarding my pride as if my pride is more precious than Love that wants to be expressed?

Oh my God. I think it might be true.

Love wants to be expressed. That's how it lives and breathes and grows. Expression is Love's purpose. It wants to be made manifest.

I've been killing myself, torturing myself and being downright cruel to myself for feeling Love. Any feelings of Love are a gift aren't they?

I remember reading a Dear Sugar column in which Cheryl Strayed told someone who loved someone unrequitedly that Love was so precious that you should savor every second of it, even if it isn't reciprocated.

I've been hating the discomfort of loving Brad. I *LOVED*. Anyone, for a moment, for a day, for a month, for a year, for a lifetime. It's LOVE. Every single occurrence of it should be celebrated and honored. I honored Love by expressing it to Brad today. I honored my capacity to do it. I honored my ability to manifest it. I honored my willingness to express it.

I honored Love.

Love wanted to find him. Love wanted to find me, just as much. Love wanted me to practice expressing it and Brad was my opportunity. Love wanted me to know that no expression of it is ever a mistake or something worth punishing one's self for.

Love wanted to make itself known to us.

Ding! Lightbulb Moment! *Aha!* I didn't fuck up. I expressed Love. I didn't allow an inappropriate person into my life, I was the conduit for Love to reach a beautiful unique man so compelling that he deserves every single spec of Love he can open to.

What kind of craziness is it that we're all walking around afraid of Love? We're afraid Love will hurt us. It can't. Love is not in the pain game. Love is in the expressing game. We shrink from it. *What if it doesn't end in marriage? What if it ends someday? One of it dies? What if it leaves me? What if it rejects me?*

God, we're so afraid of it.

And like inspiration and ideas, it's floating around us all of the time just looking for someone—*anyone*—to be open to it and be willing to express it.

Am I having a Top 5 Lifetime Epiphany moment right now?

I love. It doesn't matter who, or for how long, or when or why, or under what conditions. I love and it is a privilege worthy of honor every. single. time.

FORTY-ONE

OCTOBER 12, 2013

"**I** would like you to take a paternity test."

"Uh. Okay. I don't know what to say to that. What's happening?"

"You're a smart woman and I'm a somewhat smart man. You've surely thought of this. You have a disease called hereditary hemochromatosis. The only way you can get it is from both parents. I don't have it, so you figure it out."

"Are you suggesting that Mom had an affair and I'm not your child?"

"Yeah, that's exactly what I'm suggesting! Listen, Tracee, you're my daughter and you'll always be my daughter, and your kids will always be my grandkids, but I want a paternity test because I don't think you're mine."

"Dad, that seems highly unlike Mom."

"Lying seems highly unlike your mom, but she lies to me all the time! I'm not doing this anymore. I can't take it anymore. Your mom married me not because she was in love with me; she married me because her daddy wouldn't let her marry the man she was really in love with. I'm not going to live with it anymore. I'm leaving and we're going to get a divorce, clean out this house, and go our separate ways. I want a paternity test to prove that you're not my kid."

"I think that's a great idea, you should do that immediately. But you don't have to make Mom a cheater to say that you're unhappy and you want out."

"I know I don't have to. *I want to.*"

"Dad I think you should leave, but what will change if I'm not your daughter?"

"Nothing will change!"

"Then why do you want me to take the test?"

"Listen Tracee, the bottom line is: Are you going to take the test or not?"

"I'm not going to answer that right now. I don't know what to do with this. You've been drinking and this is crazy. You don't have to do this to leave."

"Are you going to take the test or not? If you call me back, then I will know that you are and if you don't then I'll know that you won't. Bye."

Click.

"I love you, Dad."

✑

SO. MY DAD HAS unclaimed me.

He wants out of his marriage and can't do that without a legit reason. You could say that my dad, the most fundamental male presence in my life, doesn't *want* me.

When I got off the phone, my prevailing emotion was empathy and compassion, *Oh, my parents are in so much pain.*

My dad unclaimed me two seconds after I sent a love letter to a man that I love who also doesn't *want* me. And I sent it *knowing* that he doesn't want me. I sent it *knowing* the outcome would be

344

rejection. I just wanted to give my Soul what she wants, to express love to him.

Do you know what is startling and truly an epiphany?

I'm okay. Like, totally unflinchingly okay.

My dad says I'm not his child, he's unclaimed me, and it doesn't change the essential fact of my life: I'm okay.

A man that I love isn't going to love me back and he's going to take that love and not even acknowledge it or validate it or respond to it: I'm okay.

No man will ever want me? *Puh-leeeze.*

"No one will want you now. You're a used piece of meat!" Dave Lev used to scream in my face to make me too afraid to leave him when he'd hit me. I believed him for a long, long time.

Now. Not a shred of my worth is dependent on whether my dad wants to claim me as his daughter, and not a shred of my worth is dependent on whether Brad wants me to be is girlfriend.

There's no piece of me that believes that if Alex or Brad or even my father does not love me then no one else will.

❧

I CAME TO THIS INCARNATION *to learn to love myself so much that a man can't hurt me,* echoed in my heart and vibrated my Soul. It is now true. It has taken me many lifetimes to learn this one lesson. It is now true.

A man can't hurt me. I can feel vulnerable, uncomfortable, and aggrieved by a man. But he can't really *hurt* me. I won't die. I won't crawl into a hole and refuse the other loves coming my way. I won't believe that no one will want me. I won't believe that I'm not awesome if he doesn't love me.

At forty years old and through the withdrawal of love after love, the rejection of men and the withholding of love and even the abuse at the hands of men, evidently this has happened for many lifetimes . . . *I now really know that I love myself so much that a man can't hurt me.*

❧

IS THIS A LIFE-ALTERING moment? In the sense that a person has an identity crisis and it shakes up her entire life and has to reevaluate everything now that what she believed was fundamentally true where she came from is different? You know, like in reality television and in the movies. *Eh.* Not really. I'm fine, I'm going to be fine, I'm feeling good about myself and my life, and like my core is unshakable, firmly planted and centered.

It's such a ludicrous notion to begin. And if the Universe itself cracks in half and it turns out that my mother—the good and pristine, faithful Mormon girl who married the bad boy and then feels victimized and surprised by the fact that he's really a bad boy—cheated on my father and I am not his daughter, it won't change the fact that I am fine.

My father is not an easy person to be fathered by. I've come to accept, however, that we get the fathers we need. My dad is my dad; he's the one I got. Unclaiming me is a profound act of self-hatred really. He chose the child most like himself to unclaim. That's not a coincidence. He chose the willful, unconventional, rebellious child. He chose the child who most closely followed his pattern of addiction and envelope pushing. He chose the child who rebelled against the Church. He chose the child who most reminds him of his sister, of his mother. He chose the child who doesn't back down, who gets fierce when challenged, who is loud and can be confrontive. He chose me because I reflect some things that he hates about himself. He punished me for these same "flaws" by refusing to pay for my college because I wasn't doing the "right" things. I was doing the same things as he was.

He can't hurt me, I am love.

They can't hurt me, I am love.

Do I love myself enough to let him go? Yes!

Will I be punished if I leave my family and live an unconventional life? Who gives a shit? Those people are bat-shit crazy and dangerously toxic. They're *conventional?* By who's definition? Seriously, *what?*

Here's the thing. I can run away with men, whether or not its conventional, and I'll be okay. And if they treat me badly, I can walk away from them, whether or not it's conventional. I can stand alone or stand with another. If I'm not with a man I can have a deeply satisfying life. I prefer to be in relationship because it's more fun and interesting that way. I enjoy intimacy and connection and relationship, and I want that for the pure joy of it. As is natural, normal, and true for humanity.

But if *he* doesn't love me—whoever *he* happens to be at whatever juncture in my life—I'm gonna keep right on living an exciting, interesting, and passion-filled life. I know that now.

I love myself so much that a man can't hurt me.

Not my dad. Not a not-boyfriend. Not that fucking marine who blabbed about our bizarre sexual experience *at my church* and in my social circle. Not the men on the dating websites who don't return my emails (very few considering how many email me), not the men who stand me up, not the ex-non-lovers who reduce me to "lust," or the ex-boyfriends who didn't want to claim me as their wife or their girlfriend.

They can't hurt me. I am love.

❦

NEECY: "DICK CALLED ME twenty times in the last few days. In the last hour he's texted and called me five times."

Me: "You really do need to call the cops on him."

Neecy: "I know, but I haven't had time. Have you talked to your mom about your paternity test?"

Me: "No, I haven't had time. I've been in the conference all day."

FORTY-TWO

OCTOBER 14, 2013

B rad's email: *"And the opposite of shame is courage, compassion, and connection, which you are exhibiting a tremendous amount of. This is an amazing note. More later . . ."*

⚹

I SAT IN THE LOBBY and wept. He acknowledged me. It was truly more than I had hoped for. Just to be acknowledged was such a gift. Then I got in my car and reread his message over and over, crying. Acknowledged. For courage, compassion, and connection. Exactly what I was trying to convey. The highest I had hoped for was that he would receive it. That he would allow himself to take it in. To be acknowledged for the Soul work I'm doing and the cries of my heart. It is precious.

⚹

MY HEART WAS WIDE OPEN when I left the conference, and I was extraordinarily vulnerable and in many ways depleted, but I wanted to be touched. I wanted to feel another person's hands on my skin and I wanted to be penetrated. I went to see Hottie Hank. It was nice. It was a relief to release some of my feelings through orgasm.

⁓

MY HEART HAS CRACKED wide open. There is a new portal where the Universe has cracked wide open, birthing the Divine Feminine at that conference.

Here's the thing about having a wide open heart. It's not as though there is this expansive love in the heart all the time. There is always love available. Yet, there are many other emotions too.

⁓

I'VE COME TO THE conclusion that much of the time PMS is when women open themselves to the pain of the whole world. Perhaps the grief and the pain and the struggle must be felt and during PMS women open to it, hormonally. Perhaps it is our job to feel the pain of the world and wash it up, transform it into love the best we can and send it back out into the world in a new form: that of *transfigured* love.

When I had my two babies I sobbed—without control or inhibition—I sobbed with my whole self, my expansive Soul self.

I sobbed for every terrible thing that might happen to my children, every heartbreak, every physical pain, every emotional trauma they would ever experience in this lifetime. I also sobbed for the whole entire planet. I sobbed for every witness and victim of 9/11, which I witnessed three weeks prior to my first delivery, my cervix opened wide absorbing every ounce of energetic terror, anger, and grief engulfing the city, the world. I grieved for every victim of a crime, for every hardened heart, for every person sub-

350

jected to his internal demons. I shook with grief for the grief of living, and hoping and dying. My whole Soul quaked. I lamented. I keened.

My whole body and Soul split wide open and I was the portal for all the pain in the world.

I couldn't control it. No one knew what to do with me. I could not stop for the longest time; I have no idea how long it was. The nurses, doctors, and most of all, Alex, didn't know how to respond to this feral and primal expression of grief.

I now believe that because I experienced every pain my children will go through that it made me a much more relaxed and open mother. I have never been the mother who is devastated by a mean girl saying something cruel to Madigan. I've not been the mother who winces when her child falls down or crashes a bike. I have always believed in their resilience and their ability to handle their feelings, painful or joyful. Perhaps because I've already grieved their grief and suffered their traumas and I washed them clean only minutes after they were born to their world.

Perhaps I have done that for Alex and Brad and other men in my life, my parents, and the rest of the world. Perhaps as I open my heart and there is this tender wounded feeling in my chest that I know won't kill me, but tempts me to hunch my shoulders and withdraw my heart back into its rib cage like a frightened turtle, what I am really doing is an act of selfless love and giving this unexpressed pain and grief a place to land and be washed clean.

It is my resilience that has allowed me to do this. And my comfort with pain and fear. I know both intimately, and knowing both intimately has given me a gift: I know it will not kill me. I know that I have an expansive and immense capacity to heal my own heart and to keep opening to love and beauty and gratitude, and yes, even joy.

I can do it in the face of rejection. I can do it in the face of being unwanted and unappreciated and invalidated. I can do it. I won't die from pain. I will expand and grow.

♋

My mind is blown and my heart is exposed and expanding. I feel somehow both awakened and depleted.

It is a lot to take in. The impact was unexpected and intense. Having my heart burst open and stretch itself wider in the face of such intense presence of the Divine Feminine has made me feel very, very vulnerable. I want to sit in peace and process it for a long time.

My Soul is giving me immeasurable gifts. But I am so weary by now. It's been almost two years of these cathartic Soul work gifts. Yet, I'm very tired spiritually. I'm on my knees in utter surrender again because I'm just too weary to do anything else. I may have reached my spiritual growth limit for now.

FORTY-THREE

OCTOBER 15, 2013

During my meditation this morning, I realized something important about a vital element of my sacred marriage.

I want My Man to be okay with my full range of emotions. I want a man who is able to witness me, and receive all parts of me by stepping toward me, instead of running away from me like a scared animal.

David Deida writes about massaging his woman's cervix. He says women store much of their sexual trauma in their cervix, so it is often tender and painful to the touch at first. He describes patiently touching, caressing, and massaging the cervix as his woman experiences all of the pain and hurt and rage and frustration and anger that she has stored there. He is a persistent, open witness to the pain, allowing her the honor of experiencing and releasing it, allowing it to move through her and him. It is his way of honoring her Divine Feminine essence. Eventually, having moved through and released its stored pain, the cervix opens to him, kissing his finger and his penis, as he's created trust and accessed vulnerability through persistent, healing loving.

This is what my Soul craves sexually and spiritually. I crave someone who can stand with my pain and heal me with trust and love and openness. Someone who can walk toward me and allow me to experience what I've experienced and won't shrink from the intensity of it. This description of sexuality and love is so erotic and intimate and vulnerable and exquisite to me. It bathes my Soul in desire and I crave it from deep within my heart. My Soul craves My Man's presence, his complete unwavering presence.

I want to do this for My Man, as well. I want to stand witness to his experience and his pain. I want to guard his heart as it opens and learns to heal and trust under my devotion and presence and love. I want to allow him space to open vulnerably under my loving kisses and my piercing touch.

❧

NEECY HAS GIVEN ME FEEDBACK that I really hurt Brad with my harsh words in that Facebook exchange and that just kills me. I was so hurt by him withdrawing and intellectualizing his feelings for me that I didn't consider that he would be hurt by my words. I think there's a part of me that doesn't believe men have the full range of emotions. I suppose that's based on my experience with men and their refusal to be vulnerable, or a cultural idea that they are detached and unfeeling.

I hurt him. I hate that. It hurts my heart to think of me hurting his wounded and vulnerable heart. I could feel his pain when he talked to me about how people don't understand his way of perceiving the world and communicating. I could feel his craving for intimacy and his pain about failing in relationships.

I was not tender. I was not soft.

I craved intimacy and I could feel his vulnerability, but I could also feel him decide to withdraw from that opportunity with me, for whatever his logical and prudent reasons are. I suppose I be-

354

lieved he had turned his heart off and therefore he could not be hurt by my hurt and my anger.

And I was not tender or soft with his heart.

I'm ashamed of that.

I will be softer with men from now on. Softer and more tender with their fragile hearts as they struggle to open their hearts and live more intuitively.

❧

DEAR SOUL AND GOD TEAM,

I am weary of counting my pennies. I am weary of going to the grocery store and adding up each item on my calculator, worried that if I go over I'll overdraw my account. I am weary of going to the bank for $20 to take to the pumpkin patch and worrying that I'll soon be out of $20. I am weary of clenching myself as I go into an energy session with C.J. because I'm running out of $80 to pay and I am choosing between putting gas in my car and taking care of my spiritual and emotional self.

I am weary of receiving emails about David Deida intensive workshops and not being able to attend because of the cost. I am weary of making choices like putting plane tickets to NYC for Christmas on my credit card, which goes against my money values, because Neecy already bought the tickets. I am weary of leaping off cliffs, because it takes far more energy than does just buying what I want when I want it. I am weary of feeling anxious before a sales meeting, because I'm living so close to the edge that any teeter at all will cause havoc in my life. I am weary of looking at my bank account before I make even the smallest purchase, for fear of overdrawing my account. I am weary of taking in my breath as I visit the doctor or buy the Clinique my skin needs.

I am weary of needing Medicaid to cover basic medical expenses. I am weary of not making choices I want to make about my health, not being able to take care of the birth incontinence that interferes with my ability to do simple stuff like jump rope and run and laugh. I am weary of having to worry about house trading instead of just paying for a hotel in NYC. I'm weary of worrying whether I'll be able to let the kids buy souvenirs when we go to NYC and whether or not we'll be able to go to a Broadway show.

I am weary of settling for what I can find at a good price. I am weary of worrying about how long my car will last. I am weary of staring shame-fully at the weeds that line my yard because I can't pay someone to come and landscape it yet. I am weary of the smell of dog pee and urine that emanates from my basement because I can't afford quality carpet cleaning. I'm weary of worrying about how much I spend on the gym membership and the Crossfit classes. I'm weary of feeling like I need a man to take me places. I am weary of the worry and the stress.

I'm weary of having this conversation with you. I'm weary of feeling like I'm not "making it happen." I'm weary of feeling like being poor is a skill that I've mastered. I'm weary of adding up the psychic income and trying to feel like that's abundance enough. It is not abundance enough. This weariness is taking up needed psychic space and sucking up unnec-essary energy. I'm weary of pretending that "getting by" is good enough. I'm weary of convincing myself that getting a free pass to the conference, and paying with my pen, is as good as is paying full price for the tickets to go to a conference I want to attend.

Please be different for me Universe. Provide me abundance in the en-ergy of money. I'm grateful for what I have and the abundance that you lavish on me, I am. But I'd like to spend less energy on being grateful, I'd like to stop having to look and try so hard to see and acknowledge the abundance in my life. I'd rather spend my energy doing other things, like experiencing the joy of having what I want and living what I want, and experiencing ease and effortlessness. I'd like to know what it feels like to have a big fat bank account that opens limitless choices to me. I'm ready for the having and living and experiencing that will result from limitless sources of cash flowing in and out of my life with effortlessness and ease.

And so it is.

FORTY-FOUR

OCTOBER 16, 2013

Oh Divine Mother, you may be asking too much of me.

O I check my email a hundred times a day looking for the "more later . . ." Brad promised.

I have offered my open heart. It is precious and it is tender. Will he choose to receive it?

The work right now, for me, is to remain Heart Open as I wait. And to remain Heart Open regardless of what his answer might be. My mind has played different scenarios over and over. *You're not enough, I want to date you and fuck other people; I think you're really special, but my heart is telling me that you're not the One; I don't love you, but thanks; Run away with me for the weekend; I want to see you. Let's talk about where this might go.*

I find the last one, the one where he says yes, terrifying. What if . . . we annihilated each other emotionally?

Can I still keep my Heart Open and not become bitter and closed? I've been weeping, but I'm remaining Heart Open. Even in the face of my parents putting me into the nightmare of their marriage once again.

Is it so easy for my father to not claim me as his? Does that offer him relief? Does he not consider it painful or hurtful to feel that kind of disconnect from me?

Oh Holy Mother, who wants to claim me as theirs?

Surely, there is a man in this world who wants deeply to *claim me* as his Sacred Woman. *Where is he? Is he here now?* My heart craves him. I know I'll be okay without him, without my father, and without my mother, and without my ex-husbands, and without Boulder Brad, if I must. But I crave him nonetheless.

Who doesn't respond to a love letter for four days? I can't even imagine a level of busyness that could keep me leaving someone hanging for this long with their heart hanging out in the air.

11:11

1:11

2:22

3:33

4:44

The soothing repetition of numbers appears all over my life, affirming that I am on the right track, even still.

෴

I CAN'T STOP WEEPING long enough to deliver the articles promised for attending this conference. Truly, it's cracked my heart wide open and I don't know what to do with myself. I just sit in my orange meditation chair for as much of the day as possible, save the gym, a few errands, and required appointments.

I sit here and wait for God and Goddess to make sense of me and mend me back together and determine my fate. I sit here breathing into my heart with tears welling up and spilling over. I listen to the Sea Stars' *The Unknown* album over and over.

"I won't find love if I don't give enough of my heart to this world. And it's bittersweet yet it's you and me with our hearts for the world." That's the lyric that triggered my love letter to Brad.

I can't make sense of my work. I sit in my orange meditation chair and I wait on Goddess and my Soul to direct me. *Where would you have me go and what would you have me do?*

And I weep.

Weary and weeping.

FORTY-FIVE

NOVEMEBER 1, 2013

had six days alone without the kids and they were so short and lovely that I renegotiated our parenting agreement, trading Thursday for Monday, to give me five days of child-free bliss twice a month. Perhaps the reader will think me horrible for being so damn excited to be free of my mothering responsibilities.

I look at it this way: I was a full-time, do-fucking-*everything*-with-them, 24/7/365 mom for eleven years. I did all the hard work. I laid the foundation. I was extraordinarily conscious about my mothering, and I took my role very, very seriously. I tanked my career for motherhood. In many ways that cost me my marriage.

Parenting. Burn. Out.

This is the first time I've experienced having a coparent and I love it. I LOVE it. It is such a relief of parenting burden to have him do things he's never before done, like take them to the doctor, stay home with them when they are sick, take them out to do things, hang out with them during the evenings on a school night, etc. Coparenting is a beautiful thing and I'm soaking in the benefit. I find myself so much more relaxed and able to parent effectively without all the constant stress.

The Year of YES!

❧

THE CARDS I DREW at the beginning of the week were *Crone of Transmutation, Purifier, Completion.*

I started Monday restless and anxious. This website truly does create me anew professionally. It's a bold website that declares me someone important and accomplished. This website does not shrink from my skills and talents. It puts me in a very, very big light. This website reinvents me. It takes me from one incarnation to another, much bigger, brighter, and bolder incarnation. This website is a complete transformation of me professionally. It is the death of me as the girl empowerment torch-carrier of *The Girl Revolution* and the resurrection of me as the Mastress of Manifestation, the creator of the Year of YES!, who helps people uncover their Soul purposes and helps them live their dreams.

I have ambitious and lofty goals for this website and my business to be completed by December 31, 2014. I'm really proud of the effort, persistence, and vision I've put into manifesting my new level of becoming and I'm really, really believing in my success. I feel called of God to this new coaching venture. In October I landed two new clients, and today I am landing another one.

I've also started a really exciting mastermind, by invitation only, of very powerful attractors. We call ourselves the Maxcelerators. We are using our group power to accelerate and maximize our results. Very powerful, very positive. The energy of the group together is exceptional. I'm very excited about it.

❧

BRING ME THE PERFECT MAN *for me, permission to have fun until he gets here, while repelling men who are bad for me.* Love spell refined.

One man has filtered through the refined love spell, Kenikie. On our second date, we went to Fort Collins' Zombie Fest. We dressed as Zombie Sandy and Zombie Kenikie from *Grease.*

He's a re-run. He shares an uncanny resemblance to Zeke, my first husband. He looks like him, everything from his body type, coloring, facial features, and teeth. He even smells like him and talks like him. He's bringing up stuff about Zeke that I need to process.

For the last decade or so I've put Zeke into a category, both in my head and when I talk about that relationship to other people: crackhead addict loser, stupid childhood mistake, rebelling against parents, so "that marriage doesn't count."

The truth, as I see it now, through new eyes, by experiencing flashbacks when I'm with Kenikie. . . is: *That junkie saved my life.*

In the most literal sense possible, Zeke saved me. When he stepped into my life, I was a broken mess of a little girl. I had *no one.* It's almost impossible to describe the level of aloneness that defined my life. Dave Lev had battered me physically, sexually, mentally, and emotionally for so long, deeply, and completely that I was broken. I had very little Self left and what Self there was, was shattered. He had told me how horrible I was: *I was a used piece of meat, no one would ever want me, I was not worthy of friends, and even my family couldn't stand me.*

I did not have one single friend. Not one.

My family really couldn't stand me. They wanted me punished. They wanted me out of their faces.

Dave had convinced me to go to the junior college instead of high school, where everyone was older than me and I hadn't made any friends at all.

I had slept with Poly Pete, so my old friends had banished me, and I had banished myself, as a *worthless whore* and *terrible friend.*

Zeke had hung out and done drugs with Dave during my relationship with him. He had hung around, nursing a mad crush on me. When he stepped into my life—my broken life with my shattered Self and my Self-loathing shame—he stitched me back together with unconditional, unequivocal love. His love was complete adoration. To him, I hung the moon and made the stars shine, and glowed like the sun.

Dave had filled my heart with hurtful criticism and sharp stabs of fists and words, shaming me until I pleaded, "Please don't leave me—I'll change! I promise!"

Zeke spent the next decade of my life following me around, telling me how beautiful, special, and wonderful I was. One compliment and prayer of devotion to me at a time, he stitched me back together. From the time I was sixteen, when he stepped in to heal me, until I married Alex, Zeke was a constant in my life that I could count on. Well, not in a day-to-day sense, like count on to keep a job or count on not to shoot heroine up his arms, or count on to show up on time and keep commitments, and not be a crazy motherfucker. No, he was, in *those* senses, a complete disaster as a husband and not to be counted on for one tiny second.

But when the world would wear me down, one thing was true: I could limp into his life and curl up in the fetal position and he would accept me as I was, build me back up, and fill me with his devotion—and it was unfaltering and unconditional. I would go off to other infatuations and lovers. When these relationships broke up, I would seek solace and he offered it to me every time.

Our relationship was disastrous, and technically unhealthy the majority of the time. Over that decade we would make periodic gos at "making it work." It always ended in: *No Fucking Way.*

But his love remained true. His love is true today. I can feel it stretch across the vastness of the Universe even now. If I contacted him today he'd probably drive to Colorado and cradle me, declaring his undying love and devotion.

No one has loved me like that since.

Yes, he was a junkie and a terrible husband. But . . .

That junkie saved my life.

I would not have recovered without his unconditional devotion. I just wouldn't have. I was too broken. Had I gone into another relationship where the man had been casual about me—say to Nathan, who was fun but wasn't the least bit devoted to me—I would have kept the deep wounds Dave had spent two years beating into me. I would have kept my identity as a worthless, used-meat whore whom no one would ever want again. Instead, God sent me exactly what I needed to repair and mend myself back into a full woman. He sent me someone who would make me feel unconditionally desired and valued.

Yes, the Universe sent me the perfect man for me at the time, someone blind to my faults: Zeke.

The Sacred Mother has sent me Kenikie to help me put Zeke in another category, as a Great and True Love. A perfect gift of Love. A shining example of the abundance of Love I've experienced in my life.

#yesthankyoumoreplease

A short time ago I had made a list of the characteristics from past lovers and looked at them negatively. Junky and unreliable loser, dumb, and embarrassing = Zeke. I had decided that I didn't want any of the energy of my past lovers, that I wanted something entirely new.

Possibly, God is showing me that what I'd love more would be the energy of the very best parts of my past lovers combined, without the problems that caused our relationship dissatisfaction.

If I could love someone as devotedly and passionately as I loved Dave Lev, and he could love me as devotedly and unequivocally and passionately as Zeke, that would make me very happy indeed.

But don't stop there Universe! My request in the letter S (and L): Spiritual, Sober, Successful, Sexy, and Local. I'll expand that to include that he's passionate and devoted to me, as I am to him.

FORTY-SIX

NOVEMBER 17, 2013

In January I pasted the words *Healing Arts*, with a photo that I took and published in *BellaSpark* magazine, on a story about fertility, actually. On the massage table, my Soul directed me to tithe 10 percent of my income on healing my own heart, mind, body, and Soul. I was to tithe 10 percent to *this temple of God*. Year 2012 was traumatizing, coming on the heels of my twelve-year struggle with Alex, interrupted by the traumatizing 9/11 and addiction, and Texas. Yeah, it's been a ride that I needed healing from. I knew it and declared my intention to focus on my healing and to do whatever necessary to put myself and my own well-being first, financially and energetically.

It is amazing—and I mean that in the clearest, most literal sense—that I have had the money and/or opportunity to take advantage of C.J.'s special brand of energy work, plus medical care, hypnosis, massage, and a variety of other energy work and healing techniques. At the beginning of the year, I searched for bargains and free opportunities. But I didn't like the energy of it. I preferred instead to pay full price, as a declaration to the Universe that I have enough to do this work for myself. I even stretched the definition of healing work to include pampering and maintenance, such as bikini lasering and getting regular red, sparkly shellac nail polish. I even traded for the opportunity to get an old, ugly tattoo removed from my toe. Further, I had the opportunity to go on several healing trips including Arizona, Utah, Texas, Georgia, and Cabo San Lucas. We will end the year with a healing trip to New York City with the Leas. In other words, I have fulfilled my intention for Healing Arts, and the Universe has aided me generously every step of the way.

What I didn't foresee or count on was that I would, in the midst of this healing work, be initiated as a *healer*. When my client Bina said she would be teaching a Universal White Time Energy course for level 1 certification, I immediately knew I wanted to do it.

I heal frequently. I intuitively do it when I see a need for it. I put energy into people, places, and events. I distance heal often. I've put a tremendous amount of energy into healing Boulder Brad: He energetically calls to me, needing healing, so I heal him from afar. I send healing energy to my parents, who are in such pain right now. I do hands-on healing with my friends and family when it's called for. I do healing with myself and my children.

During the course I was asked to accept myself as *chosen*. I was *chosen* to go to Sedona and receive those fascinating sexual initiations in the spirit realm. I was chosen to enter the spirit realm and bring back a gold clutch—that I now carry everywhere I go. I am chosen to become a life and business coach, teaching people the Law of Attraction and helping them manifest what they want. I am chosen to be a way-shower to other way-showers. I was chosen to bear witness and sit at the mastresses' feet at the Emerging Women Conference. I am chosen to be a Universal White Time Healer and to take part in the saving of the world. We are all *the Christ* if we accept that calling to step up and do our part in salvation.

It's an audacious thing to accept one's calling as *chosen* by the Universe, God, the Sacred Mother, Spirit, and the Great Beyond to assist in the world's salvation. It takes such audacity in the face of one's own hand to mouth financial experience to preach on the importance of attracting wealth, teaching people how to do it even. *Who am I, when I live so meagerly? I am not a millionaire yet. I do not have any idea if I can fill my 2014 Year of YES! coaching program.*

Who do I think I am? It is such audacity to think I am someone special in the face of my own cash-flow problems.

❦

OH MY GOD, I HAVE NO idea how I'm going to fill The Year of YES! For the last few weeks I've worked inspiredly and diligently, despite fear of failure and my bumping up against my Upper Limit, to create a 2014 package. It's a one-year experiment: *What would your life look like if you did everything your Soul told you to do for one year?* In fact, it's the same experiment that I took on this year, the one this memoir chronicles.

I *know* that when people sign on their lives will change significantly and never be the same. I can guarantee that. I know they will have adventures they can't even imagine. I know their Souls will never steer them wrong. I *know* beyond a shadow of a doubt, even more than a minuscule mustard seed of faith, that I can help people walk through the experiment.

What I do not know is if I can convince anyone to sign on to the program.

I have followed all the formulas. Yet I am afraid that no one will sign up. Afraid that there will be more close, but not enough, in my professional career.

I've experienced so many near misses that it's hard for me to "feel into" a major success. I don't know what such a success, or such a financial windfall feels like. I know only what putting all of my energy into an inspired project and then coming up short, being disappointed, being a *disappointment,* and utterly failing feels like.

It's been such a long time since I've experienced a real success. The one that sticks out in my mind as a major triumph is my first writing job in Tooele, Utah. It was no financial success. I was paid $7 an hour. But, I instantly won awards. It was me living my purpose. I was *writing* for a living!!! I was ballsy and confident— absurdly so for someone with no professional experience—and I was immediately rewarded with first-place writing and photography awards. And then things got hard. There were near misses. There were failures. There was running away and being afraid. There was disappointing my husband a million times. There was a promise to succeed—*I know I can do this*—and then coming up short, falling down, scraping my knees, and looking up to see his face saying, "You're such a failure. Give up. Get a job. You're of no value to me if you can't bring in money. Get over the delusion that you can make a living from these ridiculous dreams of yours. Give up. Give up. Give up."

Then to be so angry at God and the Universe and *my Soul* for requiring these things of me, only to let me fail, to falter, and to look so unworthy and absurd to my husband. To write the books that never got published. To launch the companies that no one noticed. To diligently write the blogs that never made money, year after year.

I know what that feels like. It is easy to imagine one more failure. One more near miss. One more exciting "break" that ends up being a blip of a success in the face of a failed project. One more stepping into my calling, only to find myself on my knees begging the Universe for a win.

I need a win. Please. A win.

Yes, these are the demons I battle with as I launch an ambitious program, that's really not all that ambitious in the scheme of things. It's sixteen people who are willing to pay me a moderate amount of money—enough for me to live on—to provide a service that I *know* will change their lives for the better.

That's almost too hard for me to even conceive.

I am simultaneously thrilled and excited that all of the laying my foundation work is coming to harvest. My website is going to look so good that even I find it a little intimidating how successful I appear.

This year is foundational. Next year is going to be HUGE!

❧

WHAT REALLY FRUSTRATES me to no end is how hard the money part is. I feel like one of my hands are tied behind my back because money is not flowing as abundantly as I'd like. As I know it *can* flow for me. I must change my currency. I'd like to have ridiculously large amounts of cash to buy what I want when I want it.

Case in point: I put aside $400 for the White Time Energy Healing and booked a hotel room in NYC for our vacation. This leaves me with less than $200 for the rest of the month. Well, I want to buy a cake for my Maxcelerators mastermind on Wednesday. And balloons. And copies for our project. And my refrigerator is empty. We need milk. It's just stupid, Universe—step up your game.

My currency is CASH. No more settling for bargains, free stuff, and admiration. I want all of those things, too, don't get me wrong. But it's not enough anymore. *CASH. And a fucking ton of it.*

FORTY-SEVEN

NOVEMBER 18, 2013

Nigel. Blowhard. Nigel. Nigel took me to dinner, enthusiastically. He was jovially condescending to the wait staff. He insisted I drive his brand-new, week-old Jaguar. He said he got a divorce because he didn't like the way his wife "did business." He sent me photographs of his Escalade, Jaguar, and Mercedes in the three-car garage of his brand-new McMansion. He makes his money as an oil and gas exec, negotiating mineral rights from landowners with little means. He asked if I had a passport, because within six months he'd be whisking me off to foreign resorts. He said he wanted to know how to "take it to the next level" on our second date. Because we're so dynamic, "our two dates should count as other people's six dates."

Nigel kept talking about himself being the Alpha. Nigel kept referring to my "feminism," and he kept talking about men's need to open doors for women. Nigel was short, and unattractive to me. He kissed me in front of the Bean Cycle at the beginning of our second date, in broad daylight. I felt it was a possessive move: a red flag for me. I do business at the Bean Cycle and it's full of men I may want to date. *I just met you. I'm not a tree you can pee on.*

Nigel approached me as if he was brokering a deal. "Here's the job description of Nigel's girlfriend, his trophy wife," is what it felt like. "I am the boss. You wear heels and keep your feminine quaffing up to par. If you're going to be keeping house, you have to keep house up to my standards. I'm going to be über-successful and you'll reap the benefit if we make a deal."

When I thought of Nigel, I often thought *Dad*, which does not bode well for Nigel, because I have no interest in being in a relationship with a blowhard tyrant. It's not in my DNA to do it.

Nigel is not My Man, my Soul told me and I told my friends. But it would be fun to be treated extravagantly for a few dates. I wonder what it feels like to be whisked away in a Jaguar and treated to expensive events? I would like that experience. Maybe I'll be open to what Nigel has to offer for a minute until My Man gets here.

Friday night I got all dressed up in gold glitter eye shadow, a beautiful dress, my new Cole Haan stiletto black leather boots. Nigel came to get me at 5:45 P.M. I told him I was off my game, as I had just been in a healing class and was far more open than I should be. Before we left the house, he remarked that I roll my eyes at him. I was too exhausted to argue. He had picked me up in the Jag, he was wearing a suit. He was taking me to an extravagant symphony/art show in Denver. I didn't want to be with him. But I did want to be treated extravagantly by a wealthy man. Just to see what it was like, just to have a frame of reference for what being treated like that felt like.

Stuck in traffic, for maybe five miles and thirty minutes, Nigel had quizzed me about various things like a lawyer would. He felt he was showing an interest in me, he wanted his interest to be reciprocated. He wondered why I wasn't asking him questions. He then said he felt I was "resisting his attempts at connecting with him by being harsh." He would, he insisted, break through my defense mechanisms. He suggested that I thought all men were full of shit and used harshness to defend myself from love.

"Well, this is awkward," I said. "We're too far from my house for me to walk home, and we still have an entire evening ahead of us and you have just called me *harsh* and *abrasive.*"

"Would you like me to take you home?" he asked, and then he got out of the car to pump gas while I thought about the awkward situation I was in. *Did I want Nigel to take me home? Yes.*

Nigel suggested we might have to try harder. I suggested we not try at all. "If you're bringing out the harsh in me, then this is going in the opposite direction it should be. I want a man who brings out the softness in me," I said.

He said, "I was suggesting that maybe you're afraid you'll like me too much, which is why you use harshness as a defense mechanism."

I said, "If it's hard by the third date, we should take it as a sign."

Forty-five minutes after the date began it ended with Nigel telling me more about my feminism and how I should date a more feminine man and not such an Alpha. Then I was back on my doorstep. I opened my own car door.

❧

STEPHAN. STEPHAN. STEPHAN.

Stephan is a beautiful man—tall, athletic, very handsome, very smart, very creative, and, I suspect, also very successful—who I met about twelve hours after I met Nigel. Stephan invited me for tea. We had a pleasant conversation. I enjoyed his company. He's soft spoken, kind, and unassuming. Very respectful.

Stephan was emotionally open and brought out the softness in me, encouraging me to speak with an open heart and share myself with him. Driving away from our second date, I had the thought, *Is it him? Have I finally met the One?*

Stephan has not promised to whisk me away on fancy vacations. Rather, he sent me beautiful poetic text messages, full of words I long to hear. "*You feel good to me. You're a beautiful woman in so many ways. You're a healer, bringing light, life, and love into the world. I want more. Thoughts of you are lingering. I woke thinking of you . . . what can we create together? I want to touch your hands and feel your warmth enter me. I want to kiss your lips. . . I wonder if you're thinking about me. . . What can we create together? I want to press my heart against your open heart. . . I want to explore this with you, heart open.*"

Stephan takes my breath away with his words that make me go all melty and gooey inside. His poetic wooing makes my womb flutter, my heart beat faster, and my breath catch. It is so easy to visualize Stephan in my life. It's easy to see him walking through my door. It's effortless to imagine his hands in mine, his heart pressed against me, his lips searching for me. It's easy to imagine snuggling with him, waking next to him, laying my head on his shoulder, broad and protective. It's easy to imagine being Stephan's woman. It's easy to imagine introducing him, proudly, as My Man. It's easy to imagine him being unfailingly loyal to me, and valuing me for the gifts I bring. He also looks remarkably like the man I've been painting myself with and the man that Patti painted in my commissioned piece, which is entitled *Hieros Gamos*. He's definitely attractive enough for me.

Last night he called me and we talked for three hours. Typically, I hate talking on the phone. But I wanted to know more about him and I wanted to share more of myself with him. We are playing hooky today to meet again. Likely for an unassuming lunch and a walk, where we will hold hands and kiss for the first time, to see if it feels as good as we've been visioning it.

He said he felt as though we have known each other before. In another dimension. Another lifetime.

My Soul whispers, *It will be so easy with him. So easy.*

It already feels easy. One of the ways that I know a dream or vision is meant for me is that it comes spontaneously without me trying and there's no desperation in it. I think it's what they mean when you feel as if it's already happened. With Stephan, it seems effortless to fall into each other, to grasp hands and not let go.

Of course, it's premature and there is no rush. I don't want to skip over any of the good parts. In contrast to the other men I've dated, where I instantly thought, *This is not My Man*, I find myself opening to the idea of Stephan being my Fall Boyfriend.

The Universe has been yanking men out from under me rather quickly. I hope the Universe allows this one to stay. I like him. I really, really like him. I want to touch his hands today. I want him to lean in and kiss me. I want to taste his lips and feel what kind of energy we generate together.

⁂

LOVE IS NOT A SOLITARY ACT. Love, like money, must be circulated. Ideas must be made manifest, and love must be expressed. Love cannot be contained within one person and shared exclusively with the Divine. Well, I guess it can. However, I don't believe that it can be experienced to its fullest potential independently.

Love is energy that must move. It bounces from person to person. It must be experienced, shared. Love is communal.

My fantasies lately have tended toward a sexual practice, a practice like meditation and yoga. A ritual of sex and intimacy that has limitless potential. The wordlessness and mindfulness of it is something I find extremely erotic. To dwell on a kiss. To

stare into each other's eyes. To lie side by side and circulate energy through our bodies with intention, to feel what kind of energy
we can generate together. To hold still and circulate energy while
he penetrates me. To allow him to open my cervix with his soft
and patient touch, as the deepest depths of my body and my Soul
open to him. Even in only fifteen minutes, exquisite intimacy can
be created through these means.

I crave a sexuality that is a form of worship, of communion, of
devotion. I crave the idea of coming together—he as the Christ,
me as the Magdalene—in devotion and worshipping each other as
the expressions of God that we are. I crave a holy and sacred altar
on which to lay our love and surrender to each other. I crave
sucking his cock in worship to his masculinity, as a divine offering of ecstasy. I fantasize about showering each other with our
sexual fluids as we climax in waves of pleasure. I crave coming
together in wholeness, each bringing his/her own part of yin and
yang to make a perfect circle of energy. I crave the dance of the
Sacred Feminine and the Sacred Masculine to create a whole
Godhead and a healing experience that creates intense, passionate, secure, and comforting intimacy and oneness.

No, I have no desire to sit in a meditation chair and reach
transcendence isolated and alone. My desire is to join with another, a Soul Mate, My Man, and easily and effortlessly explore
the godness within each other as we reach deeper and deeper for
each other, for God in each other, for a closeness that I have not
yet experienced with another person in this lifetime, but which I
know I'm capable of because of my past-life experience with Brad.

As good as Brad was in that past life, I know that I will reach
higher highs with My Man. He too is from a past life and he's
done his emotional and spiritual work, he's on the spiritual path
at my level and we've already taken each other to godlike intimacy
on other planes. We come together easily and everything flows

and we are in sync with each other. It will be so easy. It will be so full of pleasure, it will be contentment to the nth degree, and we will be worshipful and devoted to each other without reservation.

It's happening NOW.

FORTY-EIGHT

NOVEMBER 19, 2013

Two things. No, three things.

Stephan is NOT my guy. His smell and taste was nauseating—very acidic—maybe it was Irish Spring or something. Either way it turned my stomach. He was also an atrocious dresser. I must be with someone who I am proud to be seen with. It's the Cool Factor. My Man must be very attractive and a great dresser and have a Cool Factor.

It's amazing how a craving for intimacy will allow me to project all kinds of characteristics on a man—any man, really—who shows up and wants to play the role. After two breakfast/tea dates with Stephan, my fantasies included changing my parenting schedule to meet his, prematurely missing him and his girls the week after Christmas, plans to commission three more tree paintings for the living room, relief that money wouldn't be such a stressful problem for me, and relief that there will be someone to do the man chores. Not to mention the idea that I would be wooed and courted with the most beautiful words and we'd live happily ever after, as heart-open Soul Mates. Yes, it was so easy to imagine a whole life with him, a happy one, a less stressful one, a highly sexual one, a heart-opened one.

I'm kind of an asshole. I have a fucked up idea about men, sex, and their hearts. I would like to blame Brad, to whom I've projected an entire identity and role in my life, which he likely has no part in. I somehow believe that men want to have casual sex and don't have any real feelings about it; and that's simply not true.

❧

I DIDN'T PLAN ON IT, but when Stephan arrived he immediately kissed me. Though I knew his smell was "off" for me, the heart-open way he was with me was touching and felt good. His heart was open to me and his kiss and touch reflected that. I got aroused and brought him to my bedroom. When I got aroused, I had thoughts like, *This is not my guy, but having sex with strangers makes me feel slutty and that really turns me on.* So I took off my clothes and he gave me the best head I may have ever had.

It was passionate and lovely. He took his time and I relaxed. He kept going after I came and . . . truly it was the best head and hand job ever. Then he couldn't get it up. . . he said he hadn't had sex in two-and-a-half years because he hadn't felt like sharing his energy with anyone. He was open and sensitive and vulnerable, and I felt like I had taken advantage of him, and worried that he would think I don't want to be with him because he couldn't. He couldn't because he's sensitive and not a man whore. I, however, am a slutty barracuda who all too often assumes that men have no feelings about sex and that I can't hurt them with my words and attitudes. Afterwards, he said he wanted to create a boy-friend/girlfriend relationship with me and I had to tell him that I didn't really want to see him again.

I can be such an asshole!!! Alex's heart was so closed to me that nothing I did touched him. Brad, my first time out of the marriage, was very casual about sex and "felt bad" about women falling for him and him tossing them aside—but not bad enough, of course, not to do it, or anything "crazy" like *that*. I really need to change this attitude about men and their hearts. Men, I am discovering, are very wounded and lonely creatures, who are easily hurt and quite vulnerable.

Oh, Tracee, be softer with these poor Souls.

❧

I WOKE THIS MORNING to this message: *You can't behave down here (lower detached physical sexuality) and expect to be up here (heart open and deeply spiritually connected with emotional intimacy).* Of course, this is easier to do when I am sated. When I am ovulating and calling men toward me by the droves, or I have fantasies of being just the most wanton slut with many men, well, it's a conflict between my desires/behavior and my declaration of what I want. One option is to go back to OMing, but I find OMing less satisfying than I would like. I think celibacy is probably the prudent choice . . . but what am I supposed to do with the potent sexual energy that wants to burst forth from my pussy?

God, bring me a wealthy and successful man, with lots of time to spend with me, with the gift of poetry and seductive words, someone with eyes and heart only for me, who stimulates and elevates me in every area, who is extremely good looking, has a superb wardrobe, and has a Cool Factor. Lord, bring me the perfect man for me. The winter solstice is only one month away. Fall Boyfriend needs to hurry to make the deadline.

❧

TRANSMUTATION. CRONE of Transmutation.

For weeks this card has come up for me. Since summer, at least. It's the highest fire card. The image on it is of a female phoenix rising from flames, with a heart of fire and a pussy of fire. She has the face of a bird and wings of fire.

It is a theory Charles Darwin was made famous for: He called the transmutation of a species *evolution*. Transmutation is also a word used in alchemy, when alchemists attempted to turn base metals into gold. One of the early ideas of transmutation is that a species becomes more complex over time, adapting to their environment, and the next generation can inherit these changes.

In the field of natural science, transmutation was controversial because of the God issue. One side argued that because a species was created from an idea in the mind of God, it was unchangeable. The other argued that because it was created from an idea in the mind of God, it was ever-expanding and more complex. Nuclear transmutation is the conversion of one chemical element into another; in other words, atoms of one element change into atoms of another. Scientific attempts at transmutation was outlawed at one point, as radical and dangerous.

The Big Bang theory holds that an explosion a the birth of our Universe produced hydrogen and helium. All other elements of matter were transmutations of these.

When the Soul Awakens by Nancy Seifer and Martin Vieweg says: *"Technically speaking, the process of transformation occurs in three stages, according to the ageless wisdom. The terms used to describe these progressive stages of unfoldment are: transmutation, transformation, and transfiguration. Lifetimes are required to complete the metamorphosis that culminates at the stage of transfiguration, when the light of the Soul pours down upon the outer persona and changes it—permanently."*

Interestingly these three cards: *Transmutation, Transformation,* and *Transfiguration* have come up over and over in my cards.

Also quite fascinating is the hypothesis of *When the Soul Awakens* authors, Seifer and Vieweg, that the transmutation part of the process of spiritual awakening involves the use of *sexual energy* to create art, music, and books. The artist struggles with baser sexual desire often. They transmute the "raw material force" of sexuality into creative expression. Throughout history, they note, creative geniuses have wrestled with their lower nature in the struggle to utilize the vital forces of their personalities in service to the world. *That explains my lusty behavior and thoughts as I struggle to my Spiritual En-lighten-ment (In-Light-And-Meaning).*

Spiritual transmutation is the process by which material form comes into being from the Spiritual Realm. In other words, it's how thoughts become things. It's the ability to convert the energy around us into power. According to Melody Larson, author of *Spiritual Journey to Awakening*, transmutation is the eleventh step of the spiritual journey: mastery. She reports that only 0.5 percent of humanity chooses to continue to the eleventh step.

It is the step in which masters of energy learn how to wield universal laws and forces to perform miracles and this used to be reserved for great saints, yogis, and prophets. This step is all about learning to perform miracles and manifest instantly—or nearly instantly. *Wow.*

This stage of awakening occurs, says Larson, when one *knows*, beyond a conceptual level, that we *are* spirit, with all of the powers associated. Those in the transmutation stage are focused on POWER. The Power of Intention.

❧

KIND OF LIKE WHEN you bring a gold clutch back from heaven. Now for the $2 million.

FORTY-NINE

NOVEMBER 20, 2013

The information on transmutation has me feeling like my life could be a lot more fun. What can I do with this transmutation power I'm learning?

Madigan dropped my iPhone into the bathtub last night. I lost my shit, screamed the F-word and chewed her out. I couldn't decide if I should feel bad about being an asshole or not.

This morning I used the skills I learned at my Universal White Time Healing course. I held my hands over the phone, which was in a baggy full of rice. At the end of fifteen minutes my iPhone buzzed. It had turned itself on and was as good as new. Perfect. No problems.

❧

THE THOUGHTS AND feelings that came forward within me were feelings of love for Brad. I sent him love and energy. I felt my love for him during our past life on our ranch. Such a sweet and pure and easy love it was. I talked to him through the ether of time and space. Which I actually do a lot of, automatically and without effort. In fact, my effort is usually to resist thoughts of him so I can "get over it." As if "getting over it" is the appropriate response to a highly intense and beautiful love. *Just get over it Tracee, make it so it doesn't matter to you. Move on.* Well, it's November and that strategy is not working. So I'm giving myself over to it. I'm keeping my heart open to him. I've put it out there and I can't control what he does with it, but it is the energy of love and my heart still wants to be open to it. So I am surrendering to my natural instincts to send him healing energy, and drawing from the feelings of openhearted love I have shared with him to generate healing energy within myself.

Love generates love. Love expressed puts love out into the world. Love is a powerful energy—some say the most powerful energy in the Universe and beyond. For whatever reason. And of course I have romantic fantasies that the reason is that we're meant to be together and he will call me and insist on meeting me and we'll make love and decide to see each other as boyfriend and girlfriend and see what that is like, without high commitment pressure, and that it will be soooo easy. But my romantic fantasy is unlikely to come to fruit.

Except . . . stream of consciousness here . . . what if I can make it happen through methods of transmutation and manifestation?

What is happening here? Why haven't I been able to let this go? All of the other men I've dated—even the ones I've had sex with—have come and gone with nary a regret from me. Still, Brad. Even when I'm having sex with *them*, I'm thinking about how much more intoxicating and arousing and loving the intimacy and energy was between Brad and I. Is he pulling on me and resisting it even more than I am?

I suspect this is so. He has made a choice—a conscious choice not to fall in love with me—his words, the thought of them that makes me want to cry a little, a rejection of my Open Heart. Part of me wants to manifest that he make another choice.

Even as I call it in—that he makes the other choice, to fall in love with me because it's what his Soul wants and it's what his heart authentically feels—I keep adding the caveat If it is for my—our—highest good and only if it's EASY.

On the surface Brad and I both sensed that it would not be easy between us. There were things. Both of our direct communication styles, for one. My God, who else could tolerate our direct way of communication?

Nigel asked me, "Do you ever put yourself in someone else's shoes before you speak?"

Oh my God, I thought, *I have thought the same thing, maybe even said the same thing, to Brad. Maybe *I* have Asperger's.*

Generally I make every attempt NOT to harm people when I speak what I interpret as "The Truth." But honestly I think I did hurt Brad. Neecy has giving me similar feedback, that my mouth can be harsh and painful. I might actually have made Nigel feel bad, and I know I made Stephan feel bad.

Of course, because we're both very direct and probably too honest in our communication, you might think it would be easy for us to dole out free passes. It might even be easy for us to communicate because we have the same style. If we both approached it as tenderly as possible and were super quick with apologies and amends . . . then maybe it could be easy.

I *know* it was so easy between us once, in another realm, in another time. A time that, according to many spiritual masters, is occurring right this very second. We're making love every day and it's positively divine; we're making babies and running a ranch and we're so content and happy and in love and connected and it's sooo easy.

Look at me. Being silly. Working out a relationship that doesn't exist. He doesn't want me. He consciously chooses *not me.* I put it out there, *I love you.* He left me hanging, vulnerable and exposed, in the wind, alone.

I love him. I just do.

❧

BACK TO MY ORIGINAL thought, my hypothesis of transmutation and manifestation.

Is the Love Energy the power that manifests? Am I transmuting Love into a Gold Clutch or a good-as-new iPhone?

Is Love the Energy that generates money?

I'm close and there is no reason I'm not making a ton of money. Truly. My clients are highly satisfied and make enormous progress when they work with me. I put out a great blog and help people constantly. I am highly loving, so even when I'm being an asshole it is born of a high love energy.

My vibration is high. People instantly notice my high-energy, high-vibrational presence and they want *more* of it.

I've ruled out money as an indicator of worthiness or of value put into the world. If that were true women would be only putting in about one percent of the world's value and positive energy and men would be putting in ninety-nine percent of the world's value and energy. It's obvious this isn't true.

Yes, women have issues with money. We dare not make it our currency, that's my most recent observation/hypothesis about the energy of money.

I'm missing a piece and I know it. It's not flowing as abundantly as I need it to—as I want it to, at least. I'm so close, but somewhere I have a block that's holding it off. Somewhere it's connected to love and my revelation that love must be circulated in order to be experienced fully.

By the same token, *money must be circulated for any kind of healthy economy.* That's the fundamental basics of capitalism right there. We must make it to spend it and if it's not spent then others can't make it. I must ask for it and receive it, in order to circulate it, which then helps others. This is the foundation of the entire economy. The downward spiral of 2008, and the Great Depression of the 1920s, is the result of money not circulating. Banks stopped lending, people stopped spending, money halted its flow, and everyone felt the pain all over the entire world.

The interesting thing about this is that money is an imaginary energy. When you see those stock market numbers rolling up and clicking down, and news anchors freaking out about the fallout of a depressed economy and "losing" so much money, it's imaginary money. We made it up. We have a cultural agreement to exchange this imaginary energy for things we value, as our means of exchange for goods and services. It's a common denominator the world over, a figment of our collective consciousness.

But only a tiny percentage of all of the money and wealth in the world is physically manifest. There is not a giant building with all of the money in the stock market, waiting to fill people's pockets. No, that money is a figment of the imagination. When the stock market crashes it's because people stop circulating money and they quit imagining it in great abundance. When the markets skyrocket, it's because money is being *exchanged* at a high rate of return. Still, the money remains imaginary. Up and down our collective consciousness expands and constricts this imaginary energy that isn't even material 90 percent of the time.

Also interesting is the language we use to talk about this form of energy. For some reason that I can't put my finger on money appears to defy the laws of energy in some ways. For instance, you can earn interest on money—thus expanding the energy of money. However, the expansion of the money energy is considered less valuable—inflation—the more of it we generate, create, exchange, circulate, and imagine. This is conflicting with the way other energy works.

An opposite example is love. The more it is expressed and circulated the stronger and more valuable it gets. Between lovers, for instance, the more they express their love, the more attention they put on each other and the more they focus on the positive feelings involved—the more it expands into a greater and more fulfilling, deeply intimate love.

Why then does the energy of money lose value the more we create and put into the economy? Juxtaposed, why then does the economy become depressed if we don't put enough of it into the economy? It seems that money needs more "balance" as energy than does love.

While we're comparing the two energies—because I feel like my answer to the money puzzle I'm struggling with, is in fact, the connection between the two energies of love and money (which might very well be the same energy, except this doesn't make sense at all in the context of the gender divide)—why do people get hung up on *equality* in terms of the energy of money, but you never hear anyone say that everyone should have an equal amount of love? No one walks around bashing love either.

Well, I suppose they do, when they've suffered a heartbreak or a traumatic childhood, they constrict love and say things like, "Love sucks," and devote a tremendous amount of energy to denying love and withholding it from themselves and each other.

People also use love to distort reality and manipulate other people. I once wrote a book titled *Love Distortion* that speaks to this issue directly.

Okay. So. What we have are two energies that carry extremely powerful emotions.

Why are women so great at the Love part and men so great at the Money part?

Is love feminine and Money masculine energy?

Is the having of Love & Money like Yin and Yang? Or are women simply unaccustomed to dealing with the energy of money because it's been denied us for centuries? Do women simply need to learn how to generate money the way we've cultivated our ability to generate Love?

If this is so, do I want a man who has money, so I can learn from him how to generate the energy vibration of money and learn how to transmute the energy I'm putting out into the physical manifestation of money I bring in?

Yes.

Can I do that without a man who is great at generate the energy of money? Yes. But, will it be as fulfilling and fun? Unknown. Would it be easier? Yes. I think having a man by my side helping me learn to generate the energy of success manifested in the energy of money would be phenomenally helpful and pleasurable.

I choose that.

I want to identify the energy of money and learn how to transmute my energy *out* as money *in* so that I can teach all of my clients to do this, too.

Money is imaginary, a form of matter chosen by the collective consciousness; of this, there is no doubt. This does not make it irrelevant. It carries great power. We can make that "wrong," and many healers, spiritual people, women, and poor people do make it "wrong." However, it would be a smoother and simpler road if we learned to transmute the energy we put out into the already-agreed-upon energy of money and learned to pull it in, so we can circulate more of it.

I'm getting close with the money transmutation puzzle. I'm not there yet. But I'm getting close.

Lord, make me a conduit for the energy of money. Teach me to transmute my power, magic, and energy into the energy of money that I can circulate at my every whim with Joy and Love and Power. Manifest money in my life. So much money that I never have a list of things I want to do, but struggle to afford, again. Rather I choose to have such an abundance of cash that I am blessed with any opportunity I want to choose and every luxury that brings me joy, which I will then pass on to others.

FIFTY

NOVEMBER 26, 2013

Money. In my quest to understand the energy of money I've come across an assignment to write a letter to money. As if the Spirit of Money is an old friend. I'm supposed to apologize to that friend and ask him to come back into my life.

Apologize to money? "I should apologize to money? Are you fucking kidding me?

That's when I realized that I am really angry at money. Incensed at the idea that I should apologize to money—where is MY apology *from* money? So I guess I've uncovered some important feelings about the energy of money.

Money has been used as a weapon against me, as a barometer of my worth and value, pretty much always, and it continues to be so according to the current spiritual teachers in metaphysics.

"You get as much as you feel worthy of," they love to say.

"What you put out comes back to you . . . so put more value out into the world and money will come," they enjoy saying when you ask legit questions about the energy of cash.

"Aren't you seeing other forms of abundance in your life? Be grateful," they retort when questioned about power and green.

"Be more grateful. You don't sound very grateful!" they demand.

"Give more! You have to give to get!" they say, assuming that the richest people give the most? Is that their assumption? And that they gave before they got? *Uh. No.*

Pardon me for defying conventional wisdom and getting a little frustrated at the triteness of such things . . . but this is pissing me off. I've reached a point of frustration. I'm angry.

Money means NO. That's my earliest memories of money. *You can't have it because it costs money.*

Which is pretty typical of childhood for most of the planet, so it's not really that traumatic.

But I tell you what *was* traumatic: that my parents refused to help me in college, but paid for every one of my siblings' educations *and* sent them on expensive missions for the Church. Because they were *worthy* and I was *not.*

So, New Age gurus, were my parents right? That money believes me to be unworthy of it? That the Green God of Money knows that I am unworthy of it? Or were they both wrong and I just have to figure out where the magic pulley is that the Green God of Money pops out with a $2 million check and says, "Oh my child, you were worthy all the time, you just had to believe it!"

Is that the miracle I've been searching for?

Then we come to the other stuff. I've worked and worked and worked. I've put out 985-ish blog posts on *The Girl Revolution*, which have been available for free to millions of people. These posts have helped people a great deal. They have helped parents who were dealing with raising daughters in today's culture. They have helped thousands of women feel better about their bodies.

I know my posts have helped people because I have letters and comments and FB posts telling me that they have helped people.

Well, isn't helping people it's own reward? Isn't it enough?

No. *It's not Universe.* No. Helping people is my primary motivation, but it is not in and of itself enough. Money. I want money.

So, New Age gurus, are you telling me that Dooce, the famous blogger who spent her energies bashing her boss, put more inherent value into the world than I have, who helped hundreds of thousands of people for free? And while we're on the subject, are you telling me that other writers who have had more social media and marketing savvy from the beginning, and thus got farther than I did with *The Girl Revolution*, put more value in the world and thus are worthy of more success?

Jesus, how *worthy* must Warren Buffett and Oprah be? And Mother Teresa. Oh wait, that chick was poverty stricken on purpose, and I thought her message about worthiness was a different one . . .

Fear.

Lying in bed this morning I realized one thing. I have been afraid in my life. Sometimes completely terrorized.

Every time it was about money. Money.

Oh fine, not every time. Still, the majority of the times in my life where fear was debilitating or annoying it has been about money and the ability to provide for myself and my family our most basic needs.

Marriage.

The fundamental primary cause of my divorce was money at its most basic. I don't bring enough money in, so he doesn't value me. He certainly didn't think that readers' gratitude made the blog worth doing—that certainly wasn't enough compensation for him. No, what I did, and in fact who I am, was *worthless* because I made no money following my purpose.

Thanks for that, Spirit of Money. That didn't feel very good.

Money and Marriage again. Value. Money determined value between us, and power. He made the money, which gave him the most power. He controlled and withheld love from me with it, often sabotaging my own financial success in order to make me give up. I went without basic necessities like medicine, while he drank beer. Beer is expensive.

I go without. He indulges.

Oh wait, the Universe must value him more than it values me because he brought in more money than I did. Or he must value himself more than I value myself because he brought more money in than I did.

Right.

Time and again money has been used as the weapon to extort behavior—by my parents and by my husband, specifically. It has been used as a form of withholding of love. *If you don't do what we say, then we won't give you love or money.*

The iniquity of money is a problem, or at least it appears so. If money is a reflection of value, worthiness, or self-worth it would follow that rich people contribute more to life and the Universe and feel fantastic about themselves.

This, we know not to be true. Take Michael Jackson. The man was rich and famous and felt poorly about himself. Whitney Houston obviously did not feel good about herself. In fact, lots of wealthy people feel crappy about their lives. They say so all the time in interviews and autobiographies.

Take Nigel. He, I'm sure, brings value to the world, to his children and his coworkers. He also buys mineral rights from poor landowners for pennies so that his company can "frack" the earth—breaking open her shell and sucking the life out of her womb, contributing to the destruction of the planet, and he feels very generous for "changing these landowner's lives" by buying the mineral rights for $86,000. *Um, if you're poor and living on assis-*

tance, then yes, *$86,000 sounds like a large lump-sum payment. But the oil company will make billions, and Nigel, for his service to the world of negotiating this deal, makes up to four times that amount annually.* That money will likely pay off existing debt and maybe one kid's college education. Or be a down payment on one house. If they are savvy enough to make those choices. For this, Nigel gets compensated so much more than I, or any of the number of light bringers and healers. *Because he contributes more. Right?*

No. There's something missing here.

Something simple.

Something critical.

There's a piece of the puzzle missing here.

Unworthy people make money. People who contribute little to society make money. People who are actually doing terrible things make money. Like drug lords . . . they have money.

Many poor people contribute much to the Universe. Many poor people feel good about themselves, finding themselves worthy and of value. Poverty is not a *symptom* of low self-worth.

I hazard a guess that money is no more tied to worth, self-worth, value contributed, or gratitude than it is tied to "hard work." I think it is correlated by those who have it and those who don't, just as hard work is. But it is not a cause-and-effect relationship, otherwise it would hold true in all instances and in every case and it would be replicable across the board.

No.

I contribute. I feel good about myself. There is a reason I write and pursue coaching. It is because I know I have value and that I serve my clients very well and that I am very, very generous with my time, energy and money.

I know I give. I know I am grateful.

It *is* enough.

AND I also know that I am settling for less than the Universe has to offer me. I am grateful for what I have. AND it's not enough. Not in the sense that I can't live on it, and even live a lifestyle that's more abundant and full than the majority of the inhabitants of this planet. No, I understand that it is enough in that sense. But it is *not* enough for me to live the life *I* want to live. It is not enough for me to give my gifts to the world in as big a way as I want to give them. It is not enough to allow me to experience all of the experiences I want to experience. It is not enough for me to have the freedom to choose anything I want to be, have, or do.

No. It is not enough, because there is so much more available for the Universe to offer. The Universe could be so much softer and more generous with me.

Yesterday I found a pair of Cole Haan patent leather heels at the thrift store for $6.99. Charlie found a Bronco's pullover sweatshirt, one he's been wanting for a while, for $7.99. We were over the moon excited about it. Is it harder for the Universe to give me cash than it is for the Universe to give me designer shoes?

Both are energy materialized.

However, with cash I would have more choices. For instance, I could buy brand-new designer shoes of my choosing. I might have chosen the brown ones, or the orange ones. I might have chosen a different brand. Charlie really wanted the orange sweatshirt with blue script, not the blue sweatshirt with orange script that he found, and it was two sizes too big.

So, yes, we were grateful and even excited to have scored our thrift shop finds. Still, with cash we could have *chosen*.

I'm grateful that all of my bills are paid, that I have a hotel, airline tickets, and *Wicked* tickets bought and paid for, and that I have a house full of beautiful things that create a loving home, and we're all essentially healthy, and I have a New Rich lifestyle, and my business is being transformed, and I'm being transmuted, and I'm overall happy and filled with passion and life.

Yes, I am grateful.

I also have $44 left in my personal checking account, $0 in savings, $10,000 in credit card debt, $53,000 in student loans, and $65 in another checking account that I am about to overdraw by $1 in order to go to my energy work appointment so I can heal and allow more abundance and love into my life.

The part about this that I find so frustrating is that it's so *unnecessary*. It's unnecessary to bring me to my last cent so that my family can have a memorable vacation. It's unnecessary to allow debt to hang over my head, burdening me. It's unnecessary to give me "just enough" to survive, but only if the car doesn't break down. It's unnecessary to give me abundance in used nice things and leave me contemplating cashing in the coins in the piggy bank to put gas in the car. It's unnecessary to leave me wondering how I'll support my family if my clients don't renew, or if no one buys into my Year of YES! coaching programs (even though I followed all the rules!!!). I *try* as hard, or harder, than anyone else.

There are people for whom money flows. They are no more grateful, hardworking, worthy, or confident than I. They do not put out more "value" or "good" into the Universe than I do.

What am I missing? What am I missing? What am I missing?

I asked for clarity on this and was given three things. At the waking moment of a dream I heard: *Open Your Heart.* Which is admittedly exasperating, because I've been spending all of my money, time, and energy this year opening my heart and healing my heart and opening my ding-dang heart some more. I'll take my $65 from one checking account and proceed with more Heart Opening energy work.

Second, I was given the assignment, through a FB group I participate in, to write that letter to the Spirit of Money. I'll put that here later. The assignment brought out my anger about money. *At* money. For being kind of a bitch to me. For allowing itself to be used as a weapon. For tying itself to such things as worthiness, love, value, good or bad, enough or not enough and self-worth. For allowing itself to be used as a means to do harm in the world. For evading me. For withholding itself from me. For causing more fear in my life than any other energy. For being difficult to manage and control and for not loving me enough or allowing me to love it. For coming in the form of shoes and vans instead of wads of ample cash flowing over. For not having enough zeros. For putting women at risk. For choosing men over women to value and reward. For being inequitable.

Yes, I've been angry about money. Maybe that's the problem.

Maybe I need to forgive money. I think I'll listen to the Radical Forgiveness CD to clear some of this money stuff away.

❧

A DREAM:

My Man (I want to say my husband) gives my hand a squeeze and gives me an encouraging word. I walk on stage to speak and he stands behind me, supporting me. He's got my back. My success is his success. He wants everything good for me and he feels my work is critical to bring light to the planet and help others. He thinks my success is sexy and he's willing to back me in every way: financially, emotionally, spiritually, and physically. He's got my back.

It makes me feel so loved.

The Year of YES!

❧

I LOVE SOMEONE RIGHT NOW. I am so in love with him. We are connected so deeply I can practically feel what it feels like to *be* him. He is mine and I am his. We are one. We are intimate and completely in sync. I am seen by him. He sees me. And he loves every single spec of it. I see him. I love to look at him from body to Soul. Our love is the portal to the Universe.

He has to work something out, is a message that's been whispered to me over and over for the past few weeks or months.

He's almost ready, has been whispered to me for a few days.

❧

"MATTHEW 11:28–30."

That's what the napkin given to me at the coffee shop by a stranger said. I was complaining of being weary after all of the high-intensity spiritual work I've done over the last few years. *Rest. I need rest,* I say.

A man—it was so fast I didn't see his face—dropped a napkin on the table in front of me and disappeared: Matthew 11:28–30.

"COME TO ME, ALL YOU WHO ARE WEARY AND BURDENED, AND I WILL GIVE YOU REST. TAKE MY YOKE UPON YOU AND LEARN FROM ME, FOR I AM GENTLE AND HUMBLE IN HEART, AND YOU WILL FIND REST FOR YOUR SOULS. FOR MY YOKE IS EASY AND MY BURDEN IS LIGHT."

❧

THIS YEAR IS FOUNDATIONAL. *Next year is going to be HUGE!* says my Soul in my ear when I'm fretting about where I'm at and how fast its happening. I'm building a solid foundation for my busi-

399

ness, for my future, and things are about to take off and explode in massive success and a flood of cash.

This year is foundational. Next year is going to be HUGE!!

There are only about thirty-five days left in this year.

Oh please God, fill my Year of YES! coaching packages full in the next thirty-five days. PLEASE!!! I know it's within your power to do so. I know it's within your power to put money in the hands of the right people and compel them to sign up so they too can move to the next level.

FIFTY-ONE

NOVEMBER 29, 2013

D*ear Spirit of Money, I don't understand you. I study you (Dave Ramsey, Suzi Orman, Oprah Winfrey, Napoleon Hill, Wallace D. Wattles, and other teachers of world economics, capitalism, business, marketing, investing, personal finance, attraction, and so on) and every time I think I've figured out how to make more of you, Money, in my life, I find out I don't understand you at all.*

I get angry at your illusiveness. I get frustrated at how much you withhold yourself from me. I spin my wheels, running and working as fast as I can, like a hamster on a treadmill, and you evade me. I jump off cliffs, believing in your oh-so-close abundance, only to be rewarded with either total failure or just enough to squeak by. Actually, if I'm really honest and realistic about it, it's not even enough to squeak by because I have debt and forbearances on my student loans racking up thousands in interest year after year.

It's gotten to the point where I'm mostly frustrated and angry with you. I don't understand how to attract and harness your energy. Your refusal to flood me with the abundance and riches others experience leaves me feeling unloved and unworthy.

The people who have "supposed" to have loved me most have used you, Spirit of Money, against me. They have used it to make me power-

less, to punish me, to sabotage my dreams and ambition and to un-love me. It has hurt me deeply, Money.

Your power is unquestionable, controlling the surface power and much of the spiritual power in the world. By collective agreement you're the Spirit with which we humans have chosen to trade.

But you pick and choose who you will lavish with your love in un-predictable and unclear ways. You appear to choose men over women by astounding numbers. You trick people into thinking that you bestow your blessings on those who "work hard" or are "grateful enough" or are thinking the "right thoughts" about you. Maybe it is true that sometimes being grateful, working hard, and thinking the right thoughts and hold-ing the right beliefs about you help to attract money.

But kagillions of women work hard, are desperately and pathetically grateful in the face of horrors and atrocities committed on them by the more having among us, and they are not showered with your goodness.

What are the right thoughts about you, Spirit of Money?

What are the correct, effective beliefs about you, Spirit of Money?

I've got all sorts of healers and practitioners telling me "The Secret" about you, but most of them are poor. So I hesitate to take their "beliefs" about the Spirit of Money very seriously as the correct and most effective ones. If they knew how to tap into your vast and abundant energy, they'd be doing it already. Because it ain't no fun being poor.

Ain't no fun beggin'.

Ain't no fun jumping through imaginary hoops designed by people who think they know what they're talking about, but don't have two pen-nies to rub together either.

I do all the "right things."

If I read a book that claims to have all the answers, I follow through with the exercises and shift my belief system.

And it sorta works.

But only sorta.

Here's the thing about my relationship with you, Spirit of Money.

I don't think you're being straight with me. I think you fuck with me a lot. I think you've allowed yourself to be a weapon against my Soul, my vulnerable heart and my body too. You've been responsible for 95 percent of the fear I've experienced in my life. If I have self-worth issues you're tied into it significantly. You've sent double messages to me and my tribe for centuries. You're not very kind to women, or children for that matter. You're inconsistent and difficult to read. At times you have been cruel. Cold. Hard. Battering.

I have a client who said she is going to break up with you because it's an unhealthy relationship and that's what she would do if you were her boyfriend. God, you're practically the worst boyfriend ever! Seductive and elusive. Emotionally withholding. Giving "just enough" to get by.

I know that I've made agreements with you. Based on beliefs that I've carried over from various childhood and cultural messaging.

I've made bargains having to do with working and being a mother and agreeing to "sacrifice" so that I could be a better mom. I know that this caused Alex a great deal of stress and inflicted his own fears on him. I know that I've been bargaining, cheap, and withholding with myself in an attempt to "follow the rules" and not live beyond my means.

I confess to you right now that I don't know what the right or effective energy, thoughts, beliefs, or emotions about you is. I don't have any idea. If I did, my bank account would be overflowing with cash.

These things are true:

I have enough. I'm grateful. Enough is not good enough.

I am okay. I will be okay. I'm grateful. Okay is not good enough.

I have more money than 80 percent of the women on the planet. I drive a minivan. I live in a house. I live in a fantastic community. My children are well educated. I have freedom in a democracy. I am privileged. I do what I want for a living. I even do what I want for fun. I make my own joy. I have food in my fridge and my pantry. I have free medical coverage through Obamacare. I have wonderful friends in my life. I have a spiritual community. Many men want to date me. My house is full of beautiful art. I'm writing on a new MacBook Pro. I make calls from an iPhone. I've traveled lots of places this year. I am so successful I have subcontractors. My business is growing. I'm taking my kids to New York City for Christmas, and everything excluding spending money is already paid for.

I'm smart. I'm well-liked. The things I write, do, and say bring light into the world and change people for the better. My clients are very happy with my service and the insight I bring into their lives. I have many creative skills and talents that bring me income and great joy. I get energy work, massages, spiritual guidance, coaching, and alternative healthcare regularly. I treat myself to shellac nails and they attract men. I can afford to give my children a quality of life that 90 percent of the children on Planet Earth have reason to envy.

I have access to more educational information than I could ever consume. My business has grown from ZERO coaching clients to FOUR coaching clients, plus a ten-person Maxcellerator group in only months. My website is being redesigned beautifully. I've laid groundwork for a business that is going to thrive. Things are hopeful, wonderful, exciting.

I am grateful for ALL of this and so so much more.

It's still not good enough.

It is not as if I'm blind to everything I have, Spirit of Money. Still, I'm not blind to the more that's available to me. And I want it.

I want it for my business. I want it for my lifestyle. I want it for my joy levels. I want the more that the Universe can freely and easily give.

I think I'm on to you, Spirit of Money. I know what kind of power you offer. I don't claim to understand the parts that hang me up or the parts that wield power over others. I don't even want to understand that. But, I also know that if I have more of you—an abundance flowing over so as I can't even contain it in the small packages I have to hold your bountiful blessings—then I can do much, much greater good in the world.

Coming to me and being my consistent passionate lover will not cost you anything. I know that it won't. I understand at least that much about your nature.

Spirit of Money, I concede that I've been angry and I forgive you for that which I don't understand and do not seek to understand about your shadow side. Without having to understand my own shadow side about your nature, I surrender my shadow side to your good will, and ask you for forgiveness for whatever beliefs, thoughts, feelings, and actions I have taken that might have offended you or violated any Spiritual Laws to which you adhere and required my adherence to.

I confess. I concede. I forgive. I ask forgiveness. I surrender.

I claim a clean slate. Free of all generational, cultural, personal, relational, psychic, conscious or unconscious unhealthy paradigms, beliefs, feelings, conflicting emotions, and actions that might hold you from me.

Rather I ask that you come into my life in a flood of cash. I understand that abundance can come in many forms, and I thank you for that. However, Spirit of Money, I ask that you come into my bank account, my hands, my purse and wallet, my experience as United States currency: dollars—hundreds of thousands of them. In fact, having had my Spirit Realm experience in the Having Room, I claim that $2 million as mine in the human Earth NOW realm.

Spirit of Money, I invite you into my life to be a Joy-full experience that brings such freedom that I can express myself without restraint. That I can experience everything I wish or desire without constraint.

I call forth cash, in addition to other forms of abundance and their sweet treasures, but primarily, Spirit of Money, I wish to be showered with cash. I also declare that cash flows into my life untied to conditions such as how much worth, value, gratitude, hard work, and "right" rules I follow. I reject the claim that the Spirit of Money is tied to any of these things.

I accept and claim the reality that the Spirit of Money comes to me for no other reason than that I intend it to and have asked it to.

I will go on as I have bringing my gifts into the world, sharing my light, lifting others up, helping people find their purpose and develop the ability to serve their Soul's purpose in this human experience. I will go on being generous and kind, all the more so with greater means. I will continue to live the fullest life possible and continue my spiritual quest for purpose, meaning, connection, and enlightenment. I will continue in this way for the abundant joy it brings me.

However, none of these actions are tied to the amount of money that flows into my life. The money flows and flows and flows—in a flood of generosity that I haven't even dared imagine. It's the kind of abundance that gets one in the papers as having "been discovered" or "hit the jackpot" or "overnight sensation."

This money, this cash, comes easily and effortlessly.

Spirit of Money, I ask you to speak with clarity to my Soul about how to open the doors to this tremendous flow of cash and keep the flow coming and keep the doors and windows and secret hatches open to the incoming flow of dollars. In addition, I ask that you, Spirit of Money, direct me in your wisdom about what things I desire to do with the money for the highest good and the best outcome for myself and my family and the greater whole.

I declare it. I claim it. I welcome it. I open to it. I surrender it to you, Spirit of Money and Mother God to do as I have commanded over my life in regards to granting me this enormous flow of cash into my life.

So it is. This or something better.

Love, so much Love and gratitude,

Tracee Sioux

❧

MONEY COMES TO ME BECAUSE I INTEND FOR IT TO COME AND I ASK FOR IT. IT IS NOT TIED TO ANYTHING ELSE.

FIFTY-TWO

DECEMBER 1, 2013

I created a Money Altar, compiling all of the crystals and stones I've used to attract prosperity, my Gold Clutch and wallet, the red feng shui envelope, and the three $100 bills I've used to attract riches, the $2 million check I wrote myself after my realm hopping experience into the Great Beyond dated 1-1-2016, the world bank I use to collect my found change, my checkbooks and credit and debit cards, my bowl of mustard seeds, my business cards, and the Tarot cards I drew this week (*Crone of Transmutation* (again), *Maiden of Passion, Lakshmi, Wheel of Fortune*), iPhone, and my computer with my bank accounts and budget sheets, plus my website pulled up.

Abraham-Hick's vortex meditation on Financial Abundance has been playing since Friday morning. I used my Universal White Time Healing skills to heal my money consciousness. I intend to cleanse, balance, heal, and protect my money. I called forth all benevolent beings and spirits to assist me in whatever work that needed doing about my money consciousness. I called forth my God team: Mary Magdalene and Jesus, angels, archangels, and beings from the Great Beyond and Great Before.

I held a ritual over my money situation, forgiving money for my inability to understand it, forgiving it for perceived wrongs on my part. I asked money for forgiveness for any way in which I've misused its power and forgiveness for my inability to grasp its full nature. I released any and all beliefs, thoughts, and conscious or subconscious blocks which hold money away from me. I included beliefs that have been inherited by culture, collective consciousness, inherited from family, hidden in my DNA, from past lives and parallel lives.

I called forth cash as my currency of choice. I thanked the Spirit of Money, with real gratitude, for the many forms of abundance that come and bless my life.

Another important thing I did was to "untie" money from the conditions in which money can come to me. I untied it from time, hard work, gratitude, visioning work, "right" beliefs or attitudes, understanding of its energetic quirks, and behaviors, including how I spend it and what I must do to get it, any worth or worthlessness issues that it might be tied to, and my "value" perceived by myself, God, society, culture, or other people.

The thing is that I reject the supposition that I am ungrateful—as evidence by how ridiculously excited I am to score a $7 pair of designer shoes at the Thrift Store. I reject the insinuation that I don't put enough value into the world—as evidenced by the many, many letters and words of gratitude about the value I bring to other people through my blog posts, Facebook posts, personal interaction, and service. I scoff at the notion that I feel too "unworthy" to experience abundant money as evidenced by my stubborn insistence that I can and will make a living through my writing and coaching, even in the face of twelve years with a man who believed wholeheartedly in my failure and who consistently sabotaged any success I might have achieved. I roll my eyes at the suggestion that I don't "believe" in my success enough for the same evidentiary reason as the previous sentence.

If one does not "believe," then one does not write a free blog consistently for seven years and take the risks and leaps off cliffs that I take—with dogged and sometimes absurd persistence—as I have done without fail. I take exception to the mere notion that fear prevents one from being successful, and I hold up every single woman and man who did something that's never been done before in the face of fear, whether it's fear of failure or success.

> MONEY COMES TO ME BECAUSE I INTEND FOR IT TO COME AND I
> ASK FOR IT. IT IS NOT TIED TO ANYTHING ELSE.

Then, because the Law of Attraction works on a feeling nature, I took off all of my clothes and lay on my bed to masturbate to thoughts of rolling around in piles of cash with my lover on a yacht, repeating joyful exclamations such as, "Oh my God, we're so fucking Rich!" and "We can do *anything* we want!" and "The world is at our fingertips. There is so much freedom in this!" I visualized that we made love and basked in the joy of our liberating financial freedom in all sorts of exotic locations that cost a lot of money to be there. We rolled around in cash and we felt exquisite about our good fortune!

❧

SEXUALITY HAS BEEN USED by spiritual people for eons and we really don't talk about it enough. I find myself masturbating as a Law of Attraction tool.

If you have ever sat in meditation and tried to conjure up an emotion that is in conflict with your current experience, then you know it's pretty effortful. It takes great deal of mental trickery and energy to make yourself feel rich when you have $20 in your bank account with kids to feed and no gas in the car. It's not effortless at all and most people can't even do it. I can rarely achieve it.

However, most of us have already conditioned ourselves to become aroused quickly and effortlessly when we have an hour to ourselves in a quiet house. We do it because we want to feel good. *Feel good now*, is Abraham-Hicks' most powerful advice.

In my research on spiritual transmutation it was suggested that part of that is to transmute sexual energy—powerful feel-good energy and heightened emotions—into the physical realm.

Some religions have preached *recycling* sexual energy into spiritual pursuits. That's what religious celibacy is about. However, I wonder if the opposite methodology will produce more physical manifestation—from the Spirit into Form?

We are spiritual beings having a human experience. As such, cash and sex are an enormous part of our human experience. Imagine—and I often do—what you can attract if you are creating intense sexual energy with your lover and "agreeing" on attracting things or experiences. Each other's success, money, vacations, objects, and more feelings, such as love and joy, babies, and all other things. Even when you're not making love you're using your sexual energy together to bring things into form. Transmuting from Spirit to Form through sexual energy.

Of course, the sexual energy is more potent when it is a deeply loving and intimate sexual energy of two partners.

Interestingly, my sexual fantasies tend toward submission. I think this is a physical reflection of my craving to surrender to God. If I am the Magdalene and my lover is Jesus in the scenario, my craving is to surrender to God in Jesus. The God in me craves surrender to the God in him. I don't always want to surrender, because I'm me and leading is a natural part of who I am. But the feeling of surrender is practice in surrender to a higher power.

People don't use their sexual energy in their Law of Attraction work enough. Perhaps that's the benefits of OMing that I missed originally in my experiment. Can I use OMing as a Law of Attraction tool to attract what I want, because I will be in a heightened feeling state as I go about my life—experiencing the endorphins and oxytocin to the brain on a regular basis—with a partner who is also experiencing heightened positive vibrations?

While I would prefer for this to be with My Man, perhaps this theory is worth further exploration with Robert, my OM partner.

Even masturbating with the Financial Abundance meditation must connect the subconscious mind to experience heightened pleasure to the experience of having more money. According to every spiritual master, especially those who speak of metaphysics and Law of Attraction, it's the connection of pleasure, excitement, and joy that brings more pleasure, excitement, and joy to us.

Permission to masturbate and have a lot of sex, people! This rule does not suck. In fact, it's highly pleasurable. I commit to using it more than I do. It's an experiment in Pleasure Drenching!

FIFTY-THREE

DECEMBER 2, 2013

Intendagasm: transmuting the heightened vibration of sexual energy while agreeing on and holding an intention for the purpose of manifesting form and/or outcome.

Attractagasm: Using the feeling state of sexual arousal to attract what you want.

I went over to Robert's last night and I proposed a new ritual.

"What if," I proposed? "If the Law of Attraction works on a heightened feeling state, what would happen if during sexual stimulation we held an intention together to generate the high pleasure feeling state the Universe needs to attract what we want? Also, one of the laws is that when two or more people agree on something then it must be done, so because we're generating a heightened emotional state using pleasure energy together we then increase the power of our intention. What if we declared an intention before our sessions and held our intention. What if that works to attract what we want faster and with more power?

"We would employ digital stimulation of my g-spot because that's what really gets me off." (Penetration, even digital, is not allowed in the OMing One Taste protocol.)

Robert was all in.

My declared intentions are to manifest a beautiful relationship with the perfect man for me and to fill my Year of YES! coaching program. The broader intention was to manifest a very profitable business including the coaching and the website and to complete and manifest this book. When you start making intentions it's so fun to just go all the way.

Robert's intention is to manifest and explore his lovely relationship with his girlfriend. His professional intention is to complete one novel he's currently working on by June 2014, and in the meantime complete several more book proposals.

With that declared, we went up to the "nest" he had created in his bedroom, I took off my pants and he made me cum in about twenty to twenty-five minutes. After which, we agreed that we would abandon OM's rules around the timer because it takes me about five minutes more to cum, currently, and I'm all aroused and ready when the timer goes off and then it causes me to pull back.

In fact, we agreed that we aren't even OMing anymore because now we've completely changed the purpose, the stroke, and all of the boundaries. Rather we are participating in my own made-up ritual called Intendagasm or Attractagasm.

❧

THEN I MET AN ex-Mormon dentist with bad teeth for coffee. His voice was squeaky and unattractive. We went for coffee during the dinner hour, which I was beyond irritated about, because it was dinnertime and I thought it was cheap, and I was hungry. So I vowed not to do coffee during lunch or dinner hours again. He hinted that he has difficulty keeping it up during sex and needs medication. He did not bother to make himself presentable before arriving on our date.

Uh. No.

It was my second date of the day. The first was a man I had met at church who is rather dull. His spiritual convictions are minor, he's politically conservative and cynical, and he drives the kind of truck that screams, *I have a small penis!* He shared weird, faux-Alpha energy with the Marine and Nigel. This type of man is not resonating with me. They are gainfully employed and make decent money. But they do it in ways that I don't find appealing. They don't make me want to *open* to them. I find myself asking them a lot of questions, but evading their questions about who I really am. I find myself putting up a tough "together" exterior and deflecting their attempts at connection and intimacy.

I believe it might be their conservative view of the world that is such a turnoff to me. I mean, seriously, they don't even get where I'm coming from. They have zero conceptual framework to even understand what I'm about. There is no poetry or narrative in them. They are playing by the rules. Rules my Soul finds abhorrent. I can't be my true Genius with them. They don't even understand what I do for a living. I find it tiring and pointless to try to even explain what my business is or what my purpose in it is. To explain myself and where I'm coming from is not something I find myself wanting to invest in for even a few minutes. Either you're already there, or you aren't. I need someone who is already there.

For instance, I had this conversation on Saturday with my client and bestie, Anna. We had spent the day unpacking and organizing her entire house. We worked hard and she took me to dinner afterward. During our conversation I told her that I was working with another woman, Pat Forbes, owner of Alchemy Universal Therapies is a Mormon healer who had told me that she is working with ETs (yes, I mean extraterrestrials) whom she invites into her healing sessions. Not only that, but she is 97 percent ET DNA and 3 percent human. My client is an alien. She said that ETs regularly visit Earth to help us in our path to ascension. The fascinating part of Anna's and my conversation was that neither of us were skeptical or shocked by this information. Both of us agreed that it was likely true and that if it wasn't true, then it mattered little to us if this woman felt that it was helping her and she was using the belief to help people.

"Seven months ago I never would have had this conversation," Anna reflected. "I would have blown the woman off as crazy. But now I believe in everything. Everything that is demonstrated is true. If it's demonstrating as good in someone's life, it is true."

My job is to help Pat manifest a business vision and help her convey her Soul's purpose to the world. This should reflect who she *really* is. I can do that for an ET healer without judgment.

What I need is a man who is powerful enough not to be shocked or intimidated by my power and intensity. I also need a man who isn't going to be a cynical dick about the fact that one of my clients is ET, and is healing with ET assistance and this neither shocks me, nor do I think she's crazy, nor have I ruled it out as a possibility.

In other words, my idea of *open-minded* has stretched and I need a man who believes in all of the possibilities. All of them.

❧

THIS MORNING I DREAMED of a woman who was a badass playing small. She was an orchestrator, she was a born leader, she was powerful and strong. But she was in a role that inhibited that, and required her to hide her true essence.

There was another girl or woman—it's been two hours and the kids woke me when they came home so the details are getting fuzzy—who, at the end of the dream, confronted the woman playing small. She got in her face and pointed her finger at her fierce-ly and said, "BE. Don't worry if people don't like you. BE."

The woman who was playing small was me. The confronta-tional girl was my Soul. The message was clear.

STOP PLAYING SMALL. Just Be ME. Powerful, strong, beautiful, bossy, leader, world-changer, life-changer, perception-shifter, a way show-er to the way showers.

Stop apologizing for the big role I am meant to play in this Spiritual Game.

❧

I'VE BEEN DECLARING "EASY" over my life the past few weeks. I have ten days until we leave for New York City. Ten days to get my website complete and advertise and market my Year of YES! coaching package.

I really want to fill it. I want to have the security of the steady income to meet our basic needs without worry for the whole year. This will give me such a boost in feeling legit as a coach and I'll be able to walk sixteen women through their own Years of YES! and that idea excites me.

This coming year, 2014, will be the year that I edit this mem-oir, write a book proposal, find an agent, and get a publisher. I need the financial stability and support to be able to devote time and energy to the birth of this memoir. It's important. *This* is the book I've wanted to write and publish my whole life. I want to do it with a traditional publisher for the prestige of it. My ideal pub-lisher would be Sounds True Publishing, because I just love what they do. But I've been hearing the words *Bantam Dove* in my head for the last seven years as my publisher.

Either way. This book is going out into the world and it's go-ing to be a major hit.

I have ten days to manifest my professional transmutation. It is doable and it *is* going to happen. I'm very proud of what I've built this year. It's all coming to fruition, an entire year's worth of work building a complete business, and it's exciting. Thrilling even.

Transmutation.

FIFTY-FOUR

DECEMBER 5, 2013

Last night a wave of love for Brad hit me. My Soul started writing testimonials for the entrepreneurs in my Maxcelerators group. She enjoyed the paying it forward so much that she decided to make an open offer to write testimonials and do reviews for anyone who asked on Facebook. Quite a few people were very appreciative of the offer. So she poured out good Juju, expressing admiration, love, and appreciation in quite a number of testimonials.

I guess that opened my heart and a wave of love for him flooded me. A healing sort of love. This admission bears a little bit of shame, because, Oh My God, the reader must think me so pathetic to be hung up on him after such a short not-relationship, and to someone who appears to be a bad match, but *worse,* someone who "made a conscious choice not to fall in love with me" and who accepted my vow of love and left me hanging in the wind with a "more later" that never came. If one were keeping score, this would classify me as *pathetic.* Even in the face of real interest from many men who seem better suited on the surface.

Still. I can't deny that when my heart is opened, it is love for Brad that I struggle with. I guess I struggle because I find me silly and I want to be open to the Fall Boyfriend, but no one is lighting my fire. It is embarrassing for me to convey exactly the nature of the phenomenon that's occurring with Brad on a spiritual healing realm; for one, because this manuscript is going out into the world and Brad is sure to pick it up and read every word of my devoted worship of him and he will have a flattered ego and have so many legs up on me that he will think me beyond pathetic. And sad, probably. But what does that really cost me? Pride. My beloved pride.

I am going to go into detail about these waves of love, because my Soul is so naturally drawn to them and they involve my powers as a healer and the phenomenon of distance healing and sexuality, and of remaining open-hearted in the face of uncomfortable vulnerability.

As my heart got wide open with my positive expressing of appreciation and gratitude to those practitioners that have helped me all year, a wave started to hit me. It feels like a gentle soft meditation at first. At first my mind begins to wander to his kiss and his breath. Our synchronized breath was captivating to me. It was so in sync that it felt like my own breath with juiced up energy and God's love flowing between us.

Then I realize that's exactly what our synced breath was. It was energy that circulated through Brad's body and his chakras, especially his heart, and passed to me and circulated through my chakras, which opened my heart wide and vulnerable.

I begin to visualize intentionally flowing my breath, with all of my healing energy, through him.

I stop and ask my God team and his God team to assist me in healing what needs to be healed in him. I place my hands crossed over my heart to generate the energy I need to give him the healing energy he's calling out for.

I wonder, *Is he asking for help right now? Is he having one of his migraines? Is he longing for a girlfriend? Is he thinking about me? Does he ever? When I feel drawn to him, what is it that draws me?*

I feel pulled. My Soul responds with the most selfless love toward him, when she feels pulled from her own worldly experience, willing to feed his Soul—to whom she is a beloved in eternity—any healing, love, or blessing he needs.

I wish I knew what the event was on his end. I wish I knew if he was asking the Universe for help or experiencing feelings for me, or if he's in a particular state of pain, anxiety, or trauma when the pulling occurs. I also wish, very deeply, to know what he feels when I am healing him. *Does he fill with love as I pour it into him? Does he feel comfort and relief from pain? Is he experiencing more happiness, joy, and love in his life as this healing has extended over the course of five months now? Is he having a transmutation of his own Soul as I invest in him?*

Other questions: *Am I healing him in this incarnation or is this happening on a Spiritual Realm because he needs it here? We are undoubtedly connected in a spiritual team, and have been for 700 years (that's always my knowing), so am I healing him now because he needs it elsewhere? Is this part of our spiritual contract? Or is this my natural loving response to his calls for help that touch me across space and time—or at least across the fifty miles between Boulder and Fort Collins?*

So many questions that I don't know the answers to. I wish he would contact me so I could ask all of these questions.

In the end, the act of healing him feels so delicious to me that I surrender to the selfless act of healing him with love that's spanned many lifetimes, because right now that's what my Soul feels compelled to do.

These sessions can be very sensual and sexual. He is often nude and I am touching his body and flowing energy through him. I am participating in a form of devotion, a godly devotion. I am Goddess, offering him my heart and my energy, and my love and my spiritual-healing powers.

I imagine that I hold certain parts of his body, connected to his chakras. I will hold his cock and circulate energy from his cock to his heart, cycled through my own chakra system. Then I might place my hand on his third eye and his heart, helping him to see with clarity and to translate what he sees into his heart. Then I place my hand on his crown and connect that to his heart, helping to clear his jumbled thoughts and assisting him with sinking into his heart and allowing him to live from his heart more without intellectualizing everything.

I often hold his head between my hands and whisper, "*Shhh, ssshhh, shhhsssh,*" to him, to calm his racing thoughts.

The healing can also be more overtly sexual. Using our circulating breath I will climb on top of him and look deeply into his eyes, while lowering myself onto his cock, allowing it to sink as deeply as it will go. I might hold myself there and just breathe while we stare into each other's Souls through our eyes. I might hold my hand over his heart as I rock back and forth over his cock, bringing us both to blissful climax.

I often honor his requests for me to give him a prostate massage while licking him from balls to ass and sucking his cock. It is a form of worship of his manhood and his Soul, whom I dearly love. I take joy in giving him such intense pleasure and I get even greater joy from the edgy intimacy of the act.

Other times I allow him to enter me from behind, filling my ass completely, very slowly, with him whispering, "I love you, Tracee, I love you," in my ear. I suppose the declaration of love makes this otherwise unpleasant experience of anal sex okay for me. Because the thought that really excites me about this vision is my own feeling of declaration: *I will do anything for you, I love you so much.*

It is the act of offering myself to him that feels so pleasurable to me. During these visions my heart naturally opens to him. I can feel it expanding and widening and deepening and feeling so liberated and naked and raw and vulnerable as he looks at me or as he presses his heart against mine while making love to me, holding me open by clutching my hands above my head and the feeling of having my heart this open is exquisite. It's simply exquisite.

As I drifted off to sleep last night, I make a request of my Soul and my God team. *Tomorrow. I need a sign about my money and my man. Wait! NO! I don't need a sign. I need a SALE. And I don't need a sign about My Man either. I want to meet My Man. And/or I want contact with Brad. I want Brad to contact me tomorrow.*

Then I take the tremendous amount of energy I've generated with these effortless visions or, dare I suggest, literal out-of-body-other-realm experiences, and I shoot them to my money. Generating love over my money altar, which I am continuing to heal and bless. *I release any and all beliefs, thoughts, and blocks that are mine, are inherited, that I hold which surround my financial energy, and I heal them. I call forth money in great abundance for myself.*

I drift off to sleep asking my God team to continue the healing on my money and on Brad while I am sleeping.

When I wake, the healing energy and the compelling pull toward Brad is still present and strong. I lie in bed and place my hand around his body in this other realm.

He is still present with me while I take the kids to school. By this time, I'm entertaining thoughts that we are meant to be together. That he is the Fall Boyfriend and that by December 21 (Winter Solstice), he will contact me and ask to see me. My other-realm visions turn into present-day fantasies.

I will come into his house and he will take me into his arms and lead me to his bedroom. We will discuss our future and our boundaries as we make love, declaring our feelings for each other between kisses—I've probably mentioned how insanely arousing his kisses are, they feel at once like hope and like being on the top of a mountain peak of joy—and we will feel as one. Then all the surface stuff—we'll just figure it out.

The truth is, I tell my Soul, *that what I really want is for Brad to contact me because I want to see what this is. I want us to explore this. This is new and exciting and I want to see where it goes. I have loved him for so long.*

I put in a caveat. *I want him to contact me. But I want it only if it's for our highest good, and only if it can be easy with us.*

It almost pains me to add the caveat. I really, really want to be in this man's arms and I know what it feels like to be the recipient of his devoted attention and it's incredible. But his mouth scares me. He has wounded me deeply with few words before. *You're not my girlfriend!* still stabs at my heart and brings tears to my eyes when I think of it. My heart—so open and vulnerable at that moment, so naturally wanting to open herself to him based on our past love lives—that it cut me Soul Deep. He has the power to hurt me Soul Deep. And his heart is not pure. He tells the "truth," but his truth is the result of a jumbled and scattered mind filtered through pain and old resentments and hang-ups about perfection, which leaves me very vulnerable to his truth telling.

"Can you be soft with my open heart?" I ask him during our healing sessions. "You must be soft with my heart. That's the only way I can do this with you."

I go into my yoga class and return to the spirit realm healing. I devote my yoga practice to healing him. I think of us sharing our own passions with each other: me taking up hiking and biking and he taking up yoga and kickboxing. I see us working from home together, amiably and comfortably. Enjoying each other's work quirks, I with my candles and midday meditations, and he with his . . . whatever his work quirks are.

This time I place my hand on his heart and his throat. "A more loving heart creates a more loving truth," I whisper in his ear. "Be more loving."

I place my hand on his head and his mouth. "More loving thoughts creates a more loving truth. Think more loving thoughts," I instruct.

I place my hand on his third eye, "See deeper truths to speak deeper truths," I tell him.

I place my hand over his eyes, "See deeper, speak deeper," I say.

I go to his ears, and his mouth, "Let those that hear hear, hear deeper, speak deeper," I say.

This is profound. I feel like a holy blessing has been bestowed on him. That he has been consecrated in some way. I feel that I've blessed him on the Soul level and spoken to his Soul, helping him create a more peaceful and loving life. It is not completely altruistic. These are the things I would need him to do in order to create a loving relationship with him. I would need him to express a softer truth in order to surrender my heart—wide open and vulnerable—to him. I love him. That feels good. I want him to be My Man very much. IF it is for our highest good and if he can be soft with my heart. I know now, that I deserve that and can't settle for less. It feels really good to love him and heal him in these beautiful and sacred acts of communion.

Love, any love, is communion with God.

❧

THEN I MADE MY FIRST Year of YES! VIP private coaching sale!!!

FIFTY-FIVE

DECEMBER 12, 2013

My parents' weekend visit was full of sugar and drama free. I suppose if I have to choose between sugar and drama, I'd choose sugar, though it totally threw me off, as it always does. I've come to associate my parents with getting fat. Well, my mother anyway.

There was no Sam's Club shopping spree. Well, there was, but it was strictly to load up on ingredients for projects crafted out of sugar. There was no desperate foraging so that I could support my family.

I loved that, truly. I kept repeating the phrase, as I have repeated all year long, that Jason told my parents, "I'm an adult. I can take care of my family."

And so I am. And so I do. I like it. It feels good to me.

❦

I HAD AN ENERGY SESSION with C.J. and got some interesting insights. The world of energy is new to me. I'm like a woman stumbling awake, still so new that I'm feeling too confident, probably. I've always had intuition, but this realm-hopping and completely new level of "visualizing" that feels other-dimensional (because it *is* other-dimensional) is new.

I've made huge leaps ascension-wise, taking on the Spiritual Realm and the possibilities of transmutation as ambitiously as I do everything else, I suppose. New spiritual developments include new subtle body energy, a new auric field around my body, with a yellowish tint. C.J. says that as people move through the ascension process they open all of their known chakras and then create more chakras with subtle body energy fields—so we are always expanding and getting bigger. (Unless we're constricting, I imagine).

There were also new cross-like "structures" or "symbols" that she discovered around me or in my energy body. One was at my crown and the other was at my throat. She said these might have been placed there during my Universal White Time Healing initi-ation. However, she said they weren't vibrating high enough and were actually slowing my own vibration, so she removed them.

I also got a new guide on my God team to "light my path of creativity in my work and my relationships." Which is pretty cool. I love that there are beings stepping up to help me on my path. It makes me feel valuable and special and safer.

The part that should make me wary is that she found an incu-bus-like energy attached to my root chakra. *This* is the being I've been having my sexual healing experiences with. This energy, she says, has been tricking me into believing that he is Brad and tak-ing advantage of my potent new energy I've been developing. He's a poser. A literal Energy Suck.

How the fuck does one pick up an incubus or a spiritual being who is not for their highest good?

Traveling.

Time- and realm-traveling between dimensions during medi-tation and visioning, and while dreaming, allows one to be vulnerable energetically. She therefore advised that I create the intention to be always surrounded by my God team made of 100 percent pure light, and that I state that intention before traveling and sleeping, and that I also state the intention that I integrate what I'm learning before I return to my body.

This year I've sort of learned that this stuff *can* happen and I've also caught on that it can be *directed* by me. Which has been fun! I'll visit the *Having Room!* I'll see what sorts of magic I can create on this realm by generating energy in that realm.

It's fun. It's Cosmic Play, I guess.

I'm now learning that one must be cautious. Truly, her warnings about playing with Spiritual Beings that are not 100 percent light reminded me of the Devil warnings of Christianity.

She refused to call this incubus energy "dark." Or even to say that it had my harm in mind. What she did say is that this energy had its own agenda and that she would not want to be interacting with this type of energy. She warned that these energies are highly attracted to sexual energy, so be discriminating when I'm doing my experiments in transmuting sexual energy into physical form.

She did say, however, that my experiment—Intendagasm—with Robert was okay, but that I need to stay in my heart during the experience and to call in the God team for protection.

❧

AND THE MAN? Where is he? She heard what I heard, which is: *"He has something he has to work out."* He got seriously waylaid, she said.

There are still two men who will step up to claim me. This time she doesn't suggest a time frame.

I expressed my anxiety about being with a man that I find embarrassing to be with. She said he won't be embarrassing in the way that I'm thinking, but that I will be surprised. She said he might be nerdy and quiet and it could take a little while to get to know him, but when I do it will be amazing. She said there *will* be a mutual attraction. She scoffed at my height requirement—six foot four—saying he will be energetically big and will have many hidden skills.

She said she was being given the image of a man in her advanced energy classes, a hot firefighter with a fine body who when you got to know him has a wicked sense of humor, and no one in his life probably knew that he does energy work.

Okay, maybe it's actually him? Introduce me to him!

His name is Patrick—*I got a ping from the Universe when she said his name*—and he lives in Salt Lake City.

∾

I DID GO FOR AN Intendagasm session with Robert yesterday morning after taking the kids to school.

Before I pulled up to this house I stopped the car and called in my God team of 100 percent pure light to guide and protect me during the session. I declared my intention to fill my Year of YES! package and to open my heart to love. I invited ONLY 100 percent pure light beings to participate in my experience and to be in my energy field and energy body.

Robert and I chatted and he suggested we introduce the Hitachi Magic Wand, possibly for the second orgasm. Yes, please. Why draw the line there, right?

This experience was pure pleasure and pure heart, and all about ascending to God through sexual energy.

I played my crystal bowls chakra-opening CD and really focused on the pleasure of sensation and offered my pleasure to God, experienced my pleasure as God, and visualized the kind of love I want in my life with My Man, being one of sacred communion and a holy offering. I visualized that my pussy is the Holy Grail for My Man, and indeed several other men whom I have given access to it. I acknowledged my pussy as the portal to the Universe, the Source of Divine Light and Opening. I offered my pussy and its pleasures to the Divine. I accepted the pleasures as a Sacred gift, as part of the purpose of me being in human form. Me, in particular, who has had such fun with men in my life.

It was highly arousing. His fingers inside my pussy pressing on my g-spot, reaching up and pressing into my cervix, while his other hand stroked my clit was intoxicating. The penetration is the entire difference for me. Whatever delights those other women are getting out of strict OM stroking is lost on me. I like a good finger bang.

At the end, it was Brad again, whispering his love to me while Robert pressed the Hitachi Magic Wand against my g-spot and clitoris that finally brought me to a full body orgasm.

Which leaves me with the question. . . Brad or Incubus violating my command of protection? Did I just get vulnerable and weak out there in the ethersphere and drop my protective shield? If so, what was the God team doing while I was floating out there on Pleasure Island declaring my love for God? Isn't it their job to protect me while I'm hopping around the Spiritual Realm? Or am I really in love with, and still fantasizing about Brad?

FIFTY-SIX

DECEMBER 15, 2013

Seven first dates scheduled this weekend. One date happened. The rest cancelled or blew me off. The one date that showed up was someone I didn't want to go out with, and could never picture making love to. He was a nice guy, but that does not make a romance.

There is one lingering potential date, the one I am most excited about meeting. Will he cancel?

Bina says that people can't be around my energy if they are not of the light; they simply can't withstand the high vibration and intense power that I put out. Something will happen to prevent them from coming or they will have anxiety or be too intimidated and feel inferior around me.

They are intimidated by me. Beautiful, smart, sexy, successful, and confident, and knowing what I want. Many men (and some women) have told me this is very, very intimidating. Which means I've been the one taking the lead and making contact. And then they decide they only want to date someone in Boulder because it's a pain in the ass to commute for romance (who can blame him?), or the sitter cancels, or they have to go to Colorado Springs to pick up a stranded friend, or someone comes into town unexpectedly, or they want my personal information before meeting and get upset that I'm a hard ass when I hold to my boundaries.

The Universe is protecting me. It makes me realize just how special and unique the person I will end up must be. He will have to be to withstand my rapid expansion and spiritual growth. He will have to be of the light to withstand the light. He will have to be 100 percent committed to his own growth of his own accord because I cannot and will not wait for him to catch up or stay behind to linger in his company if he chooses not to progress.

According to the God team, there are two such men who will step up and offer these qualities. I had hoped to spend the holidays with one of them. Not that I am bored or lonely. I enjoy my time alone immensely. I enjoy reflecting and meditating and entertaining myself with creation, whether it's painting or writing or thinking up grand plans for my business.

I'VE BEEN DECLARING "EASY" over my life. I am being energetically easy about the projects that I've signed on for. I've been plucking away at them and producing quality work at an easy pace in few hours. I've been easy about sales, easy about making pitches for my Year of YES! program. Writing a commemorative journal for the program. Taking my time and surrendering—as best I can—the outcome. I have moments of anxiety about what I will do with no money when I return from New York. But I am choosing to insist that the Universe fill my Year of YES! program with five more individual clients. I don't feel that the mastermind is going to fly. Perhaps shorter masterminds are the way to go. I'll release one in February, based on the seven mindsets of 100K women.

I've stopped stressing about releasing before January 1, 2014. It will happen. The New Moon of a New Year will be a perfect time to launch myself as a woman who has transmuted into a more powerful woman and highly successful energetic presence.

EASY is my word for 2014. It will be the Year of Easy. I mentioned this on the UYB forum and they pointed out the path I've been on.

Year 2012 = Release = Real Ease.

Year 2013 = YES!

Year 2014 = EASY = A YES!

I think spiritual growth has to go in this order. You have to release what's not working in order to say YES! to what you really want, and then you have to figure out how to energetically shift to make the YES! come EASY!

Selling the Year of YES! package will come EASY! The editing of this memoir will come EASY! The agent and publisher will come EASY! The paying for my own coaching mentor will come EASY! My lover will some EASY! The courtship will be EASY! The relationship will be EASY! The money will come EASY! The marketing of the book and my business will come EASY!

This year was foundational. Next year is going to be HUGE and EASY!

FIFTY-SEVEN

DECEMBER 17, 2013

F all ends on Saturday. I changed up my online dating profiles to attract *him*.

Pay attention to who shows up in the next few days, my Soul is whispering to me. *Pay attention.*

My Online Profile

THE THIRD STAGE (OF *feminine love*) *begins when you know that you don't depend on a man, that you can make your own decisions and guide your own life, and yet you are tired of keeping up your guard; you want to relax in your feminine body and emotions. You want to stop protecting your heart. You want to swoon in the bliss of utter surrender, spiritually, emotionally and sexually.*

—David Deida, *Finding God Through Sex*

Dear Lover,

We ascend into Love, we do not fall. For us, bliss and contentment are so easy. I open to you with devotion, uncommon in the face of all of the evidence that to do so in this time with our respective romantic histories could be observed from the outside as a radical choice. Loving with abandon *is* radical, which is why we do it. Your complete presence to me, for

433

our relationship, is so intense that it allows me to surrender into Love. I trust you implicitly because my heart is your heart and you would never, ever violate that trust. Nor would I.

We effortlessly sync our lives, making our lifelong romance a priority. I have already cleared a significant space for you, in anticipation of your arrival. There is a vacancy in my heart, space in my schedule, room for you as a priority. You have done the same. Our families fall into warmth and comfort effortlessly. Our children mesh happily. We delight in each other's friends, family, and tribes. Our home is full of laughter, affection, and complete support of every member's purpose and path. We are exceedingly proud to claim the other as our own, both feeling as though we got the better end of the deal.

When I tell you of the "impossible" things that I'm creating in my business and with my work, you are present and supportive with 100 percent faith and belief that it is already happening. You not only believe in my dreams, but you can dream a bigger dream for me than I dare dream for myself. I bring all of my gifts to the table, healing you with my touch, openness, and kisses. For you, I freely offer a portal to the Universe, my body the Sacred Challis.

Our love is a sacrament, a communion. Our kiss, our touch, our connection is an offering to God, Goddess, Creation, Spirit, the Universe. The Love we create together brings Light into the world. Together we join as Yin and Yang, Divine Feminine and Divine Masculine, our love creating a form of worship to the Divine in each other.

Apart we have committed to our own spiritual growth, consciousness, and enlightenment. Together, we reach highs we can't reach alone. Finally, we realize it is connection and relationship that heals, that offers a return to wholeness, rather than an isolated independent quest for stillness.

Our paths, though colorful and sometimes rocky, brought us to each other at the perfect time and place, and for that we are profoundly grateful.

Hieros gamos, dear Lover, nothing less.

In excited anticipation,
Your Woman

Who will resonate with this love letter? Does it make me softer? Less intimidating or more intimidating? Does it make me vulnerable enough to invite My Man to step up and claim me? The man I'm looking for won't think me crazy for this letter, right? What I had before hasn't worked and today my Soul felt compared to try something new, so here we are.

&

MY MIND IS PLAYING with manifestations and visions for 2014. What do I really want?

This year I'm toying with some new concepts. What if I expanded my wishing?

What if rather than saying I want to grow my business a specific amount, or have a specific amount of money come to me, I declare, *I'm a Brilliant Businesswoman and Entrepreneur?*

I'm comfortably wearing my size 6 Levi's! Yay!

But what if instead of 125 pounds, which has yet to work in seven years of dream boards and vision statements, I assert: *I am at my natural weight, all extra melts off me?*

Neurotic eating is so annoying. What if instead of asking to be gluten-, dairy-, and sugar-free, I declared, *I can eat anything I want and my body will metabolize it easily and effortlessly?*

What if the only word on my dream board is *EASY!?*

This year I made over $31,000 in business revenues and brought in over $56,000 in total income. When I wrote my vision statement after my divorce, I wrote $50,000 because it was the highest I could dream and the lowest I felt I could live off of. I've met that goal and it's $15,000 more than I lived on last year. If you count the $6,000 that my dad gave me this year, it's over $62,600. By the end of the month I am going to clear $63,000.

Wow! I'm doing it! It's happening!!!

My writer, dreamed that I was on Oprah. Oprah. Oprah.

I will be on Oprah!!! My Soul rehearses the moment constantly.

❧

I'M STANDING AT THE END and the beginning.

This is a one-year project. Which means there are only fourteen days to allow this narrative to come full circle.

I can't imagine going back to living another way. What? After listening to and obeying my Soul for a year I go back to listening to and obeying external voices like Alex's or another man's? I go back to caring what the neighbor's think or what social convention dictates I do? I go back to allowing other people to alter my behavior by their value systems and social norms? I go back to listening to people "check my reality?" I go back to making choices from pro/con lists and rational versus irrational ponderings? I go back to living from fear, on a "safe" ledge that makes me miserable?

Never.

Through this year of practice and of committing to living Heart Open and making my choices based on what my Soul wants, it has become almost second nature. Where I might have agonized for days, weeks, months, or years over decisions to extricate myself from relationships, situations, or energetic influences, I now choose briefly and breathe a sigh of relief for having done it.

Where I once would feel bound by Alex's expectations, I no longer am bound to anyone's expectations aside from my Soul's. Where I once felt pressure to modify my beliefs, behavior, and values so as not to make my Mormon family uncomfortable, I no longer care.

What does my Soul want?

In every situation it leads to the right answer.

❧

THE BEGINNING OF 2014 holds possibilities. In Sedona, the card for my 2014 came up as *Lovers*. How delicious that will be.

I've had an invitation to a writer's group. I'm considering using it to edit this manuscript. I'm hesitant to allow those who aren't as good as I am tinker with my work, though.

I thought to hire a coach mentor, only to find that in her first year she made $10,000 and I made $32,000 and in her third year she's only clearing $55,000, where I am planning on far exceeding that number. She said she could help with my book proposal and her book has just launched, so that would be valuable.

The major turnoff was when she reality checked me. "Unless your an outlier," it takes three to five years to turn a profit and create a sustainable coaching practice.

Oh my God, it's the same story with the writing reality checks. "You know, most people never make a living at this!" everyone is so damned excited to tell you.

Don't get your hopes up too high!

I don't DO reality checks.

I don't even believe in reality.

You don't realize who I am, I think, when someone tries to limit what I can do. *Most* coaches probably NEVER turn profit, just as *most* writers probably NEVER get published or make a living or have a best-selling book, because *most* writers and coaches QUIT and fail to persist after setbacks and failures.

What happens to MOST people has absolutely NOTHING to do with me. I'm a forty-year-old woman who has made a living with my pen for the majority of my adult life. I don't quit. I persist like a motha fucka! I push through. I get smarter and more efficient and I succeed!

The question is, do I want to work with someone who is going to reality check me? NO FUCKING WAY! I want someone who will talk me out of the nonsense of "reality" when I attempt to reality check myself. I just divorced a man who wanted to chuck his reality all over me and I left home at sixteen because I wanted to untether myself to those people's depressing and sad reality.

Reality is of absolutely no interest to me. At least their version of reality.

Here's MY reality.

I bring gold clutches with $2 million back from Heaven.

I had a great, great love in a past life with a beautiful Soul who I've missed dearly this year. I love him and am loved by him in eternity. It's a beautiful gift.

I heal people from a distance.

I use sexual energy to manifest money and opportunities.

I am a highly successful life coach.

I am on Oprah in the time-space continuum as I type this and it's a fucking whole lotta fun! And I'm wearing those Louboutins.

I change people's lives.

I help people see themselves.

I bring light into the world.

I'm in love with someone right now, though I haven't met him in this lifetime yet.

Mary Magdalene gave me a logo as a gift.

This book is a *New York Times* and Amazon bestseller.

A junkie saved my life.

I do impossible things every day.

I'm a very powerful spiritual master.

My client is an alien who heals people, and I believe it's not even unlikely or implausible.

My God team speaks to me through a woman named C.J. it's the best investment ever.

Plus a whole bunch of other shit that you, my reader, has probably thought, *What the fuck? This chick is crazy,* about.

Don't fucking reality check me, bitches!

Belief is delicate. If you can't believe for me then I don't want to mix with your energy. Belief is of the highest value to me.

❧

To Anna, who has become a wonderful touchstone for me, I suggested that perhaps a spiritual coach would better serve me this year. "I don't know if you'll find one who is moving at the rate you are right now, or if you're really lacking spiritual growth in any way," she said.

What a thought. That I am the advanced player and that I am moving at such a rate that I'm a forerunner in the Enlightenment world, the Enlightenment of the World.

Obviously, there are the master masters, Oprah, Deepak, Marianne Williamson, Louise Hay, and so on. But is it a possibility that I am only steps behind and that one big success, like a bestseller, could launch me into that sphere of influence?

C.J. had told me too that I really needed to trust myself, because I'm moving so fast that I can be going faster even than my God team is going in their ascension. "You are not an underachiever," she said.

Imagine the possibilities, and risks, of outpacing your own God team, which has been spiritually designed to guide your spiritual path. Of course, a new guide stepped in to light my path to creativity in my work and my relationships. So maybe once you outpace your God team, more advanced ones step up. It's pretty likely that there will be enough people ahead of me—a mere Earth being—and God, in *Conversations with God*, is pretty clear that we're unevolved beings.

It is pretty interesting thought to imagine . . . perhaps I'm bigger even and more important even than I could ever imagine being. One day you're Liz Gilbert; the next you're *ELIZABETH GILBERT, the best-selling author*. One day you're a nerdy shame re-searcher, and the next you're *BRENÉ BROWN and teaching classes on OWN*.

This year I'm Tracee Sioux; next year I'm **TRACEE SIOUX**.

This year is foundational; next year is going to be HUGE!

Bantam Dove Bantam Dove Bantam Dove.

FIFTY-EIGHT

DECEMBER 25, 2013

My Christmas wish for the world is that everyone have at least one friendship where "that's impossible" is not allowed. The result really is miraculous. Neecy and I just took our children to New York City for a week. We did not scrimp and hoard. We bought $30 cocoa and chocolate snacks. We went to the Algonquin and paid a check of $250. We took our children to see *Wicked,* costing each of us over $400. We bought week-long subway passes. We paid entrance to Ellis Island and the Statue of Liberty. We bought souvenirs in Chinatown. We ate from China to Italy to India to Islam.

Whole 'Nutha Level, we tell each other over breakfast, on the subway, in Central Park, on Fifth Avenue, in Chinatown, at the Statue of Liberty. *We're taking it to a 'hole nutha level, H.N.L.,* Neecy says in her faux ghetto, Southern-cool accent.

We worshipped in Catholic cathedrals, and Buddhist temples, praying the same prayer in all: *Thank You, Thank You, Thank You.*

The Great Zoltar predicted our futures in FAO Schwartz.

"Your future will be very sunny.

"I see in it a chest full of money.

"Be free to spend it as you see fit.

"Because there will be plenty more of it.

"You are a fortunate person. You were born under a lucky star and that will carry you safely through all of your ventures. In time your love life will be something for the world to talk about. You will be extremely happy. There will be those who envy you and try to harm you. Just really learn who your true friends are and all will go very well with you. Your lucky stone is a ruby.

"Lucky numbers 1, 19, 16, 32, 40, 8."

The Buddhist Temple fortune has this to say:

"Probability of Success: Excellent.

"There is a tower of good height.

"It gives our guiding beacon light.

"As you have fought a stalwart fight,

"Success brings you much more delight."

᳁

MY CLIENT, BINA, HAD told me that December 21, 2013, at noon was the "Ascension" and it was a highly potent time for setting an intention. She told me to light a candle and create an intention, and the wish would come true. We decided that would be our Statue of Liberty, Ellis Island day.

I stocked my purse with candles and a lighter from the dollar store near our subway stop. We arrived at the Statue of Liberty— the epitome of New Beginnings, Fresh Starts, Liberty, and Possibility—with twenty minutes to spare. We made our way to Lady Liberty's feet and got in a tight huddle to block the wind. Each of us set an intention for our lives as we lit, then lit, then cursed the wind, then lit again our candles. The only way for our candles to stay lit was to keep one flame with all six of our candles in it.

It was so beautiful to see our SiouxTonLea Intention light up our huddle. We created a bond, a unity, unfaltering in its belief, founded in the impossible where everything becomes possible.

EASY ABUNDANCE
A Great Love
Money
Business
Love
Life/Living
Parenting
New York and Amazon Best-selling Book YOY Published
Full Year of YES! Client List

"We're due EASY, Neecy," I told her as we walked away from our candle-lighting ceremony arm in arm. "We've done the work, we've built the foundation, we've perfected striving we've struggled enough, we've made the hard calls, and we've fought the good fight. It's time for things to come easy for us. We deserve easy money, we deserve good things to fall at our feet, we deserve great romance and love to come into our lives easily and effortlessly. We're due easy abundance of all good things.

"This is the New Level. We did it. Look at us. We're here. We're not going to the new level, we're not on our way to the new level. We're on the Whole 'Nutha Level right now. This trip is it. We've transitioned. This is the moment. The light returns right now. This is the New Chapter. We're here."

❧

NEECY AND I, BOTH newly single mothers, with what feels like strapped budgets, squeezing by right under the radar, spent $1,000 on one memorable evening with our kids.

We sprinted from the Algonquin to the Gershwin Theater for the curtain call *of Wicked*. Dashing, dressed to the nines (or at least the seven-and-a-halves), up Broadway for ten blocks—it was the most fun we had the entire trip. Out of breath, going from one "Rich" event to another, wearing fancy clothes, we laughed all the way. Charlie and Cody had a sudden surge of energy burst forth and explode through the crowded streets, weaving through hoards of people, laughing heartily. Me, trailing them, cautioning them not to go so far ahead that they were out of my sight. Neecy, cheering on the stragglers, Madigan with her mismatched brown heels and brand-new thrift-store-perfect little black dress, and Ashton with his swanky New York "Look" of sophisticated arty genius with his scarf and corduroy jacket, acquired only hours before at the thrift shop. We had popped into the store "for a sec," and you could feel our collective sigh, *Aaaaahhhhh, feels like home.*

The thrift store is the place of YES! It's the place where Neecy and I can be cool moms who say YES! when the kids ask for something. It's the place where you'll find that really cool thing that no one else has that you can't find anywhere else. It's the place where you can take a fashion risk and it's no biggie if it doesn't pan out. It's the place where the kids can pretty much have anything they want! No wonder we all breathed a relaxed and contented sigh when we walked into the thrift store.

Madigan walked out with a $25 well-made designer dress. Charlie scored a very debonair tie, as did Cody. Ashton walked out with a whole new look.

444

Neecy and I were already decked out, she in a darling red lace number and me in my $15 Ross dress with my Cole Haan Nike Air pumps in the bag, bouncing at my hip as we sprinted gleefully through the Theater District.

We arrived sweaty, well-fed, overjoyed, and right on time.

We took our seats, $125 each, and were held captive by live theater in which things aren't always as they appear, the impossible becomes possible, true love wins, true friendship endures, and wicked isn't always wicked.

"I'm tired of doing things just because other people tell me I have to," says Galinda, "the Ga is silent."

Neecy opens her palm and I smack it in prayerful agreement.

❧

SO MY DEADLINE FOR my Fall Boyfriend was December 21, 2013, Winter Solstice. On December 14, I went out with a Scorpio cyclist named Scott, who fit C.J.'s description of My Man: nerdy, mutual attraction, takes a minute to get to know, and I hope wickedly funny with skills. I went out with him, for breakfast dates twice before I left as well. We've been texting and have decided to go see a movie today, *Anchor Man 2,* on Christmas Day. I'm looking forward to seeing him.

But C.J. said there were two men who were going to come into my life and I get to choose between them. There are obviously waaaay more than two men coming in and out of my life, and I am obviously choosing or not choosing them with a great deal of interference and assistance from the Universe, which is not allowing the wrong ones to linger.

Vacation Tracee is often more excitable and uninhibited when traveling, especially at the optimistically high vibration beginning

445

of a trip. I had been entertaining fantasies about meeting My Man at the airport or on the plane.

Pay attention to who shows up right now, the Soul kept whispering to me. So, Scott was texting me. A few guys that had cancelled dates, whom I was only mildly interested in, were messaging me. I was looking out for Boulder Brad, a message or email or something, I admit it.

I'm waiting in the terminal for our flight when Hottie Hank shows up. The man I'd been having casual sex with months before. His body is like a playground, buff and hairless, and his cock is pretty perfect. I had enjoyed riding him and being assertive with him. But, he's soooo boring. We don't have anything to talk about. He had gotten out of the casual sex deal, saying he wasn't interested in that anymore. But here he comes, same terminal, same time, on his way to Vegas.

Wild. Weird. What does it mean?

"We'll get together when I get back?" he asked.

"Yes, sure," I said.

❧

SOUTHWEST DOESN'T HAVE assigned seating and we had seating group C, which means we were inevitable middle seaters, and not together. I chose a seat directly behind Charlie so I could parent him while flying. Madigan sat two rows in front, absorbed in a book.

A pretty cute, age-appropriate man named Max was sitting next to me. I struck up a conversation and pulled out David Deida's *Dear Lover* for the flight. I was shooting off pheromones and high-energy vibes like firecrackers. I was brazen and flirty. He was flirty right back. He removed the arm between us so we could touch legs and arms. He busied himself with blogging and I entertained myself with peripheral touching and thinking very naughty thoughts while distractedly reading Deida's explicit descriptions of intimacy and spiritual sex. Every paragraph or so I would close my eyes and enjoy the steamy thoughts and fantasize about crawling right on top of my seat mate and fucking him uninhibitedly on the plane.

Max was feeling it. He was enjoying the touching as much as I was. About one hour outside of NYC, he put his computer away to put his attention on me. I was floating questions like, "No kids? Wife? Girlfriend?"

"I do have a girlfriend," he admitted.

"I am just going to admit that I'm pretty bummed about that."

"I'm pretty mad about it right this moment, too," Max says.

I showed him my book. He read the chapter about cervical orgasm, how to reach it, how wonderful it was, and his cock got hard. "We could just pretend that we're in a parallel reality where you don't have a girlfriend for the next hour or so," I said.

Then he put his hand on my leg and the heat from his hand rushed through my body. I focused on opening my heart and feeling his touch. My hand crept to his thigh, his hand inched its way up my thigh. I reached down and grabbed my sweater to put over our legs.

"My cock is over here, ever since I read your book."

My hand grasped his cock, feeling the thickness and the throbbing head. It was a nice cock. I wanted to suck it and I wanted to climb on top and ride it. His hand gravitated to my crotch, rubbing me through my thick Levi's.

He leaned in to kiss me. It wasn't my favorite kiss. His tongue was too hard and his breath was stale. But it was wildly exciting to French kiss a stranger on a completely packed plane, with a poor Asian woman on my right, pretending to be asleep, and my children distracted by coloring and reading only feet away. He grabbed my head, with his hands in my hair, passionately when he kissed me and that felt exotically thrilling. When he went for my breasts, my breath caught and I wanted to fuck him with abandon.

He looked at me lustily, and I returned his lusty gaze with my own wanton whore stare. I gripped and rubbed and pulled at his hard cock until he came in his cargo shorts. His passion calmed and we sat, arms entwined, stunned at what has just happened for the rest of the trip.

I was giddy and gleeful, and floaty and lightheaded. He just sat stunned and speechless, gazing into my eyes every few minutes.

"That just blew my mind," he said.

"Right? How does this even happen?" I asked.

"The Universe only has forty-eight hours left to drop a Fall Boyfriend in my lap. I thought I got so Lucky, I was about to give the Universe a serious High Five . . . and you have a girlfriend," I lamented lightheartedly.

"This can't happen again, unless my situation changes," he said.

"No, once is a vortex in the Time-Space Continuum," I agreed. "Twice is just cheating."

I really tried to stay present with his touch—his hand gripping my thigh, our upper arms intertwined, my hand on the back of his hand. "I may never see you again," I said.

"That's the wrong attitude," he warned. "Situations change."

"I'm going to give you my card and we have to take a picture because this is impossible. We just did something impossible. Who does this happen to? Way less than one percent of the population on the planet has had this experience," I mused.

He wrote me a lovely email the next morning, musing on our experience and "what we shared for an hour, it was pure and what it seemed," he wrote.

And it was. It was also highly exciting.

❧

HERE'S THE THING. It was a fabulous narrative for the Universe to deliver my Fall Boyfriend. But I couldn't keep his presence in my head for longer than a day. My mind wasn't fixating on him; I wasn't checking my email like crazy after the first day to check to see if he'd communicated with me. I even forgot his name a few times and had to rack my brain for it. Rather, Scorpio Scott was the text I was waiting for and the man I was fixating on.

I Googled Max's blog and realized he's a terrible match for me. He's a total sports fanatic and I don't want anything to do with a man who's obsessed with other things. It's just such a time suck and will take his attention away from me and us, and it's a way to avoid real connection and intimacy. The sports obsession is observation, not participation. I want someone who wants to LIVE life, not watch it on ESPN.

All of these men, Scorpio Scott, Hottie Hank, and Mile-high Max have illuminated one of my core issues with men and one of my core fears about my next relationship: I want a man who will be present with me. I don't want him to be obsessed with sports or cycling, or anything else for that matter. I don't want to compete with selfish, time- and money-sucking hobbies, I don't want to matter less than men who run around with balls and "training" for extreme sports. I want real presence and intimacy, and I'm fearful about not getting it.

The other thing Mile-high Max brought to light is that I'm afraid of boring married sex. I'm rushing to fit in exciting sexual experiences because I dread going back to dull, monotonous monogamous, passionless, and unimaginative sex. I want exciting, exploratory, and boundary-pushing sex. I want to feel wildly uninhibited and wanton, and powerful and possessed, and taken and ravished during sex. Not only in the beginning or the honeymoon phase of sex. I want enough sexual potency and creativity that my lover and myself can use Intendagasm and Extreme Intimacy to manifest what we want through the transmutation of our combined sexual energy.

This is a tall request, and I'm afraid I won't get it with My Man. Because that's what we've all culturally agreed on, right? That passion fades and we lose it the longer we are together? That the hormone high fades and can't be sustained over decades?

I have this feeling that I need to cram high-vibrational sexual experiences into this tiny window of time before I meet My Man and settle into monotonous monogamy again, because all of the boundary-pushing sex happens outside of commitment and I really, really love the boundary-pushing, exhilarating sex. *I'll need masturbatory, climax-creating material for the long, boring decades of dull and unimaginative sex in front of me*, is one of my beliefs.

The truth is that one of the greatest joys of my life has been sex and exploring it and feeling the high intensity of it and I've enjoyed it with many partners. It's like thirty-one flavors, every person and every experience has its own taste and energy and technique and flare and sounds and smell and shape and size, and I love the experience of it. I want more and more of it. I'm in my sexual peak and I want to enjoy it.

Intimacy or exquisite sex?

I want both and I don't want to choose.

Intimacy or exquisite sex?

It's a lame, false choice. I choose both.

I open myself to the idea that I can create exquisite sex with a committed and highly intimate partner who wants to indulge my boundary-pushing fantasies. My fantasies are far and wide at this moment. They are gaining potency and I want to experience the high-vibrational potency of hot sex and the intense presence that I experience within each sexual touch and kiss and lifted skirt and brazen comment, and each cock that fills me up, and each tongue that lashes at me and fingers that dig in my hole and rub down my g-spot and creep toward the rose bud of my asshole and whisper naughty things in my ear and suck on my nipples and make me surrender to pleasure and mindless exhilaration. I want the taste of cock to fill my mouth and fill me up to stretching and ecstatic energy, and I want to feel cum splash my cervix into orgasm as my lover penetrates my Soul with his eyes that don't look away when he sees me open and surrendered to love.

FIFTY-NINE

DECEMBER 31, 2013

THIS IS IT. The end of the Year of YES! experiment. I want to tie it up in a pretty bow for you. But, this is only the beginning. The Year of YES! is now the *Life of YES!* because I'm never going back to the way I lived before.

Never will I ask, "What would my husband want me to do?" instead of asking my Soul what she wants. Less and less, I'm sure, as I grow accustomed to it, will I concern myself with what "they" think about my choices. What is important to me is what my Soul thinks, feels, believes, and wants.

This IS the Next Level.

Have I gotten what I want? So much more, really. Had I started this year by deciding what I was going to heal or where my life was going to go, I know I would have gotten there. But I wouldn't have gotten *here*. I wouldn't have healed the things my Soul knew needed healing. I wouldn't have faced my past and let my destructive identities go. I wouldn't have launched the business I did launch. I wouldn't have grown in the ways my Soul wanted to grow. I wouldn't have cast off convention in favor of what I really want, which is to follow my Soul's unconventional path. No, had I not done the Year of YES! I would have missed so many unexpected and unimaginable gifts.

Trust! Tracee! Trust!

It is all about trust with me, the God team says. *Trust my Soul, trust the Universe, trust myself, trust the God team, trust God, trust life itself.*

My Soul knows where she's going.

She knows the fastest, easiest way to get there.

And she will never, ever steer me wrong.

YES!

SIXTY

THE YEAR AFTER

SO WHAT HAPPENED? How did it all turn out?

My I AM statements transmuted. After twenty-seven years of carrying shame and allowing that to dictate my choices and my self-worth, I let my identity as a *worthless whore* and a *terrible friend* go.

I am People Rich. I am a wonderful, generous, caring, and loving friend, and my life is full to overflowing with the type of friends that I wish on everyone. My Soul led me to the exact circumstances, situations, people, and experiences that would allow me to heal and release forty years of psychic garbage.

Wading through the muck of your mistakes, your shame, your deepest darkest shadow can be excruciatingly painful. Still, there's an element of it that which I believe is necessary. Grief, in all its forms, is a baptism, and if you skip it, you never feel "cleansed of your sins," or more aptly said, free of your own self-judgment of unworthiness. Judgment of Self is the primary original sin.

My eyesight returned to perfect vision. My stomach flattened. I dropped three pants sizes and got my physical strength back. As I faced what I feared, my body stabilized and returned to its natural state of health and beauty.

Boulder Brad is now a genuine friend. Go figure. Two men did show up in my life, (and many more) and I did chose: neither of them. After another period of celibacy, I extended my wildee time into 2014. I continue to explore sacred sexuality.

The Sacred Whore has played a critical role in virtually every religious and cultural tradition: Eve, Sarah, Ruth, the Virgin Mary, Mary Magdalene, Aphrodite, Venus, Shakti, and Ishtar are some examples. I'm not suggesting that all acts of sexuality are sacred religious rites. Those in which force, manipulation, and commodification of girls, women, and femininity (or boys, men and masculinity) are decidedly not. However, exerting a cloud of shame, whether individual, cultural, or religious, around feminine sexuality is a crime against femininity that is equivalent to forced sexuality. This kind of shame-based sexuality is as damaging for men and masculinity as it is for women and femininity. Women, and men, are sexual beings, and there *is* a place for sexual healing in the spiritual journey.

What I learned during my Year of YES! and my reentry into dating is that men are in desperate need of healing. Many wonderful men feel impotent in the world: powerless, hurt, and lost. They have broken hearts and have felt rejected and unappreciated by women and the world at large. Once I got over being pissed off at men as a "species," my compassion for them grew.

Almost every man I've asked has expressed that one of his primary love languages is touch. I have found that men's hearts open and heal through touch. Sex is a very healing experience for them—and us—if done with intention. Their carnal desire is truly a longing, a craving for access to the Sacred Feminine: the Chalice, the Portal to Universal Love and Oneness. Thus, is the critical role of the Sacred Whore, as it has been throughout history, myth, and theology: to heal through love and touch, to reach God through the unity of Divine Feminine and Divine Masculine.

The Godhead has two sides: Masculine and Feminine, Jesus Christ and Mary Magdalene. Together it is the Sacred Marriage: hieros gamos. To get there, we need heavy doses of healing touch.

During my Year of YES! I received mountains of sexual healing and healing from various traumas. I made my peace with my own sexual power.

I feel free for the first time in almost three decades: since the night I lost my virgin self and my identity as a good Mormon girl and harshly declared myself a *worthless whore* and a *terrible friend*. You can't know what a relief it was for me to release these terrible burdens. It is when I stopped running from my sexuality, my past traumas, my own shadow side, and instead, faced and claimed them that I freed myself of shame.

During my Year of YES! I got rich and I'm getting richer! I really did build a solid foundation for my business that year—just like my Soul promised. When success landed at my feet, I was ready for it.

I became softer, more feminine, more compassionate, and more loving. I became a better mother because I came back to wholeness and am a better example for how to be a good human.

The Universe is extremely generous with me.

#yesthankyoumoreplease

THE YEAR OF YES! COACHING

HERE'S WHAT I KNOW for sure. Everyone has a Soul and that Soul has a purpose. You came here with it. And if you're not living that purpose, you're going to have some level of discontent. No one else can live your purpose. It's yours. You can run from it, hide from it, distract yourself from it, deny it, argue with it, rationalize it, tell it to Fuck Off, sacrifice it to the gods of whatever you deem valuable, and yet . . . your purpose is your purpose.

You want what you want because it is *meant for you*—and only you.

You can try to do other things to please other people and your ego and society. You can follow the rules. You can stay in your box and color inside the lines. You can choose not to live your Soul's purpose for a variety of awesome and legit reasons. And they *are* legit. But if you bow to all the legit reasons in the world that keep you from your Soul's purpose, it will never stop calling to you, singing you a new song.

The Dare is to say YES! to your Soul's purpose anyway, and trust in these things:

1. Your Soul knows where she's going.
2. She knows the fastest and easiest way to get there.
3. She will never, ever steer you wrong.

If you take the Dare to say YES! to your Soul's purpose, you're going to come up against resistance—from your ego, from your conscious self, and from others. They'll all have something to say about any changes you attempt to make.

The ego loves *same*. If given a choice the ego will keep you at the same shitty job for 20 years, married to the same jerky alcoholic, living a lifestyle you loath, or standing in line at the food bank, because the ego confuses *same* with safe. Even if your same sucks.

The ego's will use its three biggest lies to trap you in *same*:

- You don't have enough money.
- You don't have enough time.
- You're just not good enough.

These are lies. Busyness is the number one killer of Soul purpose and it's eating our culture alive. We're the most prosperous country in the world, in history even, and we're all broke. We're busy and broke, busy being broke, perpetually. It's a collective mental illness.

If you take the Dare, you're going to be afraid and you're gonna have to deal with shit that you don't wanna deal with. You just are.

If you weren't afraid of your Soul's purpose you'd already be living it.

My advice is this: *Do not try to do it alone.* Earth is a playing field with millions of helpers, healers, and supporters. We're not playing solitaire. We're playing together.

It is my Soul's purpose to help you find your Soul's purpose. And say YES! to it.

Visit my website, www.TraceeSioux.com, to find out how you can get the support you need to say YES! to your Soul.

The Dare: Say YES!

ACKNOWLEDGMENTS

WITHOUT THE FRIENDS, HELPERS, mentors, and guides who came into my life, I wouldn't have survived my Year of YES!

Therefore, I must acknowledge and offer a special thank you to my children, Madigan and Charlie, who have thrived during the reinvention of our family with resilience, forgiveness, insight, and grace. We're a Power Family who can manifest anything.

Thank you to my co-parent for stepping up after the end of our marriage; our children are blessed that you're an involved parent.

To Neecy, thank you for never judging and for being there for my random freak-outs, and for being able to call me on my shit in the gentlest of ways. It's the family you choose.

A special thanks to Anna Koclanes, who traveled with me during the Year of YES!, becoming my first client and my first Vice President of Manifestation; without you, I wouldn't have had nearly as many Universe-all epiphanies.

To "Boulder Brad," for awakening pieces of me that needed healing, and for that Great Love Life, thank you.

Thank you to C.J. McDaniel at Lymphworks LLC, for being an integral spiritual teacher and a powerful healer.

Robert Devereaux thank you for being such a beautiful man and drenching me in pleasure, giving me practice at staying in my body.

Thanks to the Maxcelerators for allowing me to test my curriculum and leadership skills on them.

To Klint, thank you for being a shining example of masculinity and manhood; even when I didn't believe in men, I've believed in you.

Thank you Emerging Women for inviting me into the VIP section and for cracking open a portal of the Universe for the Divine Feminine to descend in her power-full-ness.

Much thanks to Katie Gray and the Sea Stars, who played the sound track of The Year of YES! Yours were voices of angels that sang me through grief to hope and love.

To Ed and Katherine Preston at Sedona's SpiritQuest, thank you for providing refuge and healing.

To *BellaSpark* magazine for giving me a spiritual travel column, which allowed me to take my own Soul Trek, much thanks.

Thank you to Valerie Moore, the feng shui artist who made me paint my bedroom pink; it really did make me much softer.

To Christine Kane at Uplevel Your Business, thanks for the business mentoring.

To Patricia Dollar at II Energy Works, thanks for taking me to realms beyond my imagination.

Thanks to the Whole Life Center for Spiritual Living for their spiritual community.

Thank you, Alexis Saint, for being a source of endless support and for being the one person who I knew should be my first reader.

Thank you to my editor, Stephanie Gunning, and Marketing Magician Audrey Christie McLaughlin for helping me birth this book.

Thank you to Noelle Drake Wood at Looking Glass Studio for bringing out the soft and feminine in me on very short notice.

Thanks to the Men for helping me heal, and for all the great orgasms.

To God, my Soul and the God team, thank you for every sweet gift.

There are so many more. Thank you.

I really am People Rich.

ABOUT THE AUTHOR

Tracee Sioux is an author, speaker, coach, radio host, and creator of The Year of YES! life coaching and business development programs. She lives with her two children in Colorado.

Contact her at yes@traceesioux.com.

Visit her website at http://www.traceesioux.com.

Manufactured by Amazon.ca
Bolton, ON

35812285R00258